THE FINAL FOUR

A PICTORIAL HISTORY OF THE NCAA BASKETBALL CLASSIC

THE FINAL FOUR

A PICTORIAL HISTORY OF THE **NCAA** BASKETBALL CLASSIC

RICHARD WHITTINGHAM

Contemporary Books, Inc.
Chicago

Library of Congress Cataloging in Publication Data

Whittingham, Richard
The Final Four.

Includes index.
1. National Collegiate Athletic Association—History.
I. Title.
GV885.49.N37P35 1983 796.32′363′0973 83-14379
ISBN 0-8092-5581-2

Published by Contemporary Books, Inc.
180 North Michigan Avenue, Chicago, Illinois 60601
Manufactured in the United States of America
Library of Congress Catalog Card Number: 83-14379
International Standard Book Number: 0-8092-5581-2

Published simultaneously in Canada by Beaverbooks, Ltd.
195 Allstate Parkway, Valleywood Business Park
Markham, Ontario L3R 4T8 Canada

Contents

1 Beginnings 1

2 Western Powerhouses 9

3 Kentucky Comes of Age 22

4 Lovellette to Russell to Kentucky Again 35

5 The Ohio Era 54

6 Enter UCLA 69

7 Reenter UCLA 77

8 Still UCLA 96

9 The Midwest Rises 114

10 Kentucky Comes Back 127

11 Michigan State and Magic 135

12 Louisville and the Doctor of Dunk 145

13 Indiana and Isiah 157

14 A Worthy North Carolina 170

15 Cinderella State 185

Appendix 201

Index 241

Other books by the author:

The Rand McNally Almanac of Adventure
The Los Angeles Dodgers: An Illustrated History
The Dallas Cowboys: An Illustrated History
The Chicago White Sox: A Pictorial History
Joe D: On the Street with a Chicago Homicide Cop
The Chicago Bears: An Illustrated History
Astronomy: A Fact Book
Martial Justice: The Last Mass Execution in the U.S.

Photo Acknowledgements

The photographs in this book, unless otherwise specified, were obtained from the universities listed below and are reprinted with permission. The author and publisher wish to extend their thanks for the courtesies and cooperation provided by the Sports Information Directors and their staffs at the following schools: Alabama-Birmingham, Arkansas, Baylor, Boston College, Bradley, California, Cincinnati, CUNY (CCNY), Dartmouth, Dayton, DePaul, Duke, Florida State, Georgetown, Georgia, Holy Cross, Houston, Illinois, Indiana, Indiana State, Iowa, Jacksonville, Kansas, Kansas State, Kentucky, LaSalle, Long Beach State, Louisiana State, Louisville, Loyola (Chicago), Marquette, Memphis State, Michigan State, Nevada-Las Vegas, New Mexico State, North Carolina, North Carolina-Charlotte, North Carolina State, Notre Dame, Ohio State, Oklahoma State (Oklahoma A & M), Oregon, Oregon State, Pennsylvania, Purdue, San Francisco, St. Bonaventure, St. Johns, Stanford, Syracuse, Temple, Texas, Texas-El Paso (Texas Western), UCLA, Utah, Villanova, Virginia, Wake Forest, Washington, West Virginia, Wichita State, and Wyoming.

The photo of Dr. James Naismith was provided courtesy of the National Basketball Hall of Fame.

To the memory of Tom "Buzzy" O'Connor, who, as a player and captain for Loyola University of Chicago's basketball team and as a coach at Notre Dame and Loyola, exemplified the very best in college basketball and amateur athletics, and was such a good friend to so many of us.

1 Beginnings

The elm-shaded campus of Northwestern University, which stretches along the western shore of Lake Michigan in Evanston, Illinois, was the site of an athletic event in 1939 that was destined to become an authentic sports classic. It was there in steamy, cramped Patten Gymnasium that the first NCAA national championship basketball game was played before a small but raucous crowd of about 5,000.

It was a time when backboards were painted white and the players often wore high-top black leather "basketball shoes," which were indistinguishable from the ones worn by boxers of the era. Players shot free throws underhand back then, the two-handed set shot was a standard, the jump shot was practically unheard of, and no one slam-dunked a basketball. Few centers exceeded 6′6″, and the hotshots of the game were the play-making, set-shot-shooting guards who rarely were taller than 5′10″. Winning scores sometimes topped 50 points, but it was not uncommon for a team to win a game with a total in the 30s or even the 20s.

If the sport is mature and sophisticated today (and it is), the days when coaches and NCAA officials were considering a postseason tournament could best be described as its adolescence. The crowds were sparse in comparison to those that fill the cavernous college fieldhouse nowadays, and the athletes often looked on the sport as an off-season diversion. A number of the college basketball standouts of the day would establish their names in

Dr. James Naismith, the inventor of the modern game of basketball. In 1891, Naismith, a divinity student at Springfield (Massachusetts) YMCA School rigged up two peach baskets, one at each end of an outdoor court. With a soccer ball and 13 basic rules, he introduced the sporting world to the game of basketball. (Photo courtesy of the National Basketball Hall of Fame.)

other areas of the sportsworld, among them Lou Boudreau (Illinois), Jackie Robinson (UCLA), Curt Gowdy (Wyoming), Otto Graham (Northwestern), and George Ratterman (Notre Dame).

Just how youthful the game was may be best illustrated by two major developments that occurred a few seasons before that first championship year: Hank Luisetti of Stanford, one of the early game's greatest players, introduced the "running one-hander" in 1936 (which would later be refined into what we know as the jump shot), and the following year the center jump after each score was eliminated. As played in those days, the game of basketball was a far cry from the sport of the 1980s.

By 1939, however, the sport had been around for almost five decades, ever since James Naismith invented it in 1891. A divinity student and sometime football player at Springfield (Massachusetts) YMCA School, Naismith had an idea for a sport that would be less violent than football but still a fast-paced team game. And so, with a peach basket hung on a pole at each end of an outdoor court, a soccer ball that would be tossed into the baskets, and 13 basic rules to govern the game, the sport of basketball was born in that New England town nine years before the turn of the century.

The sport made its informal debut on the college scene in 1895 when the Minnesota State School of Agriculture defeated Hamline College, 9–3, but with large numbers of players on the court at the same time it hardly resembled the sport we know today. The game was taken up by a number of larger and better-known schools that year as well, such as Yale, Iowa, Vanderbilt, Stanford, and Chicago (introduced there by Naismith's former football coach Amos Alonzo Stagg). The first truly recognized intercollegiate game, with five players per team on the court, was played in 1897, with Yale humbling the University of Pennsylvania, 32–10. A little more than a decade later, in 1908, the NCAA took over as the college game's rules maker and has guided and supervised it ever since.

The National Invitational Tournament (NIT) had been instituted at Madison Square Garden in New York City the year before the NCAA postseason tourney made its debut and had been a notable success. The NCAA, however, in laying the ground rules for its tournament, decided on a format different from the NIT's at-large invitational method. The nation was divided into eight geographical divisions, and from each the top team, selected by a committee from that division, would be invited to the single-game elimination tournament. The first teams to be so honored were Brown, Villanova, Ohio State, Wake Forest, Oklahoma, Utah State, Texas, and Oregon.

The two teams that survived the elimination and showed up at Northwestern that breezy late-March evening in 1939 were Oregon and Ohio State. Under coach Howard "Hobby" Hobson, Oregon battled its way to a championship in the Far West that year, the divi-

The Original Eight NCAA Districts

One team from each would be invited to the NCAA single-elimination postseason tournament. Selection would be made by a committee from each district.

1. Connecticut
   Maine
   Massachusetts
   New Hampshire
   Rhode Island
   Vermont
2. Delaware
   New Jersey
   New York
   Pennsylvania
   West Virginia
3. Alabama
   District of Columbia
   Florida
   Georgia
   Kentucky
   Louisiana
   Maryland
   Mississippi
   North Carolina
   South Carolina
   Tennessee
   Virginia
4. Illinois
   Indiana
   Michigan
   Minnesota
   Ohio
   Wisconsin
5. Iowa
   Kansas
   Missouri
   Nebraska
   North Dakota
   Oklahoma
   South Dakota
6. Arizona
   Arkansas
   Texas
7. Colorado
   Montana
   New Mexico
   Utah
   Wyoming
8. California
   Idaho
   Nevada
   Oregon
   Washington

Top left. The shortest of the "Tall Firs," guard Bobby Anet, 5'8", was the playmaker for Oregon in 1939, the first team to win the NCAA Championship.

Top middle. Forward Laddie Gale, at 6'4½", was indeed a "Tall Fir" by 1939 standards. A steady scorer and rugged rebounder, Gale scored 25 points in Oregon's three tournament games that year.

Top right. Ohio State coach Harold Olsen guided his team to a Big Nine championship in 1939 and then to the NCAA title game. The year before, Olsen had suggested the idea of an NCAA postseason tourney to the National Association of Basketball Coaches; subsequently he became a member of the coaches' committee that formulated the tournament.

Above right. Ohio State captain in 1939, Jim Hull scored the most points—58, an average of 19.3 per game—in the NCAA's first postseason tourney. Hull scored 28 in the Buckeyes' semifinal romp over Villanova, and was the team's high scorer with 12 in the final game.

Above left. Ohio State guard Dick Baker scored 25 points in the Buckeyes' first-round win over Wake Forest in the 1939 tourney. Baker and teammate Jim Hull were the only players in that tournament to score more than 20 points in a single game.

sion rightfully considered the best in the country. Besides their traditional nickname of "Ducks," the Oregon hoopsters had also been dubbed the "Tall Firs" because their baseline players were unusually tall (center Slim Wintermute was 6′8″, and the two forwards, Laddie Gale and John Dick, both were 6′4½″).

FIRST N.C.A.A. FINALIST 1939
N.C.A.A. EASTERN CHAMPIONS 1939
WESTERN CONFERENCE CHAMPIONS
1939
TOP ROW- L.W. ST.JOHN, DIRECTOR; J.E. BLICKLE, ASST. COACH; MEES; STAFFORD; H.G. OLSEN, COACH; GALL; EDWARDS; T.P. SMITH, TRAINER; HERTZ, MGR
BOTTOM ROW- MAAG; MICKELSON; LYNCH; BAKER; HULL, CAPTAIN; SHICK; DAWSON; SATTLER; SCOTT; BOUGHNER
N.C.A.A. TOURNAMENT SCORES
FIRST N.C.A.A. CHAMPIONSHIP
OREGON 46 .... O.S.U. 33
OHIO STATE BIG TEN RESULTS
OHIO OPP. OHIO OPP. OHIO OPP.
45 INDIANA 38 52 CHICAGO 25 30 NORTHWESTERN 26
38 NORTHWESTERN 33 31 MINNESOTA 30 46 WISCONSIN 38
31 ILLINOIS 45 34 INDIANA 46 42 MICHIGAN 28
45 MICHIGAN 31 53 IOWA 40 51 PURDUE 35
EASTERN CHAMPIONSHIP SCORES
O.S.U. 64 .... WAKE FOREST 52
O.S.U. 53 .... VILLANOVA 36

Ohio State's athletes, coached by Harold Olsen and representing the Midwest, were not as tall but were known to be a very high-scoring team, paced by two exceptional sharpshooters, Dick Baker and Jimmy Hull.

Both teams virtually coasted into the championship match. Oregon had knocked off Texas and Oklahoma to get there, with neither opponent coming within 15 points of them. Ohio State racked up 64 points in decimating Wake Forest (Baker contributed 25) and 53 in defeating Villanova (Hull scored 28 points that game).

Despite its prolific scoring, Ohio State proved to be no match for Oregon. Fueled by superior rebounding power and a racehorse fast break, led by a spark plug of a guard, 5′8″ Bobby Anet, Oregon simply overwhelmed the Buckeyes. At halftime Oregon held a 21–16 lead, then blew the game apart in the final period, winning it 46–33. Oregon's forward, John Dick, was the top scorer of the night with 15 points, and Anet dropped in another 10. For Ohio State Jimmy Hull was the leader with 12.

The winner's trophy was broken during the game when Bobby Anet, diving for a ball, crashed into the table holding it. The tournament showed a net loss of $2,531, a shaky start by any standard but not one that would impede the new postseason adventure.

In 1940 the two teams that made it to the

NCAA's second national championship, Indiana and Kansas, represented states destined to produce outstanding college basketball teams that would frequently visit the tournament over the next four decades. And they were coached by two men who would become basketball institutions in their own right, Branch McCracken at Indiana and Forrest "Phog" Allen of Kansas.

It was somewhat ironic that Indiana and Kansas got to the tournament in the first place. Indiana had come in second in the Big Ten that year, behind its intrastate rival Purdue, but the selection committee opted for the Hoosiers because they had defeated the Boilermakers in both of their encounters that season. And, from the Big Six, Kansas was a surprise participant in the tourney because it had not been expected to win the conference that year. But Kansas had worked its way into a season's end tie with Missouri and Oklahoma and had come out the winner in a special postseason playoff.

Indiana coach Branch McCracken played for the Hoosiers in the late 1920s, was an All-American, and was later enshrined in the National Basketball Hall of Fame. As a coach at Indiana he compiled a career record of 451 wins against 277 losses. His teams won two NCAA titles (1940 and 1953).

The pretournament favorite was the University of Southern California, which had ended the season as Pacific Coast conference champion. Its status as the favorite was substantiated when in the first round it ousted the University of Colorado, which had just won that year's NIT title. Kansas, on the other hand, had had some trouble in the first round with a much less fearsome opponent in Rice. But the Jayhawks managed to hold on and win by six points with the sterling performance of forward Howard Engleman, whose 21 points that night would prove to be the most scored in any game in that year's tourney.

Indiana drew little Springfield College, the institution in Massachusetts that evolved from the YMCA school where James Naismith had launched the game of basketball almost 50 years earlier. Indiana was a fast-breaking team, and the floor leader was guard Marv Huffman. The Hoosiers had no trouble whatsoever with Springfield, routing that team 48–24, despite Huffman's being held to a mere six points. The Hoosiers' most gifted hand that night was the other guard, Herm Schaefer, who led all scorers with 14 points.

Indiana did not have to strain in the semifinals either. It dominated another relatively small school, Duquesne, whose campus was in Pittsburgh, in a low-scoring affair, 39–30. Center Bill Menke scored the most for the Hoosiers, with 10, and Schaefer added eight.

But in the western semifinal, it was a nail biter all the way to the final buzzer. Favored Southern Cal had a one-point edge over Kansas at halftime, and the lead was traded back and forth throughout the second half. Then, with only seconds remaining in the game, Jayhawk Howard Engleman lofted a picture-perfect set shot from the corner to put Kansas ahead 43–42. Southern Cal took a time-out, but when the team came back onto the floor they only had time for a desperation half-court shot from Jack Morrison. It was almost a Frank Merriwell finish, but not quite. The ball, off target by only a fraction of an inch, hit the back of the rim and bounced out.

The championship game for 1940 was held at Kansas City's Municipal Auditorium, its

The Hoosiers of Indiana, 1940 NCAA champs. **Front row** (left to right): Jim Gridley, Herm Schaefer, Bob Dro, Marv Huffman (captain), Jay McCreary, Curley Armstrong, Ralph Dorsey. **Back row** (left to right): Branch McCracken (coach), Chet Francis, Bill Menke, Andy Zimmer, Bob Menke, Ralph Graham. Huffman was the first recipient of the tournament's Outstanding Player award and, along with teammates Bill Menke and Jay McCreary, was named to the first All-Tournament team.

seating capacity about twice as large as the little gym at Northwestern University where the game was played the year before. Practically a full house (about 10,000) was there to watch Kansas take on the Hoosiers of Indiana. For Kansas, whose campus was only 35 miles west of the arena, it was a hometown crowd. This appeared to help, at least through the first half of the first quarter, but as it turned out, Indiana was just a slow starter and that early segment proved to be the only time during the game when Kansas led. Kansas simply could not cope with Indiana's frantic fast break, and by the half the Hoosiers had built a considerable 32–19 lead. It was more of the same in the second half, and Indiana cruised to a 60–42 triumph. Marv Huffman, who was named the first recipient of the tournament's Outstanding Player award, scored 12 for the Hoosiers as did forward Jay McCreary. For the runner-up Jayhawks, Bob Allen was the top scorer with 13, and Howard Engleman had 12. Besides naming an Outstanding Player, the NCAA also selected an All-Tournament Team:

Howard Engleman (Kansas)
Jay McCreary (Indiana)
Bill Menke (Indiana)
Marv Huffman (Indiana)
Bob Allen (Kansas)

Bob Allen (13) lays in two for Kansas in this 1940 game. Looking on is Jayhawk All-American Howard Engleman (5). Engleman scored 21 points in KU's first round win over Rice, the most in any game during the 1940 tourney. He had 12 and Allen 13 in their championship loss to Indiana.

Forrest C. "Phog" Allen would become a legend at Kansas, coaching the Jayhawks for 39 seasons and winning 770 games and 24 conference titles. Allen guided his Kansas five to the NCAA finals in 1940 but lost to Indiana. He would not win the NCAA crown until 1952.

The tournament made a profit in 1940—$9,590.06, to be exact—and each of the two schools that played for the championship was awarded $750. It would be a profit maker from that day forward.

With all of Europe a battlefield and the United States warily girding for that war in 1941, sports offered a needed distraction for Americans. It would prove to be a year marked by a number of unique performances and historic moments to please fans of all persuasions. The Brown Bomber, Joe Louis, would defend his crown no fewer than seven times that year, stopping all challengers, including Billy Conn and Buddy Baer. Joe DiMaggio would hit safely in 56 straight games for the New York Yankees, a record still untouched. Greg Rice of Notre Dame would set world records in both the two- and three-mile runs. Eddie Arcaro would ride Whirlaway to the Triple Crown. And Dodger catcher Mickey Owen would drop the last strike for the last out in a game in the World Series that would become known as baseball's most famous passed ball.

But the first sporting event to garner national attention that year was the NCAA basketball championship, in its third year and already an established slice of the American sports pageant. Just as the year before, the finals were slated for Municipal Auditorium in Kansas City, Missouri. The four teams vying for the opportunity to descend on that arena were totally different from those that fought for it the year before. Reigning champion Indiana had not even made it to the tournament after losing out in the Big Ten to Wisconsin, while runner-up Kansas was beaten by Creighton University from Omaha. The cream of the proverbial crop was said to be undefeated Arkansas, which almost all observers were picking to walk off with the tournament crown in 1941.

Arkansas was among the Final Four; so were Wisconsin, the University of Pittsburgh, and Washington State. It had been a relatively easy journey for all but Wisconsin. The Badgers came disastrously close to being eliminated in the first round on their own home court in Madison. Losing most of the game to an underdog but inspired Dartmouth team, they finally took the lead in the last minute, then desperately held off a Dartmouth rally to win the game by a single point, 51–50. It was principally the play of center Gene Englund, who led the Badgers with 18 points, and forward Johnny Kotz, who dropped in another 15, including two clutch free throws in the game's last minute, that enabled Wisconsin to advance to the tournament's semifinals.

As expected, Arkansas breezed by Wyoming, a team blessed with the talents of young Kenny Sailors, a blossoming All-American. But the Razorbacks held him in check (at least to 17 points) and, behind the sharpshooting of forward Johnny Adams (26 points that night), destroyed Wyoming 52–40. In other first-round games Pittsburgh, in a slow-motion affair, defeated North Carolina 26–20 after overcoming a 12–8 deficit at halftime. And Washington State had little trouble with Creighton, winning 48–39.

Englund and Kotz were Wisconsin's two big guns, and as they went so went the fortunes of the Badgers. During the first half of their semifinal game against Pitt, they were holstered; in fact, the entire Wisconsin team could come up with only 14 points to rival Pitt's 18. In the second half, however, both Englund and Kotz found the range, and the Badgers came alive, overtook Pitt, and won 36–30.

The big surprise occurred in the second game of the semifinals. A fired-up Washington State, with an extraordinarily well-balanced attack, dominated heavily favored Arkansas. All-American Johnny Adams scored a game-high 22 points for the Razorbacks, but it was not nearly enough as Washington State, with everybody but the student manager scoring, amassed 64 points to the Razorbacks' 53.

So once again the tourney favorite failed to make it into the title contest. Because the West Coast played such top-level basketball in those days and because Washington State had so handily knocked off previously unbeaten Arkansas, Washington State was given the edge over Wisconsin. But, it was becoming very clear, things just did not turn out as they were supposed to during the NCAA tourney. The game was virtually controlled by Wisconsin. Coach Bud Foster orchestrated his methodical, patterned offense with maestrolike virtuosity, and the Badgers' tight defense was at its best. Washington State coach Jack Friel liked to have his team run, employing a fast break reminiscent of the two previous tourney champs, Oregon and Indiana. But Wisconsin didn't give them the chance, controlling the boards throughout the game. Nor could State get the ball to its big man, center Paul Lindemann, who was double-covered most of the night and held to a paltry three points. Wisconsin gained the lead early and held it up to the final buzzer. The score: Wisconsin 39, Washington State 34. Englund and Kotz teamed for 13 and 12 points respectively, and Kotz was voted the tourney's Outstanding Player.

2
Western Powerhouses

Long before UCLA became college basketball's dynasty, the land west of the Mississippi River established itself as one of the game's richest heartlands. Oregon had won the first NCAA title in 1939, Southern Cal had been expected to win the second, and both Arkansas and Washington State were favored in the third over the Big Ten team that managed to win it. Now, in 1942, the westerners were about to exert their authority forcefully. They would control the NCAA championships over the next five years.

In 1942 the star to shine was Stanford, making its first (and what would turn out to be its *only*) appearance in an NCAA postseason tournament. The Stanford Indians team that streaked through the 1941–42 college basketball season, compiling a regular season record of 25 and four, was a truly special one. The Indians were coached by Hall of Fame–bound Everett Dean, who in 1939, after 14 years at Indiana, had transferred his services to the West Coast. The Stanford squad that went to the NCAA tournament in 1942 was inordinately tall, the shortest member being 6′3″, yet it was fast, fluid, and spearheaded by a lanky forward by the name of Jim Pollard who would later team with George Mikan at the Minnesota Lakers, prove to be one of the Pro game's early greats, and be inducted into the basketball Hall of Fame.

Stanford had won the Pacific Coast Conference Championship handily and was an obvious selection for a postseason tourney invitation. The team chose the NCAA over the NIT

Forward Jim Pollard, an All-American in 1942, was the chief reason Stanford posted a 28–4 record, won the Pacific Coast Conference, and reached the NCAA finals. The team's top scorer in its first two tourney games (26 and 17 points), Pollard was benched by the flu for the title tilt. He was enshrined in the National Basketball Hall of Fame in 1977.

and headed for Kansas City. Its first opponent was Rice, a team that would give Stanford its biggest worry on the way to the national championship. Playing without the services of starting forward Don Burness, who had sprained an ankle, Stanford saw a commanding 33–21 lead at the half crumble. At one point in the second half Rice had outscored the Indians 20–4, enough to boost the team to a four-point lead. But Everett Dean turned his cagers around in the fourth quarter, regaining the lead and holding it for a 53–47 win. Pollard contributed 26 points, the most that would be scored in any game that tournament, and center Ed Voss tallied another 15.

Colorado gained the other semifinal berth in the NCAA West by knocking off a highly regarded Kansas team. But Colorado would make little trouble for the Stanford Indians, who thoroughly dominated in their match-up. Again Pollard led all scorers, this time with 17, while Voss added 10 and guard Bill Cowden another seven.

Meanwhile, in the eastern regional and semifinal contests a smooth Dartmouth team, making its second consecutive appearance in the postseason classic, coasted by Penn State, then routed Kentucky. It was a team that deserved respect, with awesome scoring potential in sharpshooter George Munroe and, up to that game, the tournament's highest scoring center, Jim Olsen (19 and 20 points respectively in the preceding two games).

Stanford was the odds makers' favorite, that is, until the announcement just before game time that star forward Jim Pollard was stricken with the flu, severely enough that he would not even dress for the championship tilt. The Indians were forced to take the floor with two subs at the forward posts that night. Replacing Pollard and Burness were Jack Dana and Fred Linari, and they would rise sublimely to the task.

The game was close throughout the first half, and when that buzzer sounded the Indians had a narrow two-point lead. But Everett Dean must have done something dramatic in the locker room at the intermission because the Indians raged back out to decimate their Ivy League opponents in the second half, outscoring them 29–16. The final score was

Outstanding Player for 1942 was Stanford's Howie Dallmar, whose leadership on the floor brought the Indians the NCAA crown in their first (and only) tourney appearance. Dallmar scored the most points in the championship game, 15.

53–38. Howie Dallmar led all scorers with 15, and substitute Dana came up with 14. Big Ed Voss had 13, and he held normally high-scoring Jim Olsen to a mere eight points. The Indians' other sub, Fred Linari, scored six. And Stanford had brought the national championship back to the West Coast. In Pollard's absence, Howie Dallman walked off with the award as the tourney's Outstanding Player.

Coach of the champion Stanford Indians, Everett Dean. After four years at Carleton College in Minnesota and 14 at Indiana, Dean coached Stanford from 1938 through 1951. He was elected to the National Basketball Hall of Fame in 1966.

Champs of 1942, the Stanford Indians. Left to right: Bill Cowden, Howie Dallmar, Ed Voss, Jim Pollard, Don Burness, Everett Dean (coach).

The next champion to come out of the Wild West was the University of Wyoming, appropriately nicknamed the Cowboys. They had a certified All-American in forward Kenny Sailors, who was one of the game's most dazzling ball handlers, and a strong, high-scoring center in 6′7″ Milo Komenich. They were coached by Ev Shelton, then in his fourth year of what would eventually be a 20-year career at Wyoming.

Wyoming had lost only two games during the 1942–43 season. The Cowboys were not, however, touted as the top team in the country going into the NCAA, though they were considered a very real threat. The team most observers felt was the nation's best was the University of Illinois. Its "Whiz Kids," as they had been dubbed, spearheaded by All-American guard Andy Phillip, had lost only one of 18 games, but the school chose not to accept a bid to the NCAA tournament. DePaul University of Chicago represented the Midwest in Illinois's stead.

The site of the regional competition for Wyoming was Kansas City, but the finals would not be held there in 1943. After three years as host the Missouri city lost out to New York City, a wise choice because twice as many basketball fans would show up at Madison Square Garden to watch the championship game as had the year before in Kansas City's Municipal Auditorium.

Texas guard John Hargis scorched the nets in 1943, scoring 59 points in two games. His average of 29.5 a game would stand as an NCAA tourney record for a decade until Clyde Lovellette would top it with 35.3. Hargis also played for the 1947 Texas team in the NCAA tournament.

The team most experts said was the best in the nation in 1943, the "Whiz Kids" of Illinois. Left to right: Andy Phillip, Ken Menke, Art Mathisen, Jack Smiley, Gene Vance. The wartime draft, however, broke up the team before it could prove its power in the postseason. The Illini were 17–1 during the regular season.

It would not be an easy road for the Cowboys during the tournament that year because in each of their three contests they would have to come from behind to win. The first narrow escape was against a wily Oklahoma team. Losing most of the first half and down 25–22 at intermission, the Cowboys finally claimed the lead in the fourth quarter and were able to hold on and win by three. Sailors was the floor leader, but he contributed only eight points that night, while the cowboys' loping center, Milo Komenich, led all scorers with 22 and forward Jimmy Weir contributed 14.

Texas earned the right to meet Wyoming in the semifinals by beating Washington, a team that many had earlier picked to win the whole thing. But Texas was fueled by All-American guard John Hargis, who scored 30 points against Washington to claim a new NCAA tournament record, breaking the old one of 28 set by Ohio State's Jimmy Hull in 1939.

Wyoming had equal trouble with Hargis when the two teams went at each other. The sharpshooting forward scored 29 points, but

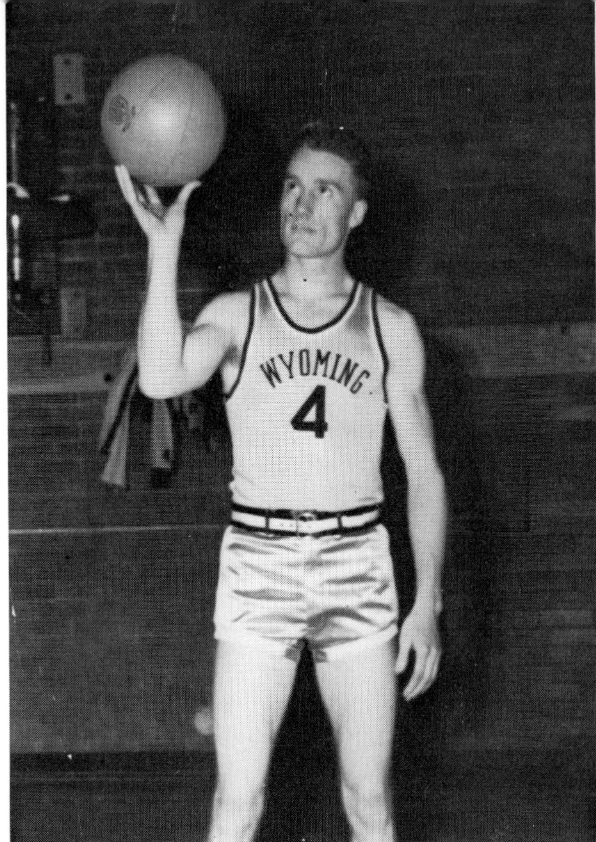

Guard Kenny Sailors was the keystone around which the Wyoming NCAA champs of 1943 were built. A superb ball handler and playmaker, Sailors was a consensus All-American that year and was selected the tourney's Outstanding Player. His 16 points were the most scored in the title game.

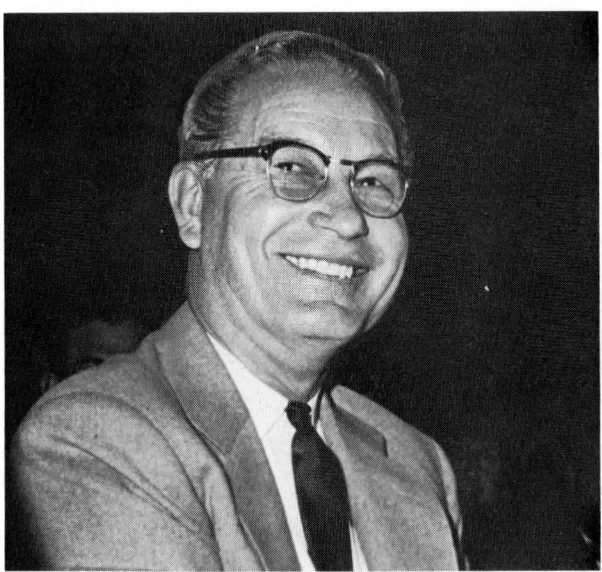

Ev Shelton, coach of the champion Wyoming Cowboys of 1943. Shelton, who would coach at Wyoming through the 1959 season and post a career record of 623 wins and 313 losses, was inducted into the National Basketball Hall of Fame in 1979.

Right. An important factor in Wyoming's 1943 fortunes was Milo Komenich. The 6'7" center was a strong rebounder and the perfect complement to Kenny Sailors. Komenich was the Cowboys' top scorer in the tourney with 48 points, 22 of which were hooped in the Cowboys' first-round come-from-behind win over Oklahoma.

Wyoming got a break—Hargis fouled out in the fourth quarter. Texas had built a solid six-point lead at the half and was in command through the third quarter, but the relentless Cowboys kept after their opponents. They eventually moved ahead, maintaining their lead with some ease in light of the absence of Hargis, and won 58–54. Again Komenich was the Cowboys' high scorer, this time with 17; Weir was next with 13, and Sailors added 12.

In the East the Georgetown Hoyas had demolished NYU by 19 points in the tourney opener, then gone on to tame DePaul, a team that boasted two men who would later become basketball legends: George Mikan, a freshman center who stood 6′10″, and Ray Meyer, a coach in the first year of an illustrious career that would extend into the 1980s. It was a game in which Georgetown had to come from behind to win and Hoya freshman center John Mahnken held Mikan to 11 points while scoring 17 himself.

When Wyoming and Georgetown met at Madison Square Garden to determine the 1943 NCAA title, both were off their game—perhaps intimidated by the crowd of 13,300, the largest yet to attend an NCAA postseason game; perhaps awed by the stakes, the national championship; perhaps overextended from their come-from-behind wins in the semifinals. Both teams were stale in the early minutes, and the score was uncharacteristically low for these two teams, which had averaged well over 50 points in each of their two earlier playoff games. By halftime the Cowboys had crawled to an 18–16 lead, but they soon lost it in the third quarter, sinking as far as five points behind the Hoyas. Once again, however, Wyoming rebounded, chipping away at the Georgetown lead until it had taken it over. Georgetown then staged a rally of its own, but the Cowboys exploded with nine unanswered points in the game's last minute and a half to win 46–34. Kenny Sailors proved to be the Cowboys' big gun that night with 16. Komenich had nine, and substitute forward Jimmy Collins came off the bench to add eight. Big John Mahnken of Georgetown was held to a mere six points that night. The Outstanding Player award went to Kenny Sailors.

Coach Ray Meyer began his career at Chicago's DePaul University in 1943 and took that year's team to the NCAA semifinals, where the Blue Demons fell to Georgetown. Meyer's first major accomplishment was the refinement of the talents of center George Mikan. Coach Meyer would guide the DePaul Blue Demons for the next 40 years.

George Mikan, DePaul's 6′10″ center, was the first of the "big men" to dominate the game of basketball. He was the nation's highest scorer in 1945 and 1946 (averaging 23.9 and 23.1 points per game). An awesome rebounder, Mikan was also a master of feeding off to guards and forwards. He is a charter member of the National Basketball Hall of Fame.

In 1943 a post-postseason game was played, pitting the winner of the NCAA against the victor in the NIT. It was called the Red Cross Classic because the proceeds of the game would go to aid that organization's wartime efforts. In basketball circles it allegedly would determine which was the premier postseason tournament, but in actual fact it would not, and for quite a few years thereafter the relative merits of each tournament and the quality of the teams that played in them would remain a point of controversy. In this contest the NCAA prevailed, Wyoming beating a highly regarded St. John's team 52–47.

By March of 1944 the war had depleted the ranks of most colleges and many of the would-be cage stars of the day were wearing entirely different uniforms from the shirt and shorts they would have worn on various basketball floors. College basketball went on despite the much more significant endeavors the nation was involved with in Europe and the Pacific, though some schools temporarily dropped the sport and others had to scrounge deeply to find players as well as other teams to play. Many of the college teams scheduled games against the military service teams that popped up around the country and were rostered with former college stars.

Probably the greatest irony in the entire history of the NCAA tournament is the fact that the 1944 title was won by the University of Utah. The school had initially turned down the NCAA's bid because the association would not guarantee to pay the team's travel expenses—although the NCAA had been making a profit each year since 1939, the war hung an economic cloud over its profit potential and the NCAA was unable to guarantee anything. The NIT on the other hand, was able to do so, and Utah accepted its bid, only to be eliminated in the first round when Kentucky gave Utah a 46–38 drubbing.

Back in Salt Lake City, Utah coach Vadal Peterson got another call from the NCAA, whose tournament was now just about to get under way—another offer. Arkansas, which had taken up the bid Utah had declined, was unable to attend the tourney after two of its top players were injured in an auto accident. So, with the chance to regain some respect after its dismal showing in the NIT, Utah this time accepted the NCAA's bid and set out for Kansas City for a regional playoff game against the University of Missouri.

Utah had one thing going for it that no other team had, and that was an 18-year-old All-American by the name of Arnie Ferrin. The freshman forward was 6′3″, a gifted shooter, and a team leader. He was by far the most imposing element on the floor in Utah's romp over Missouri, a game in which Utah was never threatened and finally won by 10 points. Ferrin was the game's high scorer with 12.

Iowa State was the team the young Utahans had to get by to go back to Madison Square Garden in New York. Winner of the Big Six and conqueror of a feisty Pepperdine team from California in the first round, Iowa State was considered a slight favorite, despite the presence of Arnie Ferrin. The odds makers were wrong, however. And even though a double-teamed Ferrin was held to six points, Utah won the game, one that was closer than the 40–31 score would indicate. Ferrin's teammates were the collective force that night, with Wat Misaka and Fred Sheffield scoring nine apiece, Bob Lewis seven, Dick Smuin five, and Herb Wilkinson four.

Dartmouth had won out East, becoming the first team in NCAA history to make a second appearance in the tournament championship game. Dartmouth had annihilated Catholic University of Washington, DC, 63–38 in the first round, then beat down a strong Ohio State 60–53. The Buckeyes of Ohio State were paced by All-American candidate Arnie Risen, but Dartmouth proved to be simply overwhelming. Dartmouth had an All-American of its own, Dick McGuire, who had been playing for St. John's and been called up by the Navy. He was sent to the Navy's officer training program at Dartmouth, which at that time made him eligible to play for that university. Dartmouth also had Audley Brindley, center and captain, a deft shooter who had scored 28 points in the school's semifinal win over Ohio State.

The clash between Utah and Dartmouth in Madison Square Garden in 1944 was a dream of a game, by far the most dramatic in the tournament's then six-year history. It was a low-scoring affair, with Dartmouth gaining a one-point advantage, 18–17, at halftime. It was neck and neck all the way through the last two quarters. Then, with only about a minute to play, Utah pulled ahead by four points. But that was reduced to two when forward Bob Gale, another military training transferee (he came from NYU) scored. Then Dartmouth snatched the ball away from Utah and got it to Dick McGuire, who lofted a game-tying two-handed set shot with three seconds left to send the game into overtime.

The extra period was just as exciting, and as the clock ran down to the final seconds it was a stalemate at 40 points. Utah had the ball and tried to get it to Ferrin for the last shot, but he was double-teamed. Open as a result was Bill Wilkinson out at the top of the free throw circle. His one-hander was perfect, and Utah was the NCAA champ.

Keystone of the 1944 national champs from Utah was everybody's All-American, Arnie Ferrin. Voted the tourney's Outstanding Player, Ferrin scored 22 of Utah's 42 points in the title game triumph over Dartmouth.

Dartmouth's Dick McGuire (11) tries to wrest the ball from a floored Arnie Risen of Ohio State in the 1944 semifinals. In the foreground is Aud Brindley (3), who scored the most points in that year's tourney, 58. Behind Brindley's 28 points Dartmouth won that night; Risen accounted for 21 of the Buckeyes' points. Number 4 is Bob Myers.

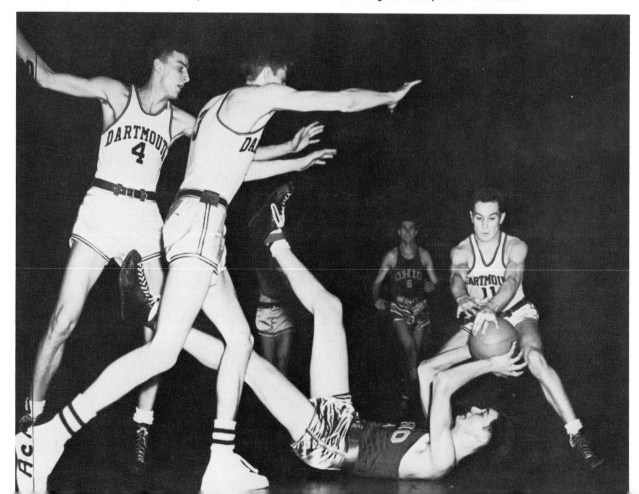

If Wilkinson added the cherry to Utah's cake that night, Arnie Ferrin had certainly iced it with his sterling performance throughout the game. His 22 points were by far the highest total, and he also could claim four of Utah's six points in the overtime period. He was an obvious choice for that year's Outstanding Player award.

As a bonus, Utah was given the chance to avenge its earlier defeat in the NIT by facing the champion of that tourney, St. John's, in the Red Cross Classic. And vengeance was theirs when the Utah cagers cleanly beat the NIT champs 43–36. For the second year in a row the NCAA champion had prevailed over the NIT winner.

Utah returned to the NCAA tourney in 1945, but without Arnie Ferrin, in fact without a single member of the previous year's championship team. And it was hardly a joyous return. In the opening game Utah went up against Hank Iba's highly touted Oklahoma A & M (today Oklahoma State) team with its seven-foot center Bob Kurland, who virtually beat Utah single-handedly. The giant Kurland controlled the backboards, dropped in 28 points, and the Aggies from Stillwater, Oklahoma, demolished Utah 62–37.

Oklahoma A & M had a very good team that year and had lost only four of its 27 regular season games. Kurland, a junior, was considered as awesome a talent as DePaul's George Mikan, and between the two they were changing the face of college basketball. For one thing, their height and jumping ability forced the NCAA rules makers to prohibit goaltending, a practice hitherto so rare that a ban on it had not been necessary.

The Aggies, however, were not *just* Bob Kurland. He was merely the core around which a fine team was constructed. Coach Iba, one of the game's most respected strategists, had devised a slow, methodical offense that took advantage of Kurland's scoring potential and developed a masterful sinking defense that forced opponents to settle for outside shots most of the time. Teams that liked to fastbreak were devasted because if they somehow managed to get a rebound it was practically impossible to throw the ball out to a guard over Kurland's outstretched arms.

Arkansas, which had in the first round scored the most points in a single game up to that time in NCAA playoff history in defeating Oregon 79–76, had hopes of running against the Aggies. But its racehorse fast break was totally neutralized by Kurland and his associates, and Arkansas never got into the game, losing decisively, 68–41. The Razorbacks had managed to hold Kurland to 15 points, but the slack was ably picked up by teammates Cecil Hankins, who scored 22, and Doyle Parrack, who contributed 16.

At Madison Square Garden the Oklahomans were to meet New York University, which had earned its spot in the finals by overwhelming Tufts 59–44 and then, with a miraculous come-from-behind effort, defeated Ohio State in overtime. NYU, coached by Howard Cann, had a prodigious scorer in forward Sid Tannenbaum. At center was Dolph Schayes, a freshman of great promise who would subsequently fulfill every measure of it in his college and pro careers.

Howard Cann's game plan was to stop Kurland, to keep him away from the basket, but then that was the plan of just about every one of the Aggies' opponents. And NYU proved to be no more successful at it than the others. It was a close game, however, and NYU threatened throughout, but in the end Kurland was dominant and the Aggies won 49–45. The towering Kurland was the game's high scorer, with 22, and Hankins added another 15 to the Aggies' fortunes. Their defense held NYU's Tannenbaum to four points and Schayes to six. And Kurland was a cinch selection for that year's Outstanding Player award.

The Red Cross Classic had all the makings of a historic confrontation in 1945—the reason being that DePaul, with its All-American center George Mikan, had won the NIT. It would be a Kurland–Mikan face-off, an unprecedented clash of the titans. But it did not turn out that way because the two giant centers lost their poise that night in Madison Square Garden. Mikan fouled out 14 minutes into the first half, and Kurland picked up four fouls

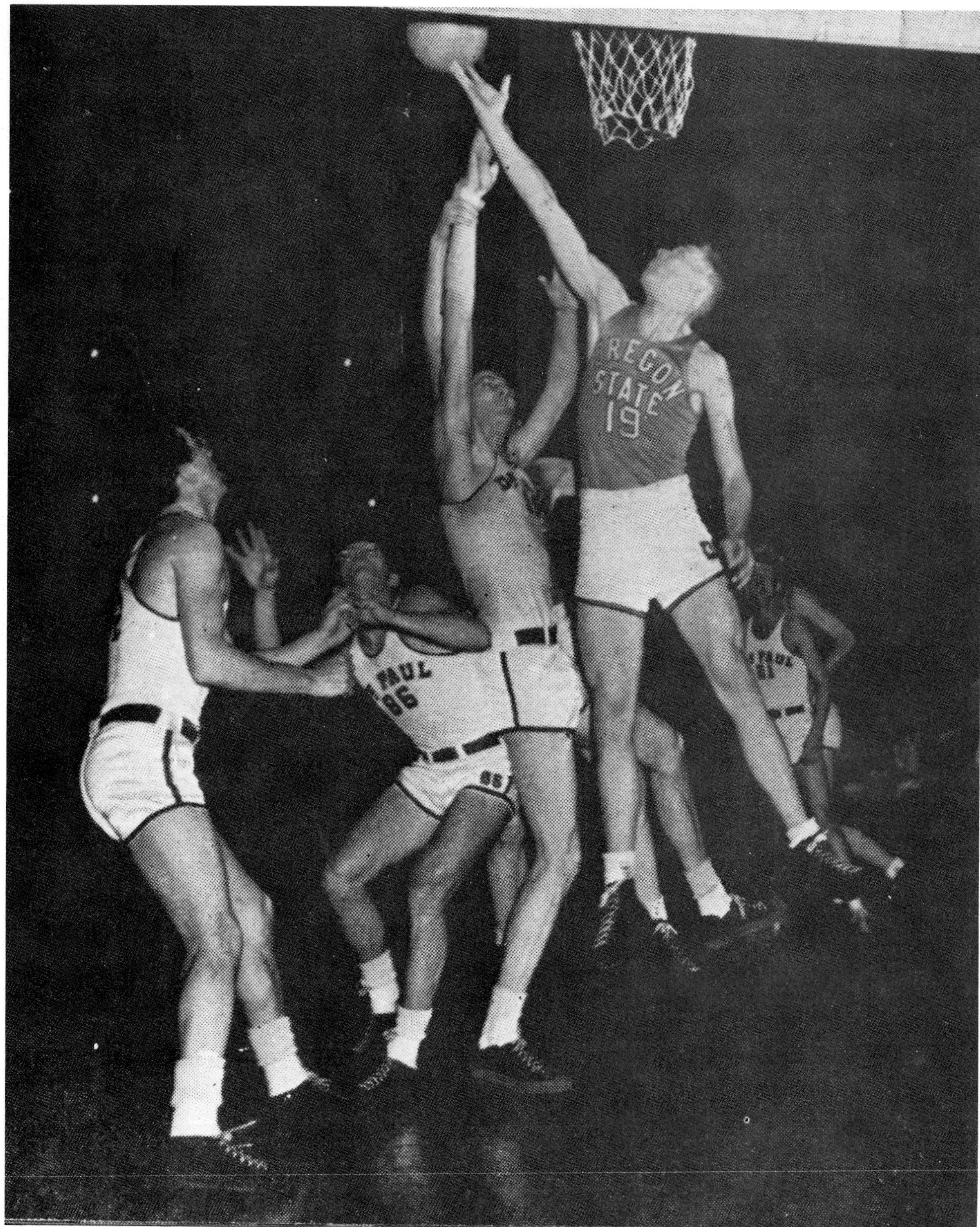

They did everything to try to stop DePaul's George Mikan in the mid-1940s. Here someone grabs his wrist to keep him from grabbing a rebound in a game against Oregon State.

Above. Champs of 1945, the Oklahoma A & M Aggies. Bob Kurland (90), at 7 feet, towered over everyone on the basketball court. He dominated both the 1945 and '46 tourneys and was named the Outstanding Player in each. Both Kurland and his coach Hank Iba (top row, far right) were elected to the National Basketball Hall of Fame. **Bottom row** (left to right): Herman Millikan (assistant coach), Cecil Hankins, John Wylie, Carl Alexander, Billy York, Weldon Kern, Art Rigg, J. L. Parks, Don Bentley, Jack Hopkins (assistant coach). **Top row** (left to right): Otis Wile (publicity), Dick Caldwell, Bill Johnson, Gentry Warren, Joe Halbert, Bob Kurland, Blake Williams, Charles Crook, Sidney Wilson, Doyle Parrack, H. P. Iba (head coach).

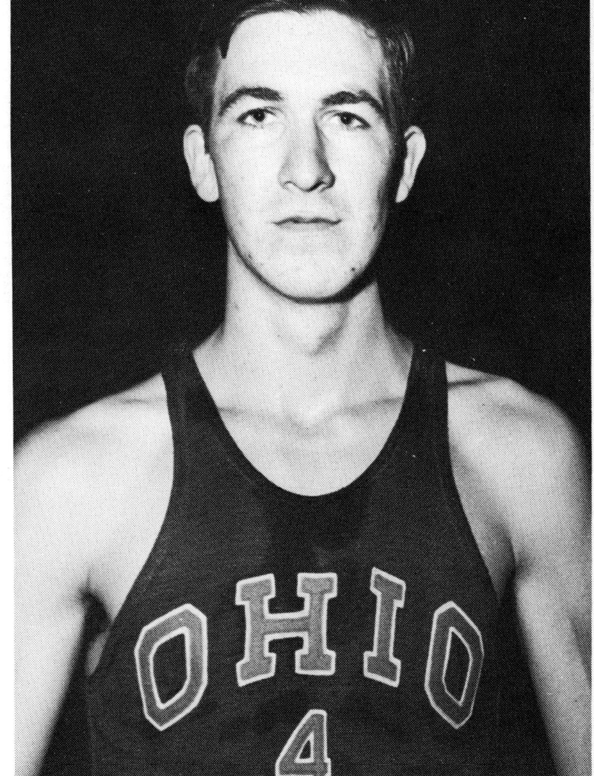

One of the brightest stars of the mid-1940s was Ohio State's Arnie Risen, the mainstay on two Buckeye teams that made it to the NCAA's Final Four (1944 and 1945). Risen's best individual effort was the 26-point performance he turned in against New York University in the semifinals of 1945.

during the same period and was forced to play a much curtailed game from that point on. When the stats were posted Mikan had nine points and Kurland 14, and Oklahoma A & M crept off with a 52–44 victory in a letdown of a contest.

At the end of the 1945–46 college basketball season the top scorer in the nation for the second consecutive year was DePaul's George Mikan, once again averaging better than 23 points a game. Not far behind was Oklahoma A & M's Bob Kurland with an average of 19. But DePaul would be absent from the NCAA tournament while the Aggies would return to it to try for unprecedented back-to-back championships. There was to be no Red Cross Classic now that the war was over, so there would be no chance of a Mikan–Kurland rematch, which basketball fans everywhere were hoping for despite their disappointment in the first encounter.

The Aggies were a true powerhouse. With one exception, they fielded the same team as the year before. Cecil Hankins had vacated one of the guard posts and was replaced by Sam Aubrey, who had just returned from wartime service. Kurland was as imposing as ever—he had scored 58 points against St. Louis in the Aggies' last home game of the season, and Hank Iba's controlled offense was even smoother than it had been the year before. The team had won 28 of its 30 games, and most basketball pundits looked upon it as the best in the nation and the favorite to win the 1946 NCAA tourney.

Their first opponent, Baylor, played a calculated game, like Oklahoma A & M, but couldn't score like the Aggies. Baylor logged only 29 points that evening while Kurland himself had 20 for the Aggies and the team posted 44 in a coaster slide of a win. Meanwhile California beat Colorado to earn the dubious pleasure of facing the Aggies for the NCAA West crown. Kurland was even more productive against that team. He scored 29 points, one short of the tournament record at that time, as the Aggies had no trouble defeating the Californians: the final, 52–35.

In the NCAA East that year it was almost impossible to pick a favorite. Ohio State was considered a powerhouse, winner of the rugged Big Ten conference, and the team had the reputation as an intimidating, high-scoring force on any basketball court, despite the fact it no longer had the services of All-American Arnie Risen. There was also the previous year's contender for the NCAA championship, NYU, which still had Dolph Schayes and Sid Tannenbaum. And making its second appearance in the tourney was North Carolina, which had inauspiciously debuted in 1941 by scoring a meager 20 points in a decisive loss to Pittsburgh. In 1946, however, the Tar Heels were looked on as second to none. They had Horace "Bones" McKinney at center, who, one writer of the day said, "ran up and down the court in sections." But McKinney was a fine center, though at 6′6″ rather dwarfed by the likes of Bob Kurland. North Carolina also had a consistently high scorer in forward John Dillon. As far as most observers felt before the tournament, the East was a toss-up among the three.

Ohio State, however, was a heavy favorite over Harvard in the first round but found the going surprisingly tough, though it finally won the game by eight points. The Tar Heels of North Carolina, on the other hand, did not have as much trouble with NYU as coach Ben Carnevale had expected. They held the previous year's runner-up in check throughout the game, allowing Schayes only nine points and Tannenbaum five. The final was North Carolina 57, NYU 49.

The semifinal game in the East was the opposite of Oklahoma A & M's cakewalk in the West. It took an overtime period to decide it, one in which North Carolina outscored Ohio State 6–3 for a 60–57 win. Bones McKinney had been held to nine points, but Dillon scored 16, high for the Tar Heels that night. After the game McKinney told one sportswriter, "I had to save some of my strength for Kurland."

Indeed he did. And he had his hands full from the moment the two centers lined up at the opening tip until McKinney fouled out of the game with a long 14 minutes left to play. Even with McKinney benched, the Tar Heels were never out of the game, and many felt the outcome might have been different if he had been able to stay around to harass Kurland until the final buzzer. As it was, however, Kurland dropped in 23 points, the Aggies a total of 43, enough to give them a three-point victory and their second straight NCAA championship. They became the first school ever to accomplish that. And Bob Kurland became the first cager ever to be named the tourney's Outstanding Player twice in a row. Over the history of the tournament only four other players would earn the award more than once: Alex Groza of Kentucky, Jerry Lucas of Ohio State, and Lew Alcindor and Bill Walton of UCLA.

Another first that year in the NCAA tourney was a face-off between the runners-up in the East and the West. They, too, were brought to Madison Square Garden to vie for third place in the tournament, and in that first consolation game Ohio State had no trouble whatsoever with California, crushing them 63–45.

Bob Kurland would graduate from Oklahoma A & M after the 1945–46 season, and the team would not make an appearance in the following year's NCAA tourney. The pendulum of basketball strength was about to swing to the East, as names like Bob Cousy, Ralph Beard, Alex Groza, "Easy" Ed MacCauley, and Paul Arizin would get the headlines instead of such westerners as Kurland, Pollard, Sailors, and Ferrin.

3
Kentucky Comes of Age

Adolph Rupp came to the University of Kentucky to take over the basketball coaching duties in 1930. He would remain for 42 years, becoming a legend in his own right and a member of the National Basketball Hall of Fame. And in that illustrious career there were certainly no more glorious days than those in the late 1940s and early '50s, when he would win first an NIT crown and then three NCAA titles in four years.

The Kentucky dynasty began to emerge in 1946 when Rupp, the "Baron of Lexington" as he came to be called, and his center Alex Groza led the team to an NIT triumph. Edging out a strong Rhode Island team by a single point in the final game, 46–45, they had earned their first postseason crown. The following year they would return to the NIT, only to be upset this time in the championship game by Utah. It would be another year before they exploded on the NCAA scene.

While Kentucky was preoccupied with the NIT, the power in the NCAA was in the process of being transferred to the East. Teams from west of the Mississippi River had dominated the tournament for five straight years, but that was about to change in 1947. How enduring the transfer would be is reflected in the fact that only one team from the West would triumph in the NCAA during the next eight years.

Unseating the West was a small but very good team from Worcester, Massachusetts, named Holy Cross. Nicknamed the Crusaders, they did not have a large enough gymnasium

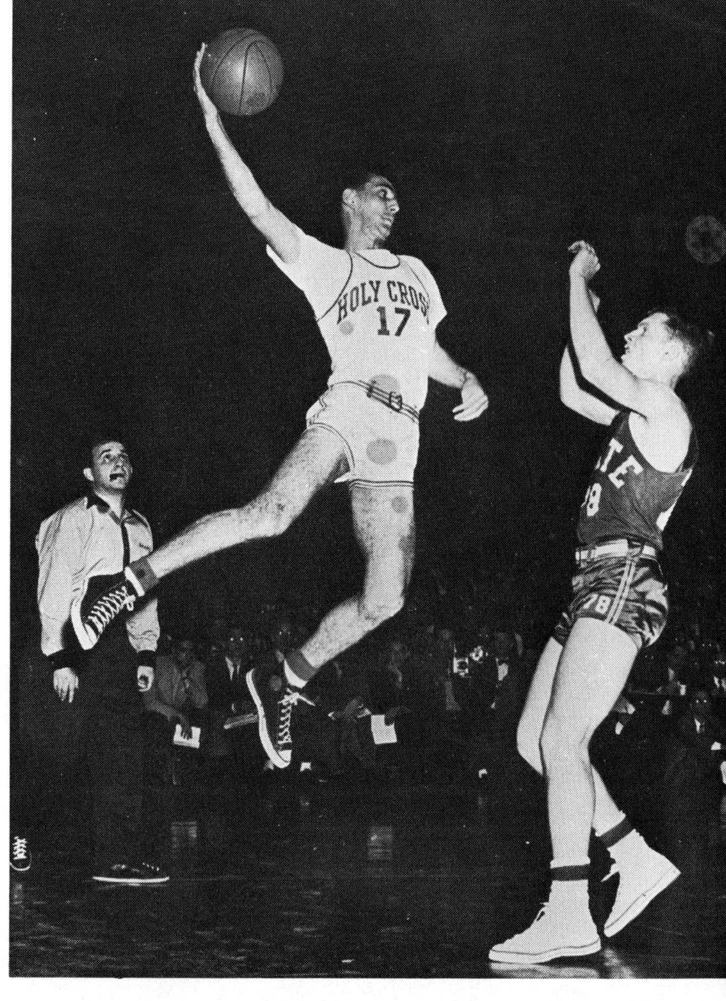

Doing what he did so well, fabled Holy Cross guard Bob Cousy rifles a leaping pass in the 1948 tourney game for third place against Kansas State. Cousy's best game that tournament was the first-round win over Michigan when he toted up 23 points. A two-time All-American and holder of the nickname "Mr. Basketball," Cousy was named to the National Basketball Hall of Fame in 1970.

for home games and therefore had to play all their regular season games on the road or at Boston Garden. They did, however, have an All-American candidate in George Kaftan. At 6′4″, he was their center and the tallest man in the starting lineup. They also had a freshman reserve guard, Bob Cousy, who played some of the time that year and was destined for basketball immortality. What they lacked in height, however, the Crusaders made up for in speed, hustle, dazzling ball handling, and an exceptionally talented group of players riding their bench.

The coach of the Holy Cross Crusaders was Alvin "Doggie" Julian, in his second year at the school. His brand of basketball was a dizzying one to watch—a lot of fast breaks, constant motion on offense with weaves and fast-paced passing, and a lot of substituting to keep the players on the court at their freshest. Navy, now being coached by Ben Carnavale, the man who had led North Carolina to the NCAA championship tilt the year before, was favored over Holy Cross in the first round, but Navy quickly found out just how volatile the Crusaders were. The score was close during the first half, with the lead often changing hands; at the intermission Navy trailed by a lone basket. But in the second half the Middies from Annapolis couldn't keep up with Holy Cross's breathless attack. The Crusaders steadily built their lead until they had Navy down eight points at the final buzzer. Guard Jim Mullaney was high scorer for Holy Cross, dropping in nine field goals for a total of 18 points, and George Kaftan added 15 points.

The jubilant Holy Cross Crusaders hoist coach Alvin "Doggie" Julian to their shoulders after thrashing Oklahoma 58–47 for the 1947 NCAA crown. Left to right: Joe Mullaney (11), Bob Cousy (17), George Kaftan (giving the "V" for victory sign), Dermie O'Connell, and Bob McMullan.

In the other NCAA East first-round game City College of New York, better known simply as CCNY, upset Wisconsin in a remarkable, come-from-behind game in which it made up a 10-point halftime deficit to win 70–56.

The first half of the NCAA East semifinal game was similar to the contest between Holy Cross and Navy, and, as in that game, the Crusaders led by two points when the first half ended. But in the second half it was all Holy Cross, George Kaftan in particular. The Crusaders swept CCNY right out of the arena, outscoring their opponents 33–20. Kaftan had 30 of the Crusaders' total of 60 points, tying the tournament record set four years earlier by John Hargis of Texas.

Texas, with Hargis still a starter at forward and a masterful guard by the name of Slater Martin, battled its way to the NCAA West semifinals in 1947 by beating Wyoming in a thriller, 42–40. Its neighbor to the north, Oklahoma, got there too, by eliminating Oregon State in an equally exciting game that was also decided by a single basket. But Oklahoma copped the ticket to the finals by nipping Texas by a single point on a last-second shot by Ken Pryor in overtime.

Oklahoma's ace was center Gerry Tucker, who had led the team in scoring in both of its previous tournament wins with 17 and 15 points. He would also prove to be the championship game's highest scorer. But his 22 points that night would not be enough. Oklahoma would blow a three-point halftime lead to the ever-exciting, second-half Crusaders who would once again show that no one ran better in the stretch than they did. They rallied

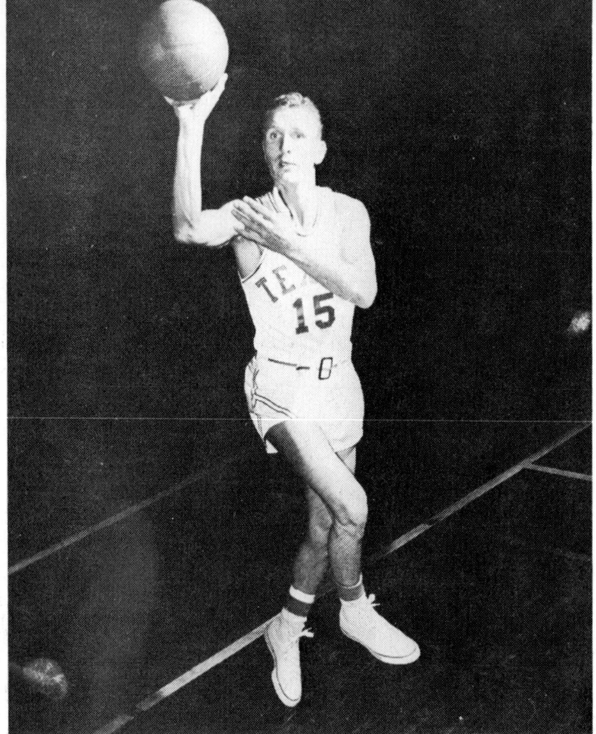

Slater Martin was the pepperpot of the 1947 Texas Longhorns. Behind his ball-handling wizardry and prolific scoring, Texas reached the semifinals where, despite his 18 points, the Longhorns lost a one-point heartbreaker to Oklahoma. He was inducted into the National Basketball Hall of Fame in 1981.

George Kaftan (12), posing here with Dermie O'Connell, was the Crusader's chief scoring threat in 1947. His 30 points in Holy Cross's romp over CCNY in the semifinals and 18 in the championship win over Oklahoma were team highs. Kaftan also played in the 1948 tournament, scoring 41 points in three games.

to defeat the Sooners 58–47. For Holy Cross Kaftan scored 18, and forwards Dermie O'Connell and Frank Oftring added 16 and 14 respectively.

George Kaftan was chosen as the tournament's Outstanding Player. Freshman Bob Cousy had contributed only 13 points in Holy Cross's three games; his time for glory was still just a little further down the road. Cousy would be back the next year as a starter; so would Kaftan, Mullaney, O'Connell, and Oftring. Holy Cross would again attend the NCAA postseason festivities, but so would Adolph Rupp's Kentucky Wildcats.

The phenomenal Kentucky team of 1947–48 was built from a melange of war veterans and youngsters not long out of high school, and it was one of the most perfect blends ever to grace a basketball court. There were three legitimate All-Americans on the team: 6′7″ center Alex Groza, guard Ralph Beard, and forward Wallace "Wah Wah" Jones. And the other two members of the starting five, forward Cliff Barker and guard Ken Rollins, certainly warranted an honorable mention in that category. But despite—or perhaps because of—all the individual talent, they worked together in perfect harmony.

Kentucky lost only two games that season, upsets at the hands of Temple and Notre Dame. It easily won the Southeastern Conference title, chose the NCAA bid over the NIT, and went to the tournament a consensus pick to win it all—which it did, and with ease.

Columbia, representing District 2, was Kentuky's first victim. Columbia was never in the game and was finally decimated 76–53. Wah Wah Jones had 21 that night, Groza 17, and Beard 15; the Wildcats' 76 points were the most ever scored in the NCAA tourney save for the 79 Arkansas rang up in beating Oregon in 1945.

The win qualified Kentucky to meet the returning champion Crusaders from Holy Cross. Almost all tournament observers agreed that this was truly the championship game, and the fact that the winner of it would have to go on to combat the western finalist was merely an afterthought. These were without a doubt the two best college basketball teams in

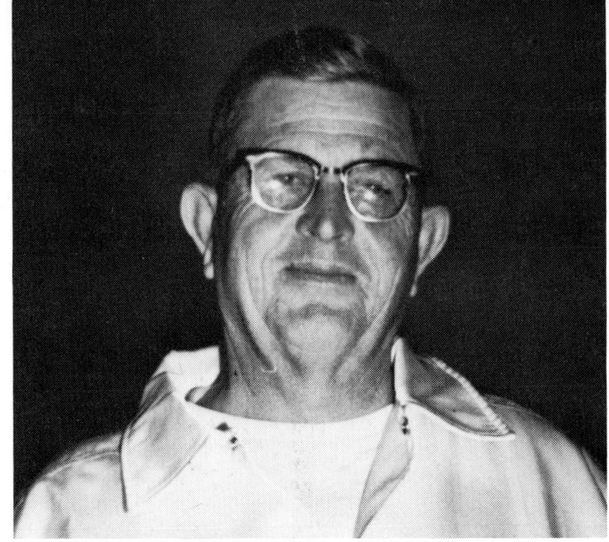

Coach Bill Henderson brought the Baylor Bears to two upset victories and a berth in the finals of 1948. But the party ended there at the hands of Kentucky, a team coached by Arnold Rupp and paced by such stars as Alex Groza, Ralph Beard, and Wah Wah Jones.

Just as Jack Kerris, Loyola of Chicago's center, dominates the boards here, the Ramblers squelched Kentucky in the quarterfinal game of the 1949 NIT tourney. The upset by Loyola denied NCAA champion Kentucky a two-tourney sweep. Number 23 for Loyola is guard Ralph Klaerich. In the background is LU's other guard, Gerry Nagle. Number 18 for Kentucky is forward Dale Barnstable.

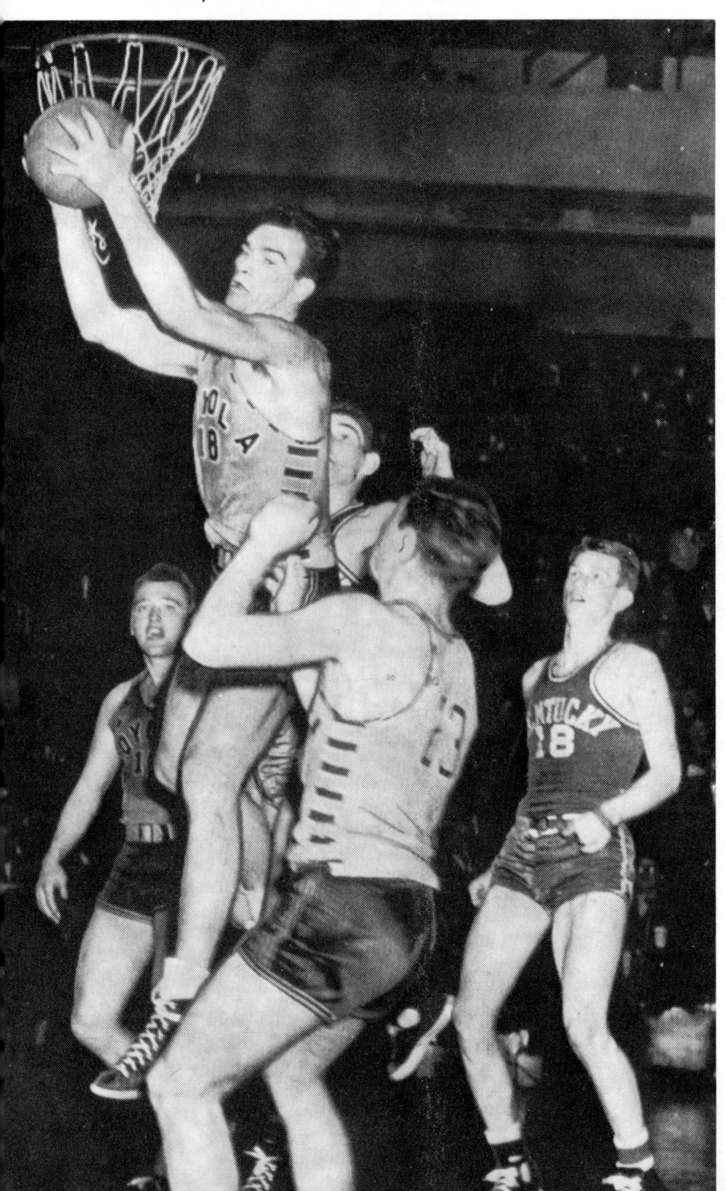

the nation that year. Adolph Rupp knew that the key to beating Holy Cross was to stop Cousy and Kaftan. Cousy had scored 23 points and Kaftan 15 in the Crusaders' first-round massacre of Big Ten champion Michigan, a game they won by 18 points. On the other hand, Holy Cross coach Doggie Julian knew his baseline players somehow had to compete well on the boards against the much bigger, stronger front court of Kentucky and somehow keep the combination of Beard and Groza in check if they were to win.

Both tasks proved too formidable for the Crusaders. Cousy was off that night, and Kaftan was overpowered in the battles under the boards. Groza was unstoppable as he maneuvered in and around the key, and Beard was all over the court on offense and defense. Kentucky won it handily, 60–52. Groza was the high scorer for the evening with 23, and Kentucky also got 13 from Beard, 12 from Wah Wah Jones, and eight from Ken Rollins. George Kaftan managed 15 for Holy Cross and Frank Oftring another 11, but Cousy was held to a mere five points.

Baylor, a team that had not been expected to get beyond the first round, had won the NCAA West but was considered a lowly underdog in the finals against Kentucky. Baylor had triumphed over Kansas State and Washington, but those competitions were minimal compared to what Baylor was to face in Madison Square Garden for the NCAA title.

It was a runaway, Kentucky posting 58 points to Baylor's 42. It was the biggest margin of victory in an NCAA championship game since Indiana devoured Kansas by 18 points back in 1940. Again Groza was the game's high scorer, though he could claim only 14 points that evening. Beard had 12, Jones and Rollins had nine apiece, and Jimmy Line came off the bench to add seven. It was not difficult for the NCAA committee to elect Alex Groza Outstanding Player. He had scored 54 points in three games, dominated the boards, proved indefatigable on defense, and illustrated to any doubter that he truly deserved his All-American credentials.

At the end of the 1948–49 basketball season the Kentucky Wildcats could claim a record of

33–1 and were deemed the best college basketball team in the country. From the previous year's championship team, they had lost only Ken Rollins from the starting lineup, and to fill that gap Cliff Barker was moved to guard, and Jimmy Line and occasionally Dale Barnstable replaced him at forward.

Kentucky accepted bids to both the NCAA and the NIT in 1949, hoping to become the first team to win *both* postseason tourneys. But that dream was quickly shattered at Madison Square Garden in the first round of the first of the two tournaments, the NIT, when the Wildcats were stunned by Loyola University of Chicago, 67–56. Loyola's strong center, Jack Kerris, outmuscled and outscored Alex Groza, and the Chicagoans' ace guard, Ralph Klaerich, tamed the Wildcats' Ralph Beard.

Adolph Rupp and his boys took that rude awakening to their vulnerability with them into the NCAA first round. They were not as cocksure as they had been going into the NIT, and it was a good thing in light of who they were playing, a very strong Villanova team, paced by one of the game's highest scorers and an All-American, Paul Arizin.

Kentucky, however, had regained its form and its poise—well enough, in fact, to wipe out the NCAA single-game scoring record by toting up a total of 85 points. The Wildcats had built an 11-point lead at the half, 48–37, then sailed through the second half, with Villanova never really threatening. Alex Groza tied the NCAA single-game scoring record with 30 points, and so did Villanova's Paul Arizin. It was the first time two players in the same NCAA tournament game scored 30 or more points, and that phenomenon would not occur again until the 1953 third place game, when Bob Hourbregs of Washington would tally 42 and Bob Pettit of Louisiana State 36. Jimmy Line also had a hot hand that night for Kentucky, scoring 21, and Cliff Barker added 18.

In the semifinals the Wildcats would face the University of Illinois, which sported its best basketball team since the Whiz Kids of the early 1940s. Paced by Dike Eddleman and Wally Osterkorn, they had gotten by a spirited Yale team, despite a 27-point performance by Eli All-American Tony Lavelli. The NCAA

A consensus All-American in 1949 was Villanova's Paul Arizin. Despite his 31-point effort, Villanova was eliminated in the first round by Kentucky, which set a tourney single-game scoring record in the 85-72 win. Arizin was named to the National Basketball Hall of Fame in 1977.

All-American Center Alex Groza of Kentucky was named Outstanding Player in both the 1948 and 1949 tourneys. He was also the top scorer in each, averaging 18 and 27.3 points respectively. His best single-game performance was the 30 points he racked up when going head-to-head with Villanova's superstar Paul Arizin in '49.

Floor leader for Kentucky's 1948 and 1949 champs was All-American guard Ralph Beard. A playmaker extraordinaire, he was also a gifted shooter.

Wallace "Wah Wah" Jones was a key figure in Kentucky's frontcourt in 1948 and 1949. A consistent scorer and rugged rebounder, the All-American candidate forward had his best single-game effort in Kentucky's first round win over Columbia in 1948 when he scored a game-high 21 points.

eastern semifinal game, however, proved to be a total mismatch. The Wildcats annihilated the Illini 76–47. Groza got 27 that night, Line 15, Beard and Jones nine each, and Barker eight.

Out West, Hank Iba's Oklahoma A & M team was back on top. It had survived a true nail biter in the first round, coming from behind in the second half to eke out a one-point victory over Wyoming, 40–39. The biggest guns for the Aggies were forward Jack Shelton and center Bob Harris. It was primarily Shelton's performance—16 points—that got the Oklahomans into the semifinals, but in that game it was a combination of Harris (23 points) and Shelton (13) that enabled the Aggies to drub Oregon State 55–30.

For the first time since 1941 the championship of the NCAA would not be decided in New York's Madison Square Garden, though that was where the eastern semifinals were held. Instead it was shifted cross-country to the University of Washington's field house in Seattle, which required Kentucky to take a 3,000-mile train trip to participate in it. The decision to move the final game would also prove a financial boondoggle as well because 6,000 fewer spectators would show up for the championship than the year before and 8,000 fewer than had attended the eastern semifinal game that year at Madison Square Garden.

Train travel apparently was no deterrent to Kentucky, however. The Wildcats took command of the championship game early and maintained it throughout the game. It was a low-scoring affair, at least for a Kentucky team which had averaged 80.5 points in its two earlier playoff games. But Kentucky's 46 points were sufficient because the Oklahoma Aggies could come up with only 36. Groza again was the game's predominant figure, scoring 25 points and controlling the boards.

With a three-game total of 82 points, by far the most scored in an NCAA tournament up to that time, Alex Groza was a cinch for the Outstanding Player award, becoming only the second player to win it twice in a row. Groza had led the Kentucky Wildcats to two consecutive NCAA titles, just as Bob Kurland, the other two-time OP award winner, had led the Oklahoma Aggies in 1945 and 1946.

Adolph Rupp, a legend in the sport of college basketball, coached Kentucky to four NCAA championships: 1948, 1949, 1951, and 1958. He was inducted into the National Basketball Hall of Fame in 1968.

When the 1950s dawned they did so on a University of Kentucky that no longer had the services of Alex Groza, Ralph Beard, Wah Wah Jones, or Cliff Barker. Adolph Rupp, as a matter of fact, had only one starter returning from the previous year, forward Jimmy Line. He did, however, have high hopes for a towering stilt of a center, seven-foot Bill Spivey, and a good ball-handling guard named Bobby Watson.

It would not be a glory year for the Wildcats, rather one of rebuilding and working out the proverbial kinks that plague a young team. The NCAA would not even choose to invite the reigning titleholders to their tournament at season's end that year, selecting North Carolina State in their stead. The NIT would, however, extend a bid, and the Wildcats would go to Madison Square Garden, only to be cut to pieces by a little upstart of a team from CCNY. The Beavers, as they were called, started one senior and four sophomores and sported a mediocre record of 17 and five for the regular season, but they totally embarrassed Rupp's Wildcats 89–50 in the NIT's second round.

CCNY was indeed a "Cinderella" team, dubbed as such by sportswriters during the postseason tourneys of 1950. The Beavers acquired the name "Cinderella" because of the surprises they wrought at the end of that basketball year. They were truly the belle of the ball, but unlike the fairy tale, their story would not have a happy ending. There would be no prince to rescue them from the scandal that would be revealed the following year and forever tarnish their mantle of victory. But in 1950 they did experience the exhilaration of triumph, even if it was short-lived.

A basketball legend, Nat Holman, a star of the original Celtics and a coach at CCNY since 1917, was the guiding light for the Beavers of City College. His youthful team was spearheaded by forward Irwin Dambrot, the only player who wasn't a sophomore. Holman's biggest man was center Ed Roman at 6′6″, but the special forte of the team was the way they played together, each member contributing an equal share.

The miraculous times began for Holman and his cagers with the NIT tournament. They were a long shot—if it were a horse race, probably about 60–1. But after they demolished tournament favorite Kentucky by 39 points at Madison Square Garden no one was taking them for granted, though no one was crying champion either. But they made it to the championship game to face Bradley, a team from Peoria, Illinois, which AP had ranked number one, at the end of the regular season. The Braves had three All-American candidates in guards Gene Melchiorre and Bill Mann and forward Paul Unruh. That did not faze CCNY. The Beavers controlled the game and defeated a surprised Bradley 69–61. Then they took their tourney trophy, put it into the school's trophy case, and went back to the Garden to compete in the NCAA playoffs.

Their first opponent was Big Ten champ Ohio State, a team that showcased one of the nation's leading scorers, forward Dick Schnittker. And the Buckeye whiz lived up to his reputation, scoring 26 points against the Beavers, but he also made the mistake of fouling out of the game. With Schnittker on the bench, Ohio State faltered and then lost by a single point, 56–55, in a true thriller of a

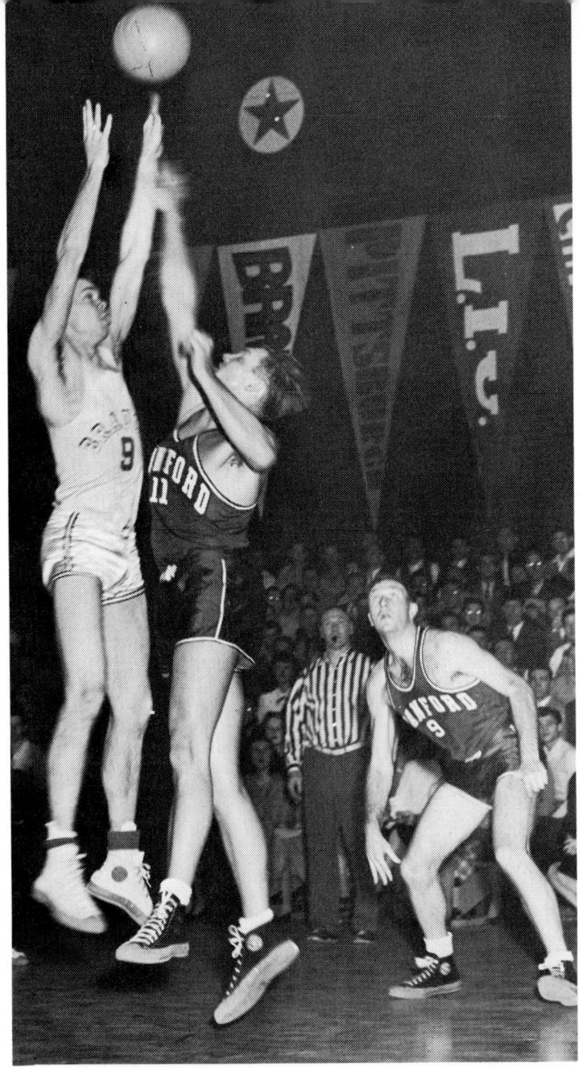

Paul Unruh (9), going up for a jumper against Stanford, was a two-time All-American for Bradley. He was held to a mere 28 points in Bradley's three 1950 tourney games, a miniscule segment of the record-setting 1,822 he logged at Bradley.

Guard Bill Mann was a key figure on the 1950 Bradley Braves, a team that went to the finals of both the NCAA and the NIT. With Gene Melchiorre at the other guard post, Bradley claimed one of the finest backcourts in the nation that year. Mann was the Braves' high scorer in their semifinal victory over Baylor but fouled out in losing the title game to CCNY.

Irwin Dambrot was CCNY's captain and floor leader in 1950 and scored the most CCNY points in the NCAA title game with 15.

game. For CCNY Irwin Dambrot was held to eight points, but Floyd Lane bucketed 17 and Norm Mager another 15, and CCNY moved on to the semifinals.

In the other NCAA eastern regional playoff North Carolina State set a new team scoring record for the tournament when it throttled Bob Cousy and the Holy Cross Crusaders 87–74, behind the prolific scoring of Sam Ranzino (30 points to tie the tournament record) and All-American candidate Dick Dickey (25). State was favored over CCNY, but then so had been Kentucky, Bradley, and Ohio State in preceding postseason games. Nat Holman knew, however, that if he was to pull off one more upset here his team would have to accumulate a lot of points. And it did, enough to win by five, 78–73. It was a true team effort, with center Ed Roman its highest scorer with 21 points, but Ed Warner contributed 17, Irwin Dambrot 13, Floyd Lane 10, and Norm Mager nine. For North Carolina State, Ranzino had 24 and Dickey 16, but it was CCNY that would go to the finals.

The NCAA championship would be a replay of the NIT title tilt, not only at the same site, Madison Square Garden, but with the same two teams as well. Bradley had mauled

UCLA and then slipped past Baylor by two points to earn its way to the final game. Needless to say, the Braves from Peoria and their coach Forddy Anderson were thirsting for revenge. And the oddsmakers thought they would get it. "There is a limit to the number of miracles in any given year," one sportswriter observed.

The game was close during the first half, but when the two teams left the court for the mid-game break CCNY had pulled to a seven-point lead. The Beavers maintained it for most of the second half, but then in the waning moments Bradley fought back to within a single point. With only about a half minute to go in the game, the Braves stole the ball, and guard Gene Melchiorre went for the lead with a jump shot from within the key, but Dambrot leaped up and blocked it. He came up with the ball, saw Norm Mager wide open, and passed the ball to him for an easy lay-up. The final score was CCNY 71, Bradley 68. It was not easy to select an Outstanding Player that year because CCNY had such a balanced attack, but it finally was awarded to Irwin Dambrot, whose 15 points had been the most for CCNY in the championship game.

Nat Holman, a legendary basketball name, was the mentor of the Cinderella CCNY champs of 1950. A player on the original Celtics in the 1920s, Holman coached at CCNY for 37 years, winning 421 games while losing only 190. He was elected to the National Basketball Hall of Fame in 1964.

The CCNY Beavers became the first and *only* team in college basketball history to win both the NCAA and NIT tournaments in the same year. All of it would be irrevocably marred when, in 1951, it would be revealed that players on the CCNY team as well as on a number of other teams, including the championship ones from Kentucky in 1948 and 1949, had players who fixed games by shaving points. At the time it was the most shocking scandal ever to hit amateur athletics, and it

CCNY, the first and only team ever to take both the NCAA and NIT crowns in the same year, 1950. **Bottom row** (left to right): Mike Wittlin, Ed Roman, Joe Galiber, Nat Holman (coach), Irwin Dambrot, Norman Mager, Seymour Levey. **Second row** (left to right): Floyd Layne, Arnold Smith, Ed Warner, Al Roth, Herb Cohen. **Third row** (left to right): Ronald Nadell, Arthur Glass, Leroy Watkins, Ed Chenetz, Larry Meyer. **Top row** (left to right): Al Ragusa (manager), Bobby Sand (assistant coach).

would forever stain some of college basketball's finest teams.

In 1951 the NCAA expanded its tournament to include 16 teams, double the number that had participated in the previous 12 postseason sessions. Still a single-game elimination format, the tourney would now be attended by the teams with the best won-lost percentages in the 10 major collegiate conferences in the nation as well as six teams selected at large.

There was no way that Kentucky could be kept out of the 1951 NCAA tourney. It had won 26 of its 28 games during the season, its two losses surprising upsets at the hands of St. Louis and Vanderbilt. At season's end Kentucky was ranked the number one team in the country and considered a favorite to win the NCAA national championship.

The big difference for Kentucky in 1950–51 was the emergence by tourney time of two freshmen on the starting lineup, forward Cliff Hagan and guard Frank Ramsey. They teamed with All-American center Bill Spivey and such other veterans as Bobby Watson at guard and Shelby Linville at the other forward position. Once again Adolph Rupp had a Kentucky team that was a perfectly tuned blend of scoring and rebounding talent.

Representing the Southeastern Conference, Kentucky went to the NCAA playoffs to face intrastate rival Louisville, one of the six at-large invitees. Determined to stop Spivey, the Wildcats' giant center, Louisville forgot about forward Shelby Linville. That was a mistake because, as a result, he rang up the most memorable game of his college basketball career, scoring 23 points that evening. Reserve guard Skip Whitaker also dropped in eight field goals while Louisville was concentrating on Spivey. Along with 14 points from Frank Ramsey, 10 from Spivey, eight from Hagan, and six from Watson, it was enough to give the Wildcats a 79–68 win and a pass to the tourney's second round.

Awaiting them at that junction was St. John's University from Jamaica, New York, long a power in the NIT and gilded in 1951 with stars like center Bob Zawoluk, and a guard by the name of Al McGuire, who would one day coach Marquette to an NCAA Championship and then as a broadcaster become college basketball's most colorful spokesman. St. John's, however, was no match for the young men representing the Blue Grass State of Kentucky. The Wildcats were slow in getting started and trailed by a point at the intermission, but in the second half they exploded, outscoring St. John's 36–19. Again, it was a team effort. Spivey was held to 12 points, but Ramsey plunked in 13, Watson 12, and Linville nine to give the Wildcats the 59–43 win.

Kentucky's biggest test in the tournament awaited the team in the semifinal game at Madison Square Garden. The University of Illinois, Big Ten champs, had destroyed Columbia and North Carolina State to reach the semifinal game. Illinois was soaring behind high-scoring forward Don Sunderlage, who had scored 25 and 21 points in the Illini's two preceding games. But unlike Kentucky's two earlier opponents, Illinois would not be able to control big Bill Spivey. The lanky seven-footer scored 28 points and was awesome on the boards in the eastern semifinal clash. Still

Coach Harry Combes (left) and captain Don Sunderlage of the 1951 Fighting Illini. Behind the talents of these two, Illinois won the Big 10 title and reached the NCAA semifinals where they lost a thriller to tourney champ Kentucky on a last-second basket. Sunderlage scored 83 points in his four tournament games.

it was a battle royal all the way. Kentucky, down by seven at the half, fought back. The lead changed hands often during the fourth quarter. Kentucky was indeed in hazardous straits late in the game because Spivey had fouled out, and so had Cliff Hagan and Skip Whitaker. But the Wildcats hung on, and with the game tied and only about 10 seconds left, Shelby Linville dropped one in to give the Wildcats a 76–74 lead. The Illini brought the ball downcourt frantically and got it to Sunderlage, who took the game's last shot and missed. Kentucky had hung on by the most tenuous thread to win the NCAA East and the privilege of going to its third national championship game. In the history of the NCAA tournament at that point only Oklahoma A & M had made as many appearances in the finals.

In the West, Hank Iba's Oklahoma A & M Aggies were making a spirited attempt to get into their fourth NCAA championship game, at least through the first two rounds. They had brushed aside Montana State and Washington and were rated a toss-up with Kansas State in the semifinals. But something happened on the way to the forum in Kansas City, and the Aggies' dream of another run at the title was convincingly demolished. Nothing would go right. By the end of the half they had scored only 14 points against Kansas State's 37. The second half offered no reprieve, and Kansas State erupted into the finals with a 68–44 devastation of Oklahoma A & M.

Kansas State was indeed a team to be reckoned with, having won a tough Big Seven conference as well as a decisive victory over NIT champion Brigham Young on its way to the NCAA finals. Kansas State was in many ways similar to the CCNY team that had prevailed in the tourney the year before. There were no national standouts on the starting lineup, no big-name scorers; instead the Kansas State team was a remarkable example of precision teamwork. Also like CCNY, it possessed a bench that could be platooned or used as a continual funnel to relieve starters who were tired or off their game. As an example, the most points scored by any K-Stater in the three playoff games before the finale was 13, racked up by Ed Head against Arizona in the

Jack Stone was Kansas State's hot hand in 1951. He led the Wildcats to the finals that year, where they succumbed to another Wildcat team, this one from Kentucky.

Big Bill Spivey was the tower around which the Kentucky champs of 1951 operated. The 7′ center was the tourney's leading rebounder, averaging 16.3 a game. In the championship win over Kansas State, Spivey had game-highs of 22 points and 21 rebounds.

first round and again by Bob Rousey against Brigham Young in the second. High scorer in the rout of Oklahoma A & M was Lew Hitch with 12, while Dick Knostman contributed 11, Jack Stone 10, and Head and Jim Iverson nine. A total of 10 Kansas State players made the box score with points that night.

Adolph Rupp knew his Kentucky Wildcats were in for a most demanding evening. He feared the tremendous bench strength of Kansas State, and he was well aware of his team's propensity for fouling. He remembered only too well that in the semifinals Spivey, Hagan, and Whitaker had been sitting next to him on the bench during the last, deciding moments of the game, each having fouled out, and that Watson and Linville had been toiling on the court under the burden of four fouls each.

On the other hand, Kansas State's coach, Jack Gardner, fretted about Billy Spivey's imposing presence on the court and Kentucky's balanced scoring attack.

The game was anybody's in the first half, with Kansas State maintaining the edge most of the way. It had a two-point lead at the half and took pride in the fact that it had virtually neutralized Spivey. But this was not to last. Adolph Rupp did something to inspire his cagers during the intermission because they roared back in the second half. There was no stopping Spivey now, and Kentucky steadily pulled ahead of Kansas State, coasting in with a margin of 10 at the buzzer, the final score 68–58. Spivey, as a result of his second-half surge, was by far the game's high scorer with 22 points. Hagan had 10, Whitaker and Ramsey nine each, and Linville and Watson eight apiece. For Kansas State Hitch scored 13 and Stone 12. Although Bill Spivey had been the dominating force in the championship game, he was not chosen as the tournament's Outstanding Player. For the first time since 1939 no such award was made.

Kentucky had now become the first team in the history of the NCAA tourney to win the national championship three times (Today only UCLA and Indiana can claim to have won it as many or more times.) By the early 1950s there were no bigger names in the game of college basketball than Adolph Rupp and the University of Kentucky. But some others

Cliff Hagan, a freshman starter at forward on Kentucky's 1951 champs, was destined for All-American status. He scored 10 points for the Wildcats in the '51 title game.

would rise with their own special glitter before Rupp would be able to bring his team back to the NCAA finals—Phog Allen, Clyde Lovellette, Branch McCracken, Don Schlundt, Tom Gola, Bill Russell, Frank McGuire, and Wilt Chamberlain, among many others.

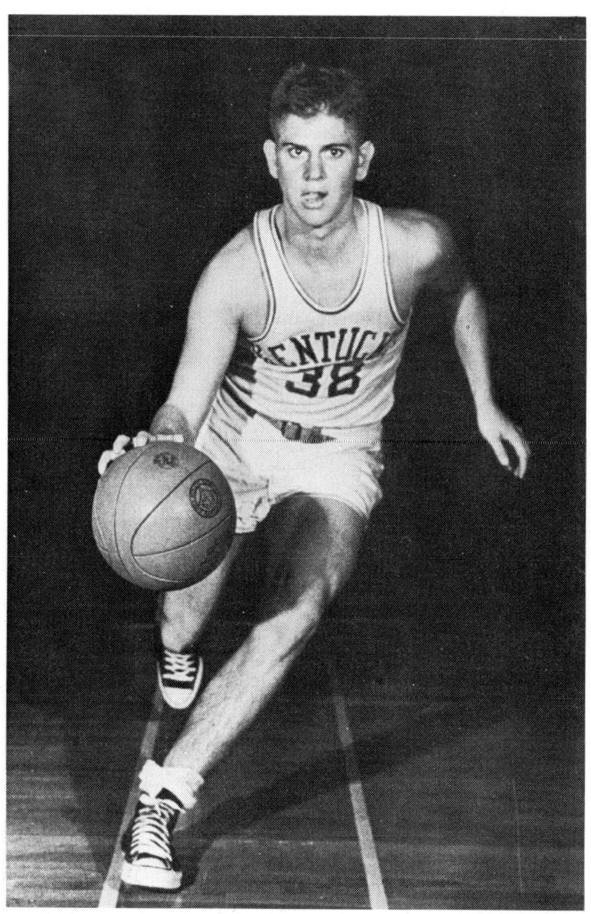

Kentucky had two dazzling guards in 1951, Frank Ramsey (left) and Bobby Watson (38). Both were superb playmakers and sharpshooters.

4
Lovellette to Russell to Kentucky Again

As the 16 teams queued up for the 1952 NCAA championship tourney, Kentucky again appeared to be the team to beat. Adolph Rupp's Wildcats had ended the regular season at the top of both the AP and UPI polls, ranked number one in the nation. Bill Spivey was gone, but Cliff Hagan had developed one of the game's most balanced blends of scoring and rebounding skills, and the 6′4″ forward was a unanimous All-American selection. Then, after their first-round devastation of Penn State, 82–54, a game in which Hagan logged 20 points, it was generally agreed that the Wildcats were indeed on their way to a fourth national championship in five years.

Frank McGuire and the St. John's team he coached did not see it that way, however. The underdog Redmen had made up their collective mind that *they* would go to that year's semifinals, that the Wildcats of Kentucky had been there often enough and now it was time for someone else. They were also bent on a little revenge after having been ousted from the tournament by Kentucky in the second round the year before.

St. John's center and highest scorer, Bob Zawoluk, was the least intimidated by Kentucky and its reputation. The year before he had held Spivey to 12 points while scoring 15 himself. Now, in 1952, he proved even more resplendent against the intruders from Lexington. There was virtually no stopping Zawoluk that night as he set a new NCAA tournament scoring record. His 32 points broke the record of 31 set a few nights earlier

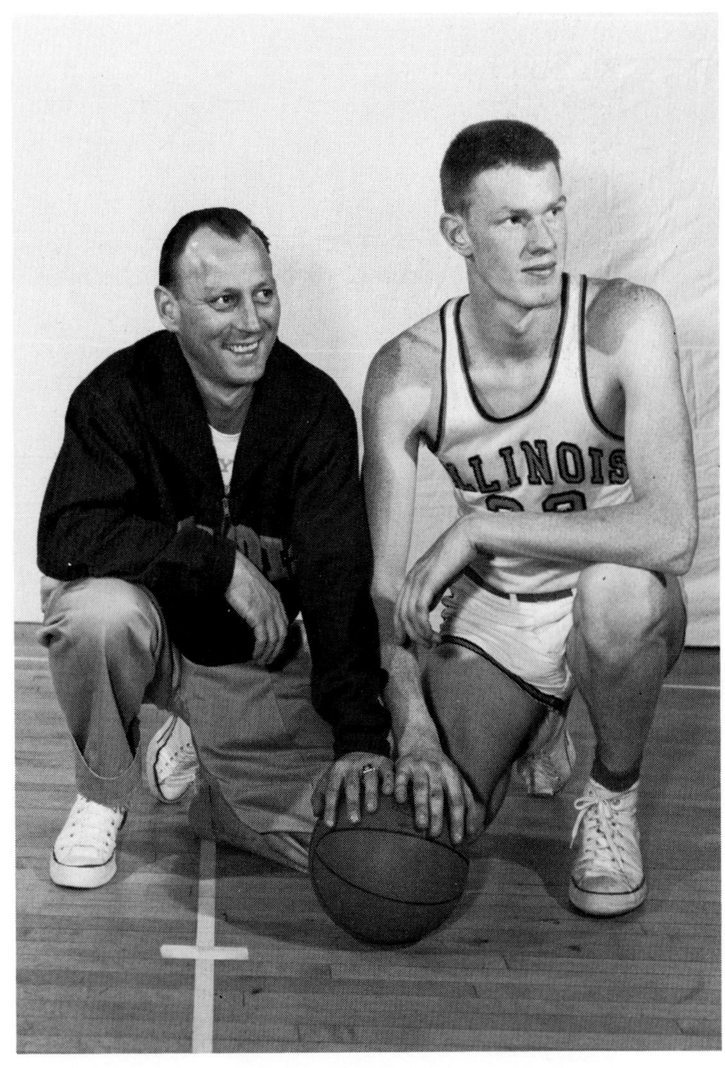

Johnny "Red" Kerr held down the pivot post for Illinois in 1952, pictured here with his coach, Harry Combes. With Kerr's rebounding and scoring, Illinois reached the semifinals but then fell to St. John's by a basket. Kerr scored 26 points in the third-place game.

by Kansas center Clyde Lovellette in a first-round game against Texas Christian. St. John's forward Jack McMahon was also hot for the Redmen as they faced down Kentucky, scoring an additional 18 points. It all added up to a 64–57 victory for St. Johns, despite Cliff Hagan's 22-point performance on Kentucky's behalf.

Bob Zawoluk's new record stood for only a matter of hours. In the Midwest regional final over in Kansas City, Clyde Lovellette reclaimed it with a spectacular 44-point performance as Kansas romped its way into the semifinals by squelching St. Louis 74–55.

In the other two regional final games Illinois defeated Duquesne, and Santa Clara pulled off its second upset of the tourney by beating Wyoming.

St. John's had the toughest task. It had upset number-one-ranked Kentucky. Now it faced number-two-ranked Illinois, which was paced by an especially strong center, Johnny Kerr, and blessed with prolific scorers like Jim Bredar and Irv Bemoras. But St. John's was on a roll. Zawoluk tossed in 24 points to lead the Redmen to their second upset victory in a row, this time squeaking by on a single basket. Kansas meanwhile decimated little Santa Clara 74–55, with Lovellette adding to his gluttonous scoring spree with 33 points.

Kansas was under the brilliant tutelage of Dr. Forrest C. "Phog" Allen, one of the game's legends and a charter member of the basketball Hall of Fame. The founder of the National Association of Basketball Coaches (in 1927), he had been at the helm of the Kansas Jayhawks continually since 1920 (he had also coached there in 1908 and 1909), and now he had an extraordinary property in uniform. Clyde Lovellette, a senior, was perhaps the most formidable presence battling under the basket since DePaul's George Mikan and Oklahoma A & M's Bob Kurland had established the big man's place in the game a decade earlier. A burly center, he stood 6′9″ and weighed in the vicinity of 250 pounds. Lovellette was punishing under the boards, as any opposing center would painfully testify,

Clyde Lovellette (16), All-American center from Kansas, goes up for an easy two in this game against Oklahoma. Lovellette set a variety of scoring records in the 1952 tourney as he led the Jayhawks to the national championship, including a 44-point performance against St. Louis.

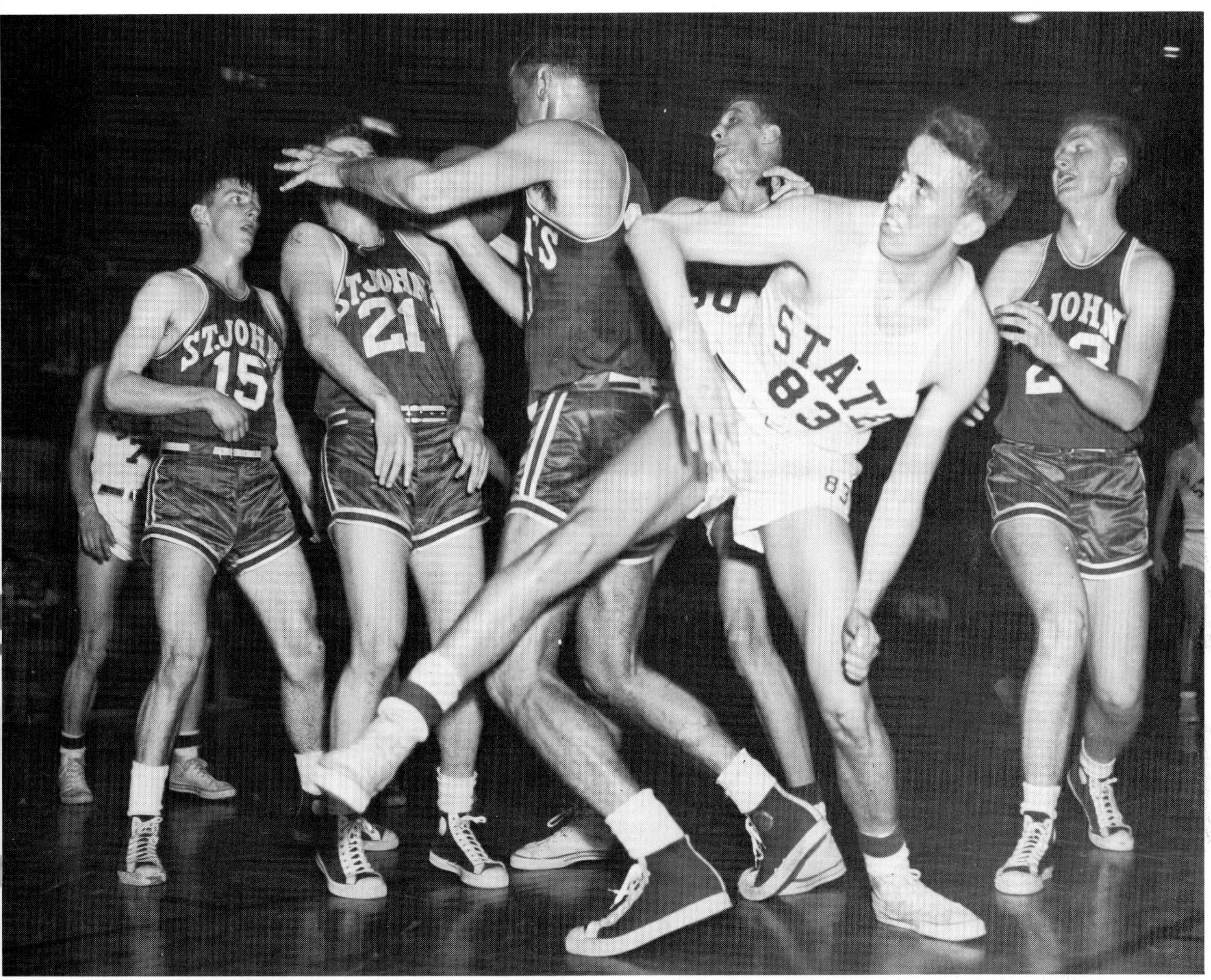

Among the horde of St. Johns' Redmen battling for the ball in this 1952 tourney encounter with North Carolina State is All-American center Bob Zawoluk, though it appears that all he is getting is the face of fellow Redman Dick McGuire (21). Number 15 is Ron McGilvray; number 23, Jim Davis.

but he was also a dynamite scorer. The 1951–52 season was his last as a collegian, and when it was over he had claim to the NCAA career scoring mark with 1,888 points, and his career average of 28.4 points per game set another NCAA record.

Now, in the postseason, he was rewriting the NCAA tournament record books. And in the championship game he was easily the predominant factor. Even the talented center for St. John's, Bob Zawoluk, could not slow Lovellette down. The imposing Jayhawk racked up 33 points, the same amount he had in the semifinal game, and Kansas was never threatened as it pummeled the Redmen from St. John's 80–63. Bill Lienhard and Bob Kenney dropped in another 12 apiece for the Jayhawks, while Bob Zawoluk had 20 for St. John's and Jack McMahon 13. The 80 points Kansas posted represented the most scored up to that time in an NCAA championship game, and the margin of victory was the highest since Indiana beat another Kansas team by 18 back in 1940.

Awards, 1952

Outstanding Player
Clyde Lovellette (Kansas)

All-Tournament Team
Clyde Lovellette (Kansas)
Bob Zawoluk (St. John's)
Johnny Kerr (Illinois)
Ron MacGilvray (St. John's)
Dean Kelley (Kansas)

Lovellette had averaged 35.3 points in the four games of the tournament, easily a new NCAA standard. He also set records for total points (141) and total rebounds (69). He was a unanimous choice for the tourney's Outstanding Player award. And Phog Allen could luxuriate in his first, and what would prove to be his only, national championship.

For the first time since 1939 an All-Tournament Team was selected, and it would become a tradition from that year forward. Needless to say, Clyde Lovellette headed the list of honorees.

Phog Allen would bring his Kansas team back to the NCAA championship tilt in 1953, but without the services of his mighty center Clyde Lovellette. Unfortunately, the tourney would not prove as hospitable as it had in 1952. The difference would be another center, a 6′10″, 19-year-old sophomore from Indiana by the name of Don Schlundt.

Kansas and Indiana could each claim one NCAA basketball championship in the tournament's then 15-year history before facing each other for the 1953 title. They had also met in the same game 13 years earlier when McCracken's Hoosiers lambasted Allen's Jayhawks 60–42 to win the NCAA's second postseason tourney.

Reigning champs or not, Kansas had not been the pretournament favorite. Indiana was considered closer to that status, but there were also a number of other excellent teams that year, all of whom had a very good shot at the tourney trophy: Notre Dame with Joe Bertrand, DePaul with Ron Feiereisel and Jim Lamkin, Seattle with Johnny O'Brien and his twin brother Eddie, Louisiana State with Bob Pettit, Washington with Bob Houbregs, among them.

Two All-Americans, LaSalle's Tom Gola (15) and DePaul's Ron Feiereisel (21) battle for a rebound here, but LaSalle's Jack Moore (8) ended up with the ball. Only DePaul would go to the 1953 NCAA tourney, where the Blue Demons lost a squeaker to Indiana, 82–80, a game in which Feiereisel scored 27 points.

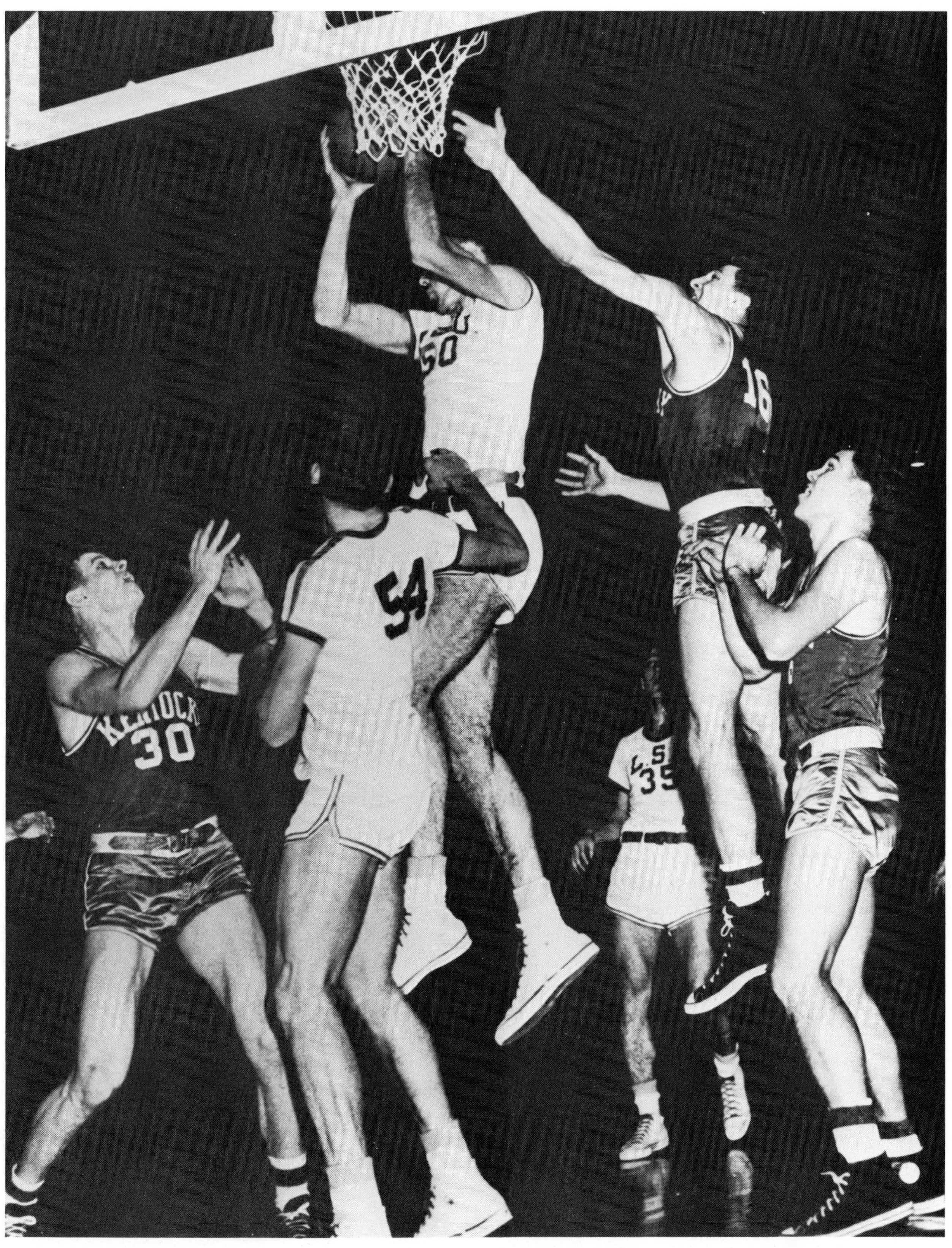

Kentucky and LSU battled for the SEC crown in 1953, but it had no bearing on who would go to the NCAA tourney because Adolph Rupp's Wildcats had been barred from postseason play. LSU made it to the semifinals but was overcome there by Indiana, 80–67. That's All- American Bob Pettit snatching the rebound for LSU.

The tournament had been enlarged in 1953 to 22 teams, adding four new conference winners and two more at-large entries. As a result 10 teams would get byes into the second round. Both Kansas and Indiana, winners respectively of the Big Seven and Big Ten conferences, were among those earning byes.

Kansas had little trouble in its first tournament game, disposing of Oklahoma City 73–65. Indiana, on the other hand, had a problem of monstrous proportions with Ray Meyer's DePaul team, one of the at-large invitees. Blowing a comfortable nine-point lead at the half, Indiana had to fight all the way to the wire to eke out a two-point victory. Schlundt scored 23 for the Hoosiers, and All-American guard Bob Leonard had 22. For the Demons of DePaul, their own All-American candidate Ron Feiereisel was the game's high scorer with 27 points while Bill Shyman contributed 17 and Jim Lamkin 15, but it was not quite enough, and Indiana triumphed 82–80.

Indiana faced another strong independent team from the Midwest in the regional finals, Notre Dame, while Kansas was pitted against Hank Iba's Oklahoma A & M Aggies. For Indiana, it was again Don Schlundt night, and what a night. He scored 41 points in leading the Hoosiers to a 79–66 win over the Fighting Irish. Schlundt's 41 points represented the fourth highest ever scored up to that time in an NCAA postseason game, closely following the 42-point performance of Seattle's 5′9″ guard Johnny O'Brien in a first-round game that year against Idaho State and the record-breaking 45 points scored by Bob Houbregs when Washington eliminated Seattle in the next round (eclipsing the record of 44 points set by Clyde Lovellette the year before).

Kansas was led to victory in its regional final by B. H. Born, who had served as the seldom-used backup center to Clyde Lovellette the year before. Born's 18 points and another 16 from Dean Kelley enabled the Jayhawks to wring a six-point victory from an otherwise determined Oklahoma A & M.

To get to the finals, both teams still had major obstacles to overcome in the semifinals. Indiana had to face LSU, a team blessed with sophomore sensation Bob Pettit, who had

Washington's All-American Bob Houbregs (25) poses here with teammate Doug McClary and coach Tippy Dye. Houbregs set an NCAA tourney record in 1953 when he scored 45 points against Seattle; both his 139 points and his 34.8 average were tourney highs that year.

racked up 28 and 29 points in his two preceeding tourney games. Kansas had an equally awesome opponent in Washington, which surged behind the rich scoring of hook shot artist Bob Houbregs. Indiana did not stop Pettit, who scored a game high 29 points, but the Hoosiers' Don Schlundt matched that point total, and Bob Leonard added another 22. It was enough to give Indiana a 13-point victory and a pass to the championship game. Kansas was able to stop the point-producing Houbregs, or at least get him into a position where he stopped himself—Houbregs fouled out in the third quarter, his total points for the night only 18. After that Kansas felt little threat from the Huskies and won it by 26 points, a game that stood as the tournament's major upset. Once again B. H. Born emerged as the Jayhawk hero of the hour, scoring 25 points, but he was ably assisted by Dean Kelley, with 18 points, and Harold Patterson, with 17.

The final game of the 1953 NCAA tournament was destined to be one of the closest, most frantic, and most thrilling in the history of the postseason classic. The two teams played to a standoff at the half, 41–41. It remained much the same through the third quarter, neither team holding a lead of more than a basket, and both teams exchanging the lead on a regular basis. The stars—Schlundt and Leonard for Indiana and Born and Kelley for the Jayhawks—were all playing well. In the fourth quarter there was no letup. The score was tied with a little less than half a minute to go in the game. Then the Jayhawks made a fatal mistake, fouling the ever-cool, hot-handed Bob Leonard. But he missed the first free throw, then made the second—a one-point lead, but the ball would now be in the hands of the Jayhawks. Kansas called a time-out, and Phog Allen told his players to hold the ball for the last shot—the ultimate gamble. Back on the floor, the Jayhawks maneuvered well, but as the seconds ticked down, the Hoosier defense tightened. Kansas was unable to get the ball to one of its best shooters, and that last infamous shot was taken by second-stringer Jerry Albers (playing for the fouled-out B. H. Born). It was not good, and the buzzer a moment later signaled Indiana's sec-

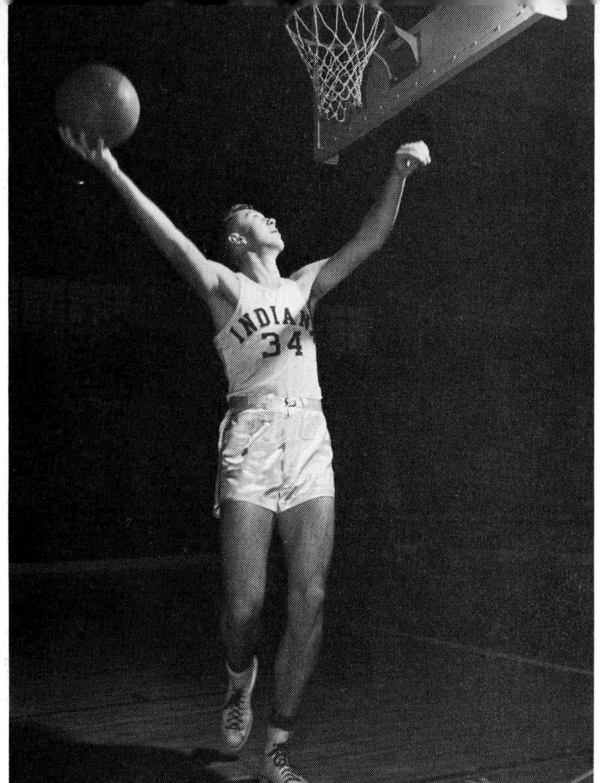

Don Schlundt, Indiana's 6'10" All-American center, led the Hoosiers to the 1953 national title with a total of 123 points in four tournament games, an average of 30.8. Schlundt scored 41 points in Indiana's regional win over Notre Dame. But surprisingly, that year's Outstanding Player award went to Kansas star B. H. Born, whom Schlundt outscored 30–26 in the championship game and by 23 points overall in the tourney.

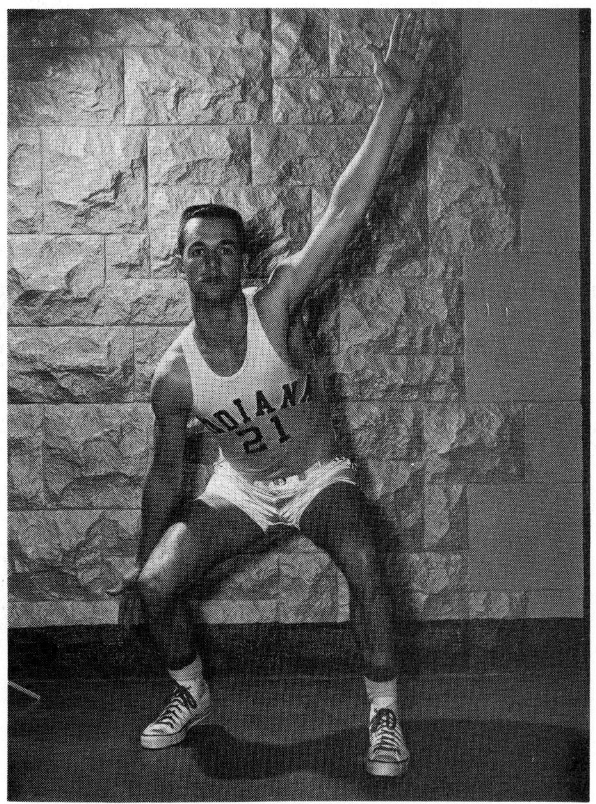

Floor leader for Indiana, national champs of 1953, was Bob Leonard. A superb ball handler, Leonard also averaged 16.8 points in the Hoosiers' four games.

ond national basketball championship; the final score, 69–68.

For the night Don Schlundt had logged 30 points, making him the game's highest producer. But despite that and his 30.75-point average in the four games of the tourney, he was not given the award for Outstanding Player. Instead it went to Kansas's B. H. Born, who had scored 26 in the Jayhawks' losing effort that night. It was the first time in the tournament's history that the award, when made, did not go to a member of the winning team. Forward Charley Kraak also turned in a sterling performance for the Hoosiers in the championship game, toting up 17 points, and Bob Leonard counted 12. After Born, Al Kelley was the Jayhawks' most productive shooter, registering 20 points.

Awards, 1953

Outstanding Player
B. H. Born (Kansas)

All-Tournament Team
B. H. Born (Kansas)
Bob Houbregs (Washington)
Bob Leonard (Indiana)
Dean Kelley (Kansas)
Don Schlundt (Indiana)

It had been a tournament of high scorers. Bob Houbregs averaged 34.8 points a game in leading the Washington Huskies to third place. And the diminutive Johnny O'Brien had averaged 32 for Seattle, while Schlundt was dropping in his 30-plus per game for the victors. Branch McCracken and Indiana could take pride in becoming only the third team to have won more than one NCAA championship, in league then with Adolph Rupp's Kentucky teams, which had won three, and Hank Iba's Oklahoma A & M Aggies, who had prevailed twice.

Indiana fielded the same team for the 1953–54 basketball season as the one that had brought home to Bloomington the NCAA championship trophy. Still, Indiana was not ranked at the very top of the polls when the regular season came to an end. That honor was afforded to the ever-powerful Kentucky, still paced by Cliff Hagan and Frank Ramsey and guided by the genius Adolph Rupp. But, as they had been the year before, the Wildcats were barred from postseason festivities, a penalty imposed by the NCAA for recruiting violations. So, as the 24 teams (two more berths were added in 1954) assembled at various arenas around the country to launch the NCAA tournament, most people's pick was Indiana to repeat.

As winner of the Big Ten, the Hoosiers drew one of the eight byes that year, then had to face intrastate rival Notre Dame in the second round. In the regional finals the year before they had destroyed a similar Notre Dame team (four of the starters for the Fighting Irish were back) and as a result were a decided favorite as the two teams took the floor. The big difference in 1954, however, was that Notre Dame had found a way to stop Don Schlundt. The Irish held the normally high-scoring Indiana center to a paltry 10 points and Bob Leonard to a mere 11. The result was that Notre Dame eliminated the tourney favorite with a 65–64 upset.

A team that did not draw a bye was LaSalle, a comparatively small school from Philadelphia whose players wore jerseys with short sleeves. They were coached by a respected strategist, Ken Loeffler, and had a legitimate superstar in junior forward Tom Gola, but despite his All-American recognition only the longest of the long-shot bettors considered putting their money on little LaSalle.

The Explorers, as they were known, were, however, almost *the* first team to be eliminated from the tourney. They barely sneaked by Fordham 76–74 in the first game of the first round. Gola, the force that night, dropped in 28 points. They followed with a more impressive win by beating North Carolina State 88–81. Gola had 26 in that game, and so did LaSalle's other forward, Charlie Singley. For the regional championship all LaSalle had to do was get by a relatively unintimidating Navy team, which had only squeaked past Connecticut and Cornell in the first two rounds. Navy was no competition for Gola and his teammates. The big forward scored 22 points for LaSalle, and Singley had another

All-American Tom Gola was the 1954 NCAA Outstanding Player, sporting an average of 22.8 points in LaSalle's five victories, Gola would also lead LaSalle in its 1955 quest for the NCAA crown, but LaSalle ran second to San Francisco that year.

Sophomore Charlie Singley was an important contributor to LaSalle's 1954 triumphs. Averaging 17.2 points in tourney play, he dropped in a game-high 23 points in the title win over Bradley.

In its first postseason NCAA appearance, LaSalle took the 1954 championship trophy, annihilating Bradley 92–76.

good game with 16, as LaSalle cruised to a 64–48 win. The Explorers packed their bags and headed for the NCAA semifinals in Kansas City. There they would face Penn State, another surprise team that year, which had upset both LSU, with its superstar Bob Pettit, and Notre Dame. In the other semifinal game Forddy Anderson's Bradley Braves would take on Southern California. The Final Four in 1954 were a surprise to everyone.

Penn State's string of upsets came to an end in the Kansas City Municipal Auditorium. The team never really got into the game, trailing LaSalle 33–22 at the half and never substantially reducing the margin during the second half. When it was over LaSalle was on the top end of a 69–54 score. Gola had 19; so did sophomore Frank Blatcher. In the other semifinal game Bradley, down by six at the half, rallied to beat Southern Cal 74–72.

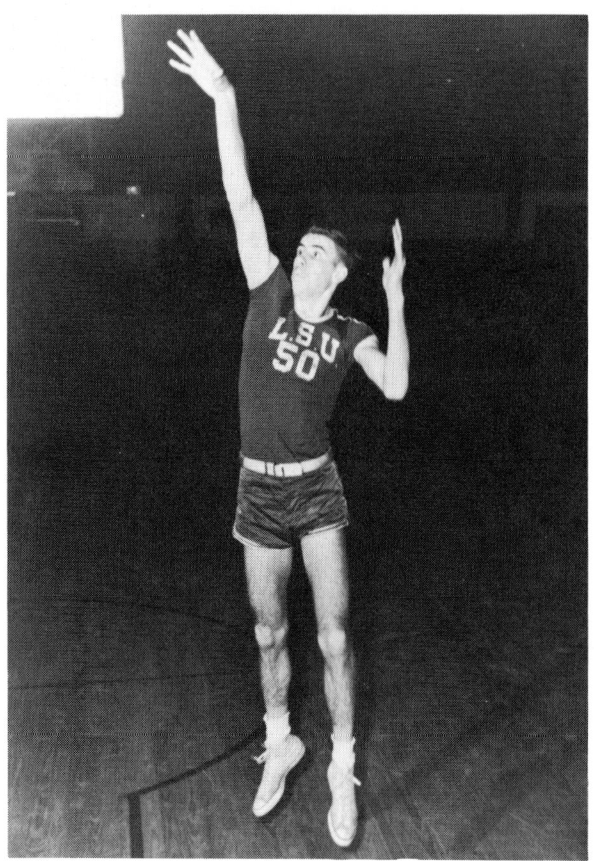

Consensus All-American Bob Pettit played for LSU in both the 1953 and 1954 tourneys, averaging 30.5 points in each. He registered a 36-point performance against Washington in '53 and tallied 34 against Penn State in '54. Pettit was enshrined in the National Basketball Hall of Fame in 1970.

Bradley had one star, Bob Carney, but he was not thought of as being as formidable as LaSalle's Tom Gola. The Braves had a balanced attack, and they had defeated some very good teams that year. To get to the finals they had to beat Oklahoma City, Colorado, and Oklahoma A & M in addition to Southern Cal. They were a high-scoring team, averaging 70.5 points in their four preceding tournament appearances. Their biggest gun, Bob Carney, had scored 27, 37, and 20 points in three of their last four games. Their major concern now was how to stop Tom Gola. And in the championship game, to an extent, they succeeded, holding him to 19 points. But other LaSalle Explorers rose to the occasion. Again Frank Blatcher broke loose, this time scoring 23 points. Charlie Singley toted up another 23. Bradley, on the other hand, could not get its scoring act in tune at all. And even though the two teams were separated by only a single point at the half—with Bradley on top—it proved to be an easy victory for LaSalle; the final score, 92–76.

Awards, 1954

Outstanding Player
Tom Gola (LaSalle)

All-Tournament Team
Tom Gola (LaSalle)
Chuck Singley (LaSalle)
Jesse Arnelle (Penn State)
Roy Irvin (Southern California)
Bob Carney (Bradley)

There was little trouble in picking that year's Outstanding Player. Tom Gola had clearly shone the brightest in the 1954 tourney, averaging 22.8 points a game as well as dominating on the boards and on defense. And coach Ken Loeffler could go back to Philadelphia comforted by the knowledge that just about the entire LaSalle team would be returning for the 1954–55 basketball season.

As the 1955 NCAA tournament opened LaSalle was ranked third in the nation and there was no more revered name in college basketball than Tom Gola. But there was a youngster playing on the opposite coast who had clearly begun the process of engraving his name in all basketball history books, a giant of a man at 6′10″ by the name of Bill Russell. A junior, he was the pivotal point of a team from the small Catholic college named San Francisco, obscure and unranked in the wire service polls at the beginning of the season but tapped as number one when it was over.

The San Francisco Dons also had another All-American candidate in the gazellelike K. C. Jones, a 6′1″ junior guard. Their coach, Phil Woolpert, had been building the team since taking it over in 1951 and by 1954–55 had established himself as a master tactician who utilized the varied skills of his players with the artistry of a symphony orchestra conductor. Russell was the keystone, however. Never before in the game of college basketball had there been as intimidating a defensive center, batting away on-target shots, slapping others back into the faces of those with the temerity to drive into his territory, and monopolizing the boards. He was fast and lithe; he could leap with the best of the leapers; in short, he was an all-around ball player whose simple presence on the court was the chief source of worry, frustration, and despair of every opposing coach.

By 1955 only one team from west of the Mississippi River had won the national championship in the preceding eight years; only Phog Allen's Kansas had been able to derail the easterners. That was about to change dramatically, but to anyone who had seen Woolpert's San Francisco Dons play during the regular season it would come as no surprise. They had lost only one of their 24 games going into the tourney, and there did not appear to be much in the way of competition for them anywhere in the West. The other alleged *creme de la crop* of the tournament was in the East: LaSalle, Kentucky (which had been ranked number two), Iowa, Bradley, and Penn State.

Out East, however, Kentucky was knocked out by Marquette, and Penn State fell to Iowa, both in the second round. Bradley then lost out in the regional finals to an inspired Colorado team. But it left two exceptionally strong

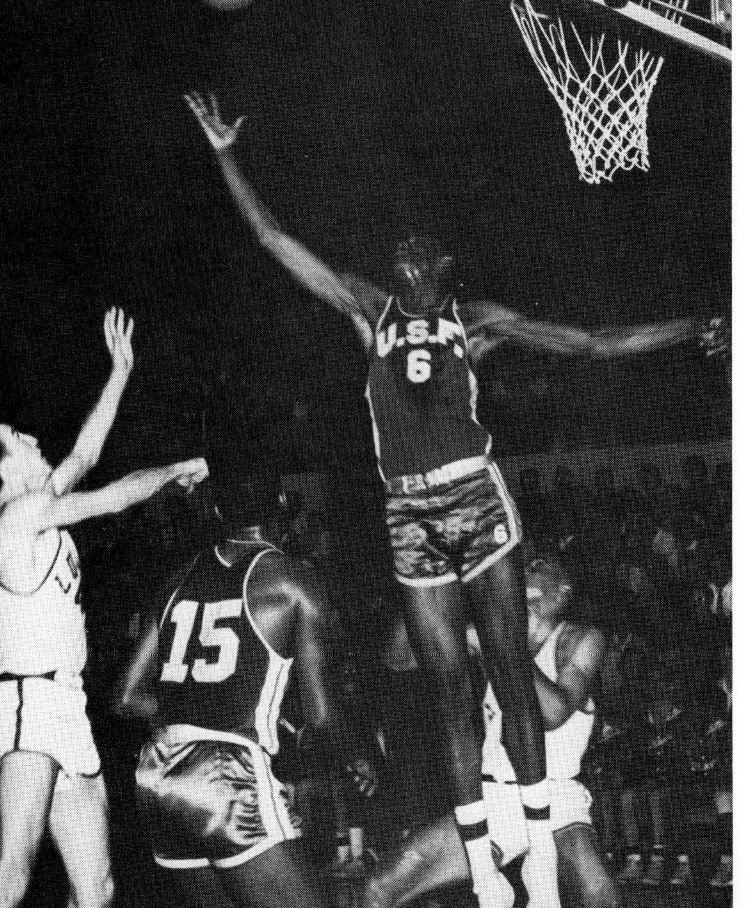

Left. The mightiest Don of all, Bill Russell (6) soars here as he did so often for San Francisco's defense in the mid 1950s. Russell led SFU to NCAA championships in 1955 and 1956, was named Outstanding Player in '55, and averaged 23.2 points in his nine NCAA postseason games.

K. C. Jones was integral to the success of the 1955 and 1956 San Francisco teams. A 6′1″ guard, he was the leading scorer in the '55 championship game with 24 points but was ruled ineligible for postseason play in '56.

eastern teams to battle in the semifinals, LaSalle and Iowa.

LaSalle had found no competition in its first three games, swamping West Virginia 95–61, Princeton 73–46, and Canisius College (in Buffalo) 99–64. Gola had scored 22, 24, and 30 points in the three games. There was little question that LaSalle was a team to contend with.

Yet so was Big Ten champion Iowa, which was spearheaded by Carl Cain, a forward of All-American proportions, and center Bill Logan. The Hawkeyes had beaten out Indiana for the Big Ten title, then in the tourney romped over a good Penn State team 82–53 and eliminated Marquette in the regional final 86–81. But as well as Iowa was playing, it was not able to stop Tom Gola when the two teams met in Kansas City to determine who would represent the East in the NCAA championship game. Principally, Tom Gola proved to be Iowa's nemesis. He chalked up 23 points and was devastating on the boards, while Charlie Singley added another 16 for the Explorers. It was enough to give LaSalle a 76–73 win.

San Francisco had a relatively easy time of it in the West, at least through the first two rounds. The Dons destroyed West Texas State 89–66 in their first game, then did the same to Utah a few nights later, 78–59. But whereas LaSalle had its biggest problem in the semifinals with Iowa, San Fransisco encountered its only real scare in the regional finals. It came from Oregon State and its skyscraper of a center, 7′3″ Swede Halbrook. Oregon State almost won it with a last-second shot, and Phil Woolpert's Dons were fortunate indeed to eke out a one-point win that night. It was their only threat, as it turned out, because they then decimated Colorado in the semifinals.

There was not an unimpressed eye in the house that had watched Bill Russell in his first NCAA tourney. The agile titan blocked shot after shot, controlled the backboards on offense and defense, and scored with impunity (29 points each in two of the three previous games). But the Dons also found a bonanza in forward Jerry Mullen, who also topped 20 points in two of the three games, as well as consistency from K. C. Jones, who not only scored in double figures but was all over the court on offense and defense as well, aiding the Dons' cause in many different ways.

The game was pegged in the press as the great college confrontation—Gola versus Russell, the former a 6′7″ forward, three-time All-American; the latter a 6′10″ center who had bedazzled the nation with his unique basketball talents. They did not go head to head, as it turned out, however. San Francisco's coach chose to hound Gola with K. C. Jones instead, and so the two superstars met only randomly during that championship game.

It was an awkward first half, neither team playing up to its proven ability; at the intermission the score was San Francisco 25, LaSalle 19. It opened up in the second half, but the momentum was surely on the side of the young men from the Golden Gate. Russell played his usually superb game, was practically invincible underneath, and when it was over had tallied 23 points. But it was K. C. Jones who proved to be the decisive factor that night. He played a magnificient defensive game, holding Gola to a relatively unimpressive 16 points, while scoring the most points of the evening himself with 24. The final score was San Francisco 77, LaSalle 63.

Awards, 1955

Outstanding Player
Bill Russell (San Francisco)

All-Tournament Team
Bill Russell (San Francisco)
Tom Gola (LaSalle)
K. C. Jones (San Francisco)
Jim Ranglos (Colorado)
Carl Cain (Iowa)

It was not a big surprise. San Francisco had been touted as the nation's top team before the tournament started, and the Dons had lived up to everything that had been written about them in the nation's press. LaSalle had comported itself in fine fashion, faltering only in the final game. It proved one thing, at least at that point in time: that the NCAA championship was not reserved for large universities with huge student bodies and lavish facilities.

There was ample room for such hitherto unknowns in the collegiate world as San Francisco and LaSalle to compete and to triumph over such stalwarts as Kentucky, Kansas, Indiana, and the other behemoths of the sport.

It would be difficult for San Francisco to improve on the overall record of 28 and one it posted during the 1954–55 basketball year (the Dons had lost only to UCLA early in the regular season). But they would do it, and the Dons would become the first college basketball team in the history of the NCAA to go undefeated all the way through the regular season and the postseason tournament. Even more impressive, they had compiled a 51-game winning streak going into the 1956 tournament, the longest rung up by any team at that point in the history of college basketball.

The primary reasons the Dons were so insuperable was that center Bill Russell, guard K. C. Jones, and playmaker Hal Perry were still wearing San Francisco uniforms, and the team had added two volatile scorers in Mike Farmer and Gene Brown.

Needless to say, the Dons were the pretournament favorites over just about anybody who could tell the difference between a basketball and a football. That isn't to say there were not other fine teams in the tourney. There were teams like Iowa, Kentucky, Southern Methodist, Temple, and Utah, and history had clearly shown that the favorite did not necessarily come out on top in the NCAA tourney. In such volatile competition anything could happen on a given night; every coach knew that. And San Francisco coach Phil Woolpert was no exception. He also would be sending out a team deprived of one of its most valuable players—K. C. Jones was ineligible for postseason play. So Woolpert did not take his team and its success for granted, though that would be a temptation in light of its undefeated status and amazing winning streak. It might be even more difficult not to become complacent after the Dons thoroughly dominated a fine UCLA team coached by John Wooden in their first tournament game; then squelched another good team, Utah, 92–77, in the regional finals; and destroyed Southern Methodist 86–68 in the semifinals. Not one of those teams had been able to bring a bead of sweat to Woolpert's brow. Bill Russell had averaged almost 22 points in each of the three contests; Gene Brown had dropped in 23 against UCLA and 18 in the Utah game; and Mike Farmer had tallied 26 against Southern Methodist. None of it prevented Woolpert from worrying about the championship game, however.

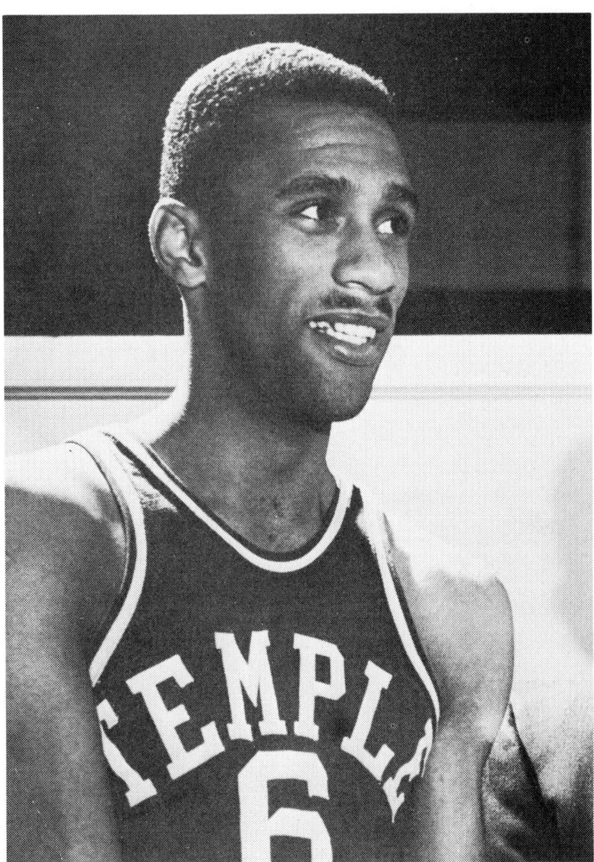

Hal Lear of Temple set an NCAA tourney single-game scoring record in 1956 when he tallied 48 points against Southern Methodist. Lear's 160-point total in that tourney was another NCAA record. He averaged 32 points in Temple's five games and was named Outstanding Player.

While the Dons were mopping up the West, Iowa was doing likewise in the East. Iowa ran up 97 points while devastating little Morehead State in the second round, then dealt stunning blows to two highly touted teams, Kentucky and Temple. The keys to Iowa's success were found in All-American Carl Cain and the high-scoring center, Bill Logan. Cain had scored 28, 34, and 20 points in the three previous tournament games, and Logan had exploded with 36 against Temple in the semifinal encounter.

Left. Carl "Sugar" Cain was Iowa's floor leader in both the 1955 and 1956 tourneys, leading the Hawkeyes to the semifinals in '55 and the finals in '56.

Right. Iowa center Bill Logan scored 36 points in the Hawkeyes' semifinal win over Temple in 1956 but was held to 12 points by San Francisco's Bill Russell in the title match. Logan averaged 19.8 points a game in the '56 tourney and 19 points the year before.

Awards, 1956

Outstanding Player
Hal Lear (Temple)

All-Tournament Team
Hal Lear (Temple)
Bill Russell (San Francisco)
Carl Cain (Iowa)
Hal Perry (San Francisco)
Bill Logan (Iowa)

The 1956 championship game was held at a new location, McGaw Hall, the impressive new fieldhouse on the campus of Northwestern University. Tiny antiquated Patten Gymnasium, where the first NCAA championship had been held 18 years earlier, was still there but now relegated to the school's intramural program. San Francisco's exalted win streak was not destined to end at McGaw Hall, though it looked like it when Iowa rushed out to an early lead (15–4 at its extreme). But Phil Woolpert's San Franciscans had poise, and it was not too long before they had reduced the lead to nothing, then assumed control of the game. At the intermission the Dons had built a 38–33 lead, then maintained it throughout the second half. At the final buzzer San Francisco had extended its phenomenal win streak to 55 games (it would end at 60 the next year) and become only the third team to win back-to-back NCAA championships (the others, Oklahoma A & M and Kentucky). The final score was 83–71.

Bill Russell was the game's highest scorer with 26 points. Also admirably aiding the Dons' effort that night were Gene Brown and Carl Boldt, with 16 points apiece, and Hal Perry, who added another 14. Russell had had a marvelous tournament, averaging 22.75 points per game, but he would not be a repeat winner of the Outstanding Player award. Instead that accolade would be bestowed on Hal Lear of Temple, who, in the game for third place, had shattered the tournament's single-game scoring record by amassing 48 points. In the five games Lear played in during the tourney he averaged 32 points.

Bill Russell departed the college basketball scene after the 1956 NCAA tourney. He was quickly replaced in the nation's limelight by another center of gargantuan proportions, 7′1″ Wilt Chamberlain, a sophomore in 1956–57, playing his first year of varsity ball for the University of Kansas. Even though he was still in his teens, Chamberlain was such an overwhelming force on the basketball floor that any team opposing him had to adapt its defense to concentrate on him.

None were all that successful in curtailing Wilt "The Stilt," as he came to be called. Chamberlain averaged nearly 30 points during the regular season, and his Kansas team, now under the guidance of Dick Harp (Phog Allen, at 70, had to retire after the previous season), lost only one game during the regular season, upset by Iowa State. There was only one major school in the United States with a better record when the regular season came to an end, undefeated North Carolina, now coached by former St. John's mentor Frank McGuire. As a result, the Tar Heels were ranked number one, but a lot of people felt they could not survive an encounter with number two Kansas and Wilt the Stilt.

The 1957 NCAA championship would provide an opportunity to test that theory. The

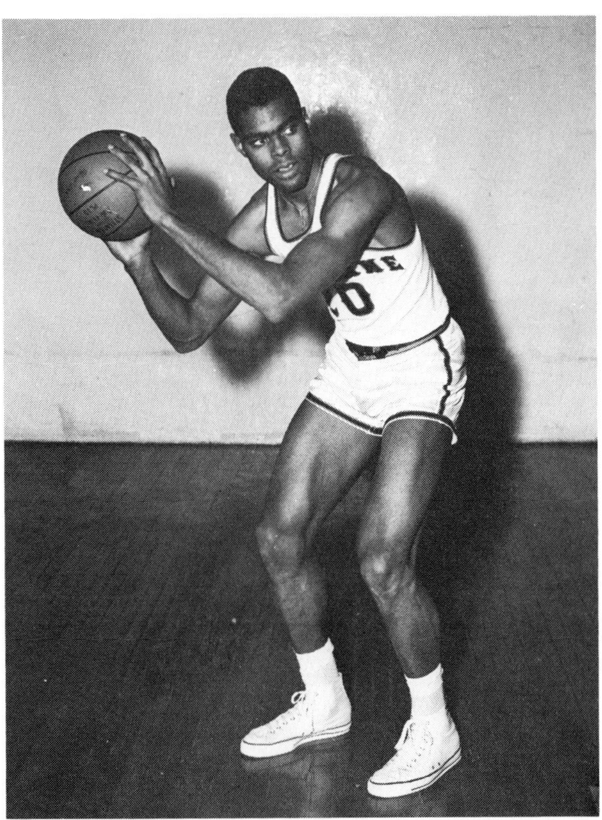

Forward Tom Hawkins, who many said had springs for calf muscles, was one of the top scorers on the high-scoring Notre Dame team in the 1957 tourney (the team averaged 86 points in three games, Hawkins 21.7).

North Carolina's top scorer in 1957 was Lennie Rosenbluth. The Tar Heel forward averaged 28 points in five games in that tourney, including a 39-point performance in a second-round victory over Canisius.

two teams would careen through their respective tournament match-ups on a course aimed at full collision in the championship game.

Kansas had a bye into the second round, where it met a strong Southern Methodist team. But with Chamberlain's 36 points, Kansas managed a 73–65 win, which qualified the team to meet Oklahoma City for the regional title. After a slow start and a subpar first half (Kansas led 27–24) the Jayhawks soared when they returned to the court and won by 20, with Chamberlain scoring 30. Phil Woolpert's San Francisco team awaited them in the semifinals, but the Dons no longer had the talents of Russell, K. C. Jones, or most of the others from their championship teams. It would have been a fabulous match-up, all basketball observers agreed, if Russell, with all his defensive skills, great strength, and agility, had still been around to face off with Chamberlain. But that battle would have to wait for the pro courts. Without the confrontation of giants, San Francisco proved no match for Kansas and Chamberlain. The Dons were blown out of the gymnasium 80–56, with Chamberlain accounting for 32 of the Jayhawks' points.

North Carolina did not have such an easy trip to the championship game. The Tar Heels were an exceptionally high-scoring team, paced by Lennie Rosenbluth, their leading candidate for All-American recognition. But everyone on the Tar Heels' starting lineup was capable of scoring in double figures in any given game. They had little trouble in the first round against Yale, winning 90–74, with Rosenbluth dumping in 29 points, Pete Brennan 20, and little 5′10″ Tommy Kearns 16. Rosenbluth racked up 39 in the next game, leading North Carolina to an 87–75 win over Canisius. In that game Kearns had 19 and Bob Cunningham, 15.

Things began to get a little tougher as North Carolina moved on through the tournament. In the regional finals the Tar Heels were surprised by a tenacious Syracuse team, which held them to 67 points, far less than they had become accustomed to scoring in a game. But they did win the game, and that enabled them to play in one of the most exciting semifinal games in NCAA tournament history, an edge-of-the-seat, triple-overtime affair. Big Ten champ Michigan State gave them a game they would never forget. Behind All-American Johnny Green, the Spartans had knocked off Kentucky and a fine Notre Dame team to get the chance at North Carolina, and those were impressive credentials. From the opening tip-off the two teams went at each other with equal ferocity. At the end of the half the score was tied at 29; at the end of regulation play it was a 58–58 stalemate. Each team scored six points in the first overtime and a basket in the second. But in the third overtime period the Michigan State Spartans faltered, and with two buckets from Rosenbluth and a pair of free throws from Kearns, the Tar Heels earned their way into the championship game, a hard-fought 74–70 win.

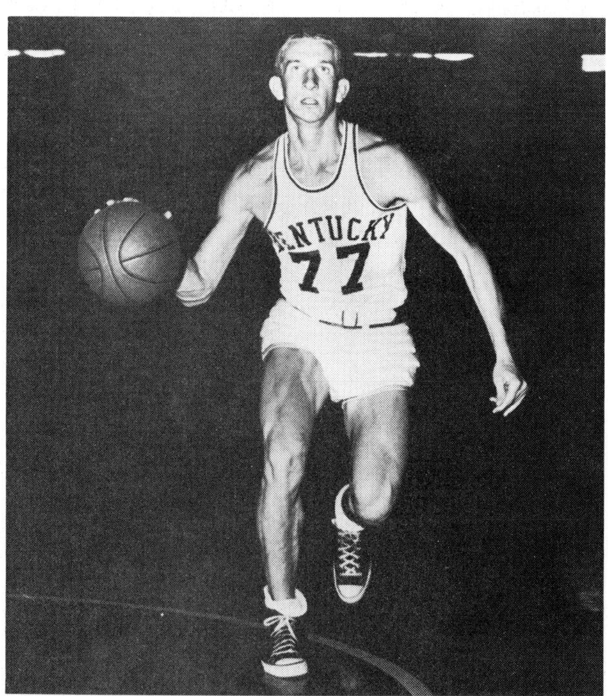

Keystone of Kentucky's 1958 champs was Vern Hatton. A deadly shooter, Hatton scored a game-high 30 points in the Wildcats title game triumph over Seattle. He also tallied 26 in the regional final win over Notre Dame.

It had all the makings of an exciting game: the explosive offense of North Carolina on the one hand and the titanic, seemingly unstoppable Wilt Chamberlain on the other. The Tar Heels were undefeated; Kansas was straddled with only a single loss—the nation's number one and number two teams were meeting for the national championship.

Frank McGuire had his defense primed for the mighty Chamberlain; he wanted to keep the ball away from him and him away from the ball and the backboards. At the same time he hoped that the strenuous triple-overtime semifinal game had not sapped the strength and the shooting virtuosity of his quintet of normally deadeye scorers.

Frank McGuire, coach of the 1957 NCAA champs, North Carolina. McGuire's Tar Heels beat Kansas and Wilt Chamberlain in three overtime periods, 54–53, for the title.

The first half was basically uneventful. Both teams were playing below standard, and the score was 29–22 at the intermission, North Carolina on top. Early jitters, some said, but no one expected that kind of basketball to continue in the second half. Chamberlain had been effectively shut down, but no one thought that would last either. And they were right. The Jayhawks were a different team the second half as Wilt the Stilt asserted himself. At the same time, North Carolina found its velvet touch, and the game finally became one of champions.

Kansas built a three-point lead with a little more than 10 minutes to go, then went into a stall. But it didn't work. The Tar Heels were able to bring it to a 46–46 tie at the buzzer, but

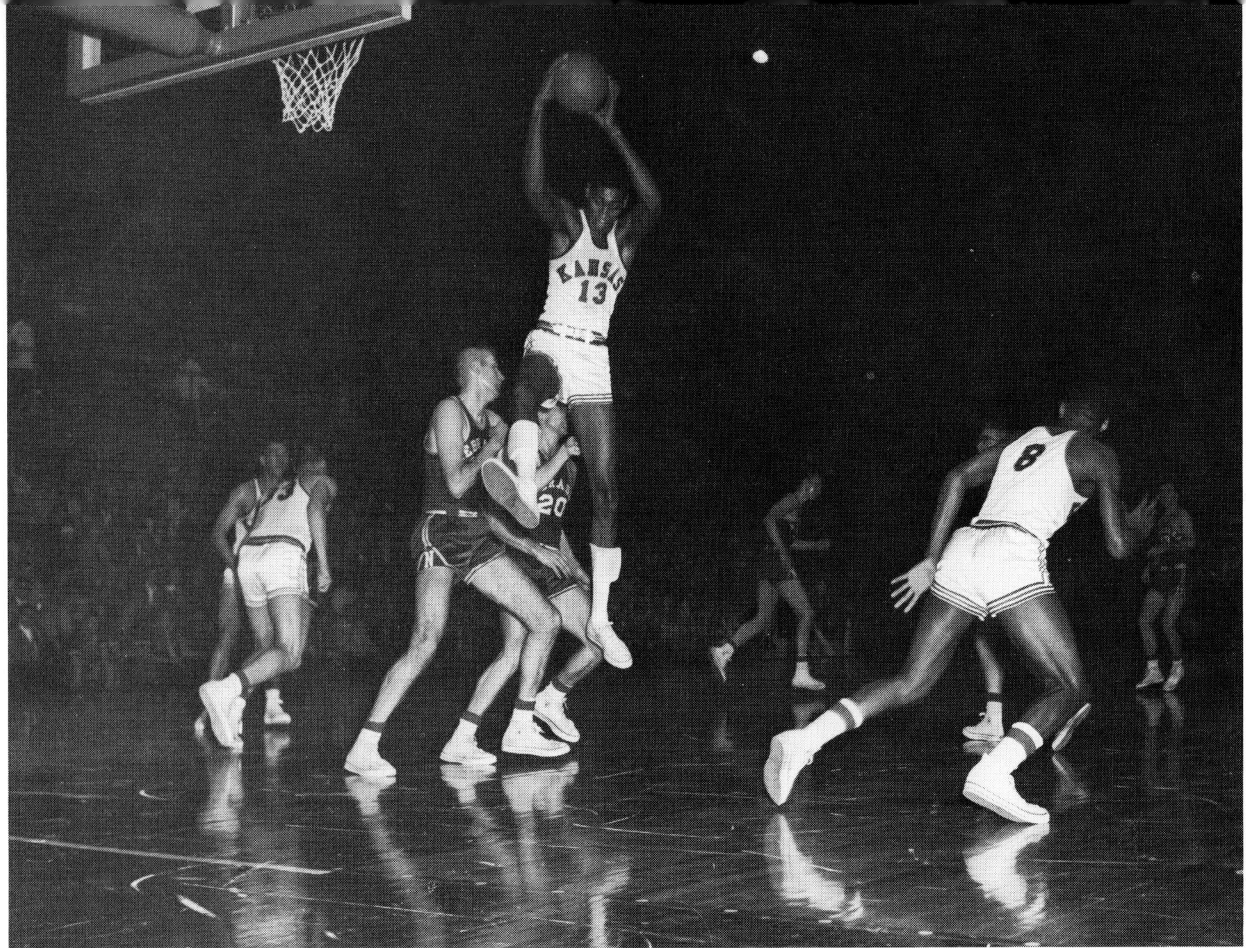

The most imposing force in basketball in 1957 was Wilt "the Stilt" Chamberlain (13), snaring a rebound here against Nebraska. The 7'1" sophomore center, everybody's All-American, led the Jayhawks to the finals in 1957, but could not get them past North Carolina. Chamberlain averaged 30.3 points and 15.5 rebounds in KU's four tourney games that year.

they had a very large problem because Lennie Rosenbluth, who had scored 20 of those 46 points, had fouled out.

In the first overtime period each team scored a lone basket, then repeated the same scenario in the second. In the third and final overtime period, however, North Carolina moved out to a four-point lead, and it appeared that they were going to win it, but the Jayhawks came back, tied it at 52 apiece, and then went ahead on a free throw by Gene Elstun. North Carolina got the ball and, with just six seconds remaining, Joe Quigg went up for a shot and was fouled. After an interminable time-out he went to the line and calmly sank both free throws, and that was the end of the scoring for the night. The Tar Heels had done it; they had stopped Chamberlain and become only the second team in history to go through the season and tournament undefeated. And they had done it, amazingly enough, by triumphing in two consecutive triple-overtime games.

Besides Rosenbluth's 20 points that night, Pete Brennan and Tommy Kearns had scored 11 each for the Tar Heels and Joe Quigg another 10. Chamberlain scored 23 for the losers, the lowest he had posted during the tourney, and Maurice King and Gene Elstun contributed 11 apiece. The Outstanding Player award was given to Chamberlain, who had averaged better than 30 points in Kansas's four games. A lot of people felt that the honor should have at least been shared by Lennie Rosenbluth, who had averaged 28 points in his five games for the Tar Heels. But he would have the consolation of a major part-

Awards, 1957

Outstanding Player
Wilt Chamberlain (Kansas)

All-Tournament Team
Wilt Chamberlain (Kansas)
Len Rosenbluth (North Carolina)
John Green (Michigan State)
Gene Brown (San Francisco)
Pete Brennan (North Carolina)

ownership of the NCAA national championship trophy, the first ever won by the University of North Carolina.

Wilt Chamberlain's appearance in the 1957 NCAA tournament would prove to be his only one; astonishingly enough, he and his Kansas team would not earn a berth there the next year, and the year after that he would go to the Harlem Globetrotters in lieu of playing out his senior year at Kansas. But when the 1958 NCAA tourney opened a number of other very big and meaningful names from the world of college basketball were present, such newly recognized greats as Elgin Baylor of Seattle, Jerry West of West Virginia, Tom Hawkins of Notre Dame, Guy Rodgers of Temple, Oscar Robertson of Cincinnati, and Bob Boozer of Kansas State. With all that talent, it was anybody's tournament.

By the end of the second round some very good teams had been eliminated, among them Cincinnati, bumped by Kansas State in an 83–80 overtime thriller; and West Virginia, upset by Manhattan 89–84. As the teams paired up for the regional finals the powerhouses appeared to be Temple, Notre Dame, and Kentucky in the East and Kansas State and Seattle in the West. Temple, out of Philadelphia, breezed by Dartmouth behind Guy Rodgers' dazzling ball handling and game-high 17 points. Then a well-rounded Kentucky team virtually thunderstruck Notre Dame 89–56, a runaway that no one would have predicted before the game's opening tip-off. Kentucky's Vern Hatton, who shot 50% from the field (11 for 22) was the game's high scorer with a total of 26 points, but the Wildcats had four other players who scored in double figures as well. Notre Dame's All-American Tom Hawkins was held to 15 points.

In the West, Kansas State, which had taken the Big Seven tourney bid away from Kansas and Wilt Chamberlain, predictably defeated Oklahoma State 69–57, with Bob Boozer contributing 26 points to the winner. And Seattle,

Notre Dame, scrapping here with Illinois, made it to the 1958 tourney. The Fighting Irish's Mike Graney, on the floor and going for the ball, gets a double take from Tom Hawkins (20), who scored 39 points that night. The other ND player is John McCarthy. For Illinois number 22 is Ed Perry and number 33 is Al Gosnell. The Fighting Irish won 81–67.

behind Elgin Baylor's 26 points and abundant rebounds, rejected California 66–62.

Kentucky and Temple had met once during the regular season, and the Wildcats had emerged victorious after three overtime periods. In the eastern semifinal the game did not go into overtime, but it was decided in the waning seconds of regulation play. Temple had a one-point lead that was erased when Vern Hatton hit a jump shot with 15 seconds left. Temple got the ball back but was unable to get a shot off, so Adolph Rupp would take a Kentucky team to the NCAA championship game for the fourth time. Sharp-shooting forward Johnny Cox had been the mainstay for the Wildcats that night, scoring 22 points, and Hatton had 13, including the clutch bucket to win the game. Guy Rodgers banked 22 points for the losers.

The game to determine Kentucky's opponent was far less breathtaking. Seattle moved ahead of Kansas State early, remained there, and won by 22. Elgin Baylor was the game's most productive scorer with 23 points.

The 1958 NCAA championship game was held at Freedom Hall in Louisville, Kentucky, ensuring at least a home-state crowd for the Wildcats, but Seattle was the betting man's favorite in the game. And it might have gone according to the betting line had Seattle's star Elgin Baylor not gotten himself into deep, dark foul trouble early. Midway through the first half he had three fouls, and he would draw another before the night was over, severely cramping his style for three-quarters of the game. Still, Seattle managed to rule the first half and went to the locker room with a three-point lead. But Adolph Rupp's halftime harangue, and Baylor's trepidations because of his foul situation, combined to change the game's momentum. Suddenly the Wildcats turned as hot as a Kentucky summer sun and outscored Seattle 48–33 in the second half, easily gaining for themselves the national championship. Kentucky became the first school to claim the NCAA crown four times.

Leader of the 1958 third-place Temple Owls was All-American guard Guy Rodgers. He averaged just under 20 points in the Owls' five games that tourney.

A look at the box score showed some of the Wildcat heroes: Vern Hatton had 30 points, Johnny Cox 24, and John Crigler 14. Elgin Baylor score 25 points for Seattle, but his shooting average from the floor was only a speck over 28% (nine for 32). Still, he had been individually effective enough to earn that year's award as the tournament's Outstanding Player. There was also another phenomenal performance during the tourney, a harbinger perhaps of what was to come, and that was the record-shattering 56 points scored by Cincinnati sophomore Oscar Robertson in a consolation game against Arkansas. The young sensation hit 21 of 36 field goals and 14 of 16 free throws that night.

Awards, 1958

Outstanding Player
Elgin Baylor (Seattle)

All-Tournament Team
Elgin Baylor (Seattle)
John Cox (Kentucky)
Guy Rodgers (Temple)
Charley Brown (Seattle)
Vern Hatton (Kentucky)

5
The Ohio Era

The question sportswriters throughout the country were asking after the 1958–59 regular college basketball season ended was: Will Oscar Robertson lead Cincinnati to the NCAA national championship; or Jerry West, West Virginia; or Bob Boozer, Kansas State? None of them would, though the three would score a vast amount of points in their separate quests. The team that would win it, on the other hand, was one not at all noted for toting up astronomical scores but instead for playing pressure-packed defense and a controlled team-oriented offense. It would be the year of Pete Newell's starless California Golden Bears.

California, winner of the Pacific Coast Conference, was not ranked among the nation's top 10 teams when its players suited up for the tournament. The Bears had a bye into the second round, where they were expected by many to be eliminated by a strong Utah team. But they were not. California racked up 11 points and held the normally high-scoring Utes to a mere 53 points. Center Darrall Imhoff, 6′10″, had monopolized the night's rebounding for the Golden Bears, and the scoring was typically well divided among the starting five, with Al Buch the leader that night, accounting for 15 points.

Most basketball eyes, however, were trained on the events unfolding in the East. Jerry West had scored 25 points in leading West Virginia to an easy 82–68 first-round win over a tough Dartmouth team. Then, a few nights later, the 6′3″ superstar of the Mountaineers chalked up 36 points as West Virginia came from behind

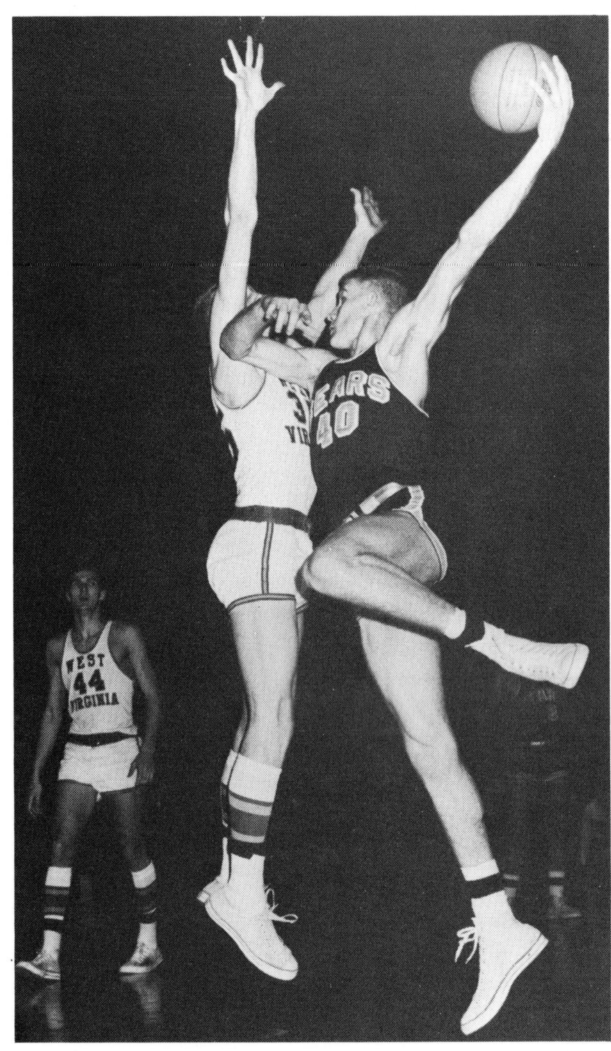

High-flying California center Darrall Imhoff (40) hooks one over a West Virginia defender in the 1959 title game. Imhoff had his best game in the semifinals, however, scoring 22 points and grabbing 16 rebounds as the Bears upset Cincinnati. Number 44 is West Virginia's Jerry West.

to nip a feisty St. Joseph's (Philadelphia) 95–92.

Cincinnati, like California, had a pass into the second round, and when it finally opened its act, its star, Oscar Roberston, shone with the luminosity everyone had come to expect. He scored 34 points, and Cincinnati needed practically every one of them to wring a four-point victory from a surprisingly tough Texas Christian team.

Kansas State, which had been ranked number one at the end of the season, massacred DePaul in its first game of the tourney, and in the process became only the third team in NCAA tournament history to break 100 points in a single game. The final was 102–70. (The other two were Utah's 108 points in defeating Seattle in 1955 and Morehead State's 107 in beating Marshall in 1956.)

Jerry West would lead West Virginia to the Final Four, and Oscar Robertson would bring Cincinnati there as well. But Kansas State would fall in the regional finals to Cincinnati, despite Bob Boozer's 32 points. Louisville, a team whose regular season record was an unimpressive 16 and 10, surprised everybody by knocking off favored Michigan State to get into the semifinals. California, which no one was paying much attention to yet, joined the others by dint of eliminating small St. Mary's of California in its regional final.

Most people looked upon California as nothing more than a two-hour exercise required of Cincinnati before the Bearcats could go to the the championship game. Only it did not turn out that way. As explosive as the Bearcats could be, and as talented a shooter as Oscar Robertson was, the young men from the city by the Ohio River had not taken into consideration Coach Newell's depriving defense. It had never been better than it was that night in Louisville. Cincinnati, averaging 81 points in its two previous tourney games, was held to a mere 58; and Oscar Robertson, averaging 29, scored only 19. Darrall Imhoff dropped in 22 for the Golden Bears and Al Buch another 18, and California stung Cincinnati by a score of 64–58.

Louisville, despite its hometown advantage, did not have that kind of fortune in controlling Jerry West. The Mountaineer scored 38 points, and West Virginia had little trouble qualifying for the finals with a 94–79 triumph.

The ultimate test for California and its now vaunted defense would be to try to thwart Oscar Robertson and Jerry West on consecutive nights. After a shaky start—California was down by as many as 10 points midway through the first half—the Golden Bears took hold, and it looked as if they would indeed shut down the high scorers from West Virginia. At intermission they had allowed only 33 points and California enjoyed a six-point lead. But West Virginia stormed back in the second half, coming within a point of the Golden Bears with less than a minute to go in the game. Imhoff, however, then boosted the California lead to three, but Willie Akers of West Virginia came back and reduced it to one. But with only a few seconds remaining the Mountaineers could not get their hands on the ball, and when the buzzer went off California had indeed pulled off the surprise of the year. With its 71–70 win, California was crowned national champion.

California coach Pete Newell, expressing a little dissatisfaction here, guided his Bears to the championship in 1959, defeating a favored West Virginia 71–70.

Awards, 1959

Outstanding Player
Jerry West (West Virginia)

All-Tournament Team
Jerry West (West Virginia)
Oscar Robertson (Cincinnati)
Darrall Imhoff (California)
Don Goldstein (Louisville)
Denny Fitzpatrick (California)

The great Oscar Robertson (12) of Cincinnati goes up for two here in the 1959 semifinal against California. Robertson scored only 19 points that night but was credited with 19 rebounds. The "Big O" averaged 29 points and 15.8 rebounds in Cincinnati's four tourney games. The defender facing Robertson is California's star forward Bill McClintock.

West Virginia's Jerry West was the Outstanding Player of the 1959 tourney. He tied the tournament record for total points, 160, set by Temple's Hal Lear in 1956, and his average of 32 points a game was the tournament high. In 1960 West would average 35 points in the Mountaineers' three games. West was enshrined in the National Basketball Hall of Fame in 1979.

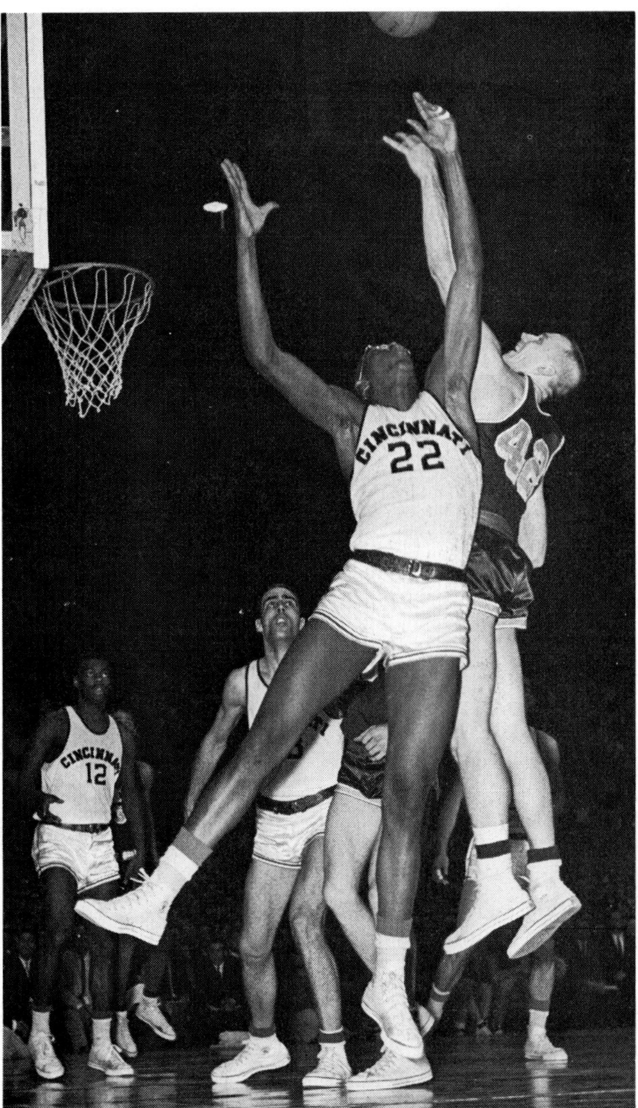

California's Bill McClintock (42) battles Cincinnati center Paul Hogue (22) for a rebound in the 1960 semifinals. McClintock scored 18 points and grabbed 10 rebounds that night; Hogue had 14 points and 11 rebounds. California prevailed 77–69. Number 12 on Cincinnati is the "Big O," Oscar Robertson.

California had not really stopped Jerry West, who scored 28 points that night; but at least his total was five points short of the average he had registered in West Virginia's four earlier tournament games. And whereas West Virginia had averaged almost 90 points a game up to the finals, California had allowed that team only 70. The 1959 college basketball crown had been earned through good defense. Once again, California's scoring was a team effort. Denny Fitzpatrick had the most points with 20, but Bob Dalton had 15 and Darrall Imhoff and Jack Grout 10 apiece. Jerry West, however, was the consensus choice for that year's Outstanding Player award, having averaged 32 points in his five tournament games.

California was no fluke as a champion, which it proved the following year. Fielding exactly the same team, the Golden Bears marched through the regular season, losing only one of their 25 games, then through the NCAA tournament all the way to the championship game. The Golden Bears were acknowledged to have the finest defense of any major college in the United States. And it was

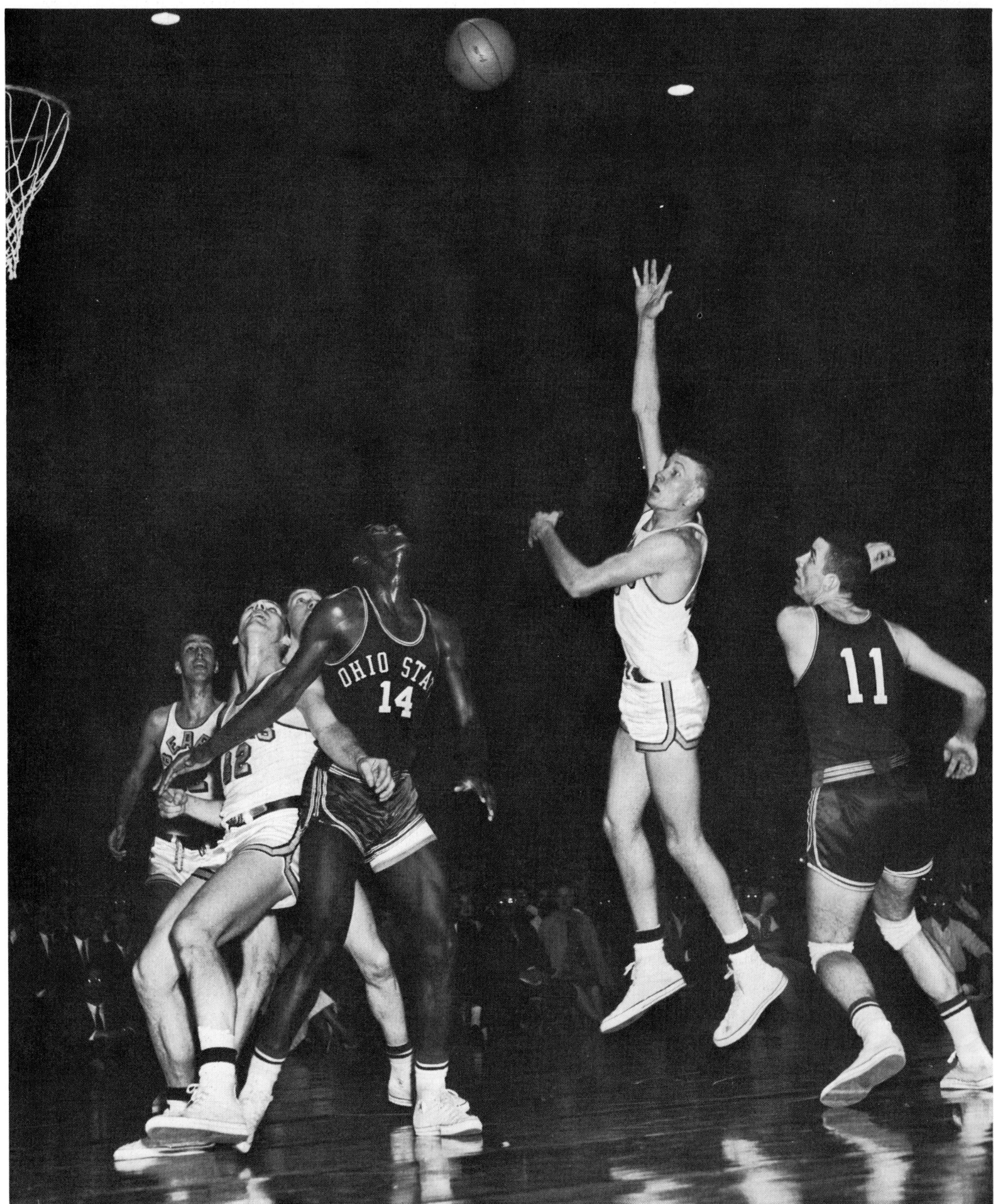

California center Darrall Imhoff loops one of his patented hook shots in the 1960 title tilt against Ohio State. Imhoff had his problems that night with Buckeye center Jerry Lucas (11), held to a mere eight points, which was far below his 17.2 tourney average. Number 14 for OSU is Joe Roberts.

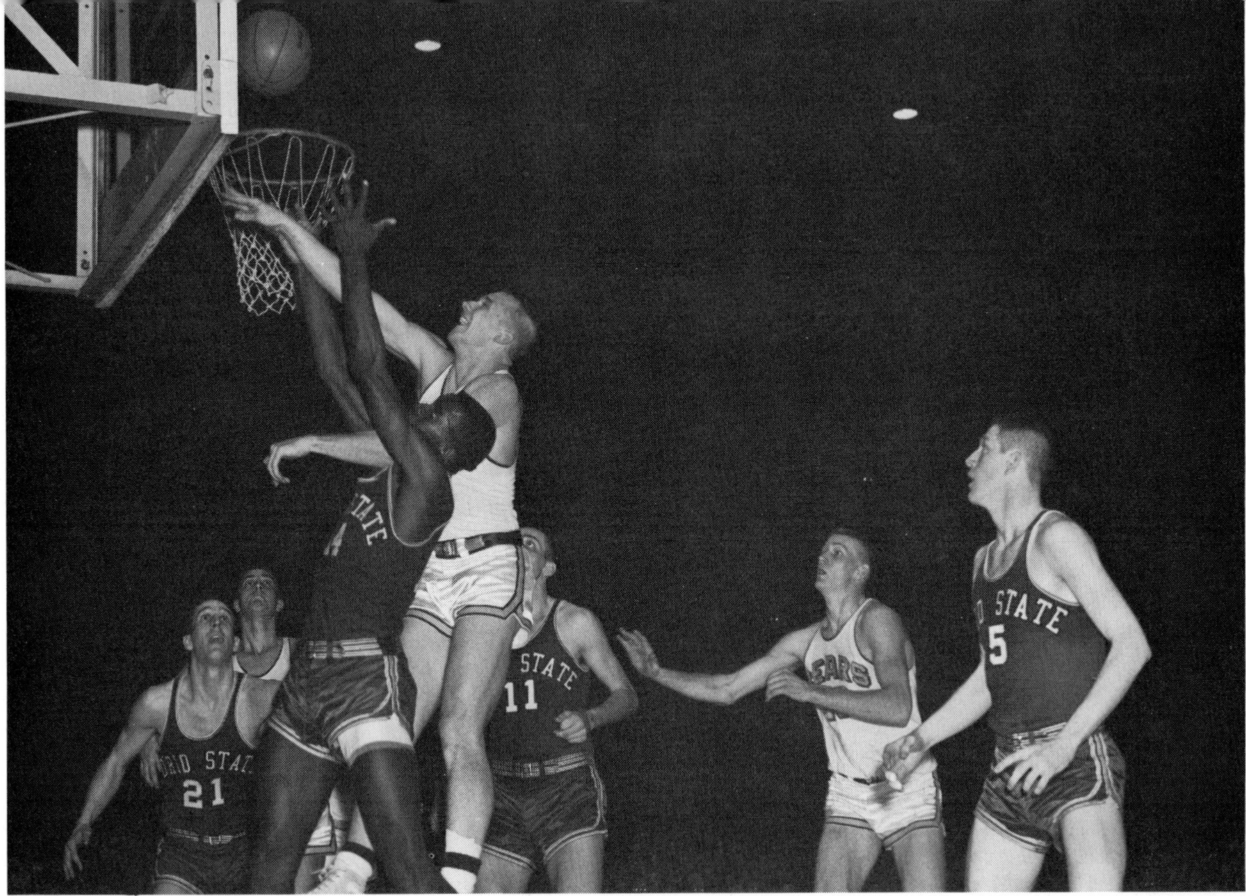

Bill McClintock soars over the back of Ohio State's much taller Joe Roberts in an attempt to tip in a rebound. The other Buckeye players, who comprised the rest of the starting lineup for the 1960 champs were: Larry Siegfried (21), Jerry Lucas (11), John Havlicek (5), and Mel Nowell.

Ohio State's All-American center Jerry Lucas (11) decisively rejects a California shot here in the 1960 championship game. Lucas, the tourney's Outstanding Player, averaged 26 points and 16 rebounds in OSU's four games. His best effort: 36 points and 25 rebounds in the Buckeyes' second-round win over Western Kentucky.

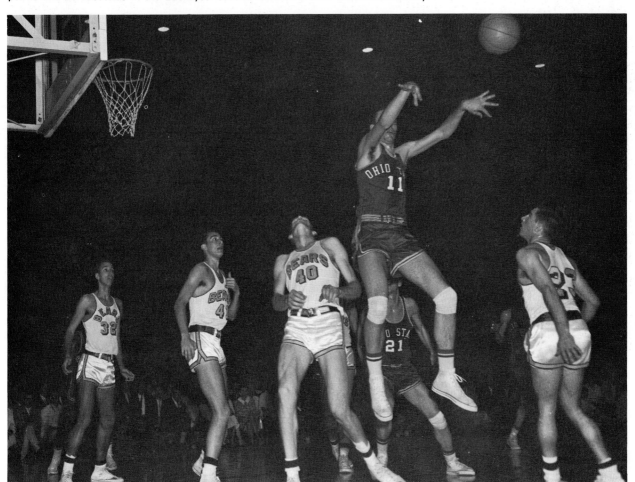

to be given the supreme test in the contest for the national championship because the team California faced, Ohio State, under coach Fred Taylor, was the highest-scoring team in the nation that year.

California, now a seasoned, smooth, and versatile team, came to the tournament with much more national respect than it had the year before. The Ohio State Buckeyes, on the other hand, came as neophytes, a team mostly made up of sophomores, though they were a remarkably poised group of youngsters. Unlike California, the Buckeyes had lost three regular season games, but they averaged an amazing 91 points per game. What made them unique was the fact that *all* of their starters were budding stars: center Jerry Lucas, forwards John Havlicek and Joe Roberts, and guards Larry Siegfried and Mel Nowell. On their bench they also had a volatile little guard by the name of Bobby Knight, who would one day coach several Indiana teams to NCAA championships.

California had to play four games to get to the finals in 1960. The Golden Bears did not draw a bye and had to take on Idaho State, winner of the Big Sky Conference, in the first round. But it was a veritable breeze. The niggardly California defense gave up only 44 points and toted up 71. Round two was hardly more of an effort; the Golden Bears easily manipulated Santa Clara, winning by 20. Oregon awaited them in the regional finals, but this, too, was a mismatch. California drubbed its fellow West-Coasters 70–49. During these prelims California showed its basic format: punishing defense and consistent scoring from all quarters. Center Darrall Imhoff was a giant on the boards; so was forward Bill McClintock, and both consistently scored in the 15-point range. But the Golden Bears usually had two or three other players in double digits as well.

Ohio State, with a bye into the second round, continued its high-scoring ways, crushing Western Kentucky 98–79, then a fine Georgia Tech team 86–69. Lucas sank 36 in the first game, with Havlicek adding 17, Newell 15, and Siegfried 14. Against the Ramblin' Wreck Lucas logged 25, Roberts 19, Havlicek 15, and Siegfried 14.

The Buckeyes certainly had the easier of the two semifinal games. They were slated to face New York University, which had pulled off a pair of upsets to get that far, defeating West Virginia (despite Jerry West's 34 points) and Duke. Ohio State would burst NYU's bubble however, in a relatively low-scoring game, at least meager in terms of the Buckeyes' usual flurry of points. With Lucas and Siegfried popping in 19 apiece, the Buckeyes won 76–54.

California, on the other hand, had to get by Cincinnati, considered by many to be *the* top team in the nation, which was still fueled by All-American Oscar Robertson, now as a senior closing out his collegiate career. And he was doing it with verve, scoring 29 points in Cincinnati's win over DePaul in the second round, then exploding for 43 in the regional final victory over Kansas. But his nemesis was California's defense. It certainly had been the year before, when the Golden Bears eliminated the Bearcats in the semifinals, and it would prove to be again. California held Robertson to 18 points, one less than in 1959, and allowed the entire Cincinnati team just 69. California's 77 were enough to move them into the finals.

It was a much talked-about confrontation: defense versus offense, representatives of the best of both in the nation going head to head. Defense had prevailed the year before, with California silencing both Jerry West and Oscar Robertson. But offense would take over in 1960. And what an offense! Ohio State virtually could do no wrong that night. Of the 19 shots the Buckeyes took from the floor in the first half, they made 16, and at intermission

Awards, 1960

Outstanding Player
Jerry Lucas (Ohio State)

All-Tournament Team
Jerry Lucas (Ohio State)
Oscar Robertson (Cincinnati)
Mel Nowell (Ohio State)
Darrall Imhoff (California)
Tom Sanders (NYU)

they had an insurmountable lead of 37–19. The Golden Bears from California were stale that night, and when it was over they had been routed 75–55. Jerry Lucas, the tournament's Outstanding Player, was the high scorer of the night with 16; close behind were Nowell with 15, Siegfried with 13, Havlicek with 12, and Roberts with 10. It was the beginning of a dynasty at Ohio State, everyone felt, as the youngsters headed back to Columbus, where most of them still had several years to go before graduating.

The state of Ohio would dominate the NCAA national championship games over the next two years. Ohio State's arrival at the classic final meeting was hardly unexpected. In 1961, the Buckeyes sent the same explosive team onto the floor—with one exception, forward Joe Roberts was now replaced by Rickie Hoyt—with the same dazzling offensive firepower that had won the 1960 national crown so easily. But the other Ohio team was a true surprise. Ed Jucker's Cincinnati Bearcats had lost the fabled Oscar Robertson to graduation after the 1960 season and so in 1961 were playing without the man who had set such a bevy of NCAA career scoring records in his three years at Cincinnati, including most career points (2,973), most field goals (1,052), most free throws (869), and highest average per game (33.8). Without the "Big O," as Robertson had come to be known, it seemed highly unlikely that the Bearcats would find their way to the championship game. After all, they had failed in that quest three times *with* Robertson, the nation's finest college basketball player during those three years. But no one ever claimed that the NCAA postseason festival was not subject to some eyebrow-lifting surprises.

Ohio State was obviously the pre-tourney favorite. The Buckeyes had gone undefeated through the 1961 season and were ranked number one in both the AP and UPI polls. Coach Fred Taylor felt his young men were at their prime.

The Buckeyes did not have to crank up their scoring machine until the second round. And then, to everyone's astonishment, they barely did, almost losing to a revved-up Louisville team, which came within a point of the favorites and held the Buckeyes to an uncharacteristic low of 56 points. It took a long jumper from John Havlicek with six seconds left to enable Ohio State to pull out a win. Normally high-scoring Jerry Lucas had only nine points, and only two Buckeyes were in double figures, Havlicek with 17 and Larry Siegfried with 14.

The next obstacle for Ohio State appeared, at first glance anyway, more formidable: the ever-threatening Kentucky under Adolph Rupp. But that year the Wildcats from Lexington were able to elicit little fear from the hearts of the Buckeyes, who in that regional final regained all their poise and momentum. With 33 points from Lucas, 20 from Siegfried, and another 13 from Mel Nowell, Ohio State ravaged Kentucky 87–74, a win that was never in doubt. They were equally devastating in the tourney semifinals. Heavily favored over St. Joseph's of Philadelphia, they made easy work of the Pennsylvanians, 95–69. This time Lucas wound up with 29, Siegfried with 21, and Nowell with 15.

Cincinnati had also earned a pass through the first round, then easily glided by Texas Tech 78–55. Since the departure of Oscar Robertson, there was no single star on the Bearcats' team. In fact, Ed Jucker had radically changed the tempo of the game his team played. The emphasis now was on defense, controlling the ball on offense, a far slower, stodgier type of play than the racehorse, high-scoring form Cincinnati fans had become accustomed to in the Robertson era. The Bearcats were extremely strong on the boards. Paul Hogue, their 6′9″ center, and 6′7″ forward Bob Wiesenhahn were the strike force beneath the basket. Scoring was a shared pursuit with everyone contributing, the leader often Wiesenhahn but sometimes Hogue or guard Paul Bouldin or forward Tom Thatcher. The playmaker was Tony Yates.

In the regional final Cincinnati was an underdog to Kansas State, but it pulled off a come-from-behind win, 69–64, with Wiesenhahn leading all scorers with 22 points. This led the Bearcats to a semifinals encounter with Utah, which was making its first Final Four appearance since 1944, the days of Arnie Ferrin when the Utes won it all. A high-scoring, fast-breaking team (averaging 89.5 points in its two previous games), Utah was also favored to beat Cincinnati. But it was not to be. The Bearcats continued their surprising ways and stunned the Utes, building a 15-point lead by the half and then sailing through the second period to post an impressive 82–67 win. Guard Carl Bouldin was high man that night for the Bearcats with 21, and Paul Hogue added 18.

The two losers in the semifinals, Utah and St. Joseph's, would, however, put on one of the most flamboyant displays of dramatic basketball in the history of that illustrious tournament. In the battle for third place they would play for 2½ hours, going through four overtime periods before St. Joseph's could wring a 127–120 victory from Utah. It was the highest-scoring game in NCAA tourney history. Eleven players scored in double figures, and Jack Egan of St. Joe's was the evening's high-point man with 42. (The win by St. Joseph's would be nullified later because of its use of ineligible athletes, and the record-high total of 127 points would be erased from the record books.)

On its heels came the championship game, an interstate affair between Ohio State and Cincinnati. The Buckeyes brought with them a 34-game winning streak and the odds makers' mark of a heavy, heavy favorite. Cincinnati's forte was defense, but Ohio State had faced the very best of that the year before, exemplified by California, and had clearly prevailed.

The game did not turn out to be the runaway that a lot of sportswriters were predicting, however. Cincinnati's defense hampered the mighty Buckeyes from the very start. By halftime only a point divided the two teams, the edge going to Ohio State. When play resumed, the lead changed hands several times. No one was in charge of the game, and it became clear that this championship was going down to the proverbial wire. At the buzzer Cincinnati had made up the one-point deficit from the half, the score 61–61. Then, in the overtime period, Ed Jucker's Cincinnatians took command and outscored the Buckeyes 9–4. A shell-shocked Ohio State team from Columbus had been upset by not-so-neighborly Cincinnati, and the Bearcats had done it without the Big O. It was a typical team effort: Wiesenhahn had 17 points, Bouldin 16, Thacker 15, Yates 13, and Hogue 9. With the exception of Jerry Lucas, who scored the game high of 27 points, the Buckeyes had been ice-cold that night, their usually prolific offense failing them. Lucas was named the Outstanding Player, becoming only the third player in the tourney's history to be so honored in two consecutive years (the others: Bob Kurland of Oklahoma A & M in 1945 and 1946 and Alex Groza of Kentucky in 1948 (and 1949).

Awards, 1961

Outstanding Player
Jerry Lucas (Ohio State)

All-Tournament Team
Jerry Lucas (Ohio State)
Bob Wiesenhahn (Cincinnati)
Larry Siegfried (Ohio State)
Carl Bouldin (Cincinnati)
John Egan* (St. Joseph's)

* Vacated, team subsequently declared ineligible.

When the lights were finally doused at Kansas City's Municipal Auditorium that long night not one of the 10,700 fans who had watched the incredible doubleheader could say he had not gotten his money's worth of college basketball.

In 1962, for the first (and so far only) time in NCAA tournament history, the same two teams as the year before met to decide the national championship. Ohio State would have the opportunity to prove that the previous year's outcome had been an upset, just one of those things than can sometimes beset a nation's top team. It would also be Cincinnati's chance to prove that they did indeed deserve the title as the best team in college basketball.

The cast of characters was slightly different. At Ohio State Larry Siegfried had graduated; Rickie Hoyt was gone as well. For Cincinnati 6′9″ George Wilson and 6′5″ Ron Bonham had replaced the departed Bob Wiesenhahn and Carl Bouldin (6′2″ Tom Thacker was moved to guard to accommodate the two taller men at the forward slots).

Ohio State was ranked number one in the nation when the regular season came to a close in 1962, though no one was predicting that the Buckeyes would waltz through the postseason festivities, as some had said they would the year before. Ohio State's first test was in the second round. Up against Western Kentucky, a team that had knocked off a sound Detroit team, which had been paced by All-American Dave Debusschere (who scored 38 points in the loss), the Buckeyes gave ample display of just how good they were. They ran up 93 points and easily claimed a 20-point win. Five players were in double figures. Kentucky was next, Adolph Rupp itching for revenge for the previous year's ouster from the tourney his team had suffered at the hands of the Buckeyes. But it, too, would be a repeat. The Ohio Staters shut down the Wildcats' All-American Cotton Nash, holding him to 14 points, and walked off with a 74–64 win. Jerry Lucas was superb that night, scoring 33 points—12 of 21 field goals and nine of 10 free throws—and collecting 15 rebounds.

Cincinnati reached the semifinals by demolishing Creighton 66–46, a game in which Paul Hogue contributed 24 points. The team followed that with a 73–46 humiliation of Colorado in the regional final. Again Hogue was the most productive with 22 points, but Wilson added 19 and Bonham 17 that night.

John Wooden's UCLA team was making that school's very first appearance in the Final Four. Paced by Walt Hazzard, John Green, and Gary Cunningham (who would become head coach at UCLA in 1977), UCLA had trimmed Utah State and a highly regarded Oregon State team to get to the semifinals. Another team making its first appearance in the Final Four was Wake Forest. Coached by Bones McKinney, who as a player had led the North Carolina Tar Heels to the 1946 NCAA national championship game, the Demon Deacons had All-American Len Chappell at forward, who had averaged 27 points in their three previous tournament games. They also had a fine guard in Billy Packer, who would make a bigger name for himself later as a television broadcaster of basketball games.

Len Chappell (50) bagging an easy two here, was the keystone of the Wake Forest offense in the 1961 and 1962 tourneys. Chappell averaged 29 points in '61 and the following year posted tournament highs with a total of 134 points and a 26.8 average. Number 25 for Virginia is Ronald Miller; Wake Forest's number 30 is Tommy McCoy.

Wake Forest was pitted against Ohio State, and Fred Taylor was not taking the youngsters from the always tough Atlantic Coast Conference lightly. Ohio State was at full surge, however, when the Buckeyes met Wake Forest at Freedom Hall in Louisville. As in each of their preceding victories, the Buckeyes were simply awesome. And as fired up as Bones McKinney had gotten his Demon Deacons, they could not stop the Buckeyes' relentless charge. Ohio State built a 12-point lead by the half, then boosted it to an 84–68 win by game's end. It was not all roses and laurel leaves, however, because All-American center Jerry Lucas had injured his knee in the second half, had to leave the game, and was considered a doubtful starter for the next night's championship game. Despite his limited play, Lucas had accounted for 19 points, but the team's high-point man was John Havlicek with 22. For the losers, Chappell had dropped in 27 and Packer, 17.

Cincinnati had a much tougher time of it in the second game of the semifinals. UCLA was a determined body of athletes, with a deep desire to keep the Bearcats from a shot at a second consecutive title. Down by as many as 14 points in the early going, the Bearcats came back strongly and went to their dressing room at the half with a 37–37 tie. The game was a deadheat through the second half, the lead going back and forth with metronomic regularity. The Bearcats did not look like the champions they were—except, that is, for mighty center Paul Hogue, having the best game of his college career and single-handedly keeping the Bearcats in the game. The nail-biter went all the way down to the last three seconds, the game tied at that point at 70. Cincinnati had the ball, and Tom Thacker went up and arced a long jump shot in desperation, a perfect shot that touched only the net and gave the Bearcats a last-second victory. When the game's stats were posted Paul Hogue had 36 points for the night as well as 19 rebounds. Ron Bonham had another 19. For UCLA John Green had been high with 27, followed by Gary Cunningham's 19 and Walt Hazzard's 12.

So, once again the two teams from Ohio would take the court to determine who was that year's college basketball national champion. A pained and somewhat hobbled Jerry Lucas was in uniform and would start for the Buckeyes, but he would not be up to his usual game, and it would hurt Ohio State immeasurably.

The Bearcats trailed in the early minutes of the game but then moved ahead and steadily built a lead that reached eight points at the half. The Buckeyes could not get anything going in the second half, with Lucas struggling and Cincinnati making no mistakes in its carefully wrought game plan. The Buckeyes, as it turned out, were not even able to make a game of it. The final score was Cincinnati 71, Ohio State 59. Paul Hogue scored the most points that evening, 22, and collected the most rebounds, 19. Tom Thacker had another 21 points, and George Wilson grabbed 11 other rebounds. For the Buckeyes Lucas managed 16 rebounds but only 11 points. As evidence of their off night, the Buckeyes' leading scorer was reserve center Gary Bradds, who had 15, and John Havlicek was held to 11.

Paul Hogue was the obvious selection as Outstanding Player. And Cincinnati gained entrance to a very elite club of those who had won back-to-back national championships, a club restricted to just three others: Oklahoma A & M, 1945–46; Kentucky, 1948–49; and San Francisco, 1955–56.

Awards, 1962

Outstanding Player
Paul Hogue (Cincinnati)

All-Tournament Team
Paul Hogue (Cincinnati)
Jerry Lucas (Ohio State)
Tom Thacker (Cincinnati)
John Havlicek (Ohio State)
Len Chappell (Wake Forest)

The stars were gone from the basketball sky above Ohio State after the 1962 season. For three straight years the Buckeyes had played for the championship, winning it once and then being denied it in the final game in the other two years. Gone now were such nationally known names as Lucas and Havlicek and Siegfried and Nowell. The Buckeyes, in fact, would not return to the NCAA playoffs until 1968.

Cincinnati would, however, come back in 1963. And this time the Bearcats would enter the competition as the tourney favorite, thought by many to be a shoo-in for an unprecedented third consecutive national championship. Unanimously ranked number one, the Bearcats had gone undefeated through the 1962–63 season. Paul Hogue was gone, but that problem had been rectified when equally tall George Wilson was moved into the center spot, Tom Thacker was moved back to forward, and Larry Shingleton joined the starting lineup at guard. The nature of Ed Jucker's defense-oriented game did not change, and the Bearcats were considered perhaps the most point-stingy team in the college game.

Playing in the West division, Cincinnati

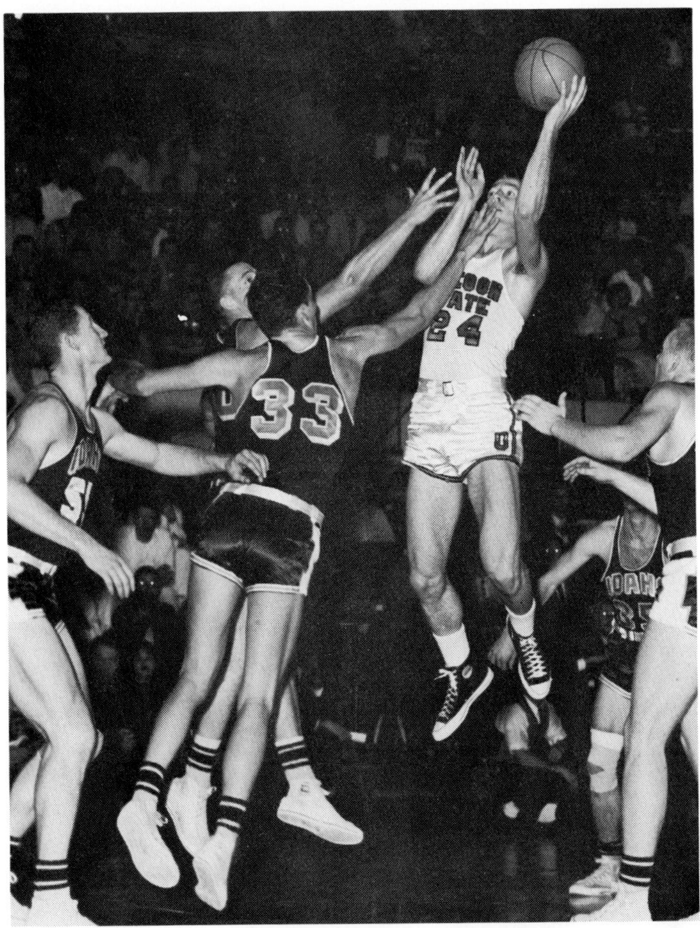

Basketball and football star for Oregon State in 1962 and 1963 was Terry Baker (24), going up for a little jumper here. In Baker's two NCAA tourneys his top performance was the 21 points he hooped against San Francisco in '63. A few months before that he received the coveted Heisman Trophy for his football prowess.

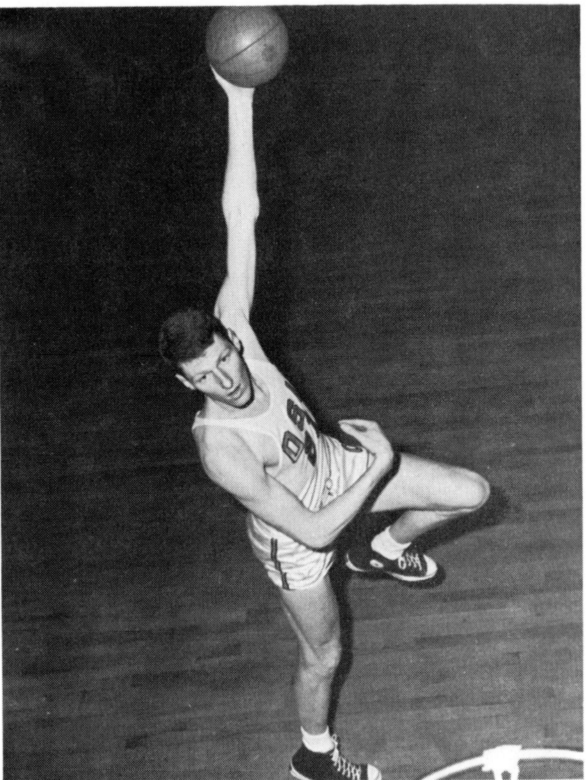

The predominant force on the Oregon State teams that played in the 1962, 1963, and 1964 tourneys was seven-foot center Mel Counts. In the nine games that Counts participated in during those years he averaged 23.2 points.

had a few teams to worry about. There was Oregon State with its seven-foot center, Mel Counts, and at guard a quarterback who had won the Heisman Trophy earlier that school year, Terry Baker. There was also a maturing UCLA team, a strong Arizona State, and unpredictable Texas. Still, the Bearcats were the class act of the division in everyone's eyes. They had more trouble than expected with Texas in their opener in the second round. It was close all the way, and Cincinnati was fortunate to escape with a 73–68 win. If it had not been for George Wilson's 25 points and Ron Bonham's 24, the two-time champs would have been heading back to Cincinnati. And Colorado was no pushover in the regional final. The Buffalos trailed only by a point at the half but finally succumbed when play resumed and lost by seven. The Bearcat scoring was dominated by Bonham with 22 points, Thacker with 18, and Wilson with 15.

Advancing to the semifinals as well was Oregon State, having knocked off Seattle, San Francisco, and Arizona State, impressive credentials because all three teams were well regarded. Lanky Mel Counts had been averaging 26 points a game in the tourney going into combat with Cincinnati, and Ed Jucker felt that Cincinnati's number one priority was to stop the big man. Jucker's Bearcats were able to slow Counts down, not stop him, but for all practical purposes they halted the rest of the Oregon State team. Counts tallied 20 points, but the entire Beaver team could come up with only 46. It was far short of Cincinnati's 80-point effort. Wilson had dropped in 24 for the Bearcats, Thacker and Bonham 14 apiece, and Yates another 12. Cincinnati moved into the finals with noticeable authority.

In the East, Loyola of Chicago, under coach George Ireland, in its first NCAA tournament ever, had earned its way into the finals. Loyola had lost only two of its 26 regular season games. The Ramblers, as they were known around Chicago, played a fast-paced style of basketball and were a sharpshooting team. At tourney time they were the highest-scoring team in the country, averaging almost 94 points per game during the regular season.

Loyola showed just how volatile its offensive attack was in the first round when it annihilated Tennessee Tech 111–42. Five players were in double figures: forward Ron Miller was high with 21; All-American candidate guard Jerry Harkness was next with 19; forward Vic Rouse and guard Johnny Egan had 18 apiece; and center Les Hunter had 17. Hapless Tennessee Tech had been able to hit only 18 of 82 field goals that forgettable night.

Loyola then marched over Mississippi State by 10 and Big Ten champion Illinois by 15. In the semifinals the Ramblers faced their toughest test. Duke, with All-American Art Heyman and high-scoring Jeff Mullins, had breezed into the Final Four and was the pick of the pundits to go to the finals. But Duke could not handle Loyola's fast break and the tiring tactic of 40 solid minutes of racehorse basketball. The Ramblers built a 13-point lead at the half, then virtually raced away with the game in the second period; the final score, 94–75. Les Hunter had posted 29 points for the victorious Ramblers, Harkness 20, and Miller 18. Art Heyman had 29 for the Blue Devils of Duke and Mullins another 21, but they would have to settle for the third place consolation game.

Cincinnati was not all that worried about stopping the high-scoring Ramblers of Loyola. After all, the Bearcats had squelched the fabled offense of Ohio State in two preceding championship tilts. And shortly after the opening tip it appeared that they were on their way to doing the same thing to Loyola. In fact, by halftime the Loyolans had scored a paltry 21 points, far below their normal output. The Bearcats, playing a slow, ball-control game, posted 29 during the same period.

In the second half it appeared to be all over, before the Ramblers ever staged any kind of threat. Ed Jucker's Bearcats stretched their lead to 15 points. But Loyola did not quit, and that perhaps unnerved Cincinnati. The Bearcats were suddenly playing with complacency, very unlike the poised veterans of a championship-caliber team, and it turned into a nightmare of errors. Now Loyola was nibbling away at the Bearcat lead. And Cincinnati stars George Wilson, Tom Thacker, and Tony Yates were in trouble with four fouls as the clock ran down. Loyola crept closer and closer. They were down by only a point with 12 seconds left when Jerry Harkness fouled

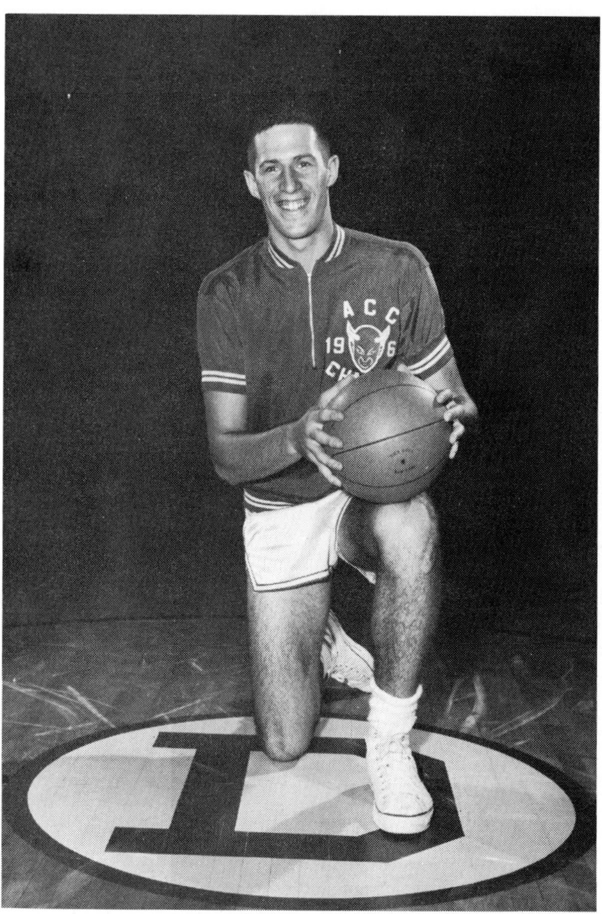

Duke's Art Heyman was the NCAA's Outstanding Player in 1963, though the Blue Devils lost in the semifinals that year to Loyola of Chicago. Heyman scored 89 points in four games.

Awards, 1963

Outstanding Player
Art Heyman (Duke)

All-Tournament Team
Art Heyman (Duke)
Tom Thacker (Cincinnati)
Les Hunter (Loyola, Chicago)
George Wilson (Cincinnati)
Ron Bonham (Cincinnati)

Jerry Harkness was the scoring spark of Loyola's 1963 national champions, averaging 21.2 points over the Ramblers' five tournament games. He also was the player many thought should have at least been named to the All-Tournament team.

Hero of the 1963 title game was Vic Rouse, whose last-second rebound and lay-up gave Loyola a 60–58 victory over Cincinnati.

Larry Shingleton in a desperate gamble to get the ball back for the Ramblers. Shingleton made the first free throw but blew the second one. Less Hunter grabbed the rebound for Loyola, then got the ball to Jerry Harkness, who drove downcourt for a lay-up to tie the game at 54. Loyola's astonishing comeback sent the game into overtime.

No longer complacent, Cincinnati was downright worried when the Bearcats came out for the extra period, their big guns in serious foul trouble. They were now going into the face of Loyola's momentum. Each team managed a pair of baskets, and then, with a little more than two minutes left, Loyola, which had the ball, changed strategy and did something rather uncharacteristic. The Ramblers played slowdown ball, the idea being to hold the ball for that long two minutes and then take the last shot. The plan was to get the ball to Harkness for that shot. The Ramblers succeeded both in controlling the ball and in getting it to their ace shooter with just seconds left. But Harkness, covered by an arm-waving Ron Bonham, could not get the shot off. So he passed the ball to center Les Hunter, who went up for a jump shot. The ball rolled across the rim, then started down, but it fell right into the hands of Rambler Vic Rouse, who went back up with it and dropped in a little lay-up before the buzzer went off. Loyola had upset the mighty Cincinnati Bearcats 60–58.

There were no standouts in the game. It was a team victory for George Ireland and his Ramblers. Hunter had scored 16 points, Rouse 15, and Harkness 14. Bonham had 22 for the losers. The Outstanding Player award was given to Art Heyman of third-place Duke, who had averaged 22.25 points in the Blue Devils' four tournament games.

Center Les Hunter was the power on the boards for the 1963 Loyola Ramblers, averaging 17.2 points a game in that year's tourney. His best game was the semifinal win over favored Duke, when he scored 29 and snagged 18 rebounds.

Left. George Ireland, coach of the Loyola Ramblers, 1963 national champs. Ireland was Loyola's head coach from 1951 through 1975, compiling a record of 321 wins and 255 losses. As a player, Ireland was a two-time All-American at Notre Dame in the 1930s.

The champs of 1963, Loyola of Chicago. **Standing:** Jerry Harkness (captain), John Egan, Chuck Wood, Vic Rouse, Les Hunter, Rich Rochelle, Jim Reardon, Dan Connaughton, Ron Miller, John Gabcik (manager), Fred Kuehl (assistant manager), Dennis McKenna (trainer). **Kneeling:** (left to right) George Ireland (coach), Jerry Lyne (assistant coach).

6
Enter UCLA

John Wooden was elected a charter member of the basketball Hall of Fame back in 1959, but as a player, honored along with just a handful of other early greats such as George Mikan and Hank Luisetti. Thirteen years later he would again be inducted into the Hall of Fame, this time for his extraordinary coaching accomplishments at UCLA. He remains to this day the only person to be so honored as both a player and a coach.

Wooden was an All-American guard at Purdue from 1930 through 1932, a playmaker and a scorer in an age when the little man and his versatility controlled the game of college basketball. In 1948 he came to Los Angeles to take over the head coaching duties at UCLA; with the 1963–64 season, he launched a dynasty that is unparalleled in college athletics. Over 12 years he guided the UCLA Bruins to 10 national championships, including seven in a row. In his 27 years at UCLA his teams won 620 while losing only 147, a victory ratio of better than 80 percent (.808, to be exact).

The team John Wooden took to the 1964 NCAA tournament was no surprise. On the contrary, UCLA had sailed through the regular season without a single defeat (26–0) and wound up at the top of both the AP and UPI polls. The latter accomplishment, however, could be disconcerting because not one team that was ranked number one at the end of the previous six seasons had gone on to take the NCAA crown. (The last to do it had been North Carolina in 1957.)

Like Loyola of Chicago, the champs who

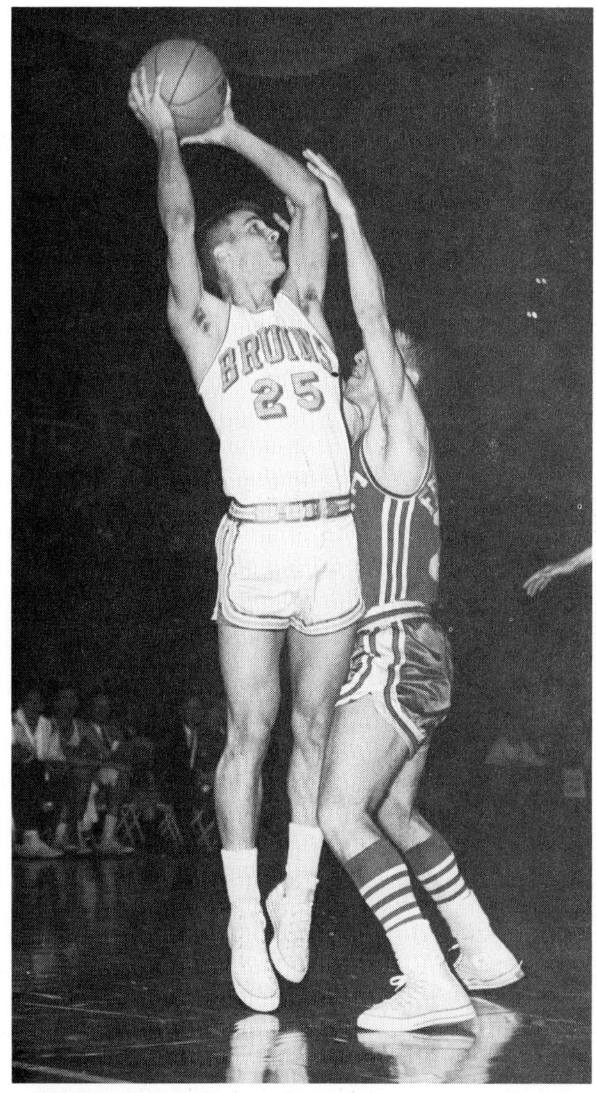

Gail Goodrich (25), UCLA's All-American guard, goes up for a jumper here in the 1964 championship game. Goodrich scored 27 points that night as the Bruins decimated Duke 98–83.

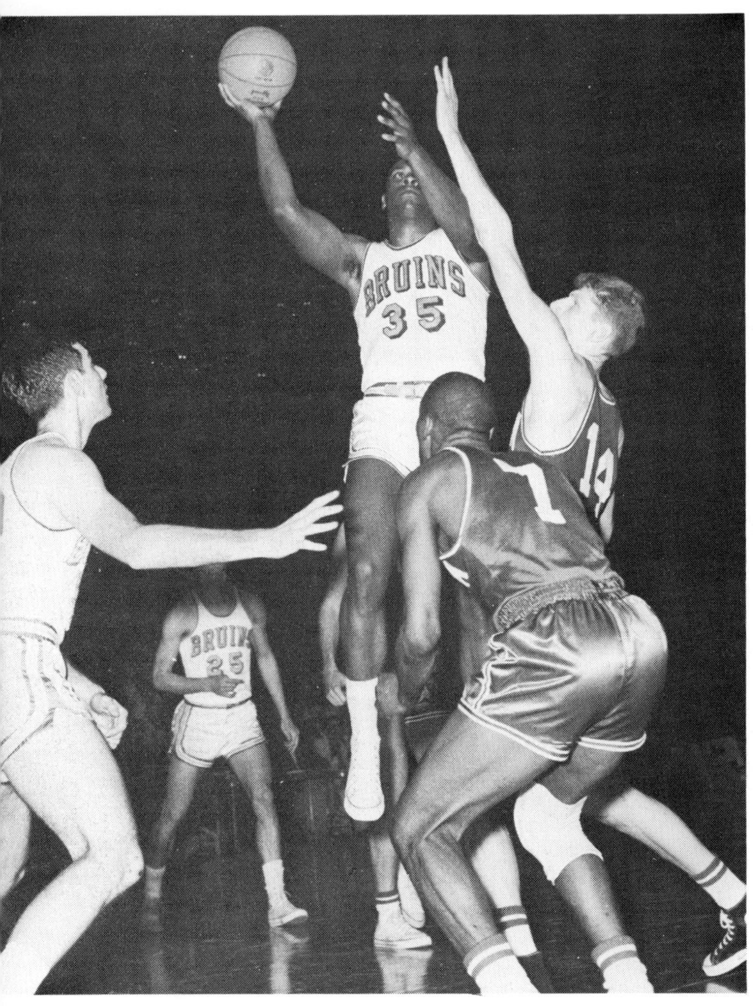

Lobbing a jumper here is Fred Slaughter (35), who worked the pivot post for UCLA in 1964. Although Slaughter averaged only 7.9 points during the Bruins' 30–0 season, he was very effective on the boards. Other UCLA players shown are Jack Hirsch (50) and Gail Goodrich (25).

Basketball legend John Wooden coached UCLA to 10 NCAA championships and 16 Pacific Coast titles. During his 27 years at the UCLA helm, and two at Indiana State, Wooden won 667 games and lost only 161. He is the only man to be enshrined in the National Basketball Hall of Fame as both a player and a coach.

preceded them, UCLA employed a run-and-gun offense. It was an uncommonly small team, its tallest starters being forward Keith Erickson and center Fred Slaughter, who were only 6′5″. They were a true anomaly in an age of 6′10″ to seven-foot centers and forwards often only slightly shorter. But they could run, score, and press so well that no one had been able to stop them, and they had knocked off some very strong teams during the 1963–64 basketball season.

Reigning champion Loyola had lost five of its 24 games that year but was still invited as an at-large tourney entrant. The only player gone from the Ramblers' starting lineup was Jerry Harkness, their highest scorer. George Ireland's Loyola squad still played racehorse-style basketball and had little trouble in the first round, leaving Murray State in its wake, 101–91. But the Ramblers could not overcome a powerful Michigan in the second round. Loyola put on a frantic rush as the game wore down, but the Wolverines were able to cope with it and eliminated the crown holders from Chicago 84–80. It was not just Michigan superstar Cazzie Russell who did the Ramblers in that night, though he did contribute 21 points; the Wolverines' big gun was center Bill Buntin, who dropped in 26.

Loyola was not the only major team in the tournament to be eliminated by the end of the second round. Kentucky was astounded 85–69 by unheralded Ohio University, and a highly regarded Oregon State had fallen to Seattle 61–57. Gone, too, were such other possible title contenders as Villanova, Texas Western, and Creighton.

UCLA had raced through its first game, a 95–90 second-round win over Seattle. The Bruins had the best guard combination in the country with 6′3″ Walt Hazzard and 6′0″ Gail Goodrich; they dropped in 26 and 19 points, respectively, in that game. Another consistent scorer was forward Jack Hirsch, and he contributed 21 points. Hirsch, Keith Erickson, and Fred Slaughter picked off 13 rebounds apiece—rather impressive against a team that virtually dwarfed them.

For the Bruins the regional finals were not as smooth. They almost blew it to a fine San Francisco team, which led them by eight points at the half and by as many as 13 during the game. The Bruins had to fight all the way to finally cadge a 76–72 win, mostly the result of the breathtaking play by their gifted guards: Hazzard scored 23 points and Goodrich 15.

Michigan, behind Cazzie Russell's 25-point night, had little trouble with Ohio. Kansas State upset Wichita State to earn a berth in the semifinals. And Duke slaughtered Connecticut 101–54 to gain the other Final Four slot. Duke's All-American Art Heyman was gone, but forward Jeff Mullins was still around—very noticeably so. In the Blue Devils' earlier tourney win over Villanova, Mullins had logged 43 points, the most that would be scored in any game that tourney and only five short of the record set back in 1956 by Temple's Hal Lear. In the regional final against Connecticut, Mullins scored 30.

The match-ups at Kansas City's Municipal Auditorium were UCLA–Kansas State and Michigan–Duke. In the first game UCLA was a distinct favorite, but this edge was not all that apparent on the court. The Bruins tried desperately to pull away from Kansas State, but the Wildcats from Manhattan, Kansas, were tenacious, gunning for their second consecutive upset of the tourney. UCLA had a two-point lead at the half, but the Bruins had to put up with a battle royal in the second period before easing ahead in the late going to take a 90–84 win. The hero of the night for UCLA was Keith Erickson, who scored 28 points, the most any Bruin would score in any game that tournament.

The second game on the agenda was touted as a much closer match, but it did not turn out that way. Duke ruled throughout, and despite 31 points from Michigan's Cazzie Russell and 19 from Bill Buntin, the Wolverines were squelched 91–80. Jeff Mullins, who tallied 21 for Duke, was aided in the scoring department that night by Jay Buckley, who dumped in 25, as well as three others who scored in double figures.

The hope of Blue Devils coach Vic Bubas was that their extreme height advantage would enable the Blue Devils to control the boards, that they would be able to overcome UCLA's devastating press, and that they would continue to score as richly as they had

UCLA Bruin forward Jack Hirsch drives past Duke's Jeff Mullins in the 1964 title match-up. Contributing 13 points and six rebounds to UCLA's winning cause that night, Hirsch had an even better game in the Bruins' second-round win over Seattle when he scored 21 and snagged 13 rebounds.

Jeff Mullins led ACC champion Duke to the finals of the 1964 tourney. The All-American forward scored 116 points, including 43 against Villanova, and averaged 29 a game, all tournament highs for '64.

in the earlier games of the tourney (they were averaging 93 points a game, and Mullins alone had averaged better than 31). If they could, he felt certain they would emerge triumphant. And had Duke been able to do that, the Blue Devils just might have handed UCLA its first defeat of the season. But they couldn't. The Bruins were at their best, their fastest, their most accurate. They rang up 50 points in the first half, enough for a safe 12-point lead, then added another 48 in the second period. Duke never got into the game; the final, UCLA 98, Duke 83.

Gail Goodrich was the most productive Bruin of the night with 27 points, and reserve Kenny Washington dazzled everyone with a 26-point performance. For the runner-up, Mullins had 22 and Buckley 18. UCLA senior guard Walt Hazzard was named Outstanding Player. Hazzard, a great playmaker, averaged 18.6 points in UCLA's four tournament games, but Gail Goodrich was the Bruins' high-point man with a 21.5 average.

Awards, 1964

Outstanding Player
Walt Hazzard (UCLA)

All-Tournament Team
Walt Hazzard (UCLA)
Jeff Mullins (Duke)
Bill Buntin (Michigan)
Willie Murrell (Kansas State)
Gail Goodrich (UCLA)

There were certainly some spectacular performances in the 1965 NCAA tournament, but then that would be expected with such incendiary stars as Gail Goodrich of UCLA, Cazzie Russell of Michigan, and Bill Bradley of Princeton on the billboard. The show of greatest magnitude was put on by Bradley. In the consolation game for third place he led his fellow Princeton Tigers over Wichita State and in the process scored 58 points, a new tourney mark. Bradley connected on 22 of 29 shots from the floor, made 14 of 15 free throws, and led all rebounders with 17. That performance, along with his other scoring feats (22, 27, 41, and 29 points in the preceding four tournament games) gave him an overall average of 35.4 points, another new NCAA tourney record, and it was enough to earn for him

The 1964 champs, the first of 10 for John Wooden at UCLA. **Front row** (left to right): Dennis Minishian (manager), Gail Goodrich, Jack Hirsch, Rich Levin, Walt Hazzard, Kent Graham, Mike Huggins, Chuck Darrow. **Back row** (left to right): Ducky Drake (trainer), Jerry Norman, Steve Brucker, Fred Slaughter, Doug McIntosh, Vaughn Hoffman, Keith Erickson, Kim Stewart, Kenny Washington, John Wooden (coach).

the Outstanding Player award, even though his team finished only third.

Princeton, the first Ivy League school to make the Final Four since Dartmouth had in 1944, was considered a good team but not necessarily one of the tourney favorites, at least at the outset. Smart money was on UCLA and Michigan.

UCLA had lost three starters from its 1964 championship team, including All-American guard Walt Hazzard, but the Bruins still had such aces as Gail Goodrich and Keith Erickson. As a team, they were as fast and as smooth as ever, and their full-court press was as inhibiting as it had been the year before. While UCLA would be defined as quick and deadly, Michigan was strong and overwhelming. Cazzie Russell was back, as were towering center Bill Buntin and intimidating forward Oliver Darden. Their coach, Dave Strack, felt that this pack of Wolverines had an awfully good chance of taking the whole thing.

Both UCLA and Michigan had byes into the second round, and neither had the slightest bit of trouble during its opening act. With Goodrich scoring 40 and Erickson another 28, the Bruins demolished Brigham Young 100–76. On the other side of the Mississippi, Michigan rolled over Dayton 98–71, getting 26 points from Buntin, 17 from Darden, and 14 from Russell.

It was not so easy in the regional finals, especially for Michigan. Down at the half to a fired-up Vanderbilt team, Michigan had to struggle back to eke out a two-point win in the final moments of the game. Russell and Buntin each accounted for 26 points in that victory. UCLA had a battle on its hands as well with San Francisco, though it was not as close a game. The Bruins' victory was the result of potent scoring, and for the second time in the tourney they broke the century mark: 101–93. Goodrich again was high for the night this time with 30, and Erickson was only a step behind with 29.

The other two teams to make the Final Four were Princeton and Wichita State. Behind Bradley's amazing shooting, dogged defense, and dependable rebounding, the Tigers from the Ivy League had beaten some of the nation's most highly regarded teams on their way to the semifinals, including two very legitimate contenders for the championship: North Carolina State, which Princeton beat by 18, and Providence, destroyed by an eye-popping 40 points.

Wichita State was paced by guard Kelly Pete, an All-American who in the tourney had scored 31 and 19 points in the Shockers' first two victories. But they were considered the weak link in the Final Four and were unlucky enough to have to line up against John Wooden's explosive Bruins in the western semifinal. UCLA took charge from the opening tip and proceeded to run up its largest score in the tournament that year. At the half the Bruins led 65–38 and at the end 108–89. Goodrich had 28, guard Edgar Lacey 24, and forward Fred Goss another 19.

As superb a player as Bill Bradley was, he was not able to push Princeton past such a powerful, well-rounded team as Michigan. He certainly tried, scoring 29 points, the most that night, but in that desperate game he was virtually too determined, and his aggressiveness caused him to foul out with a full five minutes left. And with Bradley's banishment to the bench, all of Princeton's hopes disappeared. The Wolverines won it handily, 93–76. Again Michigan was led by Cazzie Russell and Bill Buntin, with 26 and 22 points respectively.

More than 13,000 college basketball fans gathered at the Portland, Oregon, Coliseum for the final night's entertainment of the 1965 NCAA championship tourney. In the opener Bill Bradley treated them to his record-breaking scoring performance. That act would be tough to follow, but the championship contest had all the markings of a real thriller. Powerful Michigan and speedy UCLA were both dynamite teams, both capable of explosive scoring. To many it was a pick-it game. The Las Vegas odds makers appeared to favor Michigan. The majority of coaches in attendance seemed to like UCLA. Everyone thought it would be close all the way, no doubt decided at the wire.

It did not turn out that way, however. UCLA, using its press to the fullest advantage, badgered the Wolverines from the very start. At the same time the Bruins' whirlwind offense was cutting Michigan apart. At the half the

Kelly Pete (30), Wichita State's ace guard in 1965, lofts a little jumper against Southern Illinois. In that year's tourney Pete scored 31 points in State's romp over Southern Methodist, but UCLA held him to a mere 17 when the Bruins eliminated the Kansans in the West regional final.

Bruins had built a 13-point lead, and Michigan never threatened it during the second period. When it was finally over, UCLA could glory in an unpressed 91–80 victory and its second consecutive national championship.

Although overshadowed by Bill Bradley's 58-point performance earlier in the everning, UCLA guard Gail Goodrich ended his collegiate career on an exceptional note, scoring 42 points, the most at that point ever scored in the championship game, and raising his tourney average to an impressive 35 points per game. At that time, in the history of the tournament only Bill Bradley's performance the same year (35.4 average) and Clyde Lovellette's 35.3 average in 1952 exceeded Goodrich's. For the champs that night reserve Kenny Washington scored another 17 points, and Edgar Lacey had 11. For the Wolverines Russell scored 28 points, and Darden and Buntin added 17 and 14. But the glory was all UCLA's as it would be for so much of the next basketball decade.

Awards, 1965

Outstanding Player
Bill Bradley (Princeton)

All-Tournament Team
Bill Bradley (Princeton)
Gail Goodrich (UCLA)
Cazzie Russell (Michigan)
Edgar Lacey (UCLA)
Kenny Washington (UCLA)

The only year between 1962 and the decade of the 1980s that UCLA would not go to the NCAA tournament was 1966. It was the Bruins' one year of rest before they would chart seven consecutive championships, the one brief hiatus separating the school's nine of 10 NCAA basketball titles.

The rest of the college pack got their chance in 1966. And to the ultimate surprise of just about everyone, the trophy would be taken by Texas Western (today known as Texas–El Paso). The Miners, respected for their stifling defense, under coach Don Haskins, were making their third appearance in the postseason classic. In 1963 they had been eliminated in the first round, and the following year they were knocked out of it in the second. But now they were about to bring that Lone Star State's school to national prominence.

Before the tournament most people seemed to favor either Duke or Michigan, but some

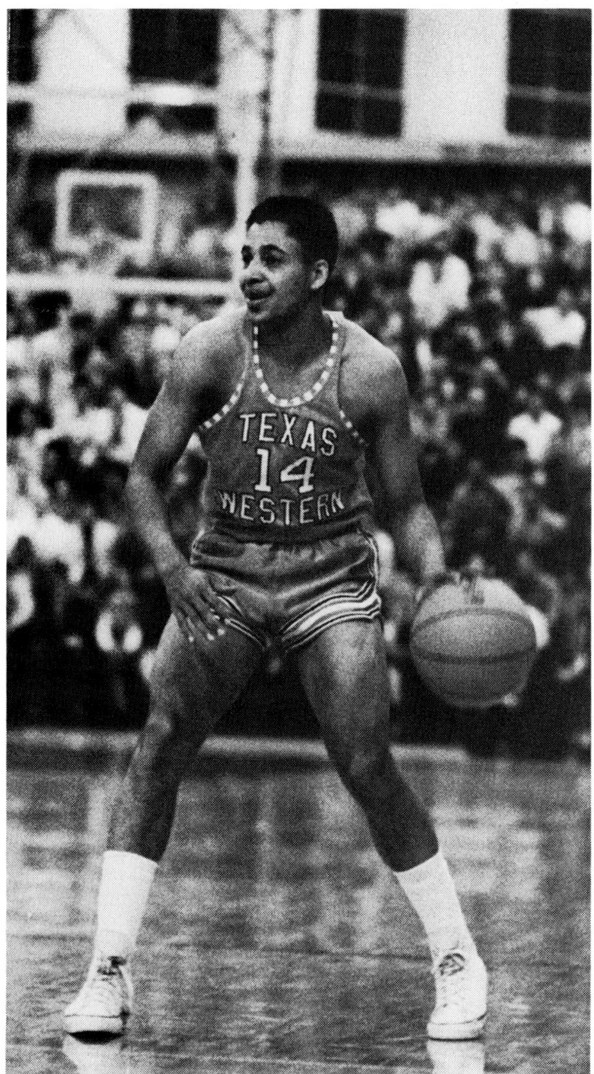

Big gun for the Texas Western champs of 1966 was Bobby Joe Hill, who averaged 20.2 points in the Miners' five games.

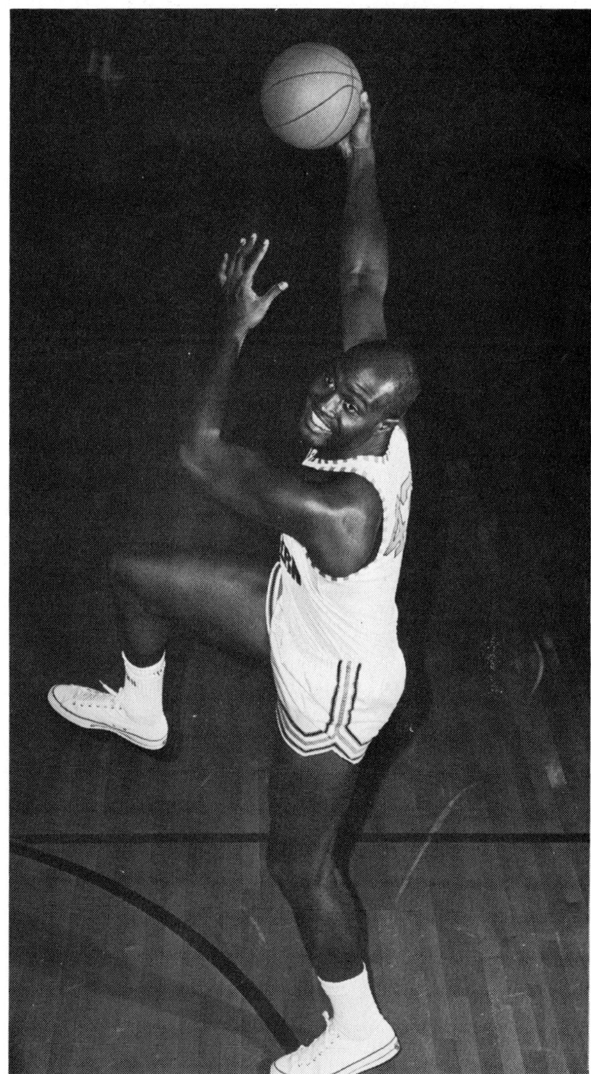

Big Dave Lattin of Texas Western was a key figure in the Texans' race to the NCAA title in 1966. Lattin's most memorable moments that tourney were the 17 rebounds he grabbed in the regional title win over Kansas and the 29 points he scored against Cincinnati.

well-informed basketball followers liked Kentucky, Kansas, Utah, or Oregon State. There was hardly a word about Texas Western though the team had ended up third in the national rankings at the end of the regular season. The wiser coaches in the tournament knew, however, that the Miners from El Paso were not a team to be taken lightly.

Michigan, with the most heralded senior in the game, Cazzie Russell, did not get past the regional finals. Despite Russell's 29 points, Michigan was waylaid by Kentucky 84–77. Oregon State was also eliminated in the regionals by Utah, who were led by the tournament's most profuse scorer that year, Jerry Chambers. In that game he had scored 33 points for the Utes, and he had earlier toted up 40 in their second-round win over Pacific. Kansas also failed to survive the regionals, losing in triple overtime to Texas Western 81–80. In that thriller, decided by a single free throw, Texas Western showed that it was capable of scoring with the best and was not just a team relying on its hound-dog defense. Its most productive point makers that night were Bobby Joe Hill (22) and Dave Lattin (15).

In the semifinals Duke was a slight favorite over Kentucky; and Texas Western, in light of its stunning performances in defeating Cincinnati and Kansas, got the nod over Utah.

Adolph Rupp had visions of his fifth national basketball championship when his Wildcats took the floor at College Park, Maryland, against Vic Bubas' Blue Devils. He had said publicly that, if they got through the semifinal match, Kentucky would indeed be champ because he did not believe that either Texas Western or Utah could beat his team. Duke, on the other hand, was a team to worry about.

The game was a true hell raiser all the way. Duke, behind the heavy scoring of Jack Marin (he would total 29 that night) led at the half 42–41. In the second period it was anybody's ball game, at least until the last few minutes. The lead was passed back and forth, but finally, with just about three minutes left, the Wildcats began to pull away. They moved to a six-point lead and eventually won it by four, 83–79. The Wildcats' hot hand of the night was guard Louie Dampier with 23, followed by Pat Riley with 19. Coach Rupp was happy, but he still would have to wait another night to celebrate.

Texas Western coach Don Haskins interrupted UCLA's monopoly of the NCAA title when his Miners took the crown in 1966 by beating Kentucky 72–65.

It was Texas Western that he would have to send his prized Kentucky team against. The Miners, even though they could not curtail Jerry Chambers, who scored a tournament-high 38 points against them, dominated the Utes and walked away with an 85–78 ticket to the finals. Don Haskins' Miners had been paced by Orsten Artis, who scored 22, and Bobby Joe Hill, 18.

The 1966 NCAA championship tournament obviously did not turn out the way Coach Rupp had imagined. Texas Western slowly but steadily built a first-half lead that rested at three points when they went to the locker room for the mid-game break. Kentucky gamely fought back in the second half, closing to within a point, but it could never get closer than that, and as the game wore down to its conclusion the Miners crept away with it. The final was 72–65, and it was Don Haskins who took his first NCAA trophy back to El Paso instead of Adolph Rupp returning to Lexington with his fifth. It was Bobby Joe Hill who tallied the most points for the Texas Western Miners with 20; Big Dave Lattin had 16 and Orsten Artis had another 15.

Awards, 1966

Outstanding Player
Jerry Chambers (Utah)

All-Tournament Team
Jerry Chambers (Utah)
Pat Riley (Kentucky)
Jack Marin (Duke)
Louie Dampier (Kentucky)
Bobbie Joe Hill (Texas-Western)

The Outstanding Player award was given to Utah's Jerry Chambers in recognition of the new NCAA record he set by averaging 35.8 points during Utah's four tournament games.

7
Reenter UCLA

UCLA swept back into the national limelight in 1967 around a seven-foot-plus fulcrum named Lew Alcindor, a recruit Coach John Wooden had to go all the way across the country to New York City to obtain. Alcindor, who would change his name to Kareem Abdul Jabbar after leaving UCLA, was now a sophomore and about to take his place among the great giant centers in college basketball history, which began with George Mikan and carried through Bob Kurland, Clyde Lovellette, Bill Russell, and Wilt Chamberlain. For three consecutive years Alcindor would be the pivot around which John Wooden built NCAA championship teams.

Just how imposing a force Alcindor was became abundantly clear in his very first varsity appearance; the long, lithe center scored 56 points to set a new UCLA record for individual scoring in a single game. Later in the season he would better it by scoring 61 points in a game against Washington State. The Bruins marched through 26 games during the regular season, arriving at the 1967 NCAA tournament undefeated and ranked number one by every poll in the nation.

Other very good teams were invited to the tournament that year, among them Houston, Southern Methodist, Louisville, North Carolina, and returning champs Texas Western. All certainly had a legitimate shot at the crown, observers felt, but UCLA remained the foremost team to beat, even though the starting five consisted of four sophomores and one junior. The Bruins had another All-American

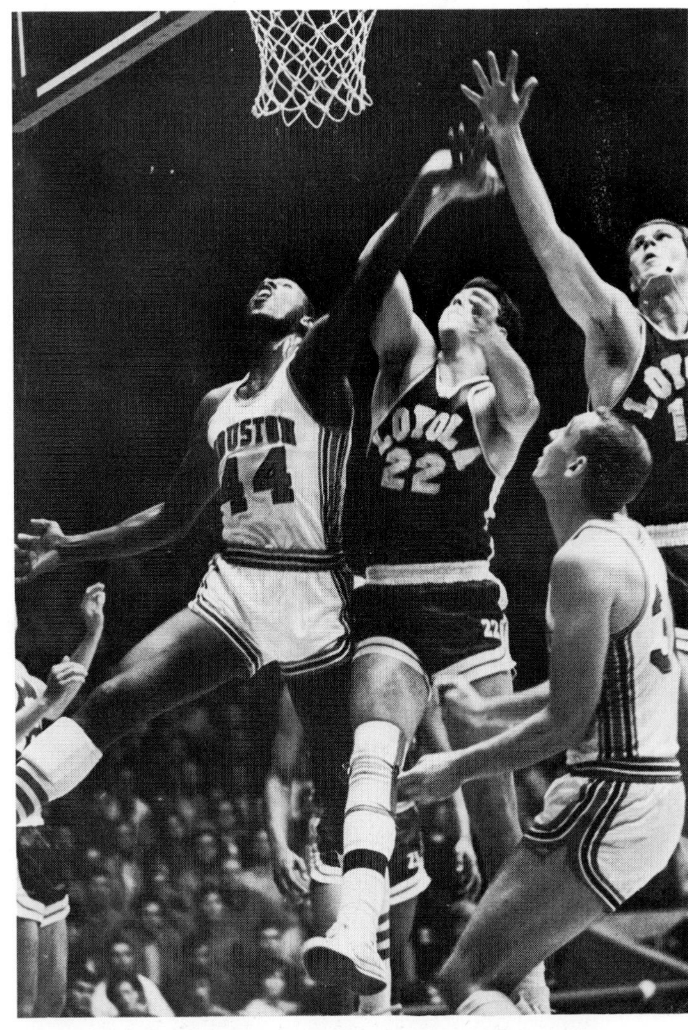

Elvin Hayes (44), Houston's superstar from 1966 through 1968, battles for a rebound against Loyola of Chicago in a first-round game in 1968. Hayes, who played in 13 NCAA tournament games over three years, is the all-time tourney high scorer with 358 points (27.5 average) and top rebounder with 222 (17.1 average). His best single-game performance was this one, in which he scored 49 points.

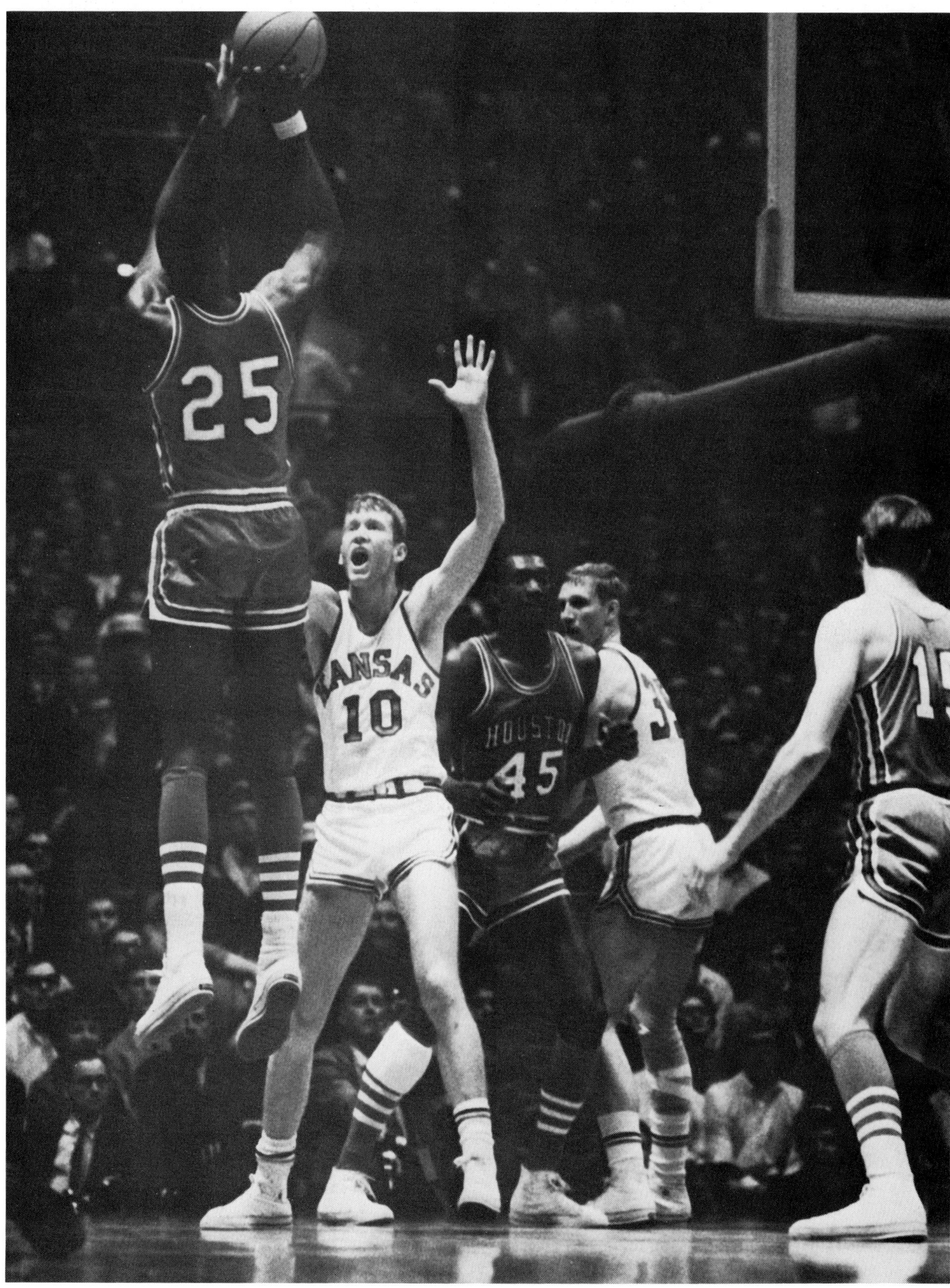

A mainstay on the 1966, 1967, and 1968 Houston squads was 6'5" guard Don Chaney (25), going up for a jumper here against Kansas in the second round of the '67 tourney. Chaney was the game's high scorer that night with 20.

The perfect picture to illustrate how intimidating Lew Alcindor (Kareem Abdul Jabbar), was during his three-year career at UCLA. Named the NCAA's Outstanding Player three times (1967–69) and the only player ever to win it that often, Alcindor ranks third in all-time tourney scoring (304 points, 25.3 average) and second in rebounding (201, 16.8 average).

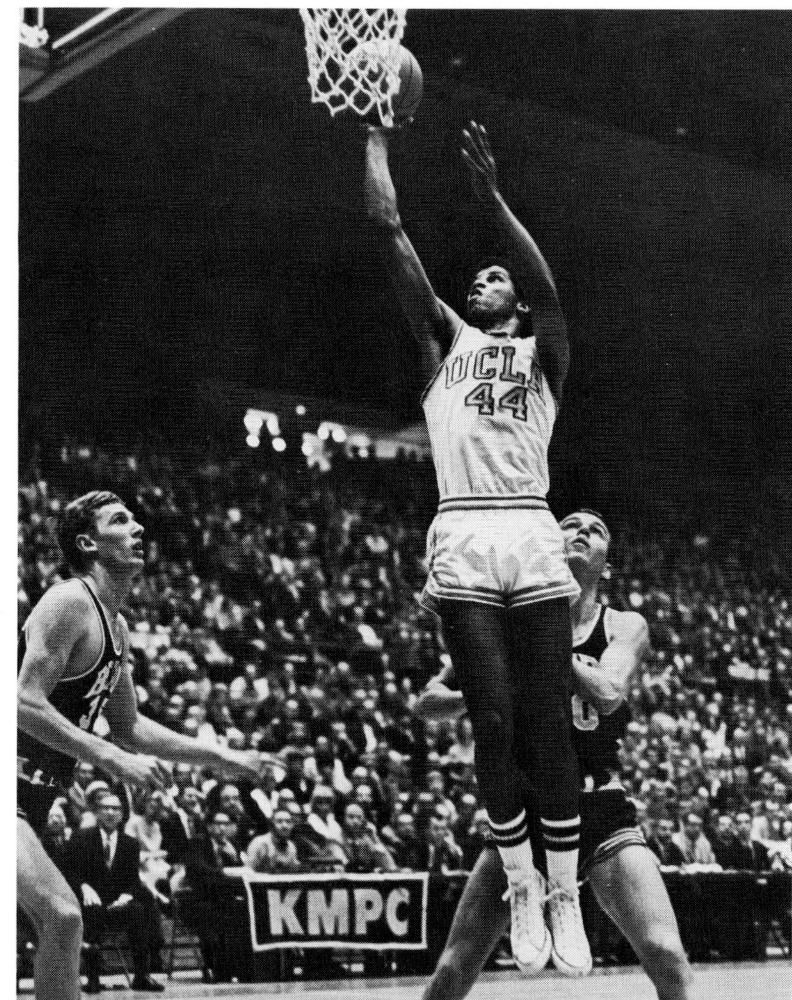

Guard Mike Warren (44) goes up for an easy two here for UCLA. A steady shooter—he averaged better than 12 points a game in both the 1967 and 1968 tourneys—and a superb ball handler, Warren won All-Conference and All-American honors in 1968. Presently he is a star on TV's "Hill Street Blues."

Below. A trio of All-Americans watch the action during the 1967 championship game: Lew Alcindor (33), Lucius Allen (42), and Don May (21). Dayton's May was the game's high scorer with 21; but UCLA, behind the 20 points from Alcindor and 19 from Allen, prevailed 79–64. Alcindor averaged 26.5 points (the tourney high mark), May 23.6, and Allen 16.

candidate in guard Lucius Allen. He was joined in the backcourt by Mike Warren (the junior), while the forward slots were held down by Lynn Shackelford and Kenny Heitz. UCLA also had a strong bench, one that gained a lot of game experience by relieving the starters in many a UCLA runaway during the regular season.

The first test of their postseason abilities came up in Corvallis, Oregon, against Wyoming. The Bruins virtually blew the Cowboys from Laramie out of the arena. With the score of 55–18 after one of the most lopsided first halves in the history of the tournament, John Wooden emptied his bench, then watched his reserves cruise through to a 109–60 victory. Alcindor had 29 points before returning to the bench, and Lucius Allen got another 15. The next battle, this one for the regional title, was not as one-sided, but UCLA had no trouble after an awful first half (they actually were down 21–17 at intermission) and pulled out an 80–64 win. Alcindor had 38 points for the night.

The going was going to get a lot rougher in the semifinals—allegedly. There, the Bruins were scheduled to meet the Houston Cougars, winners of the Southwest conference and paced by their own All-American, 6′9″ Elvin Hayes. Although Houston was thought to have the best chance at beating UCLA, the Cougars had barely gotten by the first round of the tournament. In a feverish game, they had to stage a fancy comeback to take a one-point victory from New Mexico State. But even though Houston as a team did not look like champs, Elvin Hayes did, with 30 points for the night. After that the Cougars defeated two highly regarded teams in Kansas and Southern Methodist to earn their way to the Final Four.

While all this was going on in the West, North Carolina, as expected, had forged through the eastern regionals, knocking off Princeton and Boston College along the way. The other eastern team to reach the Final Four was a surprise to everybody: unheralded, unranked Dayton out of the Mid-American Conference. Dayton had upset Western Kentucky, then gone on to beat Tennessee and Virginia Tech.

The Final Four convened in Louisville, Kentucky, for two nights of basketball to determine that year's champion. Almost everyone, however, felt that the real championship game was the semifinal match-up between the UCLA Bruins and Houston. But the game did not live up to its advance notices. UCLA breezed through it with little effort. An 11-point lead at half was turned into a 15-point trouncing by game's end. Alcindor was held to 19 points but grabbed 20 rebounds while Lynn Shackelford came up with 22 points and Lucius Allen and Mike Warren added 17 and 14 respectively. For the disappointed Cougars Elvin Hayes totaled 25 points and 24 rebounds, both game highs but unfortunately not enough.

In the other semifinal game astonishing Dayton did it again, this time stunning a highly favored North Carolina. With 34 points from forward Don May, the Flyers soared into the finals. That was not May's only fine night, either. In two of Dayton's previous three games he had accounted for 26 and 29 points.

Dayton was coached by Mickey Donoher who was justly proud of the string of miracles he and his team had pulled off in that tournament. He was also justifiably in awe of the coming encounter with Lew Alcindor and his colleagues from Los Angeles. Donoher was a realist, and he knew only too well what a monstrous opponent he had to face in the 1967 NCAA final game.

The Dayton Flyers had all the spirit, all the determination that could be mustered on that championship evening, but they did not have the resources to carry their dream beyond that last enormous obstacle. UCLA was simply too powerful, and no matter how hard Dayton

Awards, 1967

Outstanding Player
Lew Alcindor (UCLA)

All-Tournament Team
Lew Alcindor (UCLA)
Don May (Dayton)
Mike Warren (UCLA)
Elvin Hayes (Houston)
Lucius Allen (UCLA)

went at the Bruins, the Flyers were never able to come close. The Bruins of UCLA, as they had in all the other contests during the tourney, methodically destroyed their opponent. The Bruins built an 18-point lead by the half, then gave their reserves a chance to take part in an NCAA championship show. When it was finally over UCLA had a 79–64 win. Alcindor scored 20, Allen 19, and Warren 17. Don May collected 21 for the Flyers from Dayton. No one was surprised when Alcindor was named the tourney's Outstanding Player.

The dynasty was back in business.

Don Donoher, head coach at Dayton, brought the Flyers to six NCAA tourneys between 1965 and 1974. Their best showing was in '67, when they ran second to UCLA and Lew Alcindor.

Dayton would not return to the NCAA tournament the next year, but the other three semifinalists from 1967—UCLA, Houston, and North Carolina—would, and all three were bound again for the Final Four.

Crown holder UCLA had exactly the same team back, though forward Kenny Heitz was now sharing much of the playing time with Mike Lynn. Houston, too, had most of the same faces in its lineup, the most famous belonging to Elvin Hayes. But there were also the talented 6′5″ guard Don Chaney and Ken Spain, and coach Guy Lewis was delighted with the performance of newcomer Theodis Lee. The Cougars, who had gone undefeated during the regular season, were ranked number one in the nation as a result of nipping UCLA by a basket earlier in the year. The Tar Heels of North Carolina, under coach Dean Smith, were paced by forward Larry Miller and center Rusty Clark, as they had been the year before.

Joining those returnees to the semifinals was a school that was hardly a stranger to the Final Four, Ohio State, making its first appearance there since the days of Jerry Lucas and John Havlicek in the earlier 1960s. Ohio State was a definite surprise in 1968. First, it had not been expected to win the Big Ten, which it managed by upsetting Iowa in a special playoff game. Second, it had not been expected to survive its encounter with a much more highly regarded Kentucky team in the Midwest Regional final. But the Buckeyes surely rose to that occasion, curtailed the Wildcats' big guns, Dan Issel and Mike Casey, and produced three 20-point men themselves in the process: Dave Sorenson (22), Bill Hosket (21), and Steve Howell (20). Two of Sorenson's points came on a jump shot in the last seconds to give the Buckeyes a heart-stopping 82–81 upset victory over Adolph Rupp's Wildcats.

In the other regional east of the Mississippi North Carolina showed impressive power as the Tar Heels romped over St. Bonaventure, which had All-American candidate center Bob Lanier on its roster, 91–72. In the East Regional final, however, the Tar Heels were brought back to earth by an inspired Davidson team, which had the Tar Heels down by six at the half. North Carolina battled back and managed to squeeze out a four-point win, but it had been uncomfortably close, and Dean Smith, after such a near-fatal encounter, was not taking underdog Ohio State for granted.

The Houston team, especially Elvin Hayes, had a burning desire to get back at UCLA. The year before Houston had been confident it would win, but the Bruins had very deftly deflated those dreams. The Cougars had never expected to be so thoroughly routed as they

The cornerstone of St. Bonaventure in the 1968 and 1970 tourneys was 6'11" center Bob Lanier. (He had a shoe size of 19.) In '68 he scored 32 and 23 points in Bonaventure's two games. In '70 Lanier averaged 26 points in three games, but when an injury kept him from the semifinal game St. Bonaventure fell to Jacksonville.

Louisville's Wes Unseld was one of the most intimidating frontcourt players in the 1967 and 1968 tourneys. In '68 he went head to head with Houston's Elvin Hayes in the Midwest regional. The result of that classic confrontation: Hayes, 35 points and 24 rebounds; Unseld, 23 points and 22 rebounds. Louisville lost 91–75.

had been by UCLA in the previous year's semifinals. Of the teams in the Final Four, Houston had perhaps the most difficult route to navigate to get there. Houston was the only one of the four that had to play in the first round, though it felt little menace from Loyola of Chicago, who they throttled 94–76. In that game, incidentally, Elvin Hayes scored that tournament's high of 49 points, making 20 of 28 from the floor and adding another nine free throws; he also collected 27 rebounds, another tournament standard that year. A strong Louisville team lay in wait for Houston at the next juncture. The Cardinals had All-American candidate Wes Unseld at their pivot position and consistently high-scoring Butch Beard. But a determined Houston team dismembered them with little difficulty. The ever-prolific Hayes scored 35 for the Cougars in a 16-point win. Theodis Lee had 18 and Don Chaney 17 the same night. Then they simply waltzed through the regional finals, annihilating Texas Christian 103–68 in a game again dominated by Hayes, who scored 39 points.

UCLA had no trouble whatsoever advancing to the semifinals. Polished, primed veterans, they skimmed past New Mexico State and Santa Clara, two less-than-demanding warmups for their confrontation with Houston.

As thirsty for revenge as Houston was said to be, this was hardly evident that night at the Sports Arena in Los Angeles. And if the scorching the Cougars experienced the year before had been unnerving, it was minor compared to what awaited them in the 1968 western semifinal before a strongly partisan UCLA crowd. It was simple and humiliating: UCLA was hot, very hot, and Houston was cold, very cold. The Bruins manipulated the Cougars at will during the first half and pulled to a 53–31 lead at the end of that period. In the second half they increased the lead to a staggering 44 points, and from that point on a dispirited Houston team had to play out the rest of the game against John Wooden's substitutes. The final score was 101–69. Before the UCLA first stringers went to the bench three of them had tallied 19 points each—Lew Alcindor, Lucius Allen, and Mike Lynn—while Lynn Shackel-

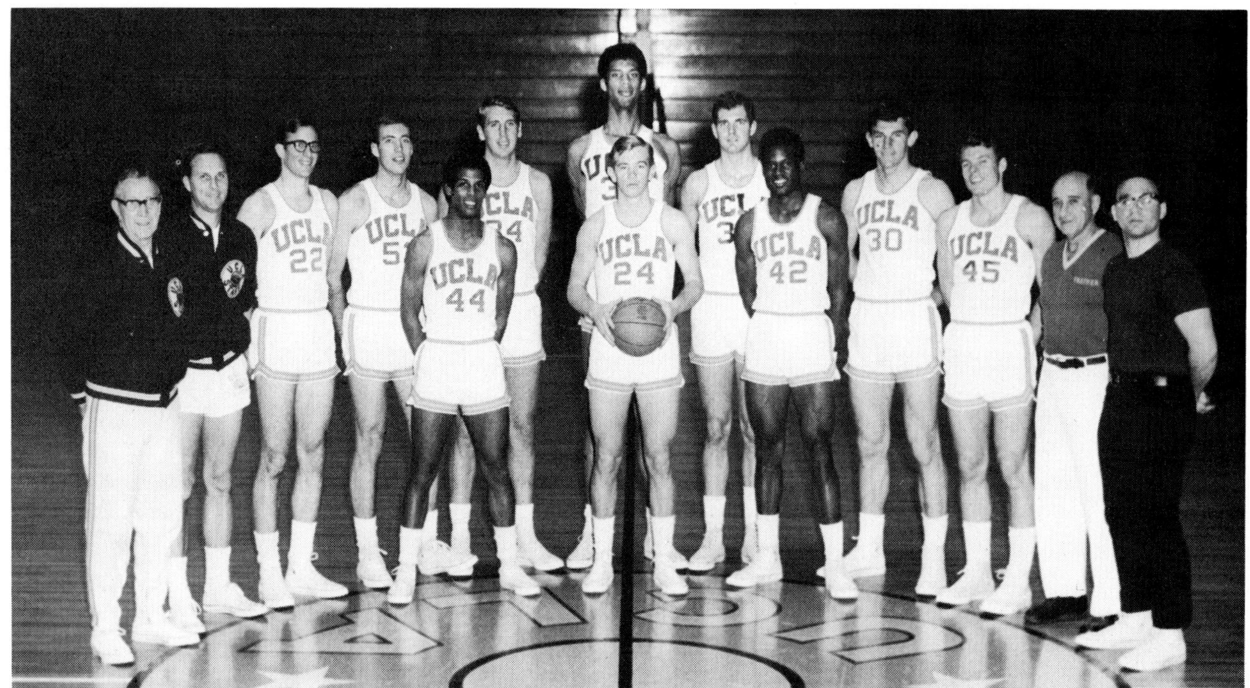

UCLA, champions of 1968, destroyed North Carolina 78-55. **Front row** (left to right): Mike Warren, Gene Sutherland, Lucius Allen. **Back row** (left to right): John Wooden (coach), Jerry Norman (assistant coach), Ken Heitz, Lynn Shackelford, Jim Nielsen, Lew Alcindor, Mike Lynn, Neville Saner, Bill Sweek, Ducky Drake (trainer), Frank Adler (manager).

ford basketed 17 and Mike Warren 14. Houston's Elvin Hayes had been totally shut down, held to a mere 10 points and five rebounds (quite a comedown from the 41 points and more than 25 rebounds he had been averaging in each of Houston's three previous games).

North Carolina was expected to beat Ohio State in the other semifinal game. And it did so with relative ease. All five of the Tar Heel starters scored in double figures (the highest was Larry Miller's 20), and North Carolina coasted to an 80-66 victory. Along with it came the dubious pleasure of encountering UCLA in the 1968 NCAA championship game.

The problem with UCLA, Tar Heel coach Dean Smith noted before the final game, was that if a team concentrated on stopping Alcindor, the other four Bruins would simply take over, run and gun them to death, and beat them in their own way. Apparently Smith chose not to try to curtail Alcindor that night, instead simply going team to team with the Bruins. Alcindor responded by dropping in 34 points and dominating the boards by taking 16 rebounds. UCLA took command at the very beginning of the game, then exploded an 11-point halftime lead into a 78-55 win, the largest margin of victory in the history of the NCAA tournament.

Alcindor was selected as the tourney's Outstanding Player, joining that select club of two-time winners which then included only Bob Kurland, Alex Groza, and Jerry Lucas. And UCLA that night became only the second school in NCAA history to win the tournament four times (the other Kentucky) and the only one to do it in a period of five years.

Awards, 1968

Outstanding Player
Lew Alcindor (UCLA)

All-Tournament Team
Lew Alcindor (UCLA)
Lynn Shackelford (UCLA)
Mike Warren (UCLA)
Lucius Allen (UCLA)
Larry Miller (North Carolina)

Lew Alcindor was playing out his last year of college basketball during the 1968–69 season, and John Wooden knew that if he was to keep his incredible dynasty going he would have to begin injecting some new blood. He also wanted the Bruins to get some solid game experience before having to take on the awesome responsibilities of replacing Alcindor's contributions in the scoring column and on the rebound chart.

Wooden's eye for talent apparently had been as sharp as ever. While Alcindor was still a lowly undergraduate it had fastened on several youngsters, who he successfully recruited. Alcindor was in the twilight of his collegiate career; theirs were about to dawn. One find was forward Sidney Wicks, at 6′8″ a fine scorer and an intimidating rebounder. Wooden also added a poem of a shooter in guard John Vallely, and an all-around athlete in Curtis Rowe. Wicks would spend most of the year apprenticing and would not make his mark until the following season, but Vallely and Rowe would be instrumental in the Bruins' fortunes of 1968–69.

UCLA's John Vallely (40) soars above a Duke defender in the 1969 semifinals to score two of his 29 points that day. Vallely was All-Tournament vintage in both 1969 and 1970.

UCLA lost only one game during the year, stalled into defeat by a mediocre but effectively tactical Southern Cal team. That loss, incidentally, ended a 41-game UCLA win streak and ended its phenomenal string of 85 straight victories at home. But it did little to deter the Bruins from their quest for a third consecutive NCAA championship.

There were some other very good teams, however, that would be vying along with them for it: such sterling clubs and stars as Davidson with Mike Maloy, Marquette with George Thompson and Dean Meminger, Notre Dame with Austin Carr, New Mexico State with Jimmy Collins and Sam Lacey, North Carolina with Rusty Clark and Charlie Scott, Duquesne with Jarrett Durham, Kentucky with Dan Issel, Purdue with Rick Mount, Drake with Willie McCarter, Colorado with Cliff Meely, and Santa Clara with Dennis Awtrey, among them.

None, however, would be adroit enough to derail the Bruins, and only one would give them any sort of game at all during the 1969 tourney. UCLA would first tromp on New Mexico State, winning by 15, then club Santa Clara into submission in a real one-sider, 90–52. After those easy workouts the Bruins had again qualified for the Final Four.

Their opponent in the western semifinal would be somewhat of a surprise, the Drake Bulldogs from Des Moines, Iowa, under coach Maurice John. The Bulldogs had won the tough Missouri Valley Conference, sported a record of 23 and four, and had decisively beaten Texas A & M and Colorado State to get a shot at the titled UCLA Bruins.

Out East the competition was a lot more heated. North Carolina fought back desperately to take Duquesne by a single point in its first game in the East regional, then held off a sharp Davidson team to eke out a two-point win in the regional final.

Al McGuire's Marquette Warriors had beaten a favored Kentucky but then found Purdue too much to handle, especially sharpshooting Rick Mount. The Boilermaker, one of the best shooters in the nation, had averaged 29 points in each of Purdue's first two tourney games.

So, in the first semifinal game at Freedom

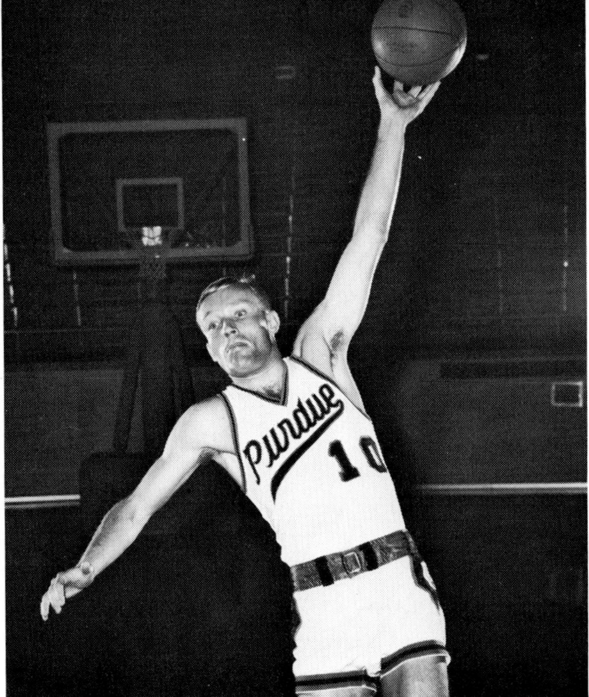

All-American Rick Mount was Purdue's principal stake in the 1969 tournament. The Boilermaker superscorer brought Purdue to the finals by logging 32, 26, and 36 points in wins over Miami (Ohio), Marquette, and North Carolina. Despite his 28 points in the title game, Purdue ran second to UCLA 92–72.

Guard Dean Meminger was Marquette's floor leader in both the 1969 and 1971 tournaments. His best efforts were the 20-point night in 1969 when the Warriors whipped Kentucky and the 30-point performance in the regional consolation game of '71, also against Kentucky.

Hall in Louisville, the North Carolina Tar Heels would face Purdue. Most onlookers favored the Tar Heels, suggesting that there would be a repeat of the preceding year's championship game because no one felt that Drake could oust UCLA in the other semifinal match. North Carolina, however, could not cope with Rick Mount. The Purdue ace dropped in 36 points, 14 of 28 from the floor and eight of nine from the line, and Purdue blistered the Tar Heels—at the half they led 53–30, then turned it into a 92–65 rout. Another Boilermaker, Bill Keller, also had a good game, accounting for 20 points.

In the second game many of the same spectators who thought the first game would be close believed this was the contest that would be a runaway. Drake seemed no match for the titanic Bruins. But it was, and it was a heated battle down to the final buzzer. With fanciful defense and a well-balanced scoring attack, the tenacious Bulldogs hung in through the first half, trailing by a lone point, 44–43, at the intermission. UCLA pulled ahead late in the second half, but Drake came roaring back in the last minute, reducing an eight-point Bruin lead to just a single point. Unfortunately for Maurice John's Drake Bulldogs, that was as close as they would get, and time ran out on their frantic comeback. The final score was 85–82, but John Wooden and his team knew they had been in a real battle. For the Bruins the big man on the scoreboard that night was not Lew Alcindor, though he did post 25 points; instead it was John Vallely, who made nine of 11 field goals and 11 of 14 charity tosses for a total of 29 points.

Drake proved it was no flash in the pan the following night when it decimated North Carolina in the consolation game 104–84, with its hotshot shooter Willie McCarter scoring a game-high 28 points.

There were two certified All-Americans in the 1969 championship game: Lew Alcindor from UCLA and Purdue's Rick Mount. Each team knew it would have its hands full with the other's star. But Purdue had nowhere near the balanced attack and depth of talent that UCLA possessed, and that was sharply evident early in the first period. The Bruins took control and built a nine-point lead at the half. Alcindor, as he had in the previous year's championship game, was rising sublimely to the challenge. It was his last game as a college player. It was, in fact, his finest performance of that year's tournament and the second most point-productive night during his three years in NCAA postseason competition.

After the second half began the Bruins were unstoppable, surging further and further ahead. The Boilermakers could not come close to making a game of it, and when the final buzzer mercifully sounded they were behind by 20 points. Alcindor had logged 37 points for the night, basketing 15 of 20 from the floor, and he also led all rebounders with 20. John Vallely posted another 15 for the Bruins, and Curtis Rowe and Lynn Shackelford were in double figures with 12 and 11 respectively. Rick Mount scored 28 for the Boilermakers.

For the first time in NCAA tourney history the same young man was named Outstanding Player for the third consecutive time; that singular honor is still solely the property of Lew Alcindor. The next year he would be a pro and would not attend the tournament, but John Wooden and another UCLA team would.

Awards, 1969

Outstanding Player
Lew Alcindor (UCLA)

All-Tournament Team
Lew Alcindor (UCLA)
Rick Mount (Purdue)
Charlie Scott (North Carolina)
Willie McCarter (Drake)
John Vallely (UCLA)

With the advent of the 1970s every college basketball team of note in the United States was gunning for UCLA. After all, the Bruins had virtually dominated the game during the past six seasons, walking off with the NCAA crown five times during those years. No team in the history of the tournament had won it so many times, nor had any team won so many games and lost so few during that long a period of time.

UCLA was not invincible, however. A few teams had beaten the Bruins in those years, though only on rare occasion, and several would, in fact, defeat them during the 1969–70 basketball season, but no one was going to succeed in dethroning them that year.

Before UCLA was able to make its annual hash of the Final Four there was another bit of pyrotechnics, supplied by the deft shooting hand of Notre Dame forward Austin Carr. In a first-round game against Ohio University he shattered the NCAA tournament single-game scoring record by tallying 61 points, a record that still stands today. From the floor Carr made 25 of 44 shots and sank 11 of 14 free throws. Notre Dame won that game easily, 112–82. Carr then took his gifted touch to the Mideast regional and applied it to the Wildcats of Kentucky, where he chalked up 52 points (22 of 35 field goals, eight of eight free throws). Notre Dame, however, lost by 10 points that night despite Carr's performance.

A true titan in the 1970 and 1971 tournaments was Jacksonville's center, 7′4″ Artis Gilmore. In '70 Gilmore tallied 30, 30, 24, and 29 in Jacksonville's march to the finals, plus an average of 19.3 rebounds. UCLA, however, held him to a subpar 19 points and 16 rebounds and beat Jacksonville in the title game.

After that there remained a consolation match with Iowa, in which Austin Carr reached his tournament nadir, held to 45 points. Iowa won that game by scoring 121 points, an NCAA single-game record. Austin Carr's average of 52.7 points a game for those three games still stands as the best scoring average in NCAA playoff history. And Notre Dame, as a team, had averaged better than 105 points a game but paradoxically still lost two of the three.

While Carr was rewriting the tournament record books, UCLA was simply winning games in what had now become a tradition to the Bruins. Steve Patterson (6′9″) had replaced Lew Alcindor at center. Sidney Wicks, at 6′8″, had broken into the starting lineup at forward, joining Patterson and Curtis Rowe in the frontcourt. Sophomore Henry Bibby landed a starting job alongside John Vallely at guard. Wooden had altered his game plan to compensate for the loss of Alcindor, and the emphasis now, as in the pre-Alcindor days, was on a coordinated five-man offensive attack, a lot of fast-breaking, and a strangulating full-court press. And it worked. There was no problem from Long Beach State in the first game of the West regional, the Bruins prevailing 88–65. Both Sidney Wicks and Henry Bibby contributed 20 points to that win, and the others did their share as well: Rowe 15, Vallely 14, and Patterson 13. Their second encounter in the regional caused no worry either, a 101–79 victory over Utah State. Wicks and Rowe contributed 26 apiece that night.

Sidney Wicks had an illustrious career at UCLA: two-time All-American (1970–71), and 1970 tourney Outstanding Player, among other honors. The 6′8″ forward started on both the 1970 and 1971 tourney champ teams, averaging 21.3 points and 13.3 rebounds in '70 and 15 points and 13 rebounds in '71.

The three other teams to make it to the Final Four in 1970 were making their maiden appearances in that select group: New Mexico State, St. Bonaventure, and Jacksonville. None of them was an especially big-name school, but they all were highly respected basketball quintets.

The New Mexico State Aggies had been invited to the NCAA tournament for the three previous years, and they had two legitimate stars in guard Jimmy Collins and center Sam Lacey. They had defeated three strong teams to reach the semifinals: Rice, Kansas State, and Drake.

Jimmy Collins averaged 23.4 points in New Mexico State's five tournament games in 1970, enough to carry the Aggies to their first and, so far, only appearance in the Final Four.

St. Bonaventure had developed a big problem. It was paced through its first three games in the tournament by 6′11″ All-American candidate center Bob Lanier. But as it was vying for the East regional title, he tore a ligament in his knee and was unable to play in the semifinal game. Lanier had scored 28, 24, and 26 points in St. Bonaventure's earlier wins over Davidson, North Carolina State, and Villanova. His loss during the semifinals would be felt severely.

Jacksonville, which St. Bonaventure had to face, possessed another center of All-American caliber in 7′2″ Artis Gilmore. It also had a high-scoring guard named Rex Morgan. Gilmore had accounted for 30 points in each of the Dolphins' first two wins over Western Kentucky and Iowa and 24 in the regional final

Awards, 1970

Outstanding Player
Sidney Wicks (UCLA)

All-Tournament Team
Sidney Wicks (UCLA)
Jimmy Collins (New Mexico State)
John Vallely (UCLA)
Artis Gilmore (Jacksonville)
Curtis Rowe (UCLA)

Notre Dame's Austin Carr (34) proved to be the tournament's all-time most explosive scorer when in 1970 he set the single-game scoring record with 61 points against an awestruck Ohio team. In the same tourney he tallied 52 against Kentucky and 45 against Iowa. The following year Carr had 52 against Texas Christian and 47 in a game with Houston. His single-tourney averages of 52.7 (1970) and 41.7 (1971) are the two best in NCAA tourney history.

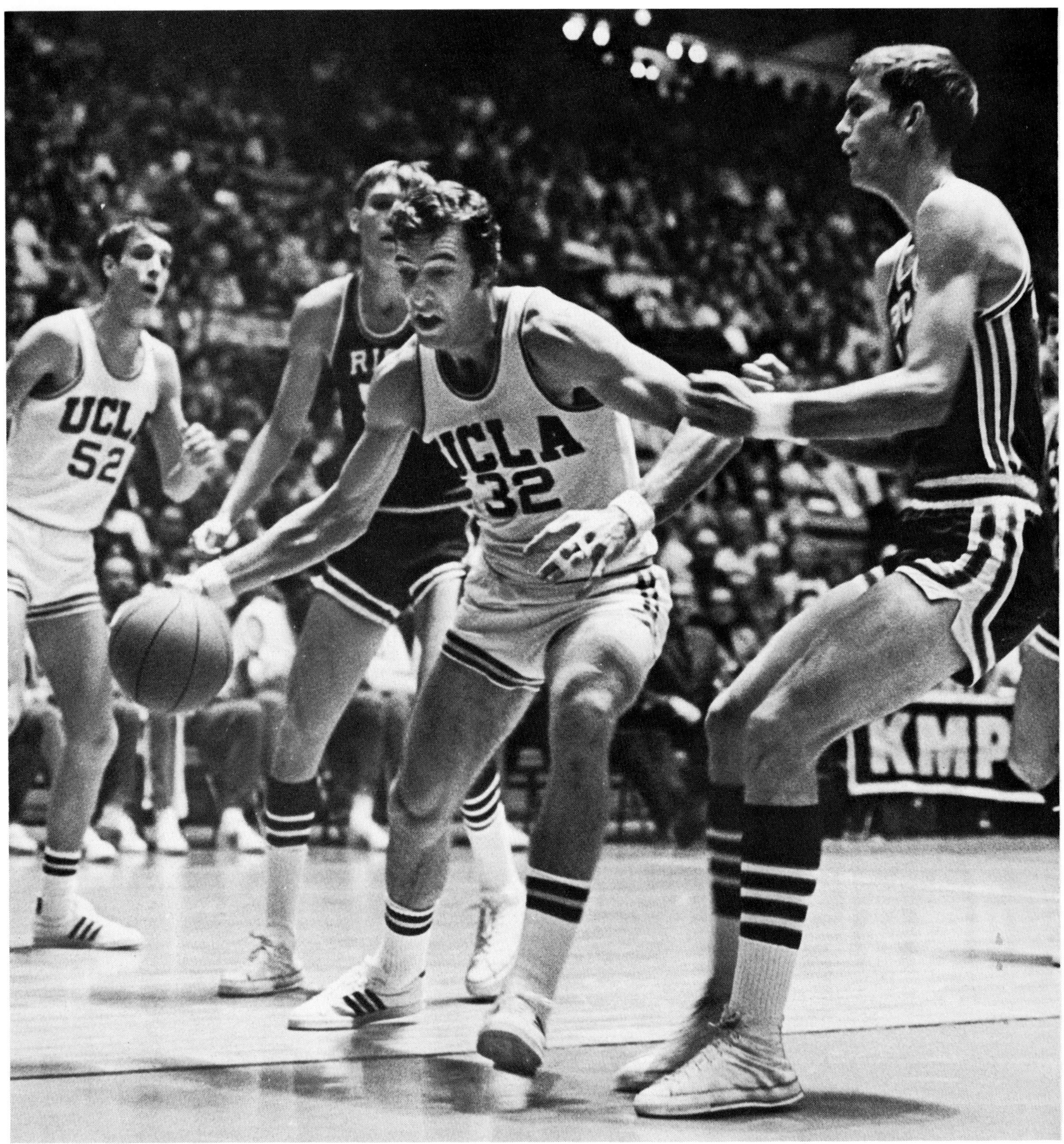

UCLA center Steve Patterson (32) drives around Rice's Mark Wehrle in this game at Pauley Pavilion. The starting center for UCLA in the 1970 and 1971 tourneys. Patterson bridged the reigns of Lew Alcindor and Bill Walton. He scored 29 points in the '71 title game. Number 52 for UCLA is John Ecker.

Curtis Rowe (30), dazzling with a hook here, started for the UCLA Bruins in three tourneys (1969–71). A versatile forward, his best single-game performance was in the '70 regional against Utah State, when he bucketed 26 points and grabbed 16 rebounds.

victory over Kentucky. Morgan had scored 24, 23, and 28 points in the three games.

Without Bob Lanier, St. Bonaventure had little chance against Jacksonville and towering Artis Gilmore. The team made a brave attempt of it, and the game was not a runaway, though the Dolphins controlled it throughout. The final was Jacksonville 91, St. Bonaventure 83. Gilmore was high man for the night with 29 points, and he also monopolized the boards, clearing 21 rebounds. Morgan had another 17 for Jacksonville.

UCLA had eliminated New Mexico State before the semifinals during the two previous NCAA tournaments, so the Aggies from Las Cruces were itching to avenge themselves. They were encouraged by the fact that UCLA no longer had Lew Alcindor. However, there was a very finely tuned five-man machine to contend with, as the Aggies found to their chagrin. UCLA's gears meshed in perfect harmony, and the Bruins methodically ground up New Mexico State's dreams. Jimmy Collins scored 28 points for the Aggies that night, the most in the game, but UCLA was never threatened in the 93–77 rout. For the Bruins, Vallely had 23 and Wicks 22; Bibby added 19, Rowe 15, and Patterson 12.

In the back of John Wooden's mind he probably thought it would be nice to have Alcindor there that championship night in 1970 to nullify Jacksonville's enormous Artis Gilmore. Still, he knew his team functioned so well as a unit and had such diversified offensive and defensive skills that one man was not going to overwhelm them, even if he was 7′2″.

UCLA quickly set the tone, as the Bruins almost always seemed to do, with their fast-paced play and intricate teamwork. Gilmore, as good as he had been during the regular season and in the previous tourney game, proved to be no factor that night. Sidney Wicks did a superb defensive job on him, and although Gilmore tallied 29 points (his lowest total of the tourney), he sank only eight of 29 shots from the floor that night. The crown holders from Los Angeles turned a five-point halftime lead into an 80–69 conclusion and UCLA's sixth NCAA title. Curtis Rowe was the high scorer for the Bruins that night with 19, while Wicks and Patterson added 17 apiece and Vallely 15. Junior Sidney Wicks was named the tournament's Outstanding Player.

The only familiar face gone from UCLA's starting five in 1970–71 was guard John Vallely, and his slot would be filled ably by Kenny Booker and sometimes Tony Shofield. John Wooden was still the team's mentor and was justifiably revered as one of the game's all-time great strategists and leaders. Once again the Bruins took the Pacific Coast Conference crown, and once again they were looked on as the force to contend with in the NCAA playoffs.

No one, however, was expecting UCLA to dance through the tourney. There were just too many good teams that year and an extraordinary cast of stars populating them. The most prolific scorer in NCAA tournament history was back and up to his old tricks. Notre Dame's Austin Carr tallied 52 points in the Fighting Irish's first round win in the Midwest regional, then posted 26 and 47 in their next two losses. His average of 41.7 points a game in 1971 stands second in tourney history only to the 52.7 average he registered the year before. But for coach Johnny Dee Notre Dame's situation was an ironic repeat of the year before: the Irish again scored richly but still lost two of their three encounters.

A number of good teams were eliminated early in the tournament. Fordham, paced by Chuck Yelverton, fell to Villanova in the first round of the East regional, and Frank McGuire's South Carolina suffered the same fate, surprised by the University of Pennsylvania. Jacksonville, with Artis Gilmore still at pivot, was edged out by Western Kentucky after blowing a 14-point halftime lead. Al McGuire's highly regarded Marquette team, with forward Dean Meminger and 6′11″ center Jim Chones, was shocked when Ohio State pulled off a one-point upset in the Mideast regional. Another tournament front-runner, Houston, which boasted such scoring demons as Dwight Davis and Poo Welch, was eliminated by Kansas in another one-point thriller.

The survivors, who earned trips to Houston to vie in the cavernous Astrodome as part of the Final Four for the ultimate NCAA spoils were Villanova and Western Kentucky from the East and UCLA and Kansas from the West.

Villanova had All-American Howard Porter on its roster, and he had averaged almost 29 points in the three previous games. Villanova also had another consistently high scorer in Hank Siemiontkowski, who also could claim one of the longest names ever to appear in an NCAA tournament box score (where it was usually abbreviated to something like "Smntkwski"). He, too, had been averaging more than 20 points a game in the tourney. Villanova had beaten three fine teams to get to Houston: St. Joseph's of Philadelphia, Fordham, and Pennsylvania (whom Villanova massacred by 43 points).

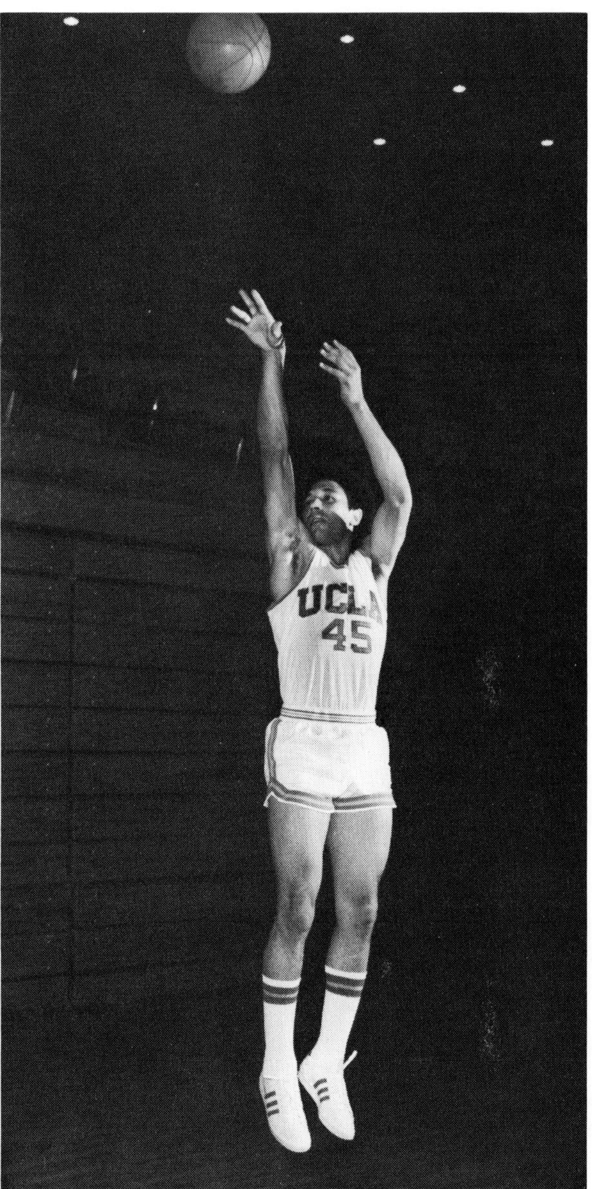

UCLA's Henry Bibby, a consensus All-American in 1971 and 1972, scored 17 points in the '71 title game against Villanova and 18 in the '72 championship match against Florida State. Bibby averaged 15 points in the eight tourney games in which he participated during those two years.

Big Jim Chones was the pivot around which Al McGuire wove Marquette's offense in 1971. Chones averaged 22 points in the Warriors' three tournament games that year, but Marquette was edged out in the regionals by Ohio State.

Western Kentucky also had to get by some stiff competition, first eliminating the previous year's tourney runner-up, Jacksonville, then Kentucky and Ohio State. The Hilltoppers of Western Kentucky had an All-American in Jim McDaniels, who had scored 23, 35, and 31 points in their three tournament wins. Another potent scorer was Jim Rose, who was consistently in double figures and had accounted for 25 against Kentucky.

If there was a team to unseat UCLA, it was the Kansas Jayhawks, many felt. They were flying high after ousting mighty Houston from the tourney, then eliminating Drake, another top-rated team. Much of the Kansas scoring punch was offered up by center Dave Robisch, who had scored 29 and 27 points in the Jayhawks' earlier wins, and there was also dependable Bud Stallworth to help in that area.

Old-hand UCLA breezed by Brigham Young, then survived a tremendous scare from a fired-up Long Beach State. UCLA pulled off a two-point victory in the last seconds of the game; it was the closest the Bruins had come to losing in the NCAA tournament since they started winning it on a regular basis back in 1964.

The first game of the semifinals, between Villanova and Western Kentucky, kept a record crowd of 31,428 fans on the edge of their seats through two overtimes (that record attendance would be surpassed the following night when about 350 more people would pass through the Astrodome's turnstiles). Western Kentucky built a three-point lead at the half, but the game had been anybody's and would remain that way through the second period. Then, with four seconds left and the score tied, 74–74, Western Kentucky's Jerry Dunn had a free throw but missed it and the game went into overtime. During that first extra segment each team scored 11 points, sending it into a second overtime period. Villanova then pulled ahead and won it by three. Hank Siemiontkowski, even though he fouled out, was the hero for the Wildcats from Pennsylvania that night, scoring 31 points and gathering in 15 rebounds. Howard Porter was also an instrumental figure, with 22 points and 16 rebounds. Both Jerry Dunn and Jim McDaniels scored more than 20 for Western Kentucky, and Jim Rose added 18, but it all went for nothing, and Villanova earned the nod to play in its first NCAA championship game.

There was no upset in game two that night. Pressing effectively, weaving their offensive pattern with infinite grace, the Bruins controlled Kansas throughout their semifinal game. At the half they led by seven; at game's end by eight. Sidney Wicks scored 21, Henry Bibby 18, and Curtis Rowe 16. Rowe led all rebounders that game with 15.

John Wooden employed an uncharacteristic tactic in the Bruins' championship game against Villanova. When he had had Lew Alcindor, Wooden's Bruins had overwhelmed opponents, crushed them. With his fast-paced, pressing teams, he had outrun and outgunned them. That night in 1971, he decided to stall Villanova into submission, a strategy UCLA had not been known for in the past. It was not an all-out freeze but instead a calculated slowdown that brought the Villanova Wildcats out of their zone and into a man-to-man defense, just what Wooden wanted, just what he knew UCLA fared best against. It almost backfired in the second half, however, because the Bruins were unable to break the game open against the Wildcats' man-to-man defense, as Wooden had hoped. On the contrary, Villanova began to close the gap, which had been eight points at the half and as many as 11 points after it. Now, as time dwindled on the scorer's clock, Villanova had reduced the margin to three. But then UCLA, so used to tournament pressure, responded like an accomplished long-distance runner, smoothly turning on its stretch kick and pulling to a six-point win.

The Bruins would not have been able to accomplish it that night had it not been for center Steve Patterson, who turned in the most memorable game of his college career. He accounted for 29 of the Bruin points and was the team's steadying factor throughout. Henry Bibby, with 17 points, was the only other UCLA player in double figures. For Villanova, Howard Porter posted 25, and he was cited as the tourney's Outstanding Player. Hank Siemiontkowski scored another 19 for the runner-up.

After the tournament, however, Porter's award would be taken away, and Villanova's second-place standing would be vacated because it would be revealed that Porter had signed a pro contract while still playing college ball, a direct violation of NCAA rules. Western Kentucky would suffer the same fate. It had edged Kansas for third place, but that

Champ of 1971, UCLA, which overcame Villanova in the finals 68–62. **Front row** (left to right): Andy Hill, Henry Bibby. **Middle row** (left to right): George Morgan (manager), Denny Crum (assistant coach), John Wooden (coach), Gary Cunningham (assistant coach), Ducky Drake (trainer). **Back row** (left to right): Larry Hollyfield, Larry Farmer, John Ecker, Curtis Rowe, Steve Patterson, Sidney Wicks, John Chapman, Kenny Booker, Rich Betchley, Terry Schofield.

Awards, 1971

Outstanding Player
Howard Porter* (Villanova)

All-Tournament Team
Howard Porter* (Villanova)
Hank Siemiontkowski* (Villanova)
Jim McDaniels* (Western Kentucky)
Steve Patterson (UCLA)
Sidney Wicks (UCLA)

* Vacated; teams subsequently declared ineligible.

accomplishment, too, would be erased from the record books because its star, Jim McDaniels, had also prematurely signed a pro contract.

There was nothing, however, to tarnish UCLA's seventh national championship in eight years.

8
Still UCLA

Just when everyone thought that UCLA would finally become vulnerable, that perhaps the time had come for the Bruins to be deposed from their perennial throne, along came Bill Walton. The exceptionally strong 6′11″ center, only a sophomore, was about to become a major force in college basketball.

It should have been a year of hope for other college basketball fives in 1971–72. After all, the UCLA Bruins had lost four starters from the previous year's champions and were allegedly faced with a rebuilding year, introducing three sophomores into the starting lineup. Gone were such luminaries as Sidney Wicks, Curtis Rowe, and Steve Patterson. Only senior guard Henry Bibby remained. John Wooden would have to go with four inexperienced hands. Walton was installed at center. Another sophomore, Greg Lee, joined Bibby at guard, and sophomore Keith Wilkes (who changed his first name to Jamaal after leaving UCLA) and junior Mike Farmer were given the forward duties. UCLA had excellent bench strength, however. Backing up Walton was 6′11″ Swen Nater, who, practically all coaches agreed, would not only have been a starter at another college but most likely a star. Walton said that Nater, who guarded him in scrimmages, was the toughest defensive center he was matched up against during the entire season. (Nater would become the only NBA *first-round* draft choice never to start a collegiate game.) There was also strong potential in Larry Hollyfield, Tommy Curtis, and Andy Hill.

UCLA's Bill Walton goes in for an unmolested two here against Indiana. The rangy center played in the 1972, 1973, and 1974 tourneys; was named Outstanding Player in the first two; and is ranked eighth in all-time tourney scoring (254 points) and fourth in rebounding (159). His finest single-game performance was in the '73 title game, when he scored 44 points.

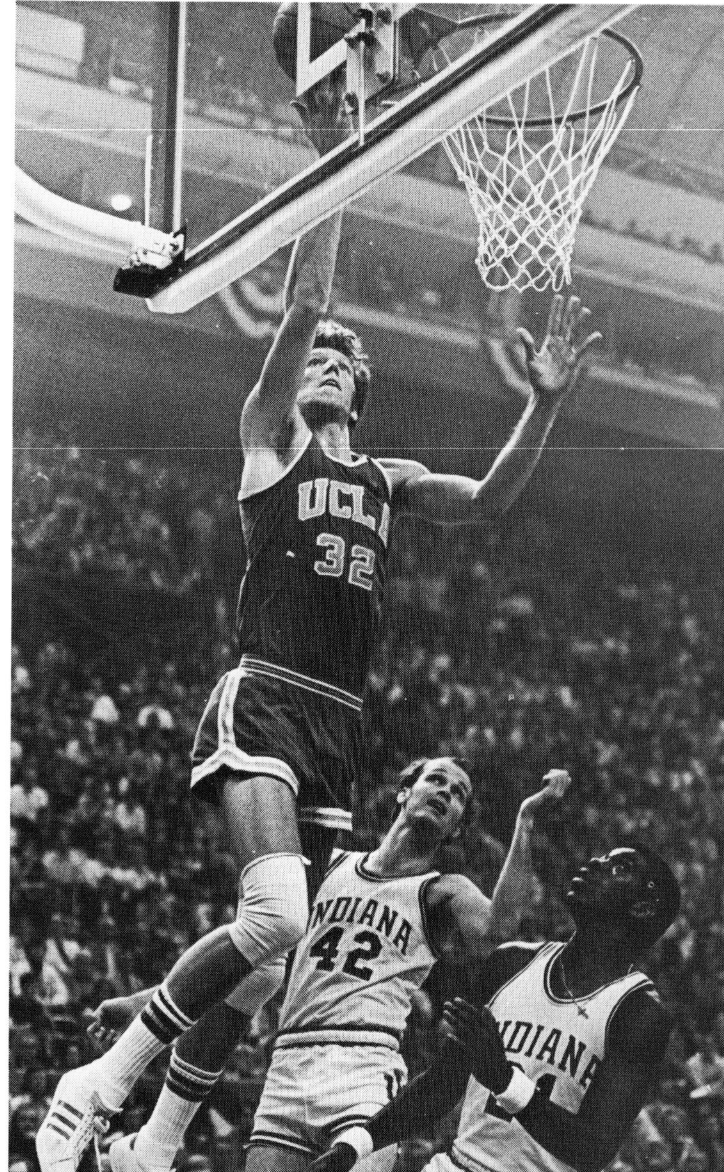

The mistakes and pains that were so much a part of the ordinary rebuilding year at other schools never seemed a part of the UCLA system. Quite the opposite; when John Wooden fielded a new team they usually appeared as if they had played together for three years. Youth and inexperience did not daunt them in the least. Proof of that was rolled out by the youngsters of 1971–72, who hurtled through the regular season without a single loss (26–0); in fact, only one team came as close as six points to the intimidating Bruins. They entered the NCAA tournament as the nation's top-ranked team and the odds-on favorite to take still another national championship.

The Bruins had no trouble at all in reaching the Final Four. They took Weber State apart in their first encounter in the West regional at Provo, Utah. Normally high-scoring Bob Davis of Weber (he had 32 in their first-round win over Hawaii) was held to 16 by UCLA's stringent defense, and the entire team could produce only 58 points. The Bruins, employing their wide-ranging scoring abilities, racked up 90 points that night. Bibby had 16, Farmer 15, and Wilkes 10. Walton, who spent much of the evening on the bench, scored only four points, but his backup, Swen Nater, contributed 12; another sub, Andy Hill, had 10.

The next hurdle brought not an extra drop of sweat to John Wooden's brow. The victim was Long Beach State, coached by Jerry Tarkanian, the same team that had come so close to eliminating the Bruins in the previous year's regional finals. Long Beach, still led by Ed Ratleff, was a highly regarded contender but one that was not going to worry this UCLA team. The Bruins took command early, built an 11-point halftime lead, then began the now almost traditional process of clearing their bench. The final was 73–57, and Bibby was high-point man for the night with 23. Walton had 19.

UCLA's opponent in the semifinals was Louisville, coached by Wooden's former assistant, Denny Crum. The Cardinals from Kentucky, paced by high-scoring guard Jim Price, had not had as easy a time as UCLA in getting into the Final Four. They had to stage a frantic comeback to overcome SW Louisiana in their first game and then watched a 16-point halftime lead over Kansas State in the Midwest regional final dwindle away to near-disaster. Still they had survived both contests, with Price averaging 25.5 points a game and center Ron Thomas 18.5.

Out East it was North Carolina all the way. Under the expert guidance of Dean Smith the Tar Heels were back in the tournament for the first time since 1969 and were considered *the* team with the best chance at derailing the mighty Bruins of UCLA. North Carolina had won the Atlantic Coast Conference and had an All-American candidate in 6′9″ Bob McAdoo. It also had other very capable scorers in Dennis Wuycik and George Karl; usually three or four Tar Heels ended a game in double figures. North Carolina had to get by two very fine teams to join the Final Four, and the Tar Heels did it with an impressive show of power. They first eliminated neighboring South Carolina, a 23-point demolition, then followed with a 14-point romp over Pennsylvania. McAdoo was a consistent scorer, rebounded fiercely, and appeared the tourney's best bet to handle Bill Walton.

North Carolina would have to get by Florida State, however, for that to happen. The Seminoles from Tallahassee, under the tutoring of Hugh Durham, had a consistent high scorer in Ron King and a fine center named Reggie Royals. They had pulled off two upsets to win the Mideast regional, first knocking off Big Ten champ Minnesota, then eliminating Kentucky in what proved to be the last college game the legendary Adolph Rupp would coach. At 70 years old he would be required to retire after 1972, and the Wildcat reins would be turned over to Joe B. Hall, an assistant to Rupp since 1965. During his long career (1930–72) as head coach at Kentucky, his teams won 879 games, making him the winningest coach in college basketball history. Besides the four NCAA championships he had captured, Rupp could also claim 27 Southeastern Conference titles.

North Carolina was a favorite to get to the finals, so was UCLA. But Florida State had gotten used to surprising everybody. They were not intimidated by versatile Bob McAdoo and the display the Tar Heels had put on during their two earlier games in the tournament. The Seminoles came on strong early and completely manipulated the first-half play, taking a 13-point lead into the locker room with them. The Tar Heels struggled back in the second period but were never able to wrest the lead from the Floridians. The final was 79–75, and the Seminoles were going to their first NCAA championship game.

UCLA was going to its eighth, all rung up in nine years. The 1972 entry was the result of a 96–77 destruction of Louisville in the semifinals. Where the Bruins had dominated in the preliminary games with cooperative scoring spread among a variety of players, the game against Louisville was dictated by Bill Walton's awesome presence. The sophomore center scored 33 points, swept 21 rebounds from the boards, and forced Louisville center Al Vilcheck to foul out. Walton hit 11 of 13 from the floor and 11 of 12 from the free-throw line. Larry Farmer bucketed 15 points for UCLA as well, with Keith Wilkes adding 12 and Greg Lee 10. For the Cardinals Jim Price had 30.

Walton was almost as predominant the following night when the Bruins took on Florida State for the 1972 college basketball crown. It just took a little longer. The "Seminole Surprise," as some referred to them, got to work right away and controlled the game in the early minutes, even built a seven-point lead near the midpoint of the first half. But that was the evening's peak for Florida State, and it was all downhill from there. Other teams might be surprised into submission, but not John Wooden's powerhouse from Los Angeles. They were not used to losing, were not even comfortable with the thought. They resolutely hacked away at the Seminole lead, continuing the momentum until they had a comfortable 11-point lead at the half. The Seminoles fought back when play resumed, but it was an impossible task. When Walton was not scoring, Keith Wilkes and Henry Bibby were. The closest the Seminoles could come to UCLA was the five points that separated the two teams at the final buzzer.

Walton was the Bruins' high scorer with 24 points and the game's leading rebounder with 20, exactly twice as many as the next most productive rebounders (Keith Wilkes of UCLA and Reggie Royals of Florida State). Wilkes scored 23 points including 11 of 16 field goals,

Top gun for the Florida State Seminoles in 1972 was forward Ron King. He scored a game-high 27 points in the championship match that year and averaged 18.4 over their five tourney games.

Pivotman for runner-up Florida State in 1972 was Reggie Royals. The big center captured an average of 10.2 rebounds in the Seminoles' five games, but had his hands full with UCLA's Bill Walton in the title tilt.

Dayton Flyer Mike Sylvester (20) soars here for two of his 36 points in the 1974 West regional against UCLA. Defending is Bruin forward Keith Wilkes (52). Despite Sylvester's sterling performance that game, Dayton lost in triple overtime.

Outstanding Player in 1974 was an easy choice, North Carolina State's David Thompson (44), going up with a picture-perfect jumper here against South Carolina. Thompson, a consensus All-American that year, averaged 24.3 points in State's four tournament games and hit for 40 in the East regional win over Providence.

Monte Towe (25), about to pass off against Duke, was North Carolina State's key ball handler and playmaker in 1974. He also averaged 15.5 points in the Wolfpack's four tourney games that year.

Maurice Lucas, up for a jumper here, roamed the key for Marquette during the 1973 and 1974 tourneys. The intimidating center scored 18 points and took 14 rebounds in the Warriors' win over Kansas in the '74 semifinals and had a game-high 21 points and 13 rebounds in the title game loss to North Carolina State.

ming the Bruins 71–70 in South Bend. In fact, when the season was over the Bruins counted three losses in their record and were no longer ranked king of the college pack.

The usurper of that title was North Carolina State, known around the Atlantic Coast Conference as the Wolfpack. State had been a powerhouse the year before, undefeated in 27 games, but had been denied admission to the NCAA postseason party because of recruiting violations. Coached by Norm Sloan and spearheaded by All-American David Thompson, a forward whose vertical jumps from a basketball floor often resembled launches from Cape Canaveral, the Wolfpack also had one of the most distinct Mutt and Jeff acts ever, with 7′4″ center Tom Burleson and 5′6″ guard Monte Towe.

North Carolina State met UCLA once during the regular season and was decimated 84–66, but as the season wore on NC State seemed to get better while UCLA got worse. So, when the NCAA tourney rolled around, it was the Wolfpack from Raleigh that the wire service polls placed on top, with UCLA a close second. How they would fare under the pressures of the postseason tournament was another question. North Carolina State had been to seven other NCAA tourneys but had reached the Final Four only once. UCLA simply could not remember losing to anyone in that tournament during the past decade.

For the first time the final game would not necessarily pit a team from the East against one from the West. Instead of the traditional East–Mideast and West–Midwest semifinal games, the Final Four would be slated differently in 1974. The winner of the West would face the champion of the East, and the Mideast survivor would pare off against the champ from the Midwest in the semifinals.

The favorite in the West, as one might surmise, was none other than UCLA. But to all those surmisers' surprise, the Bruins came precariously close to being eliminated in their first game. Facing the Flyers of Dayton, who claimed the services of high-scoring center Mike Sylvester, the Bruins found themselves uncharacteristically falling apart in the second half, a period in which they traditionally shone. Blowing a 12-point halftime lead, UCLA had to struggle to come up with an 80–80 tie at the final buzzer. The two teams went at each other in the first overtime period and came to another draw at 88 points each. By the end of the second ovetime the score was still deadlocked, then at 98 apiece. The Dayton Flyers ran out of fuel in the third overtime period, however, enabling a surging UCLA to defeat them 111–100. Dave Meyers, who had replaced Mike Farmer at forward, was the Bruin high scorer with 28 points, and Bill Walton was a step behind with 27. Walton's 19 rebounds were the game high. The most productive scorer of the night was the Flyers' Mike Sylvester, who logged 36.

There was no such scare for UCLA in the regional final, however. Their poise regained, the Bruins walked all over San Francisco 83–60 in a game in which Keith Wilkes led all scorers with 27 points.

In the East number one ranked North Carolina State lived up to its reputation, marching blithely past two highly rated foes. First it did away with Providence 92–78, as David Thompson rang up 40 points, the most any player would score in any game during the 1974 tournament. Tom Burleson captured 24 rebounds that night for the Wolfpack. Then State destroyed Pittsburgh 100–72, this time with Burleson leading all scorers with 26 points. So, with the new arrangement, the nation's top two teams would go at each other in the semifinals in 1974.

The teams comprising the other semifinal game could not, however, be taken for granted. Marquette—with center Maurice Lucas, guard Marcus Washington, and a tall, talented freshman forward, Bo Ellis (freshmen were eligible for varsity competition for the first time in 1973–74)—had disposed of Ohio, Vanderbilt, and Michigan to capture the Mideast title. And Kansas, which boasted no front-rank star but got consistent scoring from Roger Morningstar and Rick Suttle, had eliminated Creighton and Oral Roberts to carry the Midwest banner into the Final Four.

Most interest, needless to say, was centered on the UCLA–North Carolina State battle. Some observers favored the Bruins because of their vast tournament experience, others because of their desecration of the Wolfpack earlier in the year. Those touting North Carolina State cited, if not a home floor advantage, certainly an areal or conference-site advantage because the semifinal game was being played on the campus of the University of North Carolina at Greensboro, while others remembered the late-season superiority the Wolfpack had exhibited and felt the Wolfpack was peaking and the Bruins were declining.

The game was the classic everyone anticipated, one that sportswriters had been talking about for two years. Walton was stronger than Burleson, but he was also about five inches shorter; it was predicted to be a veritable clash of the titans. David Thompson going one on one with Keith Wilkes was viewed as a pure All-American confrontation.

Norm Sloan's Wolfpack certainly had the stimulus. With the opportunity to unseat UCLA, they also could wreak sweet revenge for the earlier loss to UCLA and truly justify their ranking as the nation's number one team. At the same time they were pure neophytes in the championship contest compared to UCLA, whose name was as associated with that classic as the New York Yankees were with World Series play.

It was an explosive game all the way. UCLA, as it had so many times in the past, came to the forefront in the second half. The Bruins built a lead, one that reached as much as 12 points, but then something strange happened. The Bruins did not coast to a victory as they so often had in so many other second halves. Suddenly the momentum turned and the Bruins found themselves struggling before the onslaught of a very determined North Carolina State team. Their lead continued to diminish. It became a true edge-of-the-seater as the game barreled down to its finish. The score was tied at 65 with almost a minute left. The Wolfpack had the ball and held it for the last shot. But State's last shot did not pay off, and the game was sent into overtime.

During the extra period both teams played cautiously. Two points apiece was the extent of the scoring as the clock wound down. But again the Wolfpack had the ball and a chance for a last-shot win, but again they missed and the game went into a second overtime period.

Then it appeared that State would pay for

Guard Tommy Curtis (22), a key figure on UCLA's 1974 tourney team, about to pass off here, was a fine playmaker. The Bruins got to the semifinals that year but lost to North Carolina State and for the first time since 1967 would not play in (and win) the NCAA championship game.

Right. Guard Marcus Washington played on three Marquette teams that made it to the NCAA postseason festivities (1972–74). The most memorable for Washington would be 1974, when the Warriors vied for the title with North Carolina State but, despite his fine floor leadership, lost.

A mainstay of the 1974 runner-up Marquette team was forward Earl Tatum. He would also play in the 1975 and 1976 tourneys for Marquette.

having blown two chances to defeat UCLA. The Wolfpack's world began to collapse. UCLA, on the other hand, was inspired, moving ahead by seven points with less than three and a half minutes to play. Then the momentum changed again, just as it had in the second half, and suddenly North Carolina State was surging back. That kind of action had never been written into UCLA's NCAA post-season scenario. Here was UCLA making the crucial mistakes; the Bruins were doing the struggling, turning the ball over, and fouling. David Thompson dropped in two free throws, and North Carolina State suddenly had the lead. Moments later Monte Towe made another two. And with it the game moved out of UCLA's reach. North Carolina State won 80–77, ending the Bruins' phenomenal streak of 38 straight NCAA tournament wins.

Awards, 1974

Outstanding Player
David Thompson (North Carolina State)

All-Tournament Team
David Thompson (North Carolina State)
Bill Walton (UCLA)
Tom Burleson (North Carolina State)
Monte Towe (North Carolina State)
Maurice Lucas (Marquette)

The Wolfpack would face the Marquette Warriors in the 1974 championship tilt. Al McGuire's five from Milwaukee had come from behind to drown the hopes of Kansas, a game the Warriors controlled totally during the second half. There was no particular Marquette hero that night, simply a fine team effort. But Al McGuire knew he would need much more against North Carolina State.

As many thought, the championship game was anticlimactic. The nation's two best teams had already gone at each other. As fired up as Al McGuire's team was, it was not true competition for North Carolina State. Norm Sloan's Wolfpack devoured Marquette, extending a nine-point halftime lead to a final victory of 76–64 in a game that was never out of their control. David Thompson scored 21 points for State, Monte Towe 16, and Tom Burleson and Moe Rivers 14 each. David

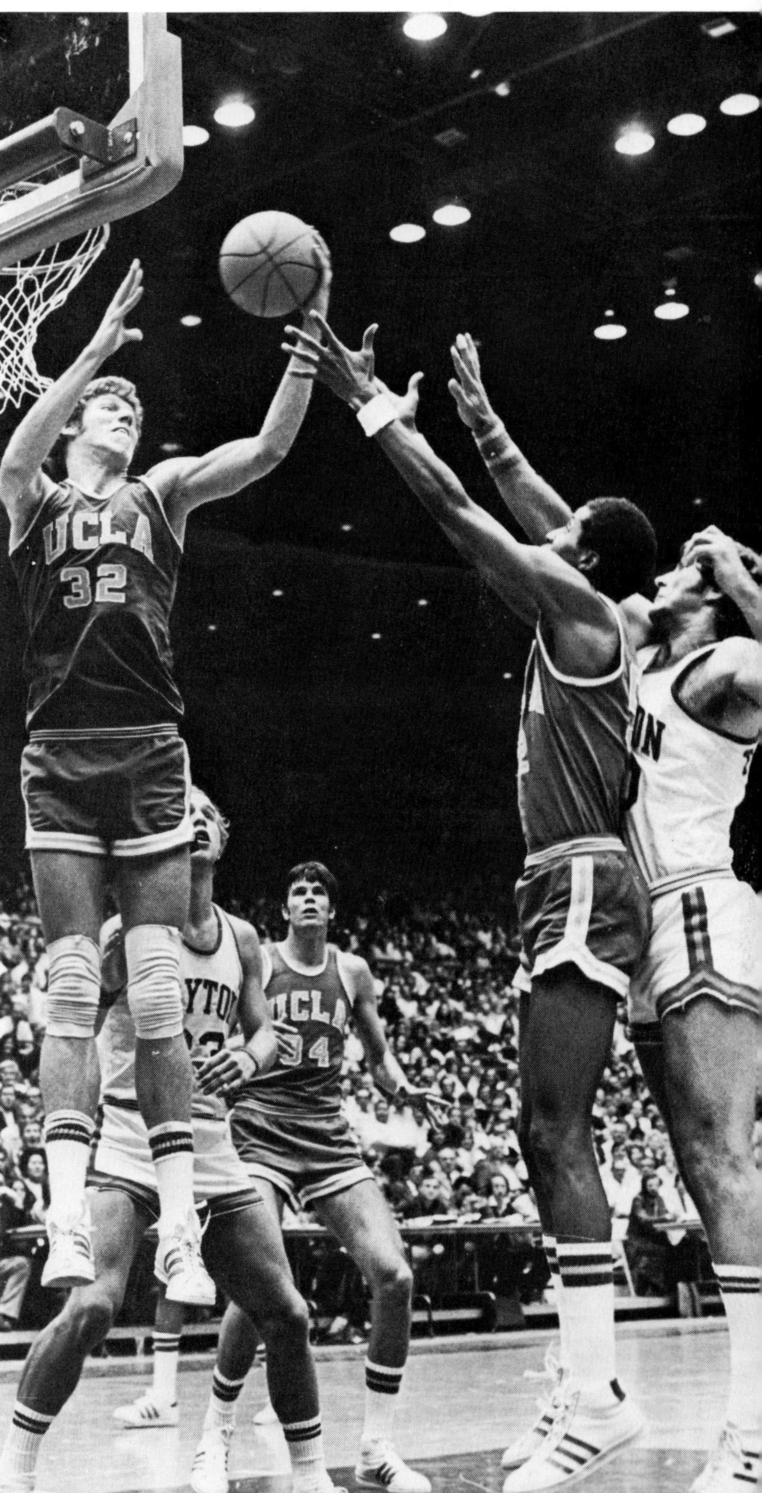

The indomitable Bill Walton (32) grabs one of his 19 rebounds against Dayton in the West regional of 1974. It took UCLA three overtime periods to wrest a 111–100 win that night. The other UCLA players are Dave Meyers (34) and Keith Wilkes. That game Meyers was high with 28 points; Walton had 27 and Wilkes 14.

UCLA pivot Richard Washington (31) challenges Kentucky's Rick Robey (53) in the 1975 championship game. The Bruins won it 92–85, their tenth title in 12 years. Washington, the tourney's Outstanding Player, scored 28 points and collected 12 rebounds in this game.

Thompson was the easy choice for Outstanding Player; he had averaged 24.25 points in North Carolina State's four tournament games. And for the first time in eight years John Wooden and his Bruins had to go back to Los Angeles without the NCAA trophy.

The Walton years were now over at UCLA, and there were rumors that 1974–75 would be the last for John Wooden. Only forward Dave Meyers returned from the previous year's starting five. Sophomore Rich Washington moved into the pivot to try to fill the large shoes of Walton. Marques Johnson was the other member of the frontcourt. The new guards were Pete Trgovich and Andre McCarter.

North Carolina State, on the other hand, turned out practically the same team as the one that won the 1974 title, with one tall exception, the departure of Tom Burleson. With the leaping and scoring of David Thompson and the deft playmaking of Monte Towe, the Wolfpack came on strong in the early season and had many people talking about a repeat national championship. But they would falter before tournament time and would not even participate, the Atlantic Coast Conference being represented by the Wolfpack's neighbor over in Chapel Hill, the University of North Carolina.

The same fate did not befall UCLA. It was perhaps just too inconceivable by 1975 to imagine a John Wooden team *not* in the NCAA postseason tourney. And true to form, the Bruins attended and ended up in the Final Four. But it was not an easy journey. In the first round they had a bevy of problems with Michigan, which was slated in the West as an at-large invitee. The Wolverines commanded a four-point lead at the half, and the normally tight UCLA defense had allowed them 50 points during that period. But the Bruins fought back and eventually regained the lead, then held on to win 103–91. Their big guns for the night were Dave Meyers with 26 points and Marques Johnson and Rich Washington with 22 apiece.

The Uclans were a heavy favorite to disman-

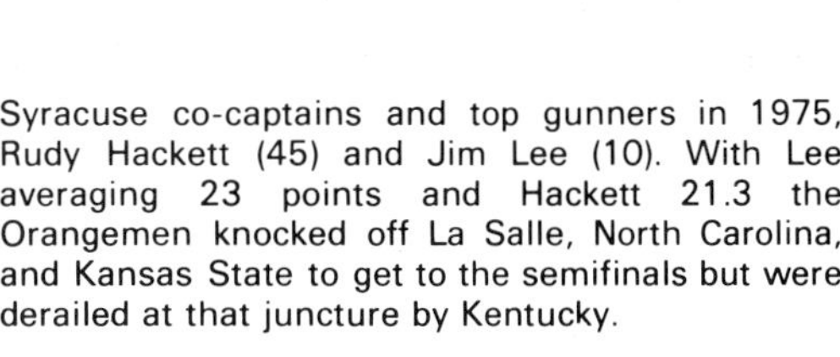
Syracuse co-captains and top gunners in 1975, Rudy Hackett (45) and Jim Lee (10). With Lee averaging 23 points and Hackett 21.3 the Orangemen knocked off La Salle, North Carolina, and Kansas State to get to the semifinals but were derailed at that juncture by Kentucky.

tle unheralded Montana in the regional final, but they almost lost that one, too. The Grizzlies were not at all intimidated by UCLA and their vaunted postseason reputation, and little-known Montana came dangerously close to upsetting the Bruins behind the 32-point production of Eric Hays. But UCLA pulled it out in the last minute of the game, 67–64.

The Final Four pairings were still rotated, and in 1975 the initial pairing was again in force, with the winner of the West facing the winner of the Midwest, which was Louisville. The Cardinals, still coached by John Wooden's onetime assistant Denny Crum, had an outstanding team, which included such consistently high scorers as Allen Murphy, Junior Bridgeman, and Phil Bond. They had beaten Rutgers in the first round of the Midwest, as expected, then trounced Cincinnati and a poweful Maryland team. In those three games Bridgeman had averaged 23 points, including a 36-point night against Rutgers.

The nation's number-one ranked team at the end of the regular season had been Bobby Knight's Indiana, but after swamping Texas–El Paso and Oregon State in the Mideast they were astounded in the regional final by Kentucky, a team they had beaten easily earlier in the year. Joe B. Hall's Wildcats edged out the Hoosiers in a heated battle, 92–90. Kentucky was a very strong, intimidating team. It had a fine center in freshman Rick Robey, and a very creditable scoring punch provided by Kevin Grevey, Mike Flynn, and Bob Guyette. The Wildcats from Lexington had slaughtered Marquette in the first round by 22 points after making up a three-point halftime deficit. They had little trouble with Central Michigan before simultaneously destroying both Indiana's title dreams and its 34-game win streak.

The fourth member of the final quartet that went to San Diego to determine the 1975 national championship was Syracuse, making its first appearance as a semifinalist, though the

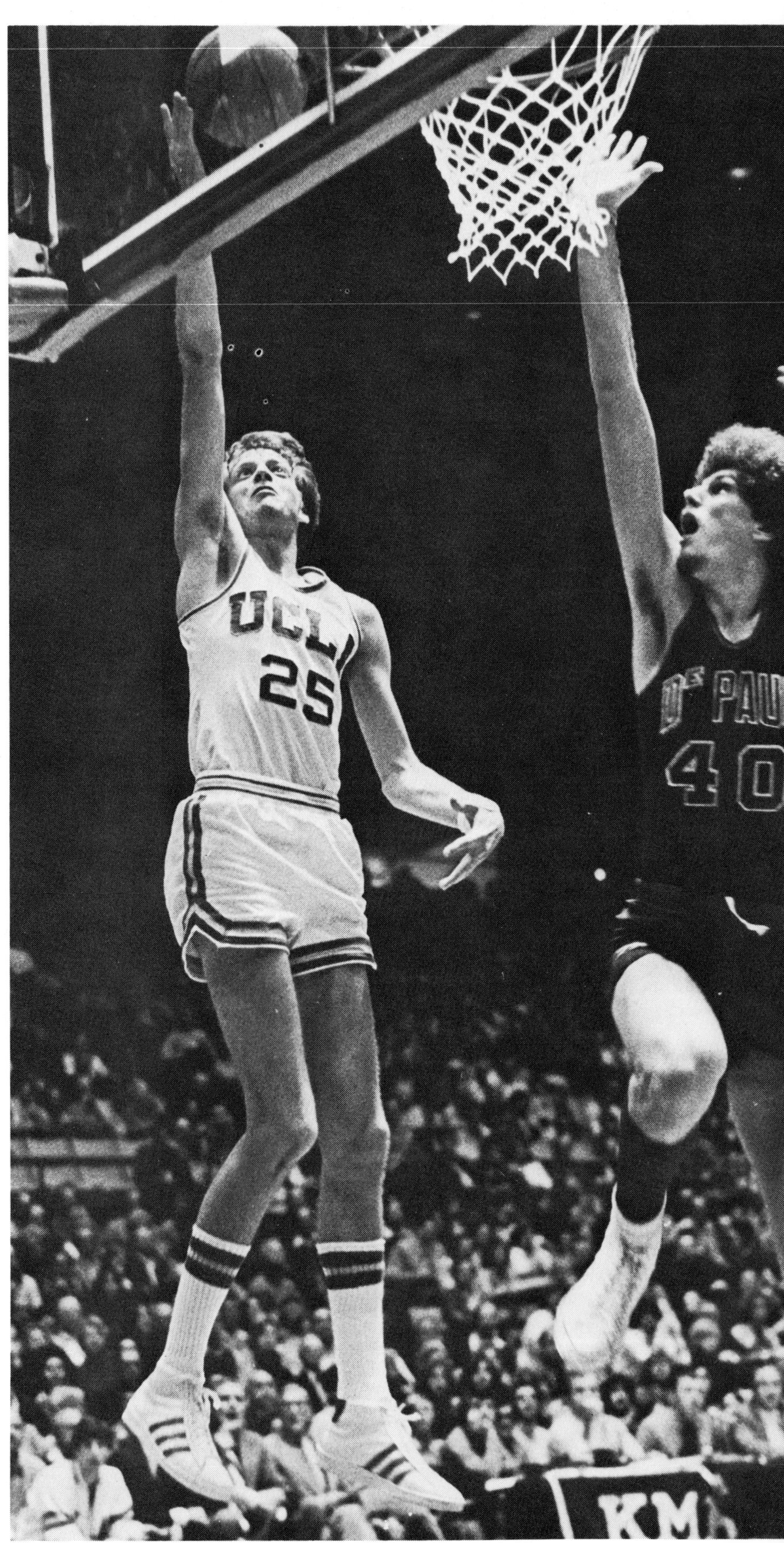

Guard Pete Trgovich (25) goes in for a lay-up despite the towering presence of DePaul's seven-foot center Dave Corzine (40). Trgovich, a starter on UCLA's 1975 championship team, averaged 13 points a game in that year's tourney.

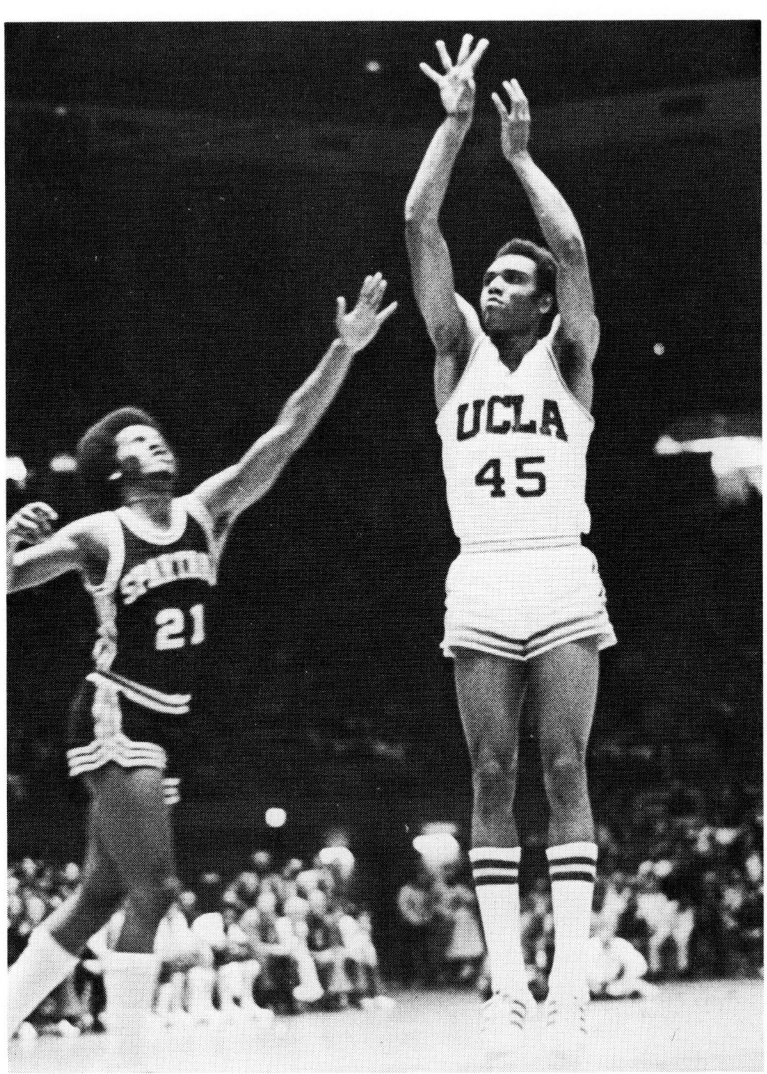

Bruin guard Andre McCarter (45) lets fly from the key in this 1975 game against San Jose State. McCarter, a superior ball handler, went to three tourneys with UCLA (1974-76) and was a starter in the last two.

school had been represented in five other NCAA tourneys. The Orangemen of Syracuse had two explosive scorers in Rudy Hackett and Jim Lee. Hackett had scored 30 in the team's first-round win over LaSalle, while Lee contributed 20 in that game. In their next encounter, Syracuse stunned a favored North Carolina and pulled off a two-point win. Lee was the high-point man with 24. Syracuse was also the underdog when the Orangemen faced Kansas State in the regional final. Down two at the half, they turned the game around and staggered the Kansans, a 95-87 surprise as Hackett accounted for 28 and Lee 25.

In the eastern semifinal Kentucky was favored to bring Syracuse back to the world of reality. And the Wildcats did it strikingly, surging to a 12-point halftime lead and then marching through the second half to post a 95-79 victory. Jack Givens, a freshman, was high for Kentucky with 24, while Jim Lee logged 23 for Syracuse.

After Kentucky's win, talk quickly spread around the San Diego arena that this might possibly be the first year in the history of the NCAA tournament that two teams from the same state would play for the national championship. That was contingent, of course, on Louisville defeating UCLA, no easy order, though the game was rated a toss-up by most. UCLA would perhaps have been a stronger favorite if the Bruins had not had such desperate trouble with their two previous opponents, both lesser teams than Louisville.

During the first half it appeared that Kentuckians of all allegiances would get their wish and monopolize the final game. The Cardinals moved quickly to the front, controlling the lead and building it to as many as nine points on several occasions. By the half they were up by four, 37-33. During the rest period, however, John Wooden got his Bruins back on track. The second half was the story of their resurgence, and the battle went right

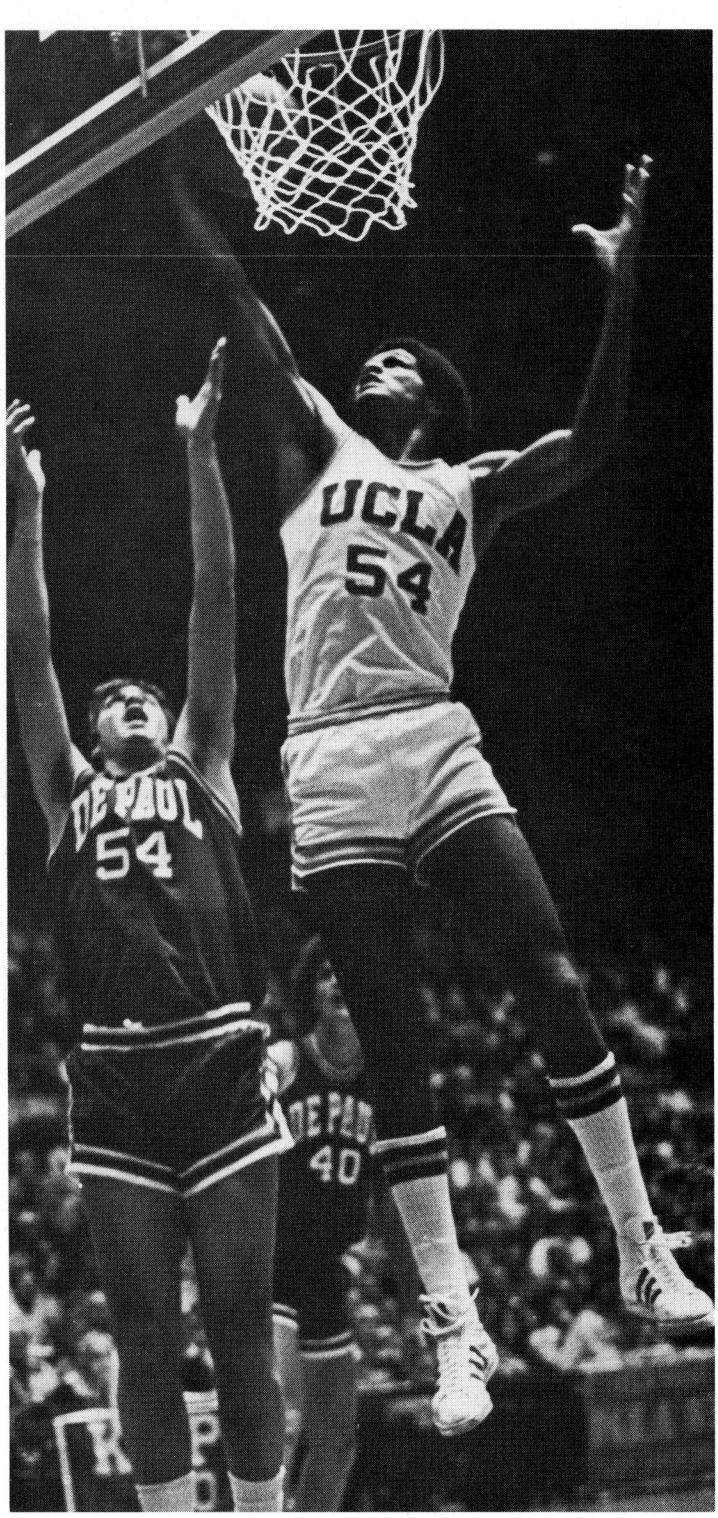

UCLA's Marques Johnson (54) goes high to snare a rebound in this game against DePaul. The multi-talented sophomore forward was instrumental in the Bruins' NCAA success in 1975 and would be named an All-American in each of the ensuing years.

down to the wire. In the waning minutes, however, Louisville regained the momentum and built another four-point lead. Then, in the game's last minute, Richard Washington sank two free throws for UCLA to bring the Uclans within a basket. The Bruins got the ball back again and Marques Johnson aced a desperation jumper to send the game into overtime. It was a fierce affair in the extra period, both teams playing sharp but frantic basketball. For the Cardinals Allen Murphy scored seven points himself, and with 20 seconds left in the game the Cardinals had a one-point lead and possession of the basketball. UCLA predictably fouled, and Cardinal Terry Howard was sent to the line with a one-and-one. But he missed the first free throw and UCLA grabbed the rebound. UCLA's one last shot was taken by Richard Washington with two seconds on the clock, a jumper from the baseline that snapped through the net, sending the Californians in the arena into ecstasy and the Kentuckians into agony.

It had been one of the most well-played, hotly contested, and dramatic games in Final Four history. Besides the last-second heroics of Johnson and Washington for UCLA, there had been other noteworthy performances. Washington scored a total of 26 points that night and took 11 rebounds off the boards. Dave Meyers accounted for another 16 points for the Bruins. Louisville star Allen Murphy had done everything humanly possible to get the Cardinals into the finals, but the team had faltered on other levels. Murphy ended the game with 33 points. Wesley Cox had another 14 and snatched 16 rebounds, and Junior Bridgeman scored 12 for the Cardinals.

John Wooden announced after the game that the following night's contest would be his last as head coach. He was stepping down after 27 years at UCLA. It was certainly a strong stimulus for his players to go out and give him one more title for his portfolio, though in that area he was already independently wealthy.

The two teams that took the floor to decide the 1975 college basketball championship had won the title more often than any other school in NCAA history—UCLA nine times, Kentucky four. The battle for it in 1975 was a dogged one, and there was no better evidence of it than in the dead-even first half. Back and forth the lead went, and UCLA edged out in front by three at the half. In the second period UCLA extended the lead to as many as 10 points, only to see the Wildcats surge back, eventually to reduce the margin to a single point. But the game's pendulum, which had been so active in the first half, swung again, and UCLA moved out, grinding its lead up to seven points, where it was at the final buzzer.

John Wooden had his 10th national championship in 12 years, a record that is not only unlikely to be broken but one that probably will not even be approached. His last Bruin team had performed superbly for him, squeezing out heartbeat-skipping wins in the preliminary three games, then prevailing in a bitterly hard-fought finale.

Awards, 1975

Outstanding Player
Richard Washington (UCLA)

All-Tournament Team
Richard Washington (UCLA)
Kevin Grevey (Kentucky)
Dave Meyers (UCLA)
Jim Lee (Syracuse)
Allen Murphy (Louisville)

The Big Bruin of the night was Rich Washington, who scored 28 points, grabbed 12 rebounds, and was the recipient of the tourney's Oustanding Player award. Dave Meyers, playing his last game as a Bruin, posted 24 points and collected 11 rebounds. Pete Trgovich added another 16 points and reserve center Ralph Drollinger 10 along with 13 rebounds.

It was a historic moment in NCAA annals, not only because of the unprecedented 10 national championships UCLA had in stock, but also because the dynasty that John Wooden had fostered was now finally over. With his retirement, UCLA's unparalleled fortunes in the NCAA championship tournaments would also disappear.

Bruin forward Dave Meyers (left) battles teammate Pete Trgovich for a rebound in this 1975 game at Pauley Pavilion. A 6'7" forward, Meyers made All-American that year and scored 24 points in UCLA's tourney title win over Kentucky.

9 The Midwest Rises

The torch of victory that UCLA had hoarded so stingily in the late 1960s and the first half of the '70s was returned to the nation's breadbasket in 1976 for the first time since Loyola of Chicago had carried it away in 1963. In fact, the championship game would be played not only between two schools from the Midwest but also between teams from the same conference, a first in the tourney's 38-year history.

There were quite a few excellent teams representing the Midwest in the 1976 NCAA championship playoffs. Foremost was Bobby Knight's Indiana Hoosiers. Strong, fast, and voracious on defense, they had bolted through the season without a loss, had defeated a Woodenless UCLA by 20 points, and were perched at the top of the polls at season's end. Knight had a beautifully rounded team. Three starters were All-American caliber: forward Scott May, 6′11″ center Kent Benson (who was also molded in the fashion of an NFL defensive end), and guard Quinn Buckner. They also had two other players of first rank in 6′7″ guard Bob Wilkerson and forward Tom Abernethy.

Besides Indiana, however, there were also Al McGuire's Marquette Warriors, close behind the Hoosiers in the national standings. Besides being the two best teams in the nation that year, Marquette and Indiana also had the two most volatile and outspoken coaches in the business. No one shouted louder or drew more technical fouls than the short-fused duo of Knight and McGuire. As a team, Marquette had a platoon of nationally ranked players,

Center Kent Benson was the 1976 NCAA tournament's Outstanding Player. An intimidating force on defense, Benson also averaged 18.8 points and nine rebounds over the Hoosiers' five games.

just like Indiana. There was the dazzling playmaker and consistent scorer, Butch Lee; an All-American forward, 6′9″ Bo Ellis; and his very able frontcourt partners, Earl Tatum and 6′10″ center Jerome Whitehead. Lloyd Watson complemented Lee in the frontcourt. Both Marquette and Indiana, however, were slated in the same region, the Mideast, so only one would get to the Final Four.

In the Midwest regional there were other local powerhouses. Michigan, runner-up in the Big Ten to Indiana and justifiably respected, was paced by Rickey Green, an All-American guard; high-scoring forward John Robinson; and intimidating center Phil Hubbard. Then there was Notre Dame, now under the tutelage of Digger Phelps, with All-American forward Adrian Dantley and such other well-known basketball names as Bruce Flowers, Bill Paterno, and Don Williams. And there was also Missouri, with hotshot shooters like Willie Smith, Jim Kennedy, and Kim Anderson. Another Midwestern team of note was at-large invitee DePaul, and the Blue Demons were scheduled to play in the East regional, considered the softest division in 1976. Under Ray Meyer, then in his 35th year as the Demons' head coach, DePaul was keyed around 7′ center Dave Corzine, but the team also had two swift guards in Ron Norwood and Randy Ramsey and two fine forwards in Curtis Watkins and Joe Ponsetto. All-in-all the Midwest was handsomely represented in the 1976 NCAA tourney.

There were, of course, other good teams from other regions. UCLA, under coach Gene Bartow, who had been wooed away from Memphis State to replace the fabled John Wooden, was once again a fearsome five. The Bruins had lost Dave Meyers and Pete Trgovich from the previous year's championship team, but they had been replaced by two outstanding newcomers, 6′9″ freshman David Greenwood filling Meyers' forward slot and Ray Townsend replacing Trgovich at guard. Andre McCarter was back at the other guard, and Richard Washington and Marques Johnson filled out the frontcourt. The Uclans had won 24 games during the regular season and lost four, but it had been enough to give them another Pacific Coast title.

There were two other formidable teams in the West that year, Arizona and Nevada/Las Vegas. Arizona was led by Herman Harris, Jim Rappis, and Phil Taylor. The youngsters from Las Vegas were spearheaded by Eddie Owens and Sam Smith.

In the East the most imposing team was undefeated Rutgers. The Scarlet Knights from New Brunswick, New Jersey, were keynoted by Mike Dabney, Ed Jordan, and Phil Sellers, all potent scorers. Another sleeper was Virginia Military Institute, which had two consistent scorers, Will Bynum and Ron Carter.

It was, however, the year of the Midwest, or really the Big Ten, as it would turn out, because it would be two teams from that conference, Indiana and Michigan, that would eventually square off in the tournament finale.

Top-seeded Indiana got to the Final Four by first drubbing St. John's 90–70, behind Scott May's 33-point effort, Kent Benson's 20, and Quinn Buckner's 15. Next was Alabama, a nationally ranked team that fell to the Hoosiers 74–69, with May logging 25 points and 16 rebounds for Indiana, both game highs.

Forward Scott May was one of the brightest lights on Indiana's national champs of 1976. He scored a game-high 26 points in the title match with Michigan and averaged 22.4 points in the Hoosiers' five games.

Then Bobby Knight's bulldozer plowed over second-ranked Marquette, turning a one-point halftime lead into a 65–56 rout. Kent Benson was the Hoosier hero that game with 18 points and nine rebounds, while Scott May added 15 and Tom Abernethy 12. Those two wins sent Indiana to the Final Four for the fourth time in the school's history.

Michigan barely got there. In the first round the Wolverines, under their brilliant coach, Johnny Orr, had to rebound from a six-point halftime deficit to sneak a one-point victory from Wichita State, then another second-half, come-from-behind win to oust Notre Dame from the tournament, 80–76. Michigan had less trouble in the regional final, however, taking to task a fine Missouri team, 95–88, despite Missourian Willie Smith's 43 points, the most that would be scored by any individual in a game during the 1976 tourney. Rickey Green had been the Wolverine's lifeblood, especially in the latter two games, when he posted 20 and 23 points. In the regional championship against Notre Dame John Robinson accounted for 21, Phil Hubbard another 20.

The East and West representatives lived up to pretourney predictions. Rutgers, after a scare from Princeton in the first round (a single-point victory), smashed Connecticut by 14, then trampled Virginia Military by 16. VMI, incidentally, had removed two highly regarded teams, Tennessee and DePaul, from the tournament, before losing to Rutgers. In the West UCLA had an easy time of it, spurring rumors of still another Bruin national championship. First, the Bruins squelched San Diego State by 10 behind Richard Washington's 25-point night and Marques Johnson's 19. Then they cleanly polished off a respected Pepperdine team 70-61. Marques Johnson was high-point man that game with 18, while Washington added 16 and David Greenwood 10. Arizona, considered to be the Bruins' most severe threat in the West, proved to be a pigeon in the regional final. The Bruins, going into the second half with a three-point lead, blew the Wildcats from Tucson out of the arena 82–66. Four players were in double digits for the Bruins: Washington 22, Ray Townsend 16, Johnson 14, and Greenwood 10.

The Final Four were gathered in Philadelphia for the 1976 finale. The big game, according to just about everybody, was the battle between the victors of the West and the victors of the Mideast; everyone, it seems, felt that the year's champion would emerge from that semifinal game. Reigning champ UCLA had virtually stormed through the West and appeared at its playing peak. On the other side was Indiana, undefeated and smirking about its humiliation of the Bruins earlier in the year.

The Hoosiers would have been more of a favorite, but the odds makers obviously remembered UCLA's fabulous tournament record over the preceding 12 years. Since 1964 the Bruins had played in 48 NCAA tournament games and lost only one of them (to North Carolina State in double overtime in the 1974 semifinals). But the magic was gone in 1976 for the legendary Bruins from Los Angeles. Their usually powerful scoring punch was reduced to a tap by Indiana's almost perfect defense. The Hoosiers allowed them a mere 26 points in the first half and only 51 all game. Indiana took control at the very beginning, held it, and won by 14. It was a true team effort. Hoosier center Kent Benson logged 16 points, Scott May and Tom Abernethy 14 each, and Quinn Buckner 12. Bob Wilkerson grabbed 19 rebounds, almost twice as many as UCLA's top rebounder, David Greenwood, who gathered in 10. Only Richard Washington and Marques Johnson were in double figures for the Bruins, with 15 and 12 points respectively.

In the other semifinal game undefeated Rutgers was considered a favorite over erratic Michigan, but Rutgers quickly found out just how rugged teams from the Big Ten were that year. The Wolverines outmuscled them on the boards (50 rebounds to 38), outshot them on the floor (35 of 70 field goals to 30 of 76), and turned a 46–29 halftime lead into an 86–70 victory.

Michigan had fallen to the Indiana Hoosiers in its two Big Ten conference encounters during the season, and most observers felt certain that Michigan had little chance. But Johnny Orr's Wolverines were inspired, at least during the first half. At the same time

Indiana coach Bobby Knight won his first NCAA title in 1976, when the Hoosiers trimmed Michigan 86–68.

Bobby Knight's Hoosiers hardly looked like they deserved their number one ranking. Michigan was the force, and Indiana was scrambling just to stay in the game. At the half the Hoosiers trailed by six, and many of the more than 17,500 spectators thought they might be witnessing the most startling upset of the tournament. But Indiana settled down in the second half and played with the quality Bobby Knight knew they possessed, and which he no doubt reminded them of in his own inimitable way during the intermission. It was all Indiana in round two; the Hoosiers outscored the Wolverines 57–33 during that period and walked away with the tourney trophy. The final score was 86–68.

Scott May was the high-point man of the night, pumping in 26 points for the Hoosiers. But Kent Benson was also instrumental in the victory, adding another 25, as were Quinn Buckner with 16 and Tom Abernethy with 11. For the disappointed Wolverines, Rickey Green contributed 18, and fellow guard Steve Grote had 12.

Kent Benson, who had averaged 18.5 points and eight rebounds in Indiana's four games and also served as the team's rallying point in the championship game, was named the Outstanding Player of the 1976 NCAA tourney. And Indiana had its third national championship; only UCLA (10) and Kentucky (4) could claim more NCAA titles in 1976.

Awards, 1976

Outstanding Player
Kent Benson (Indiana)

All-Tournament Team
Kent Benson (Indiana)
Scott May (Indiana)
Tom Abernethy (Indiana)
Rickey Green (Michigan)
Marques Johnson (UCLA)

Indiana's stay at the top would be very short-lived. With the departure of Scott May, Quinn Buckner, Bob Wilkerson, and Tom Abernethy, the Hoosiers would not win the Big Ten, nor would they return to the NCAA tourney in 1977. Still, the bastion of basketball power would remain in the nation's midsection. At the end of that year's basketball season the top-ranked team in the country was Michigan, the previous year's runner-up in the NCAA postseason classic.

The core of Michigan's team was back: guards Rickey Green and Steve Grote, center Phil Hubbard, and forward John Robinson. They came into the tournament cocky, perhaps justifiably so. They were number one, and most basketball prognosticators were suggesting that they had at least one of the very best shots at taking the entire thing. They also were playing in the Mideast, a division that was not especially strong that year. The nation's other top-ranked teams were all ensconced in other divisions: UCLA and Nevada-Las Vegas in the West; Kansas State and Wake Forest in the Midwest; and North Carolina, Kentucky, and Notre Dame in the East.

But things just didn't go right for Michigan, despite the alleged softness of its division. In the opening round, the Wolverines were down by a point to Holy Cross at the half and had to battle back to survive the first round.

Rickey Green lived up to his All-American designation by scoring 37 points against Holy Cross, the most any player would score in a game in that tournament (he shot an incredible 17 of 21 from the floor). After that the Wolverines were almost surprised by another underdog, intrastate rival Detroit, but managed to pull off an 86–81 win. That game it was John Robinson with 25 points and Phil Hubbard with 22 and an impressive 26 rebounds for the Wolverines. But then along came the North Carolina–Charlotte 49ers, coached by Lee Rose. Before the encounter the 49ers were considered little more than the next domino to be knocked down by the Wolverines on their way to the Final Four. The North Carolinians' dreams were woven around a 6′9″ center named Cedric "Cornbread" Maxwell and two other consistent scorers, Lew Massey and Chad Kinch. And, as it turned out, heavily favored Michigan was simply not ready for them. The 49ers from Charlotte dazzled the Wolverines in the first half, building a 40–27 lead, then held on to win it by seven. Cornbread Maxwell scored 25 points and took 13 rebounds from the boards, both game highs. It was short of his 32-point, 18-rebound performance earlier in the tourney when the 49ers beat Central Michigan, but it was ample enough to enable the North Carolinians to post one of the tournament's most surprising upsets and earn a bid to the 1977 Final Four.

With the structure of that year's Final Four pairings the 49ers would face the winner of the Midwest region. In that division Wake Forest was one of the major forces to be reckoned with, fueled by such volatile scorers as Rod Griffin, Jerry Schellenberg, and Skip Brown. Another was Kansas State, which could boast the talents of Curtis Reading, Mike Evans, and Larry Dassie. There was also Marquette, still under the guidance of Al McGuire and still exhibiting one of the finest rosters in the country. Returning starters included guard Butch Lee, forward Bo Ellis, and center Jerome Whitehead. Jim Boylan nailed down the other guard slot, and Bernard Toone gained the start at forward. But the Warriors' performance had been erratic, if not chaotic, during the regular season, and they had lost seven of their 27 games. They were deemed a

Cedric "Cornbread" Maxwell deposits a lay-up here for North Carolina–Charlotte in its 1977 regional title win over Michigan. Maxwell scored 25 points and snatched 13 rebounds that night, both game highs. He also scored the most points in that year's tournament, 123; had the highest average, 24.6; and collected the most rebounds, 64.

North Carolina–Charlotte's Chad Kinch goes high for a jumper here in the 1977 tourney. Kinch averaged 15 points in UNCC's five games, including a 30-point performance in the third-place consolation game against Nevada–Las Velas.

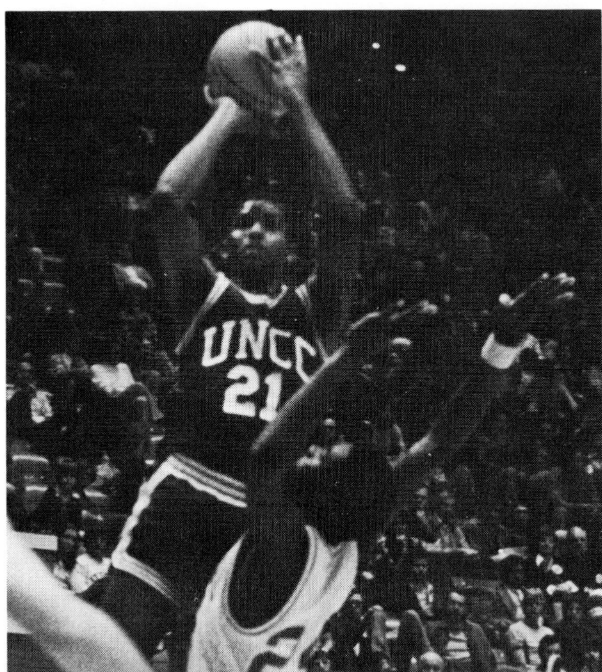

threat by many, but such an unpredictable one that it seemed unlikely that the Warriors could get it all together and survive the pressures of the playoffs.

It appeared, in fact, as if Marquette would not even get through the first round. They were slight favorites over Cincinnati but in the first half were outplayed and trailed by three at that period's buzzer. Under Al McGuire's not so gentle urging, however, the Warriors went on the warpath in the second period and took total command of the game. At the end they were 15 points ahead. Only three Warriors scored in double figures: Bo Ellis with 17, Jerome Whitehead with 15, and Butch Lee with 13. Their big test awaited them in the next round, where they faced Kansas State. Behind Curtis Reading's 32-point performance, Kansas State had rallied to beat Providence in the first round. Once again, Marquette could not get its act in gear during the first half, this time falling behind by eight points. But once again the Warriors fought back. Spurred by the inspired play of Butch Lee, they made a game of it, then took control. The little guard, on whom Al McGuire relied so heavily for floor leadership, came up with 26 crucial points. Bo Ellis added another 19, and that was enough to allow Marquette to come out on top of a real squeaker, 67–66.

One more major obstacle remained for the Warriors in the Midwest regional: Wake Forest. The Demon Deacons from Winston-Salem, North Carolina, had emerged from a 13-point halftime deficit to beat a tenacious Arkansas team in the first round, then came back again to defeat an unheralded but very tough Southern Illinois–Carbondale team 86–81. (SIU's Mike Glenn had averaged 32.5 points in his two tourney games and almost led the Illinoisans to a dramatic upset of Wake Forest.) For Wake Forest, Rod Griffin had scored 26 and Skip Brown 23 against Arkansas, and Brown had 25 and Griffin and Jerry Schellenberg 22 each in the triumph over SIU.

In the regional final Marquette, for the third straight time in the tourney, trailed at the half, this time 35–31. But, as before, the team responded and rallied, on this occasion with special verve, outscoring Wake Forest 51–33 in the second period. McGuire's Warriors walked

Big Bo Ellis started for Marquette teams in four tourneys (1974–77). In the Warriors' championship year, 1977, the 6'9" forward averaged 14.8 points in the five tourney games.

Ever-steady guard Jim Boylan was an integral part of the 1977 champion Marquette Warriors. Boylan scored his tourney high 14 points in the title game.

off with an impressive 14-point win and the right to meet the 49ers from Charlotte, North Carolina, in the semifinals at the Omni arena in Atlanta.

The victors from the East and the West would also face off in that Georgia edifice to see who would be the other team to go to the NCAA championship game of 1977. North Carolina, Dean Smith's explosive team from the ever-tough Atlantic Coast Conference, would represent the East. They were paced by All-American guard Phil Ford but also had dependable scorers in frontcourt players Mike O'Koren and John Kuester. The Tar Heels were a favorite in the East, but it was an especially rugged division that year and Smith's youngsters had to endure some real brawls to get to the Final Four. First there was a fired-up Purdue team that led the Tar Heels through the first half of their first-round encounter and hung in all the way to the last minute. But North Carolina was finally able to wring out a three-point victory, much the result of Phil Ford's 27-point performance. Then there was Digger Phelps' Notre Dame team, notorious for derailing acknowledged winners. The Fighting Irish had almost the same team returning from the year before, only All-American Adrian Dantley was absent from the starting five. Rich Branning replaced him, joining Bruce Flowers, Bill Paterno, Don Williams, and Toby Knight in Notre Dame's impressive starting lineup. In this game the Tar Heels were forced to overcome an imposing 10-point margin at halftime; they managed it behind Phil Ford's 29 points, the 16 contributed by Mike O'Koren, and the 14 from John Kuester. But it was close all the way, and the difference was a single basket at game's end.

One of the reasons North Carolina reached the 1977 championship game was Mike O'Koren. O'Koren tallied 31 points in the semifinal victory over Nevada–Las Vegas.

The win enabled North Carolina to meet Kentucky, a powerhouse in its own right and one of the nation's top-ranked teams. The Wildcats had hot-hand forward Jack Givens as well as able center Rick Robey. In this game, however, Dean Smith got his Tar Heels going from the opening tip-off, even though his superstar, Phil Ford, was hampered by a painful elbow injury. North Carolina built a 53–41 lead by halftime, then maintained it smoothly through the second period. The final was North Carolina 79, Kentucky 72. Walter Davis, who had played in only one of the Tar Heels' previous two games, rose to the occasion and led all North Carolina scorers with 21. John Kuester had 19 and Mike O'Koren 14, while troubled Phil Ford was able to contribute only a lone basket. Jack Givens was high with 26 for the defeated Kentucky Wildcats.

UCLA, as everyone had grown to expect, was back again in the West regionals. The Bruins beat a fine Louisville team in the first round, but they were shocked in the second session by high-flying Idaho State. The Bengals from Pocatello turned around a six-point halftime deficit and sneaked off with a one-point win over the favored Bruins. Steve Hays was the big gun for Idaho State, dropping in 27; he also scored 29 in his team's first-round decimation of Long Beach State. For the surprised Bruins, Marques Johnson had tallied 21 and David Greenwood 20, but UCLA was eliminated from the tourney.

The most dazzling display of offensive basketball in that year's tournament was being staged by Jerry Tarkanian's Nevada-Las Vegas. The team had rung up 121 points in its first-round slaughter of San Francisco, which tied the NCAA single-game scoring record set by Iowa when it defeated Notre Dame 121–106 in 1970. In this game six Nevadans scored in double figures: Reggie Theus, 27; Eddie Owens, 22; Glen Gondrezick, 21; Sam Smith and Robert Smith, 14 each; and Lewis Brown, 10. After that the high rollers from Las Vegas shredded Utah's dreams of advancement, 88–83, this time with only five players in double digits, the highest Robert Smith with 21. Tarkanian's team had its only flirtation with trouble in the first half of the regional title game with Idaho State, and the cagers went to the locker room a point down. But they exploded in the second half with 56 points and registered a decisive 107–90 victory. Eddie Owens had 24 that night, and reserve Tony Smith (not to be confused with teammates Sam and Robert) had 18.

Forward Eddie Owens was the key scorer for three Nevada-Las Vegas teams that went to NCAA tourneys (1975–77). In 10 postseason games Owens averaged 20.2 points. His best effort was the 1977 consolation win over North Carolina-Charlotte, when he scored 34 points.

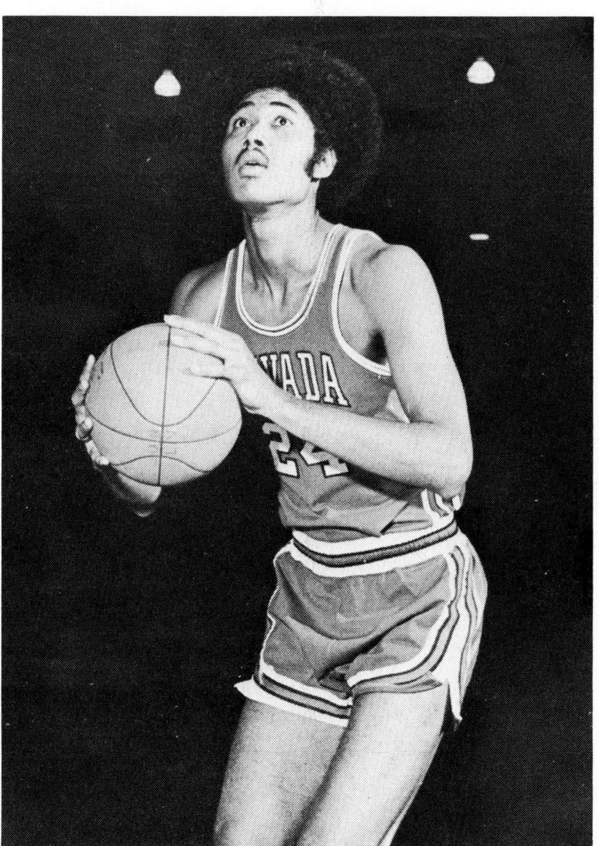

So the come-from-behind Tar Heels of North Carolina would face the explosive scoring of Jerry Tarkanian's Nevadans in one semifinal encounter, and come-from-behind Marquette would take on surprising North Carolina-Charlotte in the other.

Dean Smith knew he would have to slow the game down if his Tar Heels were to get by

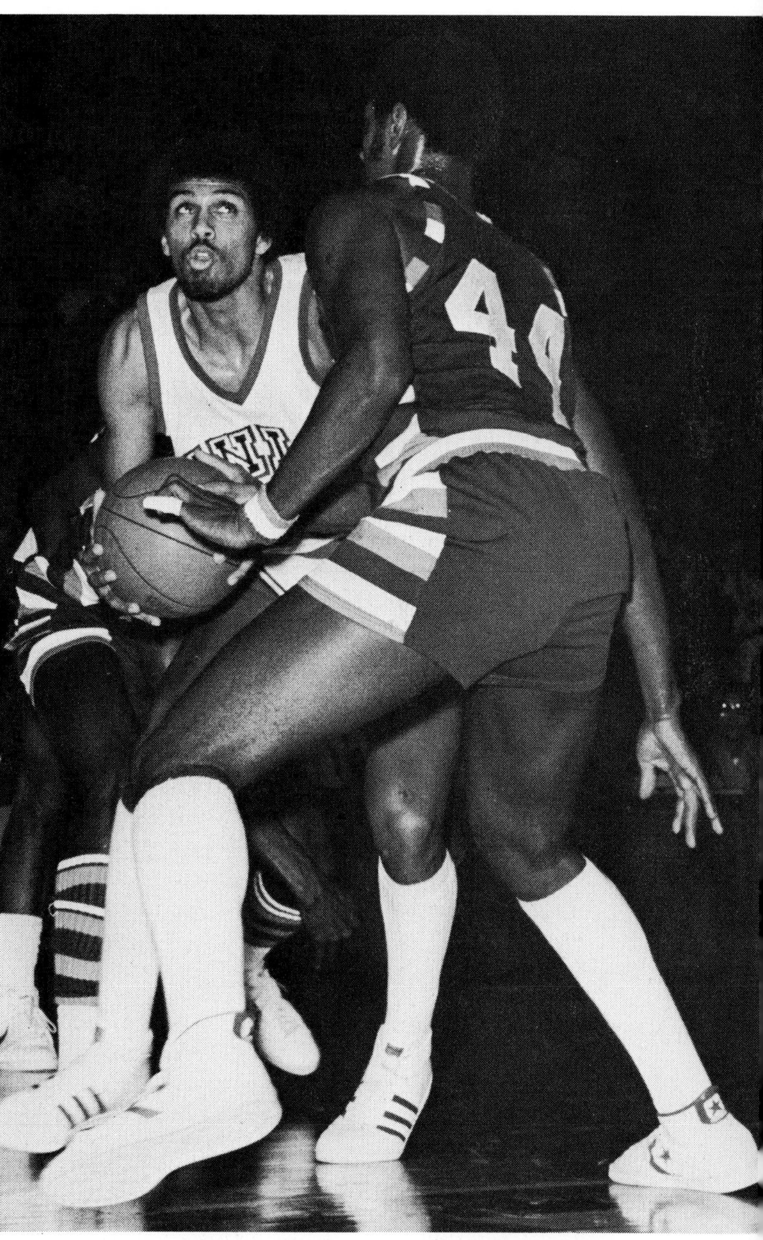

Reggie Theus, eyeing the basket here, was one of the principal reasons Nevada-Las Vegas got to the 1977 tourney and advanced to the semifinals. He averaged 17.8 points in UNLV's five tourney games, his best effort being 27 points against San Francisco.

Nevada-Las Vegas guard Sam Smith goes up for a contorted jumper here in a 1977 first-round game against San Francisco. With Smith's help the Rebels won 121–95. Smith's most productive game was the semifinal loss to North Carolina, however, a game in which he scored 20 points.

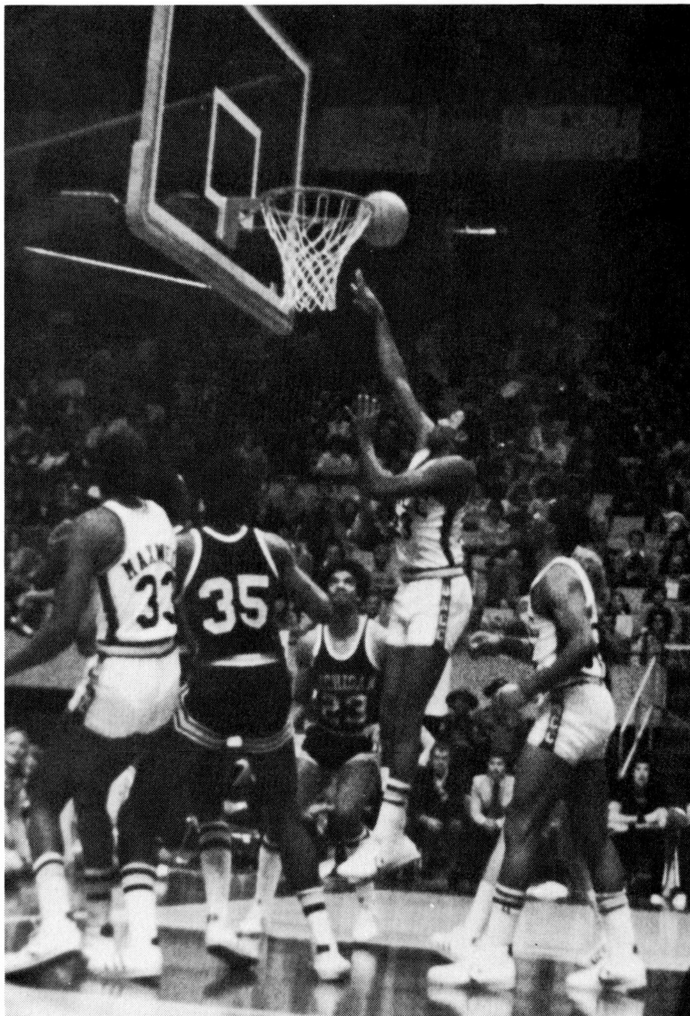

Lew Massey tips for two in North Carolina-Charlotte's 1977 win over Michigan on its way to that year's finals. Massey scored 19 points that game and took 11 rebounds.

Nevada-Las Vegas, but he was not able to do that in the first half and North Carolina trailed 49–43 at the mid-game respite. In the second half, however, his team was able to manipulate the game, at least to some degree, and the Nevadans were prevented from running off with it as they had in so many games earlier that year. The Tar Heels worked their way to a three-point lead with just seconds remaining, the result principally of their steady hands at the free-throw line in the game's final minutes. The final score was 84–83, and Dean Smith would be taking North Carolina on that school's fourth trip to the NCAA championship game. The best performance from a Tar Heel that game came from freshman Mike O'Koren, who scored 31 points (14 of 19 from the floor). Also contributing to the North Carolina fortunes were Walter Davis with 19, Phil Ford still bothered by his elbow injury had 12, and Rich Yonakor another 11. Sam Smith was the high-point man for Nevada-Las Vegas with 20.

Marquette did not have to come from behind to win its semifinal game. Surprisingly enough, the Warriors held a three-point lead over Lee Rose's youngsters from Charlotte, North Carolina, at the half, though they had scored only 25 points. Neither team showed any more offensive spunk in the second half, and Al McGuire's Warriors, who lost the lead in the second half but then regained it, hung on to win the game. But it was a battle all the way to the game's last seconds, and there, just a fraction of a second before the buzzer, Marquette's center Jerome Whitehead laid up the

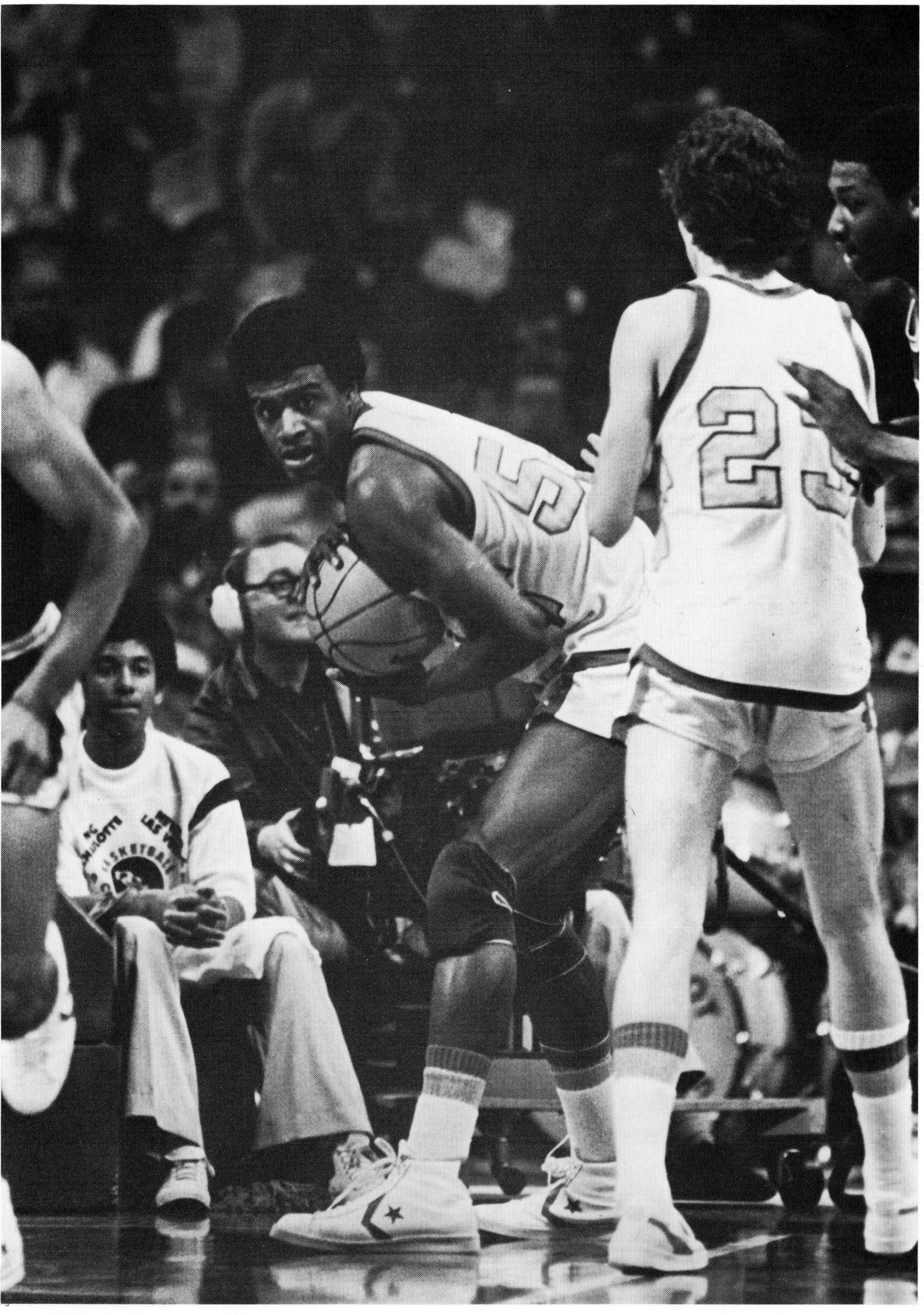

Marquette's Jerome Whitehead guards a rebound in the 1977 semifinal victory over North Carolina–Charlotte. The 6'10" center raked in 16 rebounds and scored 21 points that night, both game highs. Number 23 for Marquette is Jim Boylan.

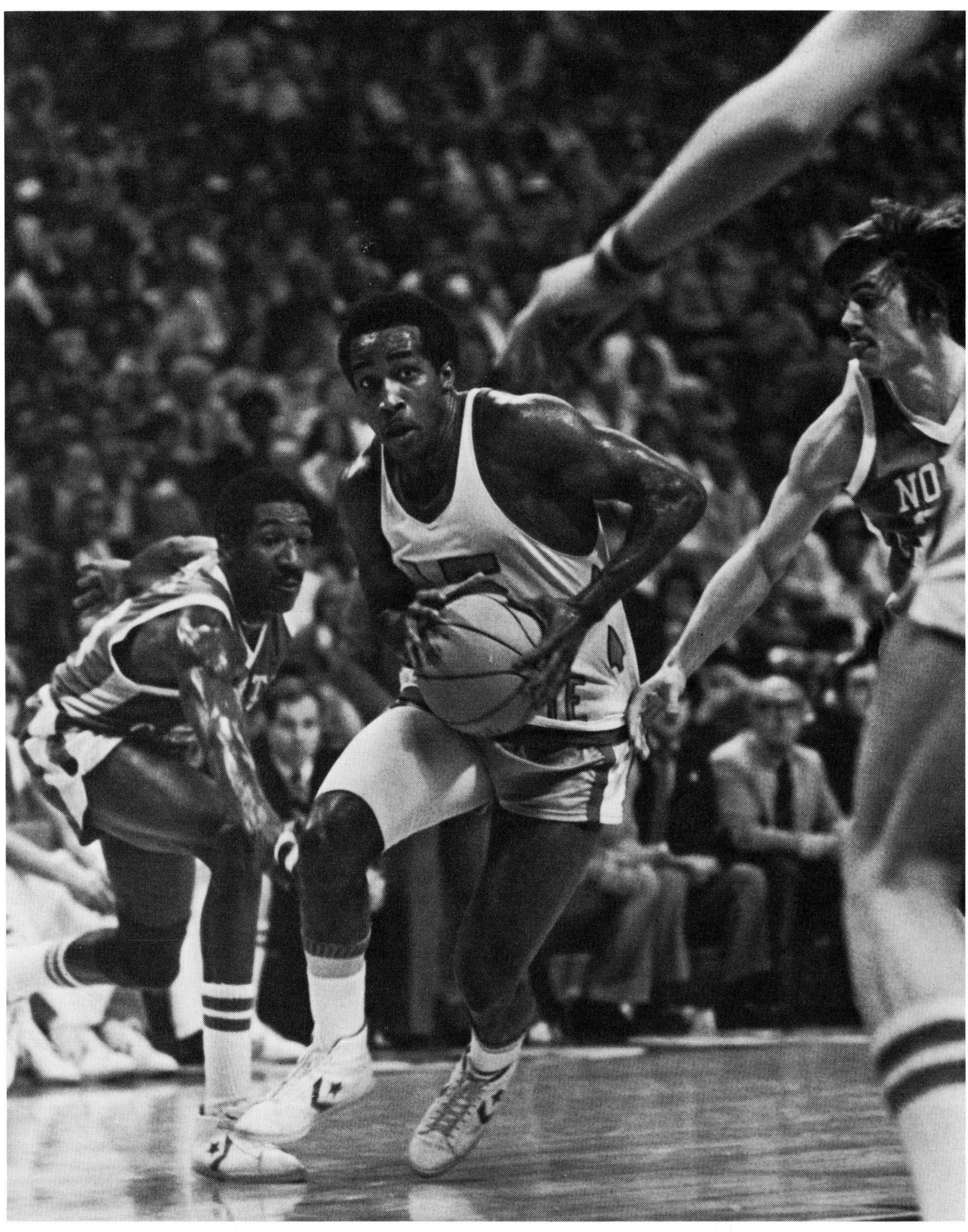

The sparkplug of Marquette's 1977 national champions was guard Butch Lee, driving against North Carolina here. Named the tourney's Outstanding Player, Lee was both floor leader and a volatile scorer, averaging 17.6 points in the Warriors' five tourney games.

game-winning basket. The final score was 51–49, and the Warriors earned the opportunity to make the school's first NCAA championship appearance. The one player most responsible for getting them through the semifinal match was Jerome Whitehead, whose 21 points and 16 rebounds were both game standards, and who held the 49ers' star center, Cornbread Maxwell, to 17 points and 12 rebounds.

Both teams that took the floor for the 1977 championship game had established postseason reputations for rebounding from first-period adversity. Both had had to battle back valiantly through all but one of their three preceding games just to be there (the only game of the six in which one of them did not have to rally from a halftime deficit was Marquette's win over North Carolina-Charlotte in the semifinals, and even there they had to come from behind during the second period).

North Carolina's appearance was no real surprise on the floor of the final game. Marquette's was. Not that the Warriors didn't have the talent or the coaching genius; it was simply that they had not functioned consistently well during the year. They had been up, down, streaking, then faltering, scoring copiously in one game, then seemingly unable to buy a basket in another. In the final game—or the final analysis, for that matter—however, there was one pervasive influence: Al McGuire. It was to be the last college basketball game he would coach because he had announced earlier that he was retiring after the 1976–77 basketball season. As much as he wanted to go out on the wings of victory, his players equally wanted to give Al McGuire his ultimate moment of triumph.

The Marquette Warriors, however, had their hands full with the Tar Heels that night in Georgia—but not until the second half. Marquette came on strong during the first period and built an intimidating 12-point lead by intermission, the score 39–27. North Carolina

The 1977 champs: Marquette whipped North Carolina for the trophy 67–59. **Front row** (left to right): Greg Stack (manager), Ulice Payne, Gary Rosenberger, Butch Lee, Jim Boylan, Robert Byrd, Tom Hayden (manager), David DuChateau (manager). **Back row** (left to right): Rick Majerus (assistant coach), Bill Neary, Jim Dudley, Bernard Toone, Craig Butrym, Jerome Whitehead, Bo Ellis, Hank Raymonds (assistant coach), Bob Weingart (trainer). **Inset:** Al McGuire (coach).

Coach Al McGuire got the ultimate retirement gift in 1977, the NCAA championship. He brought nine Marquette teams to the postseason classic and finally won it all in '77.

fought gamely in the second period but was handicapped by Phil Ford's nagging elbow injury. Still the Tar Heels battled back and eventually took a 45–43 lead. Then it was Marquette's turn to rally, and after the Warriors regained the lead they held it with a great show of clutch free-throw shooting. When the game was over and Marquette could boast a 67–59 victory, the Warriors could also take pride in having sunk 23 of 25 free throws, including 14 crucial ones in the game's last two minutes.

For the Tar Heels, Mike O'Koren, who had taken up so much of the team's scoring slack that resulted from Ford's injury, was held to 14 points. Walter Davis, the Tar Heels' other potential scoring threat, did get 20, but he was the only other North Carolina shooter who was productive that night.

Awards, 1977

Outstanding Player
Butch Lee (Marquette)

All-Tournament Team
Butch Lee (Marquette)
Bo Ellis (Marquette)
Jerome Whitehead (Marquette)
Mike O'Koren (North Carolina)
Walter Davis (North Carolina)
Cedric Maxwell (UNC–Charlotte)

Marquette simply did what it had to do to give Al McGuire the sweetest of retirement gifts, a national championship. It was a fine team effort. Butch Lee scored the most points with 19 (including seven of seven free throws), and Bo Ellis and Jim Boylan contributed 14 apiece. Jerome Whitehead swept 12 rebounds from the boards. The award for Outstanding Player was voted to Butch Lee, who had averaged 17.6 points in the Warriors' five tournament games and had been the spark plug around which Marquette had rallied to redeem early tournament games, enabling them to prevail in the final one. Al McGuire, like UCLA's John Wooden before him, retired with an NCAA championship as his last memory of college coaching.

10
Kentucky Comes Back

The Final Four from 1977 were nowhere to be found when the Final Four of 1978 convened at the Checkerdome in St. Louis to determine who would take that year's NCAA national basketball crown. North Carolina-Charlotte and Nevada-Las Vegas did not even make it to the tournament. National champion Marquette, despite the fact that it had four returning starters—Butch Lee, Jerome Whitehead, Jim Boylan, and Bernard Toone—was eliminated in the first round in a surprise upset by Miami of Ohio, 84–81. The same fate befell 1977 runner-up North Carolina, still claiming stars Phil Ford and Mike O'Koren, which was similarly stunned in the first round by underdog San Francisco 68–64.

The team that had been ranked number one in the nation throughout most of the season was there, however. Kentucky had its entire team back from the year before and despite a grueling schedule had won all but two of its regular-season games. The Wildcats' most prodigious scorer was still All-American forward Jack Givens, and dominating the boards was the imposing Rick Robey, who played either at center or at forward as the situation dictated. Also back were Truman Claytor, Mike Phillips, Jim Lee, and Jay Shidler. And a sophomore guard named Kyle Macy had broken into the Wildcats' starting lineup. They would have to be ranked as the pretournament favorite but only by a hair, because there was an incredible array of competition spread throughout that year's playoff slates.

Joe B. Hall, heir to the legendary Adolph Rupp, guided Kentucky to the 1978 NCAA tourney championship.

Joe B. Hall, heir to Adolph Rupp at Kentucky, had been a masterful and successful coach in the four years he had guided the Wildcats, but he had yet to win the coveted NCAA crown. Now, in 1978, he had a clear shot at it, just as he had in their unsuccessful bid against UCLA in his first year at the helm back in 1975. He also knew that '78 was a crucial year in that most of his players were seniors and would be gone after the tourney, such notables as Givens, Robey, and Phillips among them.

Kentucky was slotted in the Mideast where lurked some rather auspicious opponents, foremost among them reigning champ Marquette and Big Ten ruler Michigan State. Hall's seasoned Wildcats, however, had a lot of trouble in their first-round game against Florida State, and for a while it looked as if the Seminoles might just oust Kentucky from the proceedings before they got anywhere near St. Louis. Behind the talented touch of Mickey Dillard, who shot eight of 10 from the floor and five for five from the free-throw line, the Floridians controlled the first half and built a hefty 39–32 lead. It took a determined effort and some lucky breaks in the second half for the Kentucky Wildcats to pull the game out. Normally productive Jack Givens was held to 11 points, and high-point honors went to Truman Claytor, who scored 16.

The rest of the regional was held in Dayton, Ohio, where Kentucky was pitted against Miami, which had the advantage of a large contingent of home state rooters but perhaps more importantly the recognition of having knocked off a highly favored Marquette in the first round. Miami was fueled mainly by the scoring of Randy Ayers, John Shoemaker, and Rick Goins, but the team was not prepared for a revitalized Kentucky team, which had little intention of allowing Miami to stage back-to-back upsets. Rebounding from its first-round scare, the Wildcats did just about everything right that evening in Dayton. They surged to a 16-point halftime lead, which enabled them to empty their bench in the second period, and coasted to a 91–69 victory. Again Givens was below par with a mere 12 points, but Mike Phillips tallied 24 and Rick Robey 14 before they took seats next to Joe B. Hall on the Wildcat bench.

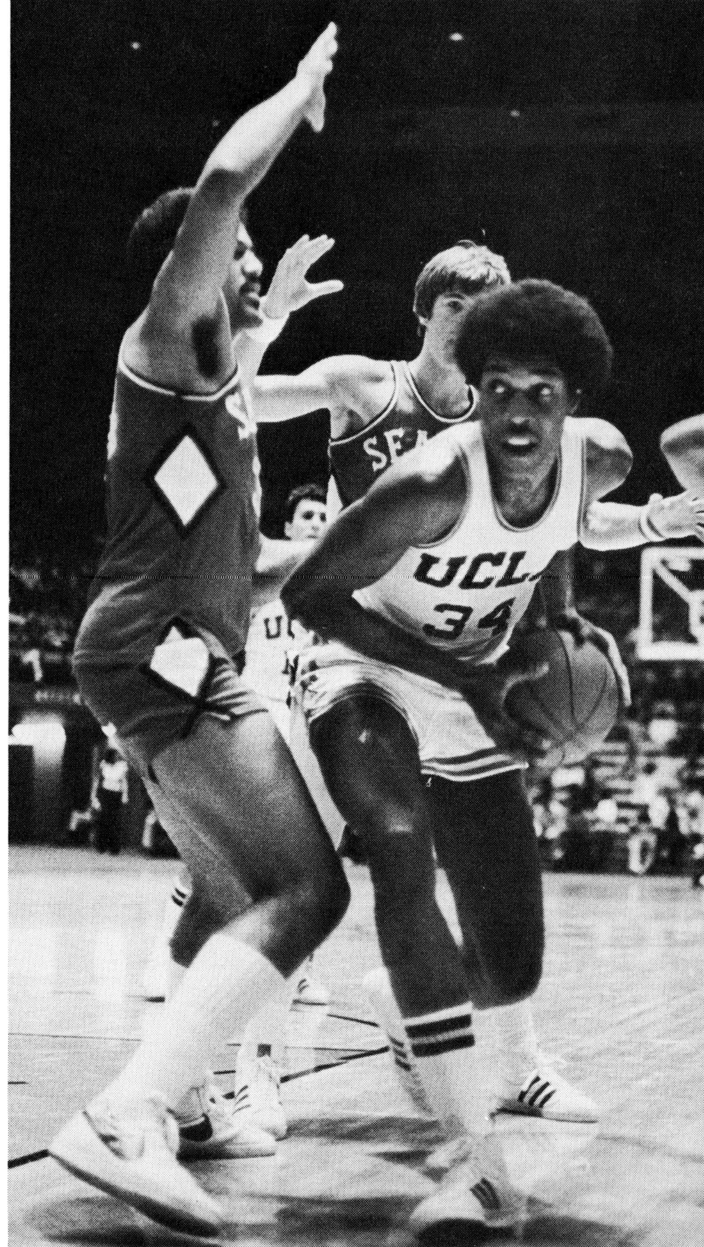

David Greenwood, driving against Seattle here, has the distinction of having started on four UCLA teams that played in NCAA tourneys (1976–79). The 6'10" forward, a two-time All-American, had his best game in the Bruins' 1979 regional loss to DePaul when he accounted for 37 points.

It wasn't really as easy, however, in the regional final. Michigan State which had polished off two very good teams—Providence, 77–63, and Western Kentucky, 90–69—earned the shot at Kentucky. The Spartans had top talent in Greg "Special K" Kelser, Bob Chapman, and Jay Vincent and tremendous promise from a freshman guard named Earvin "Magic" Johnson. Kelser had averaged 23 points in State's first two games, and Chapman had netted 23 in the Western Kentucky game. Coach Jud Heathcote was satisfied that he had a solid contender when the Spartans took the floor to do battle for the Mideast regional title.

Despite all the scoring potential that both teams had, the game was a very low-scoring affair. Michigan State controlled the first-half activities and built a 27–22 lead, but Kentucky pecked away at it in the second period and finally evened the game at 35 points. From that point on it was close indeed, and it was eventually decided on the deft hand of Kentucky's diminutive guard Kyle Macy, who dropped in several key jumpers and 10 of 11 clutch free throws (including six straight in the last three minutes of the game). When the buzzer sounded Kentucky was on the happy end of a 52–49 score. Macy had totaled 19 points for the Wildcats, while Givens added 14 and Phillips 10. Greg Kelser had the Michigan State high with 19, but Magic Johnson, rounding out an awful tournament, sank only two of 10 shots from the floor (in the previous game against Western Kentucky he had hit only three of 17). It was a big disappointment for Jud Heathcote, but his Spartans were young, and they would be back the following year when their fortunes would be decidedly different. For 1978, however, Kentucky for the eighth time in the school's history was going to the Final Four. There, the Wildcats would face the winner of the West regional. Doing battle in that division were such teams as UCLA, Arkansas, North Carolina, and a California team by the name of Fullerton State, which could hold its own against any of the bigger-name schools.

North Carolina, however, surprised in the first round perhaps more by its own lackluster play than by San Francisco, posed no threat. And the UCLA Bruins, despite stars like David Greenwood, Roy Hamilton, and Ray Townsend, were manhandled in the second round by Arkansas. That, however, was not a surprising upset. Arkansas was roundly respected as one of the nation's finest college basketball teams, ranked number five at the end of the regular season. The Razorbacks, guided by coach Eddie Sutton, had three players of All-American caliber in Sidney Moncrief, Ron Brewer, and Marvin Delph. Arkansas had destroyed Weber State in the first round, getting 20 points from Delph, 19 from Brewer, and 16 from Moncrief. Against UCLA, whom they in fact dominated even

Kentucky's Jack Givens was the 1978 tourney's Outstanding Player. Sharpshooter Givens scored 41 points (18 of 27 from the floor) in the Wildcats championship win over Duke. He had 23 in the semifinal triumph over Arkansas.

Playmaker for Kentucky was sophomore guard Kyle Macy. He also scored a team-high 18 points in the Wildcats regional final win over Michigan State in the '78 tourney.

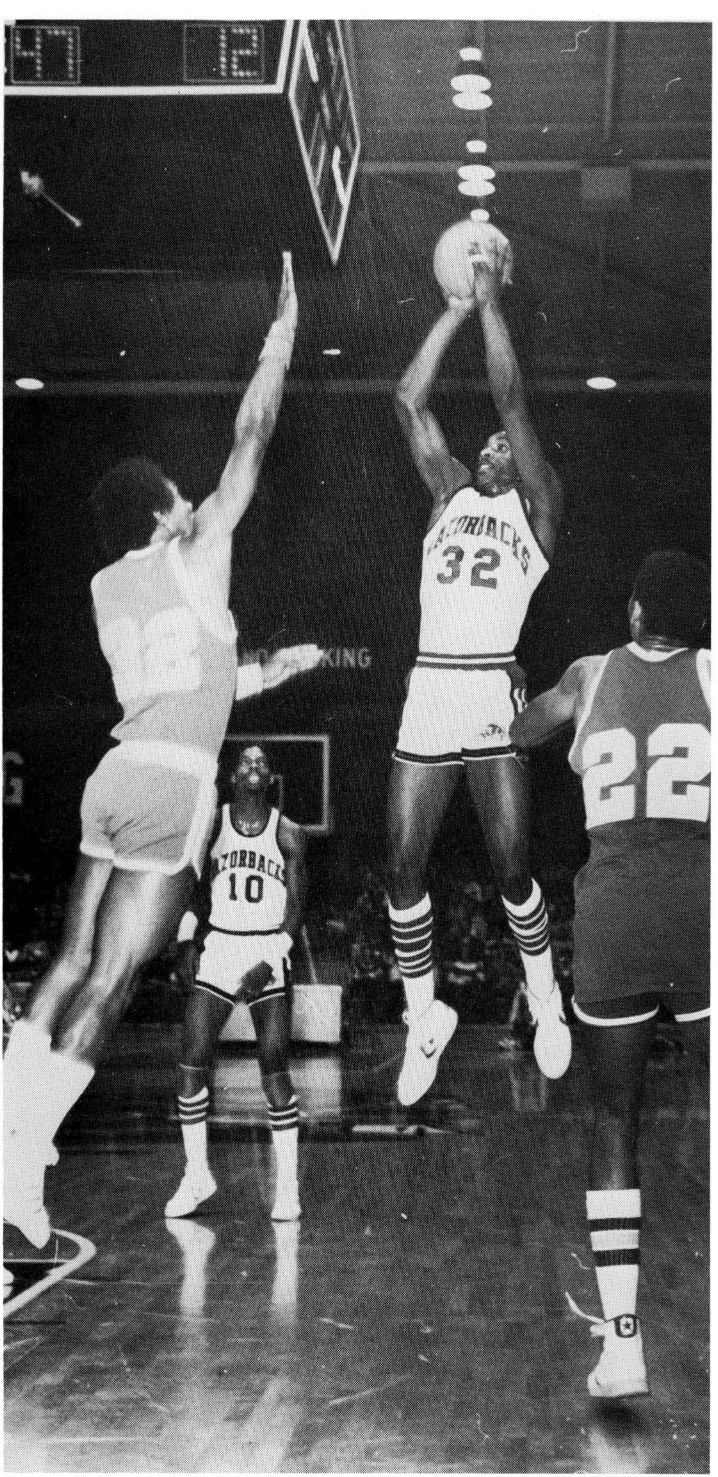

Sidney Moncrief (32), soaring for a jumper, spearheaded the Arkansas Razorbacks' attack in both the 1978 and 1979 tourneys. Moncrief averaged 14.2 points in '78, but Arkansas lost to Kentucky in the semifinals; his '79 average was 23.3. In the background is another Razorback superstar, Ron Brewer (10), who averaged 19 points a game in the '78 tourney.

though the final margin was just four points, Delph again was high, accounting for 23, while Moncrief added 21 and Brewer 18.

Meanwhile Fullerton State was in the process of making its basketball team known throughout the country. With such excellent basketball players as Keith Anderson, Kevin Heenan, and Greg Bunch, the team had beaten New Mexico and San Francisco. It was the school's first trip to the postseason classic, though it was somewhat of a surprise that they made it all the way to the regional title game. There Arkansas lay in wait for them. The Razorbacks, who seemed to get better with each game, bolted to the front in the first half and piled up a 39–24 lead. But the cagers from Fullerton did not give up and instead came roaring back in the second half to make an exciting game of it, but at the final buzzer they still trailed by three. Keith Anderson of Fullerton State was the game's high scorer with 23 points, and teammate Greg Bunch collected the most rebounds with 10. For the triumphant Razorbacks, Ron Brewer scored 22 and Marvin Delph had 14. It was a fine tournament debut for Fullerton State, but Arkansas was simply too strong that night.

In the East the consensus favorite was Duke, even though the Blue Devils had not won the Atlantic Coast Conference (North Carolina had, but Duke won the conference playoff tourney). The rest of the division did not summon a great deal of enthusiasm from the odds makers. Duke, coached by Bill Foster, did have certified superstars in guard Jim Spanarkel, center Mike Gminski, and forward Gene Banks. But it almost did not get past the first round. Against unranked Rhode Island, the Blue Devils trailed by a point at the half, then in a breathless finish eked out a 63–62 win despite Rhode Islander Sly Williams' 27-point effort. Had it not been for each of Gminski's 25 points, Spanarkel's 18, Banks' 14, and six from Jim Suddath, the only Blue Devils to score that night, Duke would have gone back home to Durham, North Carolina.

The second round was no easier for Duke. A strong Pennsylvania team, keyed around the talents of Keven McDonald (he scored 37 in the team's first-round win over St. Bonaventure) and Tony Price, made the Blue Devils

It was with the hot hands of these three players—guard Gene Banks (left), forward Jim Spanarkel (below), and center Mike Gminski (right)—that Duke made it to the 1978 championship game. Gminski scored 29, Banks 22, and Spanarkel 20 in the Blue Devils' semifinal win over Notre Dame, and each of them logged 20 or more in their title game loss to Kentucky.

work their proverbial tails off to earn an 84–80 victory. Spanarkel and Banks were the most productive that game for Duke with 21 points each.

To get to the Final Four, Duke had to overcome Villanova, a high-scoring team that had been quite impressive in knocking off LaSalle and Indiana in two earlier tourney encounters. Keith Herron was Villanova's chief scorer, and he had posted 24 and 23 points in those two games. But they were no match for Duke in the East regional final. The Blue Devils, hotter than they had been in previous games, surged to a 14-point halftime lead, then glided on through with hardly a worry. The final was 90–72, with four Blue Devils in double figures: Spanarkel, 22; Gminski, 21; Banks, 17; and Kenny Dennard, 16. Keith Herron scored 20 and Reggie Robinson 16 for Villanova.

If the outcome in the East was somewhat of a foregone conclusion, the Midwest regional was truly up for grabs. There were three teams that had equally good chances at winning it, all of them sporting fine rosters with big names. DePaul, an independent from Chicago, had seven-foot center Dave Corzine, an All-American candidate, as well as high-scoring guard Gary Garland, playmaker Randy Ramsey, and two seasoned forwards, Curtis Watkins and Joe Ponsetto, and were coached by the grand old man of college basketball, Ray Meyer. There was also a fearsome Notre Dame team whose frontcourt was perhaps as burly and brutalizing as the front line of the school's football team, which had won the NCAA crown in its sport earlier in the school year. The Fighting Irish were getting much of their scoring from forward Kelly Tripucka, center Bill Laimbeer, and guard Don "Duck" Williams. But there was also scoring potential from guard Rich Branning and forward Dave Batton. The third team of note was Louisville, led by Darrell Griffith, Rick Wilson, Larry Williams, and Bobby Turner, all fine scoring threats.

A surprising Creighton team came very close to smashing DePaul's hopes in the first round. The fired-up quintet from Omaha, Nebraska, built and then frittered away a 14-point halftime lead and finally lost to DePaul by a basket. Ray Meyer's youngsters had turned in a fine second half, however, ending up with five players in double digits (the most points from Gary Garland, 20, and Dave Corzine, 19). The Blue Demons' next encounter proved to be the most exciting game of the tourney and certainly one of the most entertaining and dramatic in any of the NCAA playoffs. DePaul and Louisville went through two overtime periods before the outcome was decided. The lead went back and forth, reaching a 74–74 stalemate at the end of regulation time. In the first overtime period each team came up with eight points, sending the contest into an additional period. It was almost as close in that period, but DePaul managed one extra point and a 90–89 win. Center Dave Corzine had been the chief difference, scoring 46 points (18 of 28 field goals and 10 for 10 from the line), the most points that would be scored in any game that tournament.

Notre Dame, behind its mesomorphic frontcourt, destroyed Houston in the first round 100–77, with Bill Laimbeer posting 20 points and Don Williams 19. The Fighting Irish raised no more of a sweat in their 69–56 drubbing of Utah in the next round; this time Kelly Tripucka took the scoring honors with 20 points.

Digger Phelps felt that Notre Dame's frontcourt could handle the towering Dave Corzine. He was right. The big center was effectively neutralized by their beef trust. Behind a balanced scoring attack, the Irish took a four-point halftime lead and turned it into a 20-point rout. Kelly Tripucka collected 11 rebounds and Bill Laimbeer 10 to Corzine's seven. Tripucka was Notre Dame's top scorer with 18 while Rich Branning added 15, Don Williams 14, and Bill Laimbeer 12. For DePaul Gary Garland accounted for 18 and Corzine for 17.

The Final Four for 1978 was among the most equally balanced in tourney history. Each team had a very legitimate shot at the crown, and it was generally felt that just a few breaks might be all that was necessary to bring the tourney trophy to one of the four teams. The pairings were Arkansas versus Kentucky, Notre Dame facing Duke.

One semifinal game had all the promise of a scoring bonanza. Both Arkansas and Kentucky could put myriad points on the board when the occasion called for it. But it did not turn out to be that kind of a game. Instead it was an awkward, slowed-down affair, keynoted by a proliferation of fouls, which hurt Arkansas the most. Kentucky edged ahead by two at the half and then simply outlasted the Razorbacks in the remaining period. Such normally productive Arkansas scorers as Sidney Moncrief, Marvin Delph, and Ron Brewer contributed only 13, 15, and 16 points respectively. Kentucky's Jack Givens was the only player to evince any offensive magic, scoring 23. The final was 64–59 in favor of Kentucky.

Bruce Flowers (34), grabbing a high pass here against West Virginia, roamed from center to forward for Notre Dame in the 1977, 1978, and 1979 tournaments.

A far better game was staged by Duke and Notre Dame. But the excitement didn't come until late in the second half. In fact, the first half was merely an embarrassment to Notre Dame. The Fighting Irish could not do anything right and trailed by a seemingly insurmountable margin of 43–29. But Digger Phelps's cagers were far from through. They staged a magnificent comeback in the second half and almost overcame Duke. The last four minutes of the game were chaotic. Notre Dame worked its way to within a basket of the Blue Devils but then were forced to foul in an effort to get possession of the basketball. Duke's deadliness from the free-throw line was what saved the game for them. Blue Devil shooters sank 10 straight from the line in the game's last minutes (they were 32 of 37 for the night) and took a 90–86 win. Notre Dame would not get the opportunity to become the first school ever to win NCAA championships in football and basketball during the same year. And Bill Foster would bring Duke to the championship tilt, for the second time in the school's history (Duke lost there to UCLA in 1964).

Heroes of the semifinal game for Duke were center Mike Gminski, who scored 29 points; Gene Banks, who had 22 and grabbed 12 rebounds (the latter a game high); and Jim Spanarkel, who contributed 20 points, including 12 for 12 from the free-throw line.

Kentucky was rated as a slight favorite in the championship game. The Wildcats would probably have been a greater favorite if judged solely on the two teams' performances during the regular season, but Duke had been so impressive in the tournament that no one was discounting the Blue Devils.

As predicted, it was close in the early going, often no more than a point dividing the two teams. But as the game bore down on the half, Kentucky edged away. There was a seven-point difference in Kentucky's favor when the second half began, and it was a lead the Wildcats would not relinquish that night. It grew to as many as 12 points in the second period before Duke fought back. With the advantage of playing against mostly Kentucky reserves, Duke narrowed the Wildcat lead to four points, but then the regulars returned and Kentucky held on to win 94–88.

There was little question as to who would

Forward Kelly Tripucka shouldered many of the hopes of Notre Dame fans in the 1978, 1979, and 1980 tourneys, but the closest the Fighting Irish would come was their fourth-place finish in '78.

Awards, 1978

Outstanding Player
Jack Givens (Kentucky)

All-Tournament Team
Jack Givens (Kentucky)
Ron Brewer (Arkansas)
Mike Gminski (Duke)
Rick Robey (Kentucky)
Jim Spanarkel (Duke)

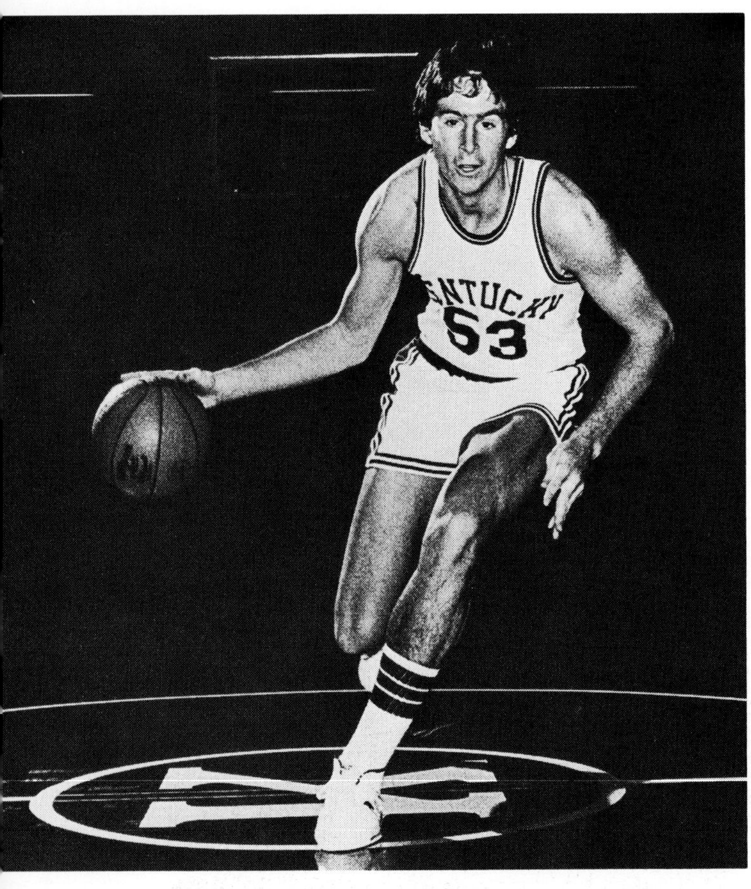

Rick Robey alternated between center and forward for Kentucky in 1978. Always a power on the boards, the 6'11" Robey pulled in a team-high 11 rebounds and scored 20 points in the '79 title game.

receive the Outstanding Player award. Jack Givens provided the Kentucky Wildcats with 41 points that championship night (18 of 27 from the floor), and he was the easy choice. Another star was Rick Robey who accounted for 20 points and 11 rebounds. The Blue Devils' "Big Three" had also scored well, though not quite well enough: Gene Banks had 22, Jim Spanarkel 21, and Mike Gminski 20 (along with a game high 12 rebounds).

Joe B. Hall no longer would have to live in the overwhelming shadow of the legendary Adolph Rupp. He, too, had reached the very top, enabling the University of Kentucky to take pride in owning its fifth national basketball championship. Only UCLA has won more.

11
Michigan State and Magic

Sophomore Magic Johnson, as colorful a personality as he was a basketball sensation, described his team inimitably and, as it turned out, correctly when he spoke to a *Sports Illustrated* writer early in the 1979 NCAA championship playoffs: "We got a team that can kill you from the outside, and we got a team that can kill you from the inside. If we're on top of our game, ain't nobody in the world can beat Michigan State."

Going into the tournament, the Spartans from Lansing, Michigan, were a highly respected team, but not everyone shared Magic Johnson's supreme optimism. After all, State had lost six of its 27 games during the regular season and had to settle for a three-way tie for the Big Ten title that year. But Magic Johnson, the 6′8″ guard who moved to forward during the season, had blossomed into a superstar, a status he shared with Michigan State's other high-scoring forward, 6′7″ Greg Kelser. Before the postseason drama got underway, it was conceded that Jud Heathcote's team had a good shot at taking the crown, but there were a number of teams that actually commanded more favorable odds.

First, there was Indiana State and everybody's All-American forward Larry Bird. The Sycamores from Terre Haute, who were attending their very first NCAA tournament, went undefeated through the 1978–79 season and were heralded number one in both the AP and UPI polls when the playoffs got under way.

From out of the West there was number-

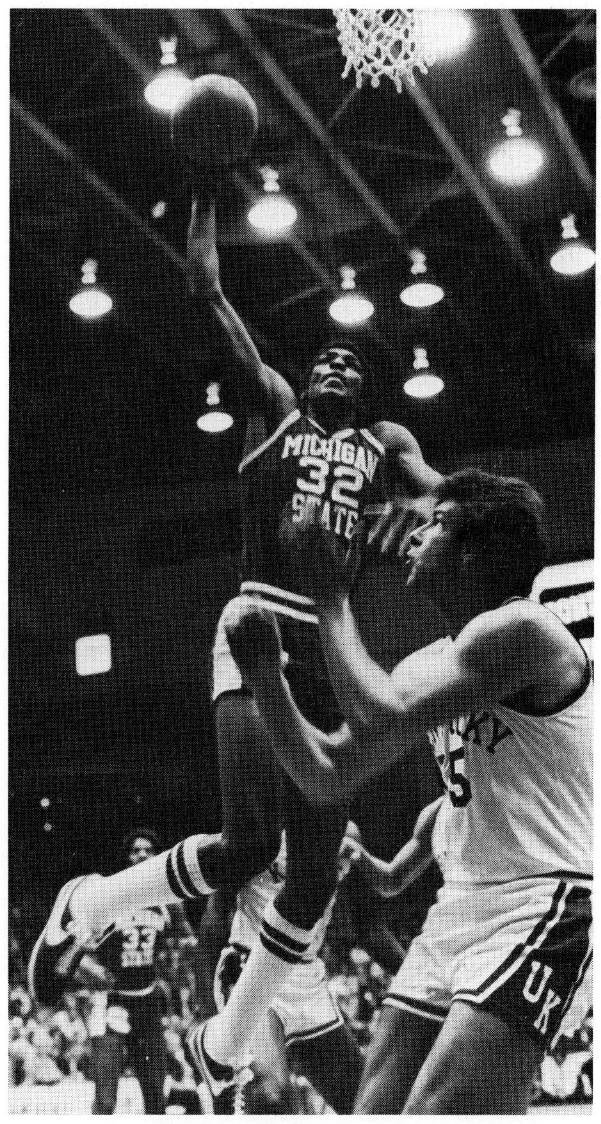

Spartan Greg Kelser goes up for a slam-dunk against Kentucky. Kelser was Michigan State's top scorer in the '79 tourney: 127 points, an average of 25.4 per game.

two-ranked UCLA, a team dubbed that year as the best shooting team in college basketball history, the result of a most impressive seasonal percentage of .555. Coached by former UCLA player, Gary Cunningham, now in his second year at the helm, the Bruins had on their roster such luminaries as forwards David Greenwood and Kiki Vandeweghe and guards Roy Hamilton and Brad Holland. From the opposite coast was third-ranked North Carolina. Dean Smith's Tar Heels had again conquered the mighty Atlantic Coast Conference and still had the services of steady scorer Mike O'Koren.

Not more than a basketball bounce or two behind those front-runners were several other top-touted teams. Among them was Arkansas, with All-American guard Sidney Moncrief. Under coach Eddie Sutton, the Razorbacks were nationally ranked and were considered Indiana State's biggest threat in the Midwest regionals. In the Mideast a powerful Notre Dame lay in wait for Michigan State. Digger Phelps' Fighting Irish had a slew of familiar names on the roster, such as Kelly Tripucka, Orlando Woolridge, Bruce Flowers, Rich Branning, Bill Hanzlik, Tracy Jackson, and Bill Laimbeer. Notre Dame was widely acknowledged to have the best bench in college basketball that year.

All-American forward Mark Aguirre was the star many thought would guide DePaul to the 1979 NCAA title. He did average 23.4 points in DePaul's five tourney games, but the Blue Demons could not contain Larry Bird and Indiana State in the semifinals.

Lodged in the East was sixth-ranked Duke, runner-up to North Carolina in the ACC and still paced by Jim Spanarkel, Miki Gminski, and Gene Banks. To worry UCLA in the West were no less than three top teams. Ray Meyer's independent DePaul Blue Demons had had a fine season behind the superstar freshman, 6′7″ forward Mark Aguirre (he had averaged 24.1 points a game in the regular season) and their fine guards, Gary Garland and Clyde Bradshaw, and consistently high-scoring forward Curtis Watkins. Marquette, another independent invitee now being coached by Hank Raymonds, Al McGuire's former assistant, also claimed a host of stars: Bernard Toone, Sam Worthen, Oliver Lee, and Odell Ball. San Francisco also was a very real threat with 7′ 1″ All-American center Bill Cartwright dominating every key he entered.

As so often is the case, there were a number of eyebrow-raising surprises in the early rounds. None perhaps were more striking than those carried out in the East. First Duke was rebuffed by St. John's, the last of the 40 teams invited to that year's tournament. If that was not a hard enough blow to the prestige of the ACC, heavily favored North Carolina was likewise stunned in the tourney's second round, edged 72–71 by Pennsylvania.

In the Mideast Iowa, one of the teams to share the Big Ten crown in 1978–79, did not expect to be eliminated by Toledo, but it was. And in the Midwest a solidly favored Texas team was trounced 90–76 by its border rival Oklahoma.

Michigan State, however, found no trouble in the early going. First it took on Lamar, a middle-sized school from Beaumont, Texas, and devastated them 95–64. They went inside that night, as Magic Johnson would have described it, principally to slam-dunking Greg Kelser, who racked up 31 points and took 14 rebounds. Johnson himself scored only 13 points for the Spartans but cleared a game-high 17 rebounds and was credited with 10 assists. The other powerhouse in the Mideast, Notre Dame, also won handily, taking Tennessee by six points.

In the Midwest, Indiana State was living up to its notoriety. With Larry Bird and Carl Nicks contributing 22 points each, Indiana State easily disposed of Virginia Tech 86–69. Arkansas deftly handled Weber State, getting 19 points from Sidney Moncrief and 18 from Steve Schall.

The displaced midwesterners, DePaul and Marquette, sailed through their first encounters on the West Coast. DePaul, with Curtis Watkins scoring 27 points and Mark Aguirre 25, defeated Southern California by 11 points. Marquette annihilated Pacific 73–48, getting 18 points apiece from Bernard Toone and Sam Worthen. At the same time the Californians were advancing in the West. UCLA had a much tougher time with Pepperdine than expected, having to come back from a two-point halftime deficit, but the Bruins did so and won 76–71. David Greenwood was the predominant force that night, leading the Bruins with 18 points and 10 rebounds. Meanwhile towering Bill Cartwright and his teammates from San Francisco overwhelmed Brigham Young 86–63, and Cartwright was the game's high-point man with 24.

If events in the Midwest, Mideast, and West were turning out as most basketball pundits had figured they would, the same could not be said about the goings-on in the East. After the astonishing blows dealt to North Carolina and Duke, the perpetrators of them continued their surprises. With the regional staged at Greensboro, North Carolina, St. John's met a favored Rutgers team and shocked them in the same manner it had the Duke Blue Devils. Down four points at the half, the amazing Redmen from New York rebounded to sink Rutgers when center Wayne McKoy dropped in a tie-breaking bucket with only five seconds left in the game. The 67–65 St. John's win was also much the result of the 22-point performance by Redman Reggie Carter. The other East Coast giant killer, Pennsylvania, had an even tougher opponent in Syracuse. The Orange-

Coach of the 1979 champs from Michigan State, Jud Heathcote.

Bill Cartwright (24), San Francisco's 7'1" center, taps in an easy two here against Notre Dame. Cartwright's average of 29 points a game in the 1979 tourney was tops that year.

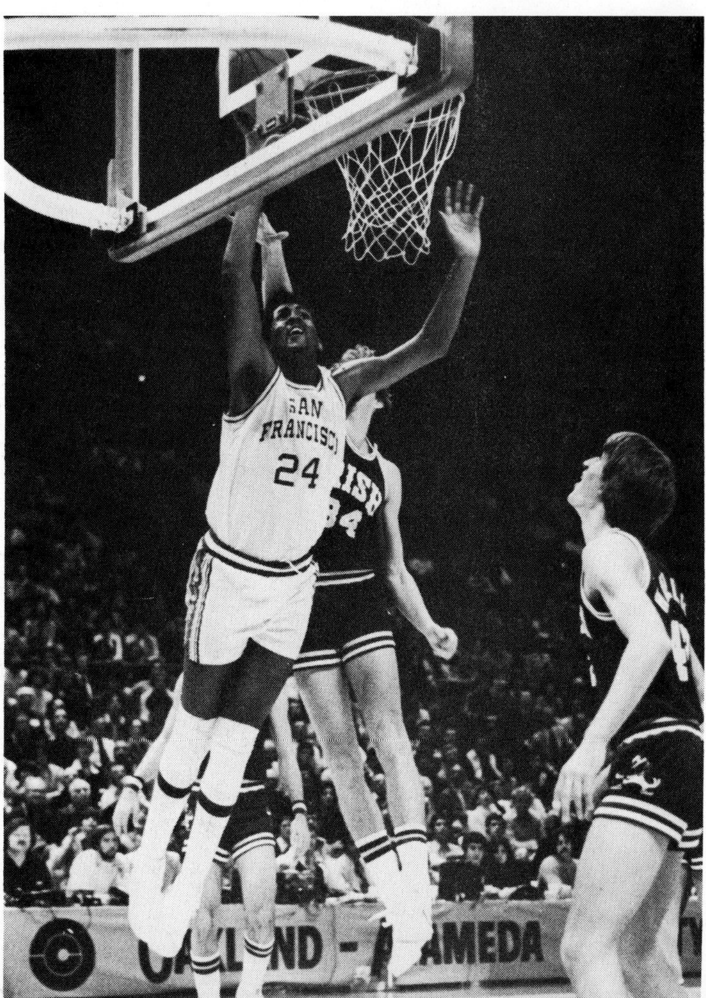

men were, after the demise of the ACC teams, the pick of the odds makers to represent the East in the Final Four. But the Quakers from Philadelphia had forward Tony Price, a prize of a ball player. He had scored 25 in Penn's upset of North Carolina and 27 in its first-round win over Iona. Price was again the game's top scorer when the Quakers took on Syracuse, this time posting 20 points. Along with 18 from fellow forward Tim Smith and 14 from guard James Salters, Penn astounded the Orangemen from Syracuse 84–76.

So two surprising upstarts would face off to determine who would represent the East in the Final Four. Most observers viewed the Quakers as a slight favorite, but many also felt that this particular game was totally unpredictable, that the game would simply be decided by who shone brighter that night, Penn's Tony Price or St. John's Reggie Carter. It was slow

Tony Price (15) All-American from Pennsylvania, was the tourney's high scorer in 1979 with 142 points, an average of 23.7. Here he puts a move on DePaul's Curtis Watkins (30) in the consolation game for third place that year, which DePaul won despite Price's 31 points.

going through the first half, and the only thing shining in the arena were the overhead lights. Penn finally ended up ahead by three at intermission, 29–26. It was close throughout the second period, but every time the Redmen made their run at Penn the Quakers were able to hold them off, at least until the final minute. Then it came down to the proverbial wire. With less than 30 seconds remaining, the score was tied at 62 apiece. James Salters, however, was sent to the line for the Quakers and neatly dropped in two free throws, which proved to be the winning margin. In the game, Tony Price, who made seven of 11 field goals, was the high scorer for the Quakers, with a total of 21 points. A similar number was tallied by forward Ron Plair for St. John's, while Reggie Carter accounted for only four. So it was Pennsylvania, playing in its ninth NCAA tournament that would for the first time go to the Final Four.

In the Mideast, Michigan State had to get by Louisiana State, winner of the Southeast Conference, and Notre Dame had to dispose of Toledo, if those two teams were to go head to head in the regional final, as so many predicted they would. And they did just that. The Spartans, playing absolutely first-rate basketball, bowled over LSU 87–71. Spartan scoring honors went to Magic Johnson this time (24 points), though the game high was the 25 toted up by Jordy Hultberg of LSU. The Fighting Irish had just as easy a time advancing, controlling Toledo throughout and turning a 10-point halftime lead into a 79–71 victory. Kelly Tripucka scored 24 for Notre Dame, and Jim Swaney had 26 for Toledo.

It promised to be a very close and very physical game. Both Michigan State and Notre Dame were strong and fast, and both had been performing at their peaks so far during the tourney. But, as it turned out, the deciding factor was the special harmony created by the interplay of Magic Johnson and Greg Kelser. They were virtually unstoppable in the regional final at Indianapolis. One moment it was Johnson's lob pass and Kelser's "Alley-Oop" slam dunk; the next a drive by Johnson and a perfect feed underneath to Kelser for the lay-up or a fake by Kelser and a drop-off pass back to Johnson for a jumper. Their precision had never been more in tune. Behind the two State surged to a 34–23 halftime lead and never let up afterward. The game was never in doubt, and when the final buzzer rang Notre Dame was humbled 80–68. Greg Kelser had his most productive game of the tournament, 34 points (15 of 25 field goals) and 13 rebounds, both game standards. Magic Johnson had 19 points and 13 assists, many of them to Kelser. It would be Michigan State's first trip to the Final Four since 1957, a less than enduring memory because the team ended up fourth that year.

As devastating as Michigan State had been thus far in the tourney, Indiana State, under coach Bill Hodges and behind the magnificent talents of Larry Bird, was proving to be just as awesome a winner in the Midwest. To get to that regional final the Sycamores had to eliminate the Oklahoma Sooners, a task that proved to be no problem whatsoever. With Bird scor-

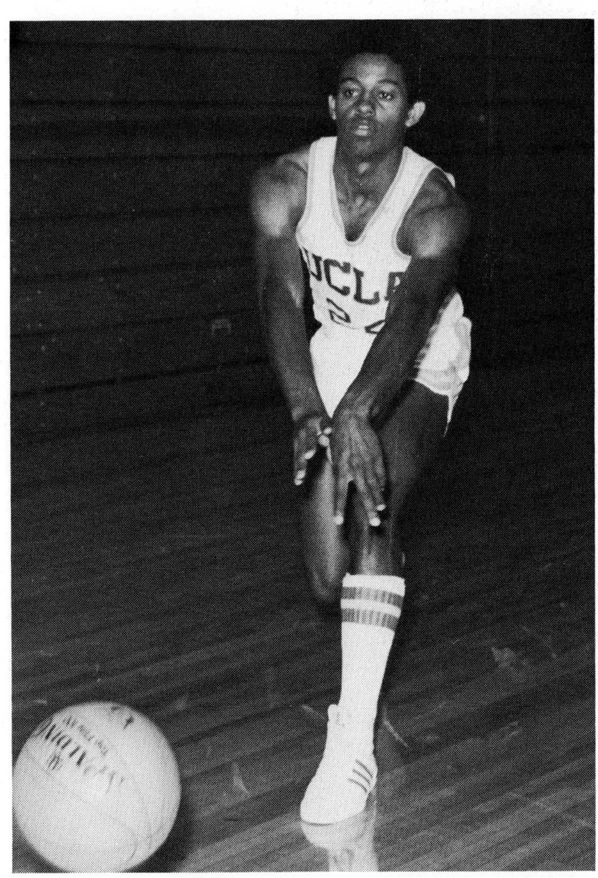

Roy Hamilton was one of the key figures on the UCLA teams from 1977 through 1979. In '79 he scored 36 points in the Bruins' regional win over San Francisco, his finest postseason performance.

ing 29 points and grabbing 15 rebounds, both game highs, and Carl Nicks adding another 20 points, State crushed the Sooners 93–72. And already there was talk about a championship clash of the superstars, Larry Bird and Magic Johnson.

Arkansas, with its own superstar in Sidney Moncrief, however, appeared a very real barrier to Indiana State. That was surely substantiated when the Razorbacks tore apart a respected Louisville team in the regional at Cincinnati. With Moncrief scoring 27 and collecting 12 rebounds Arkansas had a 73–62 win and the right to try to chop down the Sycamores of Indiana State.

A confrontation between Larry Bird and Sidney Moncrief would be an All-American one in its own right but an unorthodox one in that Bird was a 6′9″ forward and Moncrief a 6′4″ guard. But it did come about in the second half. That was when Razorback coach Eddie Sutton assigned Moncrief to guard Bird. The result was successful as Bird was neutralized under the breathless and dogged pursuit of Moncrief. The normally unintimidated Bird scored only six points in the last 13 minutes of the game while Moncrief was guarding him.

The game was close all the way. Arkansas led at the half by a basket, but Indiana State came back strong and built a lead in the second period. With Bird bogged down by Moncrief, the Razorbacks forged back, and in the last few minutes it became anybody's ball game. With less than two minutes left, the score was tied at 71 points, and Arkansas had the ball. The Razorbacks quickly went into a ball-control game, hoping to hold the ball for a last shot. But they failed, and Indiana State got the ball from them with just more than a minute remaining. The Sycamores, to no one's surprise, adopted the same strategy. And they were successful, though there were some deviations from the original plan. The obvious plan was to get the ball to Larry Bird for the last shot, which they did with 11 seconds on the scoreboard. But Bird was so hounded by Moncrief that he couldn't get a shot away. He at least got rid of the ball, however, and with only two seconds remaining reserve Bob Heaton, a right-handed shooter, threw up an off-balance left-handed shot that bounced around the rim and fell in.

Both Larry Bird and Sidney Moncrief had played a fine basketball game. Although slowed in the game's last quarter, Bird accounted for 31 points, his most productive output so far in the tournament. Moncrief scored 24 and was the Razorbacks' leading rebounder with eight. It was a heartbreaker for Arkansas, but at least the team had been part of the Final Four the year before. Now it was Indiana State's turn, a team that had truly earned it.

The pairings in the West regional at Provo, Utah, called for two more games, and their outcomes were anybody's guess. DePaul and Marquette would go after each other in the first game of that doubleheader, and UCLA and San Francisco would wind up the night's entertainment. DePaul was a slight favorite, partly because the Blue Demons had edged the Warriors by a point during the regular season and had looked quite good in beating a tough Southern Cal team earlier in the tourney. In addition, there was some definite sentimental stimulus to bring the revered Ray Meyer, then in his 37th year as head coach of the Blue Demons, a national championship. But DePaul's team did not respond with anything that approached alacrity after the game got under way, and their sluggish play left them on the short end of the score by as many as nine points in the early going. The Blue Demons came back, however, and were able to take a three-point halftime lead. Then it was a return to lackluster play in the second period, and their lead vanished. Marquette pulled ahead, this time by as many as eight points. Although playing below par, the Demons were determined, and again they came back to regain the lead. They were able to hold it this time and finally took a 62–56 win. It was hardly one of their more impressive victories, but it did give Ray Meyer's Blue Demons the chance to play for the regional championship. In defeating Marquette, DePaul's biggest guns were Curtis Watkins and Mark Aguirre, who scored 19 points each, and Gary Garland, who added 15. For the losing Warriors from Milwaukee, Bernard Toone, their only player in double figures, posted 26 points.

In the second game UCLA looked like the Bruins of NCAA playoffs past. San Francisco, however, was no easy mark, graced with the nation's most lauded center, Bill Cartwright. The Bruins, who had been ranked second nationally at the end of the regular season, were a shade favored in the game. The Dons were impressive in the opening segment, and UCLA had to struggle just to stay in the game. San Francisco took a two-point lead into the second half, but then UCLA exploded. It was as if John Wooden had returned and his patented second-half rallies had suddenly materialized, and the Bruins were once again the tourney's indomitable masters. Guards Roy Hamilton and Brad Holland had a touch to their jumpers that could only be described as golden as shot after shot touched nothing but net. And between David Greenwood and Kiki Vandeweghe, the Bruins stifled Cartwright and controlled the inside. The game was virtually ripped out of San Francisco's hands as the Bruin marksmen shot 73 percent in the second half and surged to an impressive 99–81 victory. For UCLA, Hamilton, who made 15 of 20 field goals that night, scored 36 points, Holland another 22, and Greenwood 19. The game's leading rebounder was Vandeweghe with 13. Big Bill Cartwright managed 34 points for San Francisco but was credited with only nine rebounds. After UCLA's electric performance most observers felt that the Bruins would have little trouble keeping the West's crown in the West and out of the hands of interloper DePaul.

But the UCLA effervescence went flat when the Bruins took the floor against DePaul in the NCAA West regional final. All the fire and fury was generated by the Blue Demons, who outran, outshot, and outrebounded UCLA and surged to a 51–34 halftime lead. Still, Ray Meyer knew this UCLA team's reputation for dazzling shooting and second-half miracles. With his comforting lead, Meyer wanted to slow the game down and keep the volatile Bruins as contained as possible. His squad did manage to slow the game down, but at the same time the Bruins nibbled away at the lead. Almost all the scoring was coming from an inspired David Greenwood, who was simultaneously doing the work of a forward and a

All-American Larry Bird soft-touches an easy one in this game against Bradley. The 6'9" forward, with one of the game's most accurate shots, led Indiana State to the 1979 championship game but was unable to get the Sycamores past Michigan State. Bird was the tournament's second-highest scorer with 136 points, averaged out to 27.2 in the Sycamores' five games.

center. And for a brief moment it looked as if the Bruins might just work another second-half miracle when in the waning minutes they pulled to within a basket of DePaul. But that was as close as they were to get; the Blue Demons held them at bay in the closing minutes and won 95–91. For the bereft Bruins, David Greenwood had turned in the most productive night of his college career, 37 points, and led with 10 rebounds as well. But it was not enough to offset the beautifully balanced scoring of DePaul: Curtis Watkins and Gary Garland scored 24 apiece, Mark Aguirre 20, James Mitchem 14, and Clyde Bradshaw 13. So Ray Meyer, on the wings of an impressive triumph, would soar with his fast-paced Blue Demon team to the Final Four competition at Salt Lake City, bringing DePaul there for the first time since 1943.

Michigan State, which hardly had to exert itself in its three previous tournament games, was the decided favorite in the semifinal match against Pennsylvania. Jud Heathcote did not want his Spartans to become overconfident, however, and made a point of reminding them of what the Quakers had done to North Carolina two weeks earlier. But he needn't have worried. His cagers took the game seriously and played it flawlessly. They raced to a 50–17 halftime lead, then roared through to win 101-67, the biggest rout in Final Four history. Perhaps Larry Keith, writing in *Sports Illustrated,* summed it up best: "Penn was so shaken by the bright lights that it committed all the usual mistakes and even invented a new one when Vincent Ross passed to James Salters, who was standing out of bounds." For Michigan State, the dynamic duo of Greg Kelser and Magic Johnson once again did their dastardly act, and Penn could do nothing to thwart it. Johnson scored 29 points (nine of 10 field goals, 11 of 12 free throws), his best performance of the tourney, snatched 10 rebounds, and had 10 assists. Kelser had 28 points and nine rebounds. Penn's star Tony Price was held to his tournament low of 18 points.

The second semifinal contest was no runaway, however. DePaul and Indiana State went practically basket for basket down to the final buzzer in a true heart stopper of a game. Sycamore Larry Bird turned in a grand performance, his best of the tourney, but DePaul's smooth spread of scoring was also precisely effective. Through the first half the game was especially close. At 15 different junctures the score was tied, and when the buzzer ended the period Indiana State led by three. That margin was increased to 11 when the two teams came back onto the floor, but then DePaul began to chip away at it methodically. And with just under five minutes remaining, the Blue Demons took the lead 73–71. Ray Meyer sent them into a four-corner delay, but it backfired. A costly turnover gave the ball back to the Sycamores, who tied the score when Larry Bird rifled a pass to reserve Bob Heaton underneath for an easy lay-up (the same Heaton who dropped in the last-second basket to beat Arkansas in the regional final). With that the game turned frenetic, but neither team could capitalize on a possession. Then Blue Demon guard Gary Garland was fouled and calmly dropped in the first free throw with only a little more than a minute and a half left in the game. But Larry Bird cleared the board when Garland missed the second charity toss. The Sycamores, trailing by a point, maneuvered for the right shot as time ticked away. Suddenly there was Bob Heaton alone again under the basket, and he dumped in another easy lay-up. With the one-point difference now in Indiana State's favor, DePaul chose to go with the ultimate gamble and hold the ball for that last decisive shot. A win or a loss rode solely on it. Mark Aguirre took it from 20 feet out with four seconds remaining, but the ball bounced away from the rim and Indiana State came up with it. An immediate foul by DePaul enabled the Sycamores to put another point on the scoreboard, and the game ended with Indiana State victorious 76–74. It could have gone either way, but one team had to come out on top; as Larry Bird said after the game to a *Sports Illustrated* writer: "Today we was lucky. We was very lucky."

Heading the game's final stats was Larry Bird, with 35 points and 16 rebounds, both game highs. For DePaul, Mark Aguirre and Gary Garland scored 19 apiece, and Curtis Watkins had 16. A disconsolate but always gentlemanly Ray Meyer accepted the heart-

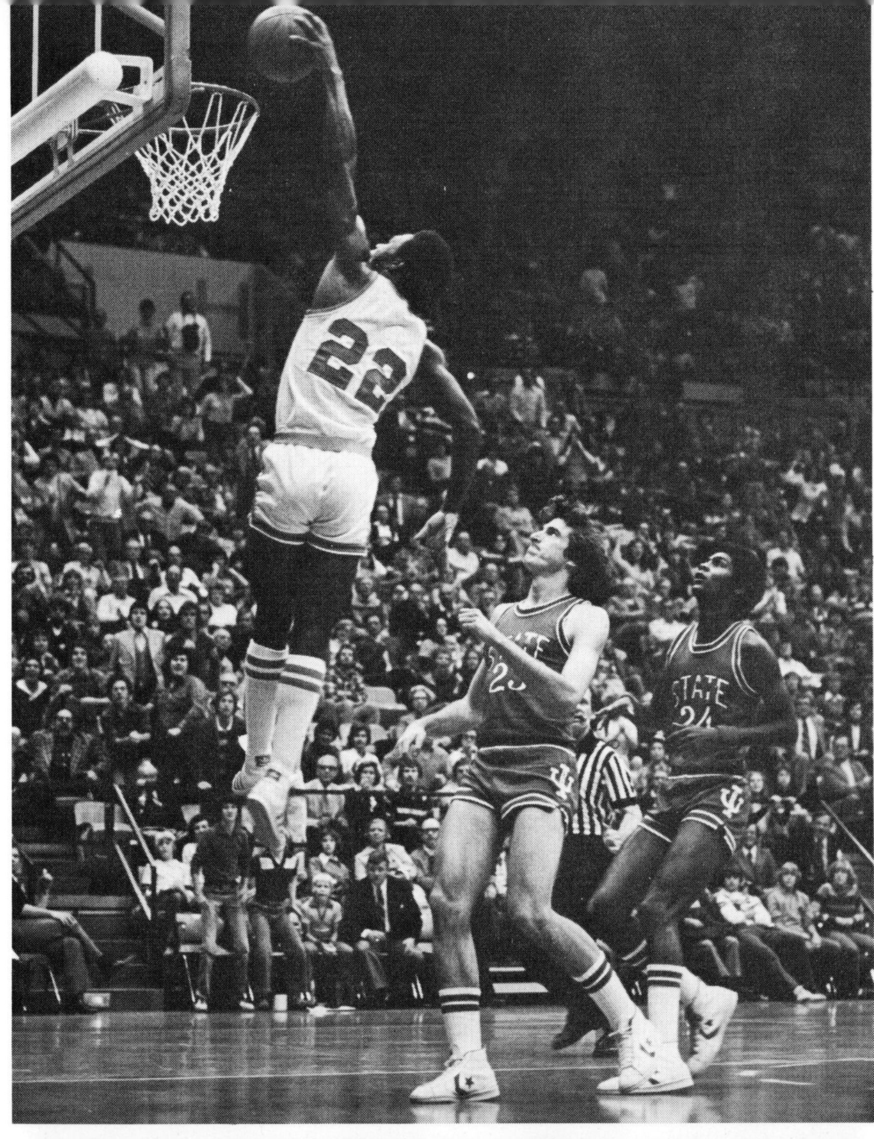

Soaring for a slam dunk here is Indiana State's Carl Nicks (22). The high-flying guard was the sixth-highest scorer in the 1979 tourney with 82 points, an average of 16.4.

A meeting of the superstars, both numbered 33. Michigan State's Earvin "Magic" Johnson, with the ball, is confronted by Indiana State's Larry Bird in the 1979 championship game. Bird averaged 27.2 points in his five games, Johnson 21.8, but Magic outscored him in the title tilt 24 points to 19.

breaking loss, while Bill Hodges started to get his top-ranked Sycamores hyped up for the national championship game against Michigan State.

The confrontation basketball fans everywhere had been awaiting—Bird versus Johnson—was now to be a reality. But in reality it would simply be a Bird-centered Indiana State against a Johnson/Kelser-cored Michigan State. Still it was the perfect matchup for the 1979 NCAA title. Undefeated Indiana State and soaring Michigan State were two teams that had unique abilities to bring even the most lethargic fan off his chair with a whirl of basketball brilliance.

The obvious strategy for Spartan coach Jud Heathcote was to stop Larry Bird. In the other corner the Sycamores' coach Bill Hodges' tactic had to be to disrupt the interplay between Magic Johnson and Greg Kelser and to contain both at the same time. Neither team had a very easy task before them. But Michigan State, a team that rose from a relatively unimpressive regular season to full blossom in the postseason, was up to the chore. The Spartans alternately stymied and frustrated the great Larry Bird, forcing him into his poorest performance of the tourney. The same Bird who had scored 35 points and collected 16 rebounds against Arkansas in the semifinals, who had averaged 29.25 points and 13.5 rebounds in his four tournament games, was held to a mere 19 points (making only seven of 21 shots from the floor). In addition, throughout the game he maneuvered awkwardly and threw passes away; he simply did not have it that night at Salt Lake City. As a result, Indiana State was in trouble for the entire game. The Spartans took the lead with fewer than five minutes elapsed in the first period and never gave it up. They moved smartly to a 37–28 halftime lead, and after that the Sycamores never came within six points of them. The final score was Michigan State 75, Indiana State 64. The surprisingly lopsided game closed out Indiana State's victory streak at 33 and give Michigan State its first national basketball championship ever.

If the game was to be viewed as the consummate confrontation between Magic Johnson and Larry Bird, as so many sportswriters had dubbed it, Johnson would have to be considered the victor. He scored 24 points for the Spartans, the most by any player that night, and was his usual dazzling self as floor commander. Greg Kelser had 19 points, and guard Terry Donnelly added another 15 for Michigan State.

The Outstanding Player honors for 1979 went to Magic Johnson, but a lot of observers felt they should have been shared equally with tandem star Greg Kelser. The most points scored in the tourney, however, came from the gifted hands of Tony Price of Pennsylvania, who scored 142 in six games. Close behind was Larry Bird with 136, which he chalked up in only five games. The best scoring average belonged to San Francisco's Bill Cartwright, at 29 points, but he participated in only two games, while Larry Bird was next with 27.2 points over five games. Bird also grabbed the most rebounds in the tourney, 67, far ahead of runners-up Greg Kelser and Tony Price, who claimed 53 each. The most points scored in a single game were the 37 David Greenwood rang up for UCLA in its loss to DePaul in the West regional final.

Awards, 1979

Outstanding Player
Earvin Johnson (Michigan State)

All-Tournament Team
Earvin Johnson (Michigan State)
Larry Bird (Indiana State)
Greg Kelser (Michigan State)
Mark Aguirre (DePaul)
Gary Garland (DePaul)

Only two of the 1979 Final Four teams would be invited back to the 1980 NCAA championship tournament, DePaul and Pennsylvania, and they would not be a factor that year at all. Also gone would be such memorable college basketball names as Magic Johnson, Larry Bird, Greg Kelser, Sidney Moncrief, David Greenwood, Bill Cartwright, and Tony Price. But there would be a bevy of new names and new talents and just as much excitement.

12
Louisville and the Doctor of Dunk

When the 1980 Final Four met at Market Square Arena in Indianapolis to vie for that year's NCAA basketball crown there were more than a few looks of astonishment on the faces of those who came to report the proceedings. Only one team seemed to have any business being there at all: Louisville, which had ended the regular season with a record of 28 and three and was ranked number two in both wire service polls.

The invitations extended to the other Final Four teams, just to the tournament itself, raised more than a few eyebrows. UCLA, sporting its worst regular-season record in 15 years, 17 and nine, had ended up in fourth place in the Pac-10 Conference. Then there was Iowa, which had lost eight games and was stuck in a tie for fourth place in the Big Ten. And filling out the quartet was Purdue, which had come out on the short end of final scores nine times, though it ended the season one place higher than Iowa in the Big Ten standings. The Final Four had registered 29 regular season losses among them, 26 of them credited to UCLA, Iowa, and Purdue, the total being the second highest in the tourney's history (in 1954 Bradley, LaSalle, Penn State, and Southern Cal counted 33 losses).

Iowa, perhaps the biggest surprise of all, arrived to represent the East, amazingly making it despite the fact that its one certified superstar, guard Ronnie Lester, was just coming back from knee surgery and had been severely hampered throughout the earlier regional rounds. But somehow Iowa had risen

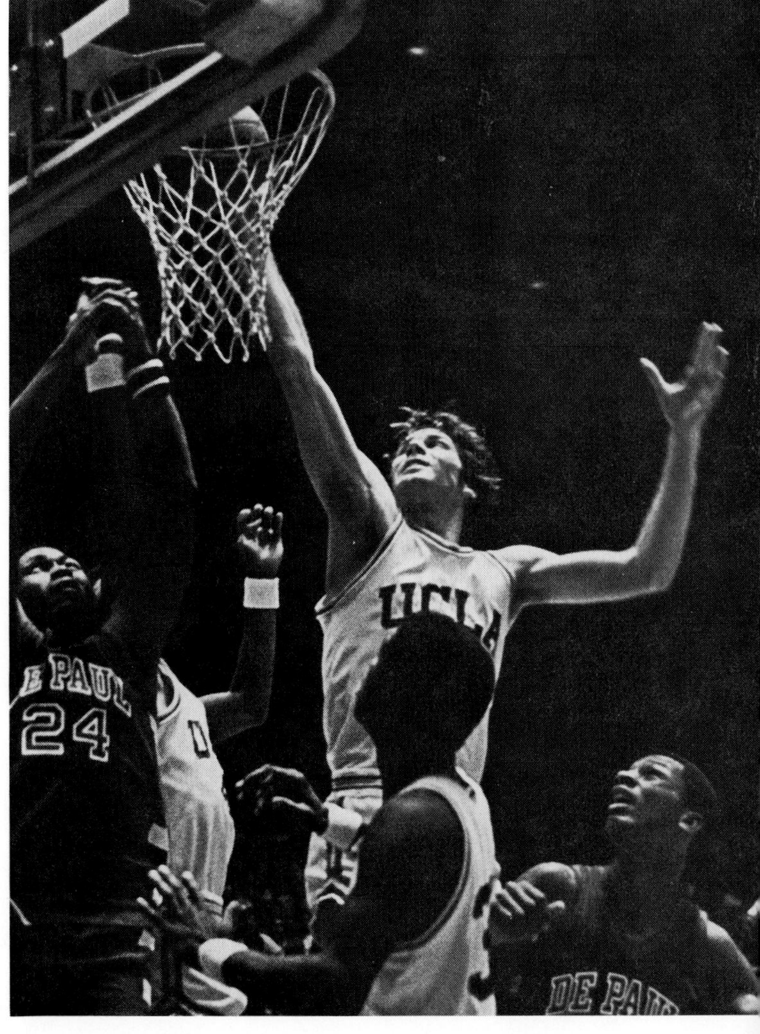

UCLA's Kiki Vandeweghe drops in two here against DePaul. The Bruins lost this regular-season game but came back in the 1980 tournament to stun favored DePaul 77–71 in the second round of the West regional. For DePaul number 24 is Mark Aguirre; at the lower right is Terry Cummings.

above adversity in a division that boasted such nationally ranked teams as Syracuse, Georgetown, and Maryland.

Lute Olsen, in his sixth year as head coach of the Iowa Hawkeyes, had obviously inspired his cagers because they clearly played far better during the tourney than they had in the regular season. Their first-round opponent was Virginia Commonwealth, a team they beat soundly, 86–72. Picking up the scoring slack for the hobbled Ronnie Lester was fellow guard Kenny Arnold, who banked a game-high 23 points. Lester, forward Kevin Boyle, and center Steve Waite added 17 apiece.

The road would become rougher in the second round. There Iowa encountered North Carolina State, representing the always dynamic Atlantic Coast Conference. The Wolfpack from Raleigh gave Iowa a rugged time in the first half and had the Hawkeyes down by three. But in the second period it was all Iowa, much the result of its full-court press, which caused a number of turnovers, and the play of reserve Vince Brookins, who came off the bench to score 17 points for the Hawkeyes. Along with 18 from Kenny Arnold and another 17-point performance by Ronnie Lester, the Hawkeyes finished on the high end of a 77–64 final score.

Besides the Hawkeyes, Syracuse, Georgetown, and Maryland advanced to the regional semifinals in Philadelphia. The Orangemen of Syracuse were a distinct favorite to remove the Hawkeyes from the tourney in the first game of the regionals. But that was not destined to be, despite a 25-point, 16-rebound performance from Syracuse center Louis Orr. To the dismay of most, Iowa surged to a seven-point first-half lead, then battled desperately through the second period and eventually prevailed 88–77. Again, many of the heroics were provided by substitute Vince Brookins, who contributed the most Hawkeye points, 21, including a clutch 11 of 12 from the free-throw line. Three of those charity tosses enabled the Hawkeyes to regain the lead that they lost midway through the second half. Also helping the Hawkeye cause was Kevin Boyle with 18 points and Steve Krafcisin, who added 14.

Georgetown, which could claim the largest coach in the college game, John Thompson at

Much of Iowa's hopes in the 1980 tourney were focused on All-American Ronnie Lester (12), leaping here for an uncontested two points. Injuries, however, curtailed Lester's play, and Iowa had to settle for third place that year. Lester averaged 12.2 points in the tournament.

6′10″ and 300 pounds, extended its winning streak to 15 games when it defeated Maryland in the other regional semifinal at Philadelphia. The Hoyas, from Washington, D.C., had the services of one of the nation's better guards, Eric "Sleepy" Floyd. Earlier they had eliminated Iona, a fine team which had decimated Louisville by 17 points during the regular season. Now Georgetown was expected to

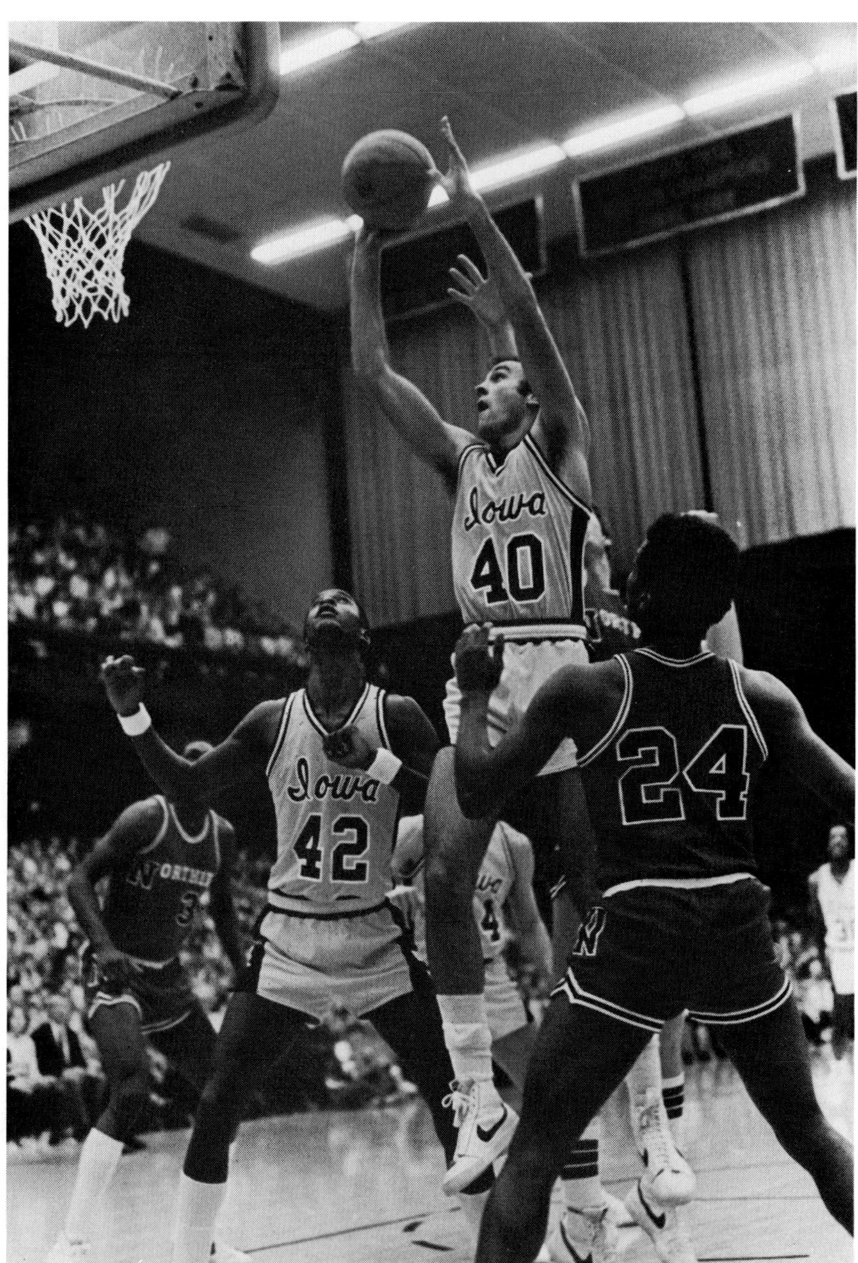

Kevin Boyle (40) was one of Iowa's steadiest performers in 1980, shown here dropping in an easy two. Boyle averaged 10.8 points in Iowa's six games and collected a total of 37 rebounds.

do the same to Iowa in the East final. And it certainly looked like that would be the case. Georgetown controlled the first half and led by 10 at that period's buzzer. But once again Lute Olsen ignited his Hawkeyes during the intermission, and a seemingly different team took the floor. Suddenly the full-court press was working, Hawkeye shots were raining through the nets, and the momentum of the game was noticeably shifted. In the waning minutes of the game Iowa took the lead, but then Georgetown tied it with just more than two minutes remaining. Lute Olsen told his Iowans to hold the ball for a last shot, and for a long two minutes they succeeded in doing just that. As the seconds wore down, center Steve Waite got himself open and Kevin Boyle fed him the ball. Waite was fouled as he made the lay-up and then converted the free throw for a three-point lead. The Hawkeyes then let the Hoyas drop in an uncontested last basket.

With an 81–80 win Iowa left the floor to contemplate the joys of joining the Final Four, the first time that school had so succeeded since 1956. The game's high scorer had been Sleepy Floyd, who had 31 for the Hoyas.

In the Iowa stats it was again Vince Brookins who stood out. He had 22 points, while Steve Waite contributed 15 and Kevin Boyle 14. Overall, Iowa had shot 61 percent that night (71 percent in the second half) and made 19 of 20 free throws.

Iowa would have to face the winner of the Midwest regional in the semifinals, and that would be no less than Denny Crum's Louisville Cardinals. Crum was no foreigner to the Final Four; he had brought two other Louisville teams there, in 1972 and 1975, but both times they had fallen in semifinal games to his alma mater and former boss, UCLA and John Wooden respectively.

In 1980 Louisville was one of the pretourney favorites. The chief reason was an incredibly high-flying guard, known as the "Doctor of Dunk," 6′4″ Darrell Griffith. A senior, he was a consensus All-American and the nucleus around which the Cardinal team was built. Although his high scoring and gravity-defying theatrics often overshadowed the contributions of his teammates, they too were a fine blend of top-notch basketball players. The front line of Derek Smith, Rodney McCray, and Wiley Brown were not tall by 1980 standards, but they were strong and competed well on the boards. There was also a fine tandem guard in Jerry Eaves and a hustling sixth man named Roger Burkman, whose method of play was described nicely by the press as "frantic" and not so nicely as "maniacal," and who in action often seemed more like a free safety than a basketball player.

Louisville's first test in the 1980 tourney came in the second round against Kansas State, and the Cardinals found more trouble there than they had anticipated. The Wildcats took them all the way down to the final buzzer of an overtime period before Louisville reserve Tony Branch made his only basket of the night, a long jumper that gave the Kentuckians a breathtaking 71–69 win. The Doctor of Dunk had been held to 18 points by the Kansas State defense, but Derek Smith filled in with 20 that game.

The Midwest regional semifinals were held in the Summit at Houston, where Louisville encountered a harshly partisan Texas crown and the Texas A & M Aggies from nearby

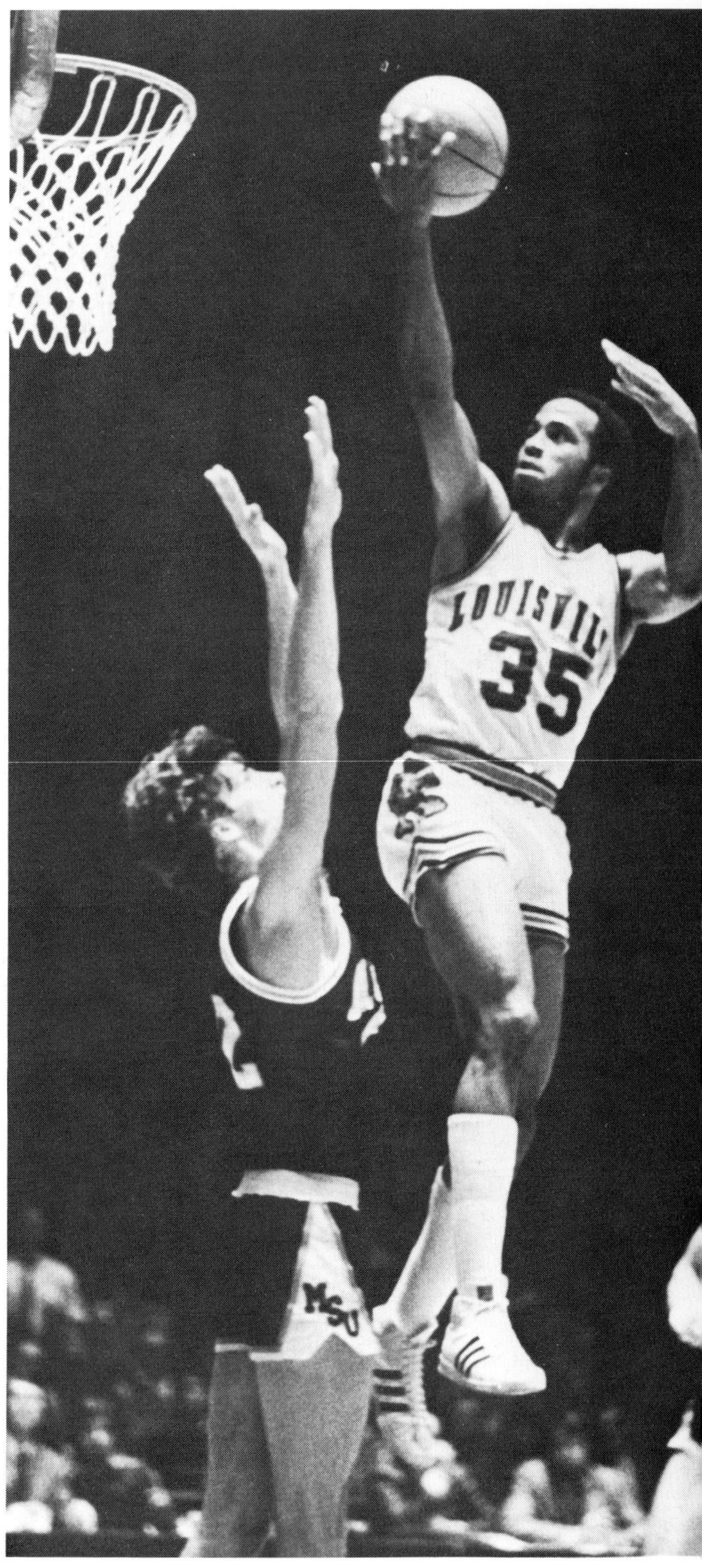

The "Doctor of Dunk," Louisville's sensational Darrell Griffith (35) goes up for a graceful two points here. A dazzling leaper, Griffith led the Cardinals to the 1980 championship, averaging 23.2 points a game and earning the Outstanding Player award. His best single-game performance: 34 points in the semifinal win over Iowa.

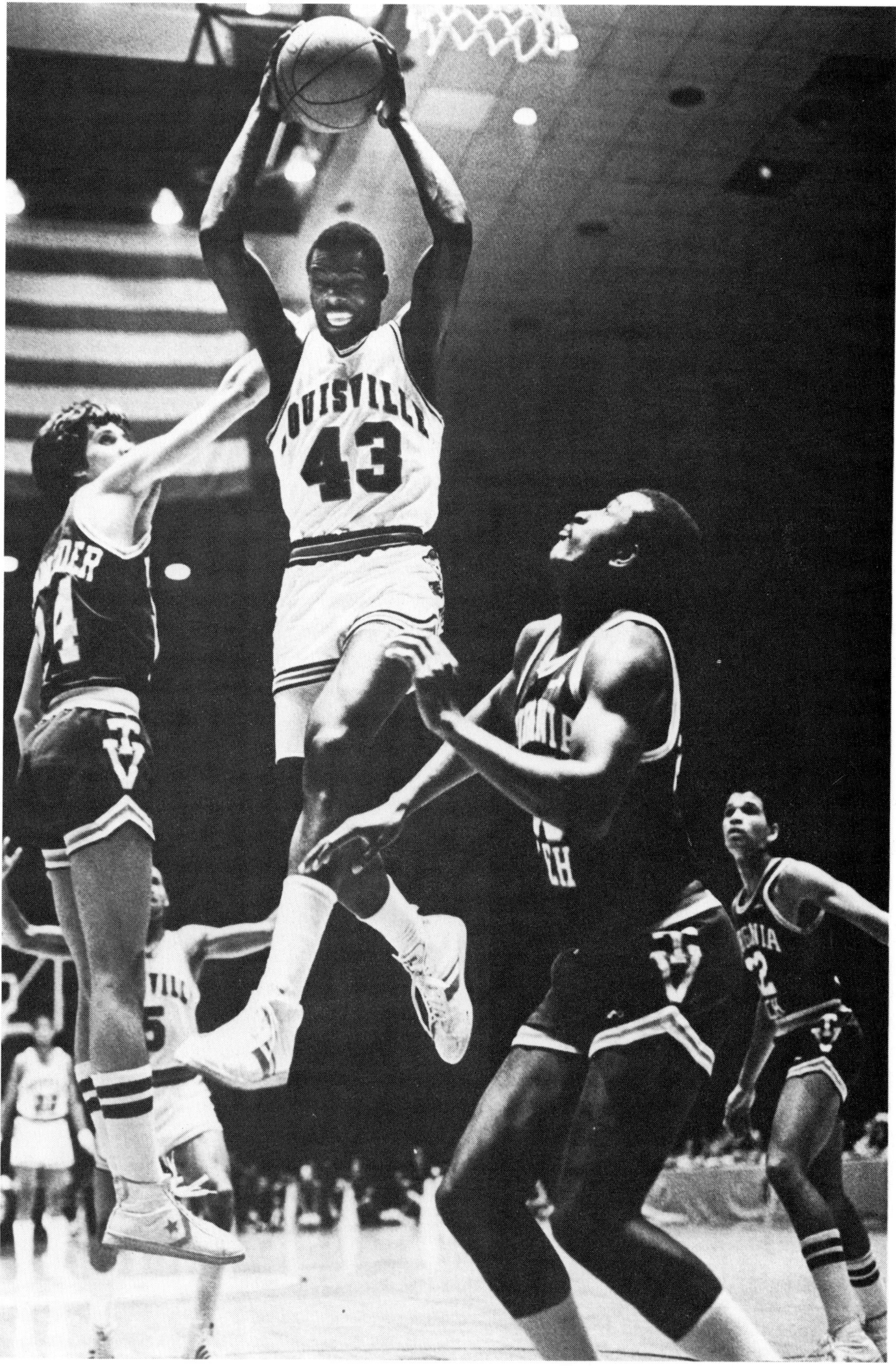

Forward Derek Smith (43) was one of Louisville's most consistent threats on both offense and defense in 1980. He averaged 12.2 points in the Cardinals' five tourney games that year.

College Station. To get there the Aggies had beaten a favored Bradley team by a basket, then astounded a heavily favored North Carolina in double overtime in the second round. In that game Texas A & M set an NCAA tournament record that likely will never be matched when it scored an incredible 25 points in the second overtime period. But the Aggies ran out of miracles when they came up against Darrell Griffith and his fellow Cardinals. The game went into overtime, but there were no 25-point flurries for the Texans that day at the Summit. Instead, the Cardinals hounded them mercilessly in the extra period, allowing the Aggies a mere two points while they posted 13 themselves. The final was 66–55, but the Aggies, like Kansas State before them, had thrown a very real scare into Denny Crum and his Cardinals during the game.

In the other Midwest regional semifinal a highly regarded Louisiana State battled back to beat Missouri and would face Louisville for the regional title. The Fighting Tigers from Baton Rouge were led by a leaper almost in Darrell Griffith's league named DeWayne "Astronaut" Scales. They also had proven scorers in Jordy Hultberg, Willie Sims, and Rudy Macklin. LSU was in fact seeded higher in the region than Louisville and had beaten Alcorn State in its first tourney game 98–88, in which Macklin tallied 31 points and Sims 30. LSU's explosive scoring fizzled somewhat in the Missouri game, totaling only 68 points; in fact, the Tigers trailed at the half, then came back to win by five. DeWayne Scales was high for the Tigers with 17.

LSU's scoring punch also deserted the team when they took the floor against Louisville. They could muster only 29 points in the first period, then were outscored 55–37 in the second half. The rout ended with Louisville winning it 86–66. The second half had been sheer disaster for LSU; not only were they unable to slow down suddenly white-hot Louisville but they committed a barrelful of fouls and turnovers on their own. LSU shot only 42.6 percent from the floor, converted only eight of 13 free throws, and were outrebounded 42–35 that night. The Cardinals, on the other hand, shot 57.7 percent and cashed in on 26 of 39 free throws. LSU was charged with 31 personal fouls to Louisville's 17. Darrell Griffith was the Cardinal high-point man with 17, though he played only 18 minutes because he had gotten into foul trouble early. Wiley Brown had another 16 for the Cardinals. So Denny Crum would take his third Louisville team to the Final Four. He could rest somewhat securely in the knowledge that his old boss John Wooden was retired and would not be there to haunt him. And even if UCLA made it to the Final Four in 1980, the Bruins could not dash Crum's hopes in the semifinals anyway because the winner of the Mideast, Louisville, was slated to face the champ of the East, which happened to be Iowa.

UCLA could destroy Denny Crum's dream of a championship in the finals, however, because the Bruins, despite their disappointing play in the regular season, flared in the West regionals and surprised everyone by earning passage to the Final Four for the 14th time in 19 years. The Bruins were now coached by Larry Brown, coming to the Los Angeles campus after coaching the pro team in Denver for five years. Brown was the third head coach in the five years since John Wooden shelved his clipboard and whistle. UCLA had only one starter returning from the previous year's Pac-10 champions, the multi-talented forward Kiki Vandeweghe. James Wilkes now filled the other forward slot, and Mike "Slew" Sanders was at center, while freshmen Rod Foster and Michael Holton had won the backcourt duties. Because of their uninspiring record, UCLA had to play in the first round, but they had little trouble there, coasting by Old Dominion 87–74 in a game in which Vandeweghe scored 34 points and Sanders bagged 18 rebounds.

The win gave the Bruins the right to meet the nation's number-one-ranked team, DePaul. Ray Meyer's Blue Demons had won 26 of their 27 regular-season games and had a consensus All-American in their 6′7″ cherubic forward Mark Aguirre, a superstar freshman in 6′9″ Terry Cummings, a much improved center in 6′9″ James Mitchem, and two fine guards, Clyde Bradshaw and Skip Dillard. They were a substantial favorite to hand UCLA its 10th loss of the season and send the Bruins back to the City of Angels. But for all their talent, the Blue Demons went absolutely stale when they met the Bruins, and they turned in their worst game of that year. Most disappointing was All-American Aguirre, who never really got going, making only eight of 18 from the floor and three of six from the free-throw line. UCLA had a two-point lead at the half and hung on through the second period, though DePaul managed to tie it at 67 points, but then the Bruins pulled steadily away to win 77–71. It had been a collective effort on UCLA's part. Five players scored in double figures: Rod Foster, 18; Mike Sanders, 15; Kiki Vandeweghe, 13; and Cliff Pruitt and James Wilkes, 10 each. Sanders was the prime force on the boards, grabbing 12 rebounds, and Wilkes was the defensive juggernaut who bottled up Aguirre. The only respectable performance by a Blue Demon was turned in by freshman Terry Cummings, who scored 23 points and got eight rebounds. A disappointed Ray Meyer, who thought that in his 38th year guiding DePaul he might finally win the gilded cup, went back to Chicago empty-handed while an exhilarated Larry Brown escorted his Bruins to Tucson for the West regional semifinals.

Guard Clyde Bradshaw was a starter on three DePaul tournament-bound teams (1979–81). A skilled playmaker, he witnessed the victimization of the Blue Demons in their first tourney games in '80 and '81, both stunning upsets.

Another midwestern team awaited UCLA there, this one Ohio State, one of the four Big Ten teams to be invited to the 1980 NCAA tourney. The Buckeyes were spearheaded by guard Kelvin Ransey, a high scorer and fine ball handler. They also had proven scorers in center Herb Williams and forward Clark Kellogg. Under coach Eldon Miller the Buckeyes had demolished highly rated Arizona State earlier in the tourney and now were considered a definite favorite over UCLA.

When the game was over, on paper it would appear that Ohio State had beaten UCLA. The buckeyes outshot the Bruins 54.4 percent to 42.3 percent from the floor. Kelvin Ransey was far and away the hot hand with 29 points, and Herb Williams snatched the most rebounds with 10. But Ohio State lost the game for two reasons: the Buckeyes fouled too much (27 personals to UCLA's 14), and the Bruins were prolific from the line, making 28 of 35 that night, while the Buckeyes could count only six of 11 free throws. Those were the two elements that enabled UCLA to advance in the West; the final score, 72–68. Aiding the Bruins' cause that night were Rod Foster and Mike Saunders, who both scored 19 points.

The Bruins were not so much the underdogs when they queued up against Clemson, because the Tigers from South Carolina were also a fourth-place finisher in their conference, the ACC. And UCLA was on a tear, getting better with each game, and that was no more evident than in the West regional title game. The Bruins dominated Clemson from the very start, worked up to a 46–35 halftime lead, then held on to win it 85–74. The Bruins got 22 points apiece from Kiki Vandeweghe and Mike Sanders and another 12 from Rod Foster. And UCLA was on its way to yet another Final Four convention.

The Big Ten fared better in the Mideast regional—where they had two entries, Indiana and Purdue—than they had in the West. But also in the Mideast were three recognized powers to contend with: Kentucky, Duke, and Pennsylvania. Purdue, because of its undistinguished record during the regular season, seemed the least likely team to advance, and many felt they would not get by their first-round encounter with LaSalle. But the Boilermakers were coached by Lee Rose, a court strategist who had guided North Carolina–Charlotte to the Final Four in 1977 and did have a most imposing force in 7′1″ All-American center Joe Barry Carroll. Just how great a force he was became clear in Purdue's first game. Amid a forest of tall, strong LaSalle frontcourters, Carroll managed 33 points and 13 rebounds, both game highs. Another steady star for the Boilermakers was forward Keith Edmonson, who contributed 18 points in the LaSalle game, while guard Drake Morris posted 21. Purdue squelched LaSalle 90–82. The massive Carroll was even more destructive when Purdue took on St. John's in the second round. This time he ended the night with 36 points and 12 rebounds. With 21 from Edmonson and 19 from Morris, Purdue had an easy time of it, 87–72, and a ticket to the regional semifinals at Lexington, Kentucky.

The quest for the Mideast title for 1980 produced two distinct surprises. First, Kentucky, which had been that division's favorite from the start, was hosting erratic Duke on its own home court, an ostensible advantage. The Wildcats had an impressive roster, headlined by 7′1″ center Sam Bowie, ace playmaker Kyle Macy, veteran guard Jay Shidler, and two topdrawer forwards in Fred Cowan and LaVon Williams. But with everything that Joe B. Hall's Wildcats had going for them, they still came up short. Duke, which had lost eight times during the regular season and had tied for lowly fifth place in the ACC, astounded them. The Blue Devils still had 6′11″ center Mike Gminski and ace forward Gene Banks as well as veterans Kenny Dennard and Vince Taylor. In the first half it was a lopsided 37–23 in favor of the Blue Devils, who then held off a desperate Wildcat rally and gained a 55–54 win. Big Mike Gminski scored 17 for triumphant Duke and Fred Cowan 26 for stunned Kentucky.

Purdue was also considered an underdog to Bobby Knight's Indiana Hoosiers. During conference play earlier in the year the two intrastate rivals had each won a game, but

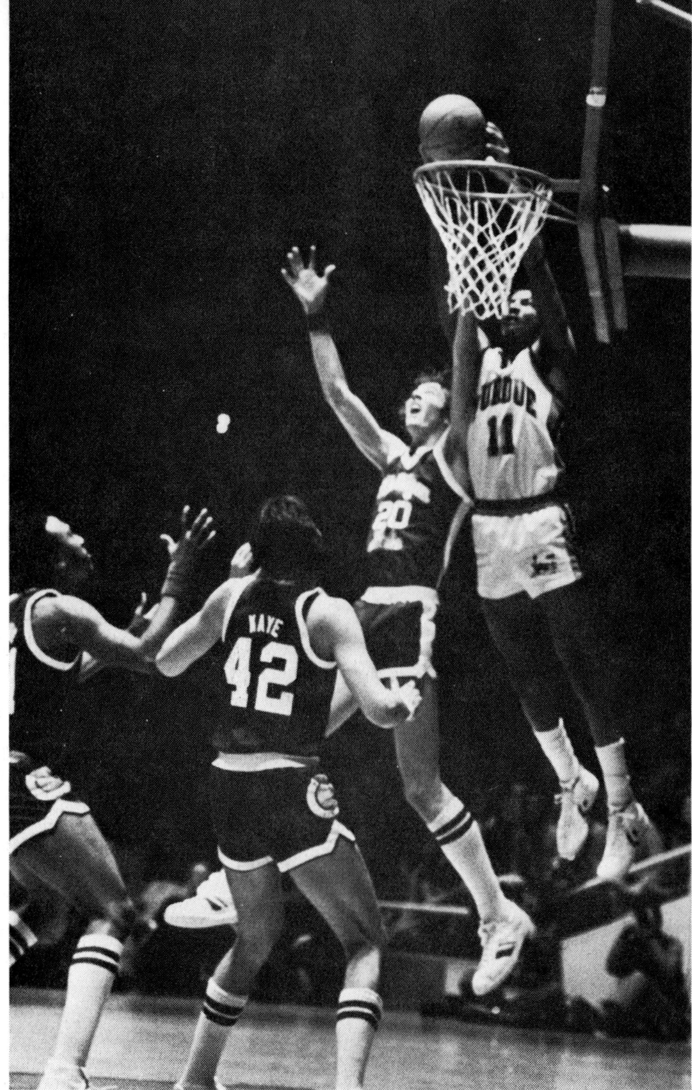

Keith Edmonson (11) is about to complete part two of the Alley-Oop here. A great leaper, Edmonson also scored 111 points for Purdue in the 1980 tourney, fourth best that year.

Driving Drake Morris (33) was an important cog in Purdue's 1980 third-place squad. Morris scored 89 points in the Boilermakers' six games, the sixth best in the tournament.

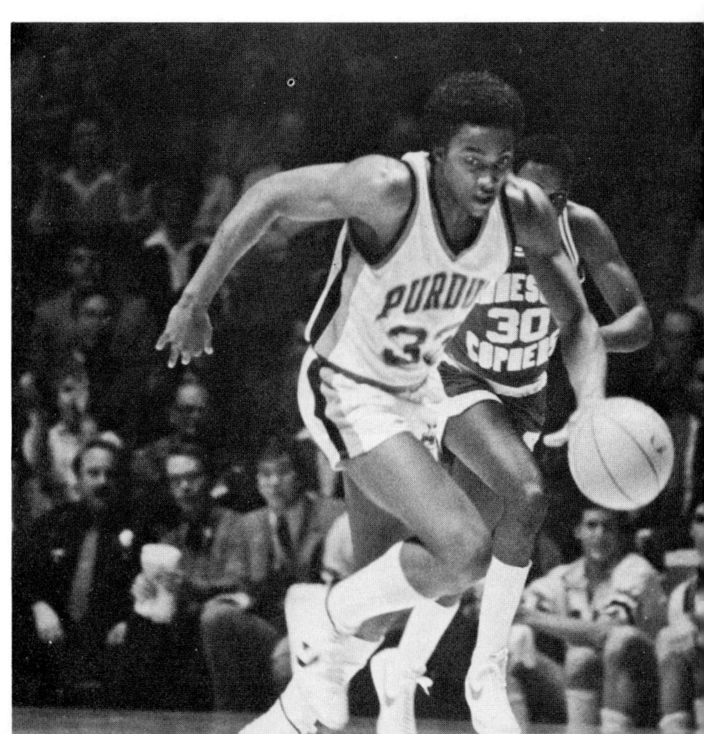

Indiana had ended up with a better record and a higher Big Ten standing. They had a brilliant freshman guard in Isiah Thomas and strong players in Mike Woodson, Ray Tolbert, and Butch Carter. Bobby Knight knew he had to stop Purdue's Joe Barry Carroll, that was his first and foremost objective. He succeeded, holding the big center to a mere 11 points. The problem was that in stifling Carroll he could not subdue the rest of Lee Rose's Purdue cagers, who rallied magnificently to the cause. Keith Edmonson and Drake Morris both had 20 points, and Mike Scearce came off the bench to drop in nine of 11 free throws and a basket. Purdue won it 76–69. And the two underdogs, the Duke Blue Devils and the Purdue Boilermakers, with 17 regular season losses between them, pared off to decide the Mideast title for 1980.

It was billed as a battle of the centers, Joe Barry Carroll versus Mike Gminski, though there were other fine players in attendance from both squads. But the game turned out to be more of a fiasco than a battle. If either team had played as poorly in their previous regional encounters, neither would have reached the final. Both Duke and Purdue shot identically from the floor, 23 of 52 field goals, a less than impressive 44.2 percent, and each team turned the ball over to the other with regularity. Purdue won it on the strength of its free-throw shooting, 22 of 29, giving the Boilermakers an eight-point advantage in that aspect of the game. As far as the combat between the centers went, Joe Barry Carroll came out on top, scoring 26 points to Mike Gminski's 17, but the Duke pivot out rebounded Carroll nine to six. Lee Rose was not at all pleased with his team's performance but still had to be delighted with the outcome.

The four regional champs would take to the neutral floorboards of Market Square Arena in Indianapolis paired thusly: East would take on Midwest first, Mideast against West in the second game. In the opener, it was Iowa versus Louisville (or, as some suggested, Ronnie Lester versus Darrell Griffith). The Cardinals were a solid favorite, not only to beat Iowa but to win the tourney as well. Lute Olsen hoped his Hawkeyes could continue their Cinderella act in the tourney and redeem with ultimate honor their otherwise frustrating season. But it was not to be a fairy tale finish for the Buckeyes, which was apparent from the very beginning.

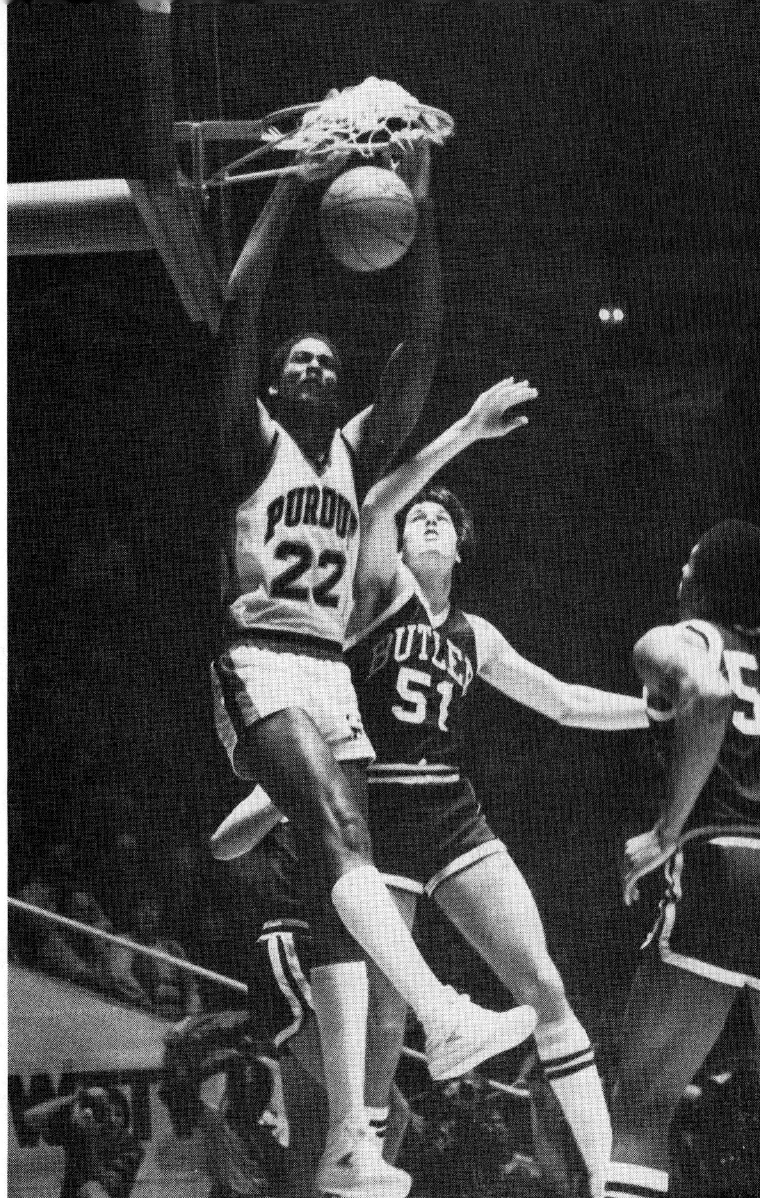

Purdue's 7'1" center, Joe Barry Carroll (22), slam-dunks one, something he made a habit of doing during the 1980 tournament. Carroll scored the most points that tourney, 158, and logged the most field goals, 63.

Louisville controlled the early game, then gained a guarantee of the outcome a short while later when Ronnie Lester, after colliding with Roger Burkman, crumpled to the floor, reinjuring his knee. He left the game for good. At the half the Cardinals led by five, but the margin did not really denote the domination that the Doctor of Dunk and his teammates were exerting over their foes from Iowa. The Hawkeyes simply did not have the touch that night. Normally steady-scoring Kevin Boyle did not make a single one of the eight field goals he attempted in that game, and Vince Brookins, who had had such a hot hand in earlier tourney games, could sink only six of 18 shots. Ken Arnold was the only Hawkeye to have a respectable night, scoring 20 points. Without Lester the Buckeyes had little hope of controlling Darrell Griffith. From jumpers to slamdunks, he stung the nets, compiling 34 points (14 of 21 from the floor and six of eight from the line). Rodney McCray added 14 and Derek Smith 13 for the Cardinals in their 80–72 triumph.

The Big Ten fared just as badly in the next semifinal contest, though Purdue was not the underdog that Iowa had been. Many felt that the UCLA Bruins could not stop Boilermaker center Joe Barry Carroll. One notable exception to that way of thinking, however, was UCLA coach Larry Brown. He had faith in his shorter but still very strong frontcourt. He did not feel they would be outmuscled or outfought underneath. Among Mike Sanders, Kiki Vandeweghe, and James Wilkes, alternately harassing Carroll and working the boards with exceptional determination, Brown felt he could turn Lee Rose's dream of a Purdue championship into a nightmare. And he was right; the Bruin frontcourt did it. They held Joe Barry Carroll to 17 points and eight rebounds, and the result was that they led decisively in the first half, then staved off Purdue's rally in the second half (the Boilermakers came as close as a point) and finally retired with a 67–62 victory. The Bruins had played a meticulous game, shooting 50 percent from the floor and sinking 21 of 25 free throws. Kiki Vandeweghe was one of the most vital forces, with 24 points and spirited defensive play. Mike Sanders was the only other Bruin in double digits with 12. So Larry Brown, in his rookie head-coaching season, was taking UCLA to the NCAA championship game where the school had been so at home during the preceding decade and a half.

Denny Crum obviously had to be experiencing a strange set of feelings going into the championship game. For one, he had to remember what UCLA had done to his Louisville Cardinals in their two previous trips to the Final Four. This game could prove to be a third disaster or an opportunity for sweet re-

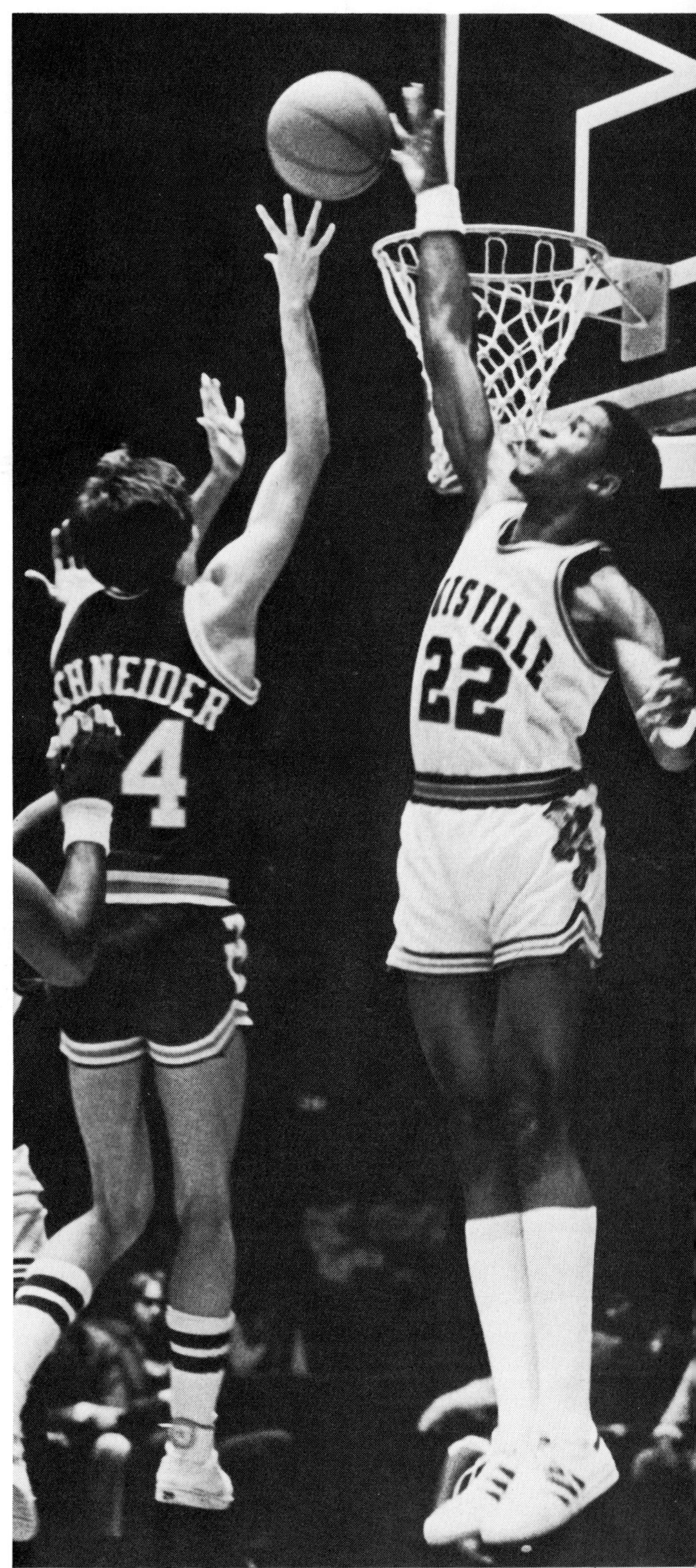

Rodney McCray (22) migrated between forward and center for the 1980 champions from Louisville. Here he demonstrates some of his defensive skills. McCray dominated the boards in the Cardinals' championship win over UCLA.

venge. And there was some consolation in knowing that his team was a strong favorite, though at the same time he knew only too well how often that meant so little in the heat and drama of national championship competition.

Once the game began it appeared as if all Crum's worst fears were to become reality. The UCLA jinx came crashing down on the Cardinals, and he watched with fevered frustration as the Doctor of Dunk and the other Louisville cagers made mistakes, missed shots, and generally played as if John Wooden sat somewhere sticking needles into little Louisville voodoo dolls. At the half the Cardinals were on the depressing side of a 28–26 score.

The second half was even more disheartening, as the Bruins maintained control and pulled to a five-point lead with just fewer than 6½ minutes left in the game. The Bruins had also been able to curtail the usually uncontrollable Darrell Griffith, the cornerstone of Denny Crum's NCAA hopes and aspirations. Crum harangued his Cardinals in the time-out huddle and from courtside. Finally it took effect and the Cardinals got their on-court act together. With a brilliant surge in the last few minutes of the game they caught UCLA, then moved ahead and stayed there. The final was 59–54, and Louisville had moved out from under the blue-and-gold cloud that had so shadowed its previous NCAA fortunes.

Although he was off his game in the first half and part of the second, Darrell Griffith was the determining factor in the final analysis. He was the only Cardinal in double figures with 23 points. His efforts and those of his teammates were summed up best by Curry Kirkpatrick in *Sports Illustrated:*

Louisville head coach Denny Crum expresses a little displeasure during part of the proceedings of the 1980 tourney. But just about everything else went his way that year as his Cardinals posted a record of 33–3 and took the national championship.

> Oh, there were other heroes for the Cardinals. Rodney McCray, who had a game-high 11 rebounds; Wiley Brown, who left his famous artificial thumb on the breakfast table and had to have it retrieved from a hotel dumpster; Roger Burkman, whose lip was sliced open by a team manager's clipboard late in the game; and Jerry Eaves, the overlooked second guard who played with two good thumbs, two good lips, and consummate poise. Brown and Burkman took down the key late rebounds, and Eaves made two clutch baskets to tie the game at 54-all with 2:54 remaining. But it was Griffith who came through when all the freshmen and sophomores on both sides weren't up to the task. "Just his presence out there was the big fac-

tor," said UCLA coach Larry Brown. "We were trying to guard the greatest player in the country."

When all the stats for the 1980 NCAA tourney were posted, five players had scored more than 100 points: Darrell Griffith did it in five games (116 points); the others in six games—Joe Barry Carroll (158), Kiki Vandeweghe (119), Keith Edmonson (111), and Kenny Arnold (104). The highest-scoring average of the tourney was 27 points, logged by Ohio State's Kelvin Ransey, but Joe Barry Carroll was only a fraction behind with 26.3 for his six games. Mike Sanders of UCLA was the top rebounder with 60, and Carroll again was close behind with one less. Kiki Vandeweghe of UCLA set a tournament record for the most free throws in a six-game series, sinking 39 of 46 (84.8 percent). And Joe Barry Carrol established a new standard for the most field goals in a six-game series, making 63 of 98 (64.3 percent).

Darrell Griffith, the Doctor of Dunk, with an average of 23.2 points a game, was voted the Outstanding Player, and Denny Crum had the distinct pleasure of bringing back to Louisville its first national championship trophy.

Awards, 1980

Outstanding Player
Darrell Griffith (Louisville)

All-Tournament Team
Darrell Griffith (Louisville)
Kiki Vandeweghe (UCLA)
Joe Barry Carroll (Purdue)
Rod Foster (UCLA)
Rodney McCray (Louisville)

13
Indiana and Isiah

After the second round of the 1981 NCAA playoffs, a number of surprised and chagrined teams trotted, tails between their legs, back to their respective campuses instead of moving on to the regional semifinals as had been expected of them. Among them was crown holder Louisville. Denny Crum's Cardinals fell in round two to the Arkansas Razorbacks, a team that had just barely gotten by little Mercer University from Macon, Georgia, in the first round.

True, Louisville was without the services of the Doctor of Dunk, Darrell Griffith, who had taken his fabled leaps to the NBA's Utah franchise. And true, Arkansas was by no means a stepping-stone. Still, the Cardinals were a favorite. And they had a one-point lead with only a solitary second left in the game. Then disaster came in the form of a fairy tale ending that couldn't have been written more fittingly by Hans Christian Anderson. It was an inbounds pass to Razorback U. S. Reed at half-court, who lofted a long, looping desperation shot that dropped through the net, a 49-footer just as the buzzer sounded. The final was Arkansas 74, Louisville 73, and an incredulous Denny Crum and his team were out of the tournament.

Perhaps more surprising was Georgetown's fate at the hands of little-known James Madison University. The cagers from Harrisonburg, Virginia, took on All-American candidate guard Eric "Sleepy" Floyd and the rest of the highly favored Hoyas and taught them a little lesson in steady basketball play. Their

Outstanding Player in 1981 was Indiana's masterful guard Isiah Thomas. A dazzling ball handler, Thomas was also the tourney's second-highest scorer, amassing 91 points and averaging 18.2

methodical, consistent game kept Georgetown at bay and resulted in a six-point win for the Madisonians, who, to everyone's amazement, simply outplayed Georgetown, especially outshooting the Hoyas from the floor 53.7 percent to 44 percent and from the free-throw line 17 of 20 to 11 of 19.

More shocking than the demise of Georgetown was the fate of Oregon State, the powerhouse in the West. Considered one of the two or three front-runners that year to win the tournament, the Beavers, under coach Ralph Miller, anticipated only minor annoyances at most from the Kansas State Wildcats. The Oregonians were big, strong, high scoring; had lost only one game during the regular season; and had won the Pac-10 two years in a row. They had one of the nation's strongest centers in 6′11″ Steve Johnson. But they did not have their usual poise when they met coach Jack Hartman's Kansas State team. Although the play was sloppy in the first half, Oregon State did manage a 26–19 lead at the intermission, one they enriched to 10 points in the second period. But with mistakes, untimely fouls, and cold shooting they saw it fritter away as the game wore down to its conclusion. With a little less than 3½ minutes left the score was tied at 48. The score was the same with two seconds left, when K-State star Rolando Blackman let fly a 16-foot jumper that swished through to snatch the game from Oregon State 50–48.

And most astounding of all was the event taking place in the Mideast. There, unseeded St. Joseph's of Philadelphia, coached by youthful Jimmy Lynam, a team that had come from behind to eke out a two-point victory over Creighton in the first round, was about to ring up the most surprising upset of that year's surprise-filled tourney. The odds of the unheralded Hawks getting beyond the second round were astronomical because they were slated to meet DePaul, a team ranked number one in the nation for most of the regular season and certainly one of the top tourney favorites. Ray Meyer had four of his starters back from a team that had gone 26 and two in 1979–80, including consensus All-American Mark Aguirre. In the regular season just past the Blue Demons had lost only one of their 28 games. The odds makers referred to DePaul as a "prohibitive favorite." But where some teams rise from obscurity in postseason play, others for some mysterious reason sink to ignobility.

Nowhere was that more evident than in the St. Joseph's–DePaul game of the 1981 NCAA tourney. Here, where Ray Meyer's nationally regarded Blue Demons were supposed to annihilate the Hawks of St. Joe's, the favored sons fizzled like a Fourth of July dud. DePaul, playing awfully, maintained the lead through most of the second half but not by much. Superstar Mark Aguirre was effectively shut down, and his play, at the most generous, was described as lackadaisical. With 13 seconds remaining in the game, however, the Blue Demons still had a one-point lead, and Skip Dillard, their best free-throw shooter, was at the line with a chance to ice the game if he made both ends of his one and one. But he missed the first, and St. Joseph's cleared the boards. They brought the ball down and got it to freshman Lonnie McFarlan in the corner, who in turn found forward John Smith open under the basket. He rifled the ball to him, and with three seconds left Smith laid in the winning basket: St. Joe's 49, DePaul 48. Just how bad DePaul was that night is only partially recorded in the box score, where Aguirre registered a paltry eight points and only one rebound and where the high-point man was Skip Dillard with 12 points. As summarized in *Sports Illustrated:* "The resolute Philadelphians out-shot, out-hustled, out-poised, and outbrained the conceited, haughty Blue Demons." And it was another disappointing end to an otherwise successful season for Ray Meyer.

While the unexpected was happening in certain quarters of the 1981 postseason convention, elsewhere other strong teams were advancing and taking their places in the columns of tourney favorites. In the Midwest Louisiana State, under the tutelage of Dale Brown, was the most feared. It had one of the college game's best forwards that year in Rudy Macklin, a high scorer and exceptional rebounder as well as a brutalizing, sometimes terrorizing center in Greg "Cookieman" Cook,

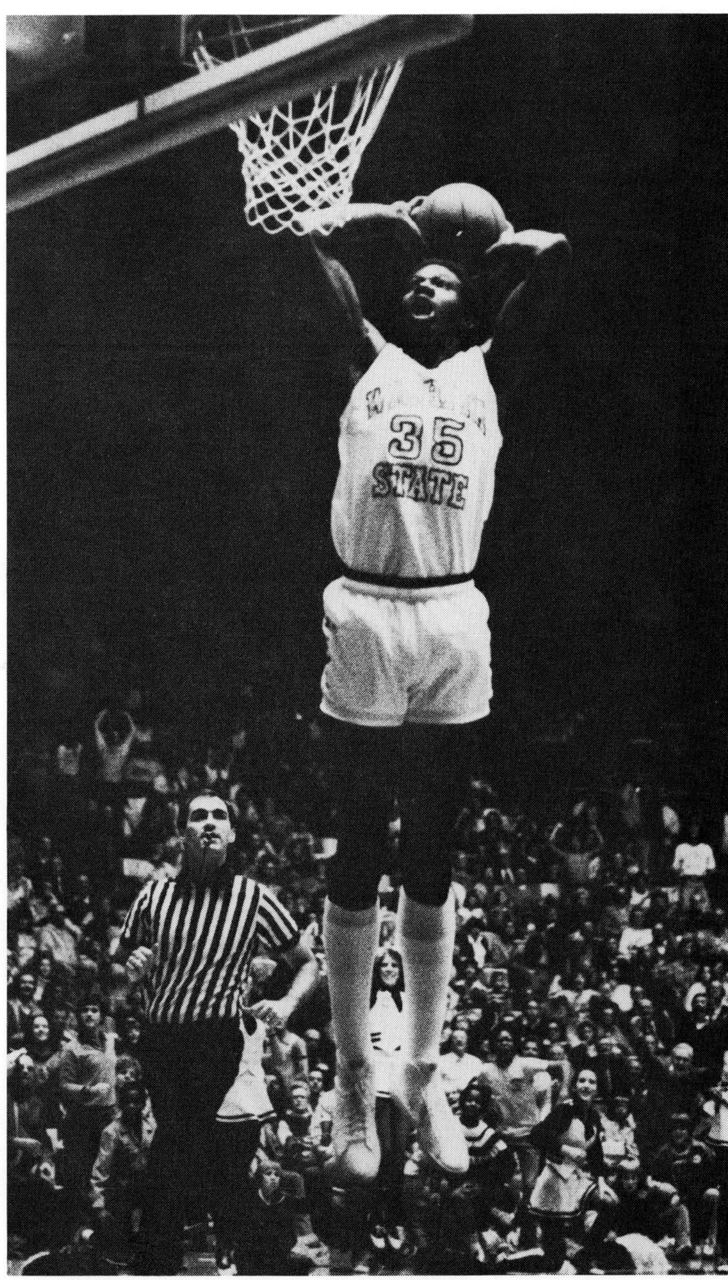

Wichita State's Antoine Carr, about to sear the net here, was the sixth-most-productive scorer in the 1981 tournament, with 76 points and an average of 19. He was the game's high scorer with 22 in the Midwest regional final, but Witchita State still could not get by LSU that night.

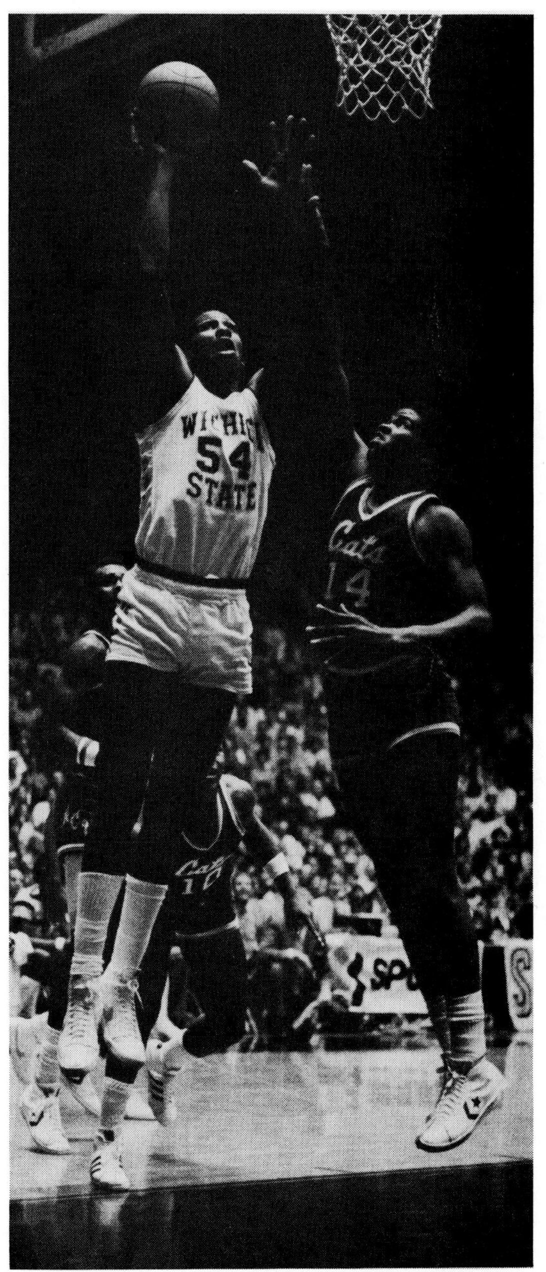

Cliff Levingston (54) of Wichita State, going up for two, collected the most rebounds in the 1981 tourney, 53 in four games. He also averaged 21.5 points a game.

and solid scorers in forward Leonard Mitchell and guard Howard Carter. In their opener the Tigers routed Lamar 100–78, Macklin scoring 31 points and grabbing 16 rebounds and Carter adding 26 points on 13 field goals.

With Louisville eliminated from the Midwest, LSU's toughest opponent appeared to be Wichita State. But LSU first had to get by Arkansas in the regional semifinal. Eddie Sutton's Razorbacks had given LSU one of its only three losses earlier in the season, and though it was an upset, it stood as a reminder of mortality and vulnerability, and Dale Brown was not taking Arkansas lightly. LSU had another advantage in that the game was being played at the Superdome in New Orleans, which would be filled to capacity with Louisiana rooters. The game got off to an embarrassing start; after five minutes of play neither team had scored more than two points and between them had missed 16 of 18 shots. Then Louisiana State found itself, and Arkansas remained lost in the glare of the Superdome lights and the dazzle of the LSU offense. In fact, the Razorbacks put only 18 points on the scoreboard by the half, while LSU rang up 34. The Tigers continued to dominate in the second period, and Arkansas never was able to get in the game. The final was 72–56. LSU's high-point man turned out to be playmaker guard Ethan Martin, who scored 16; Macklin had 15 and a game-high nine rebounds.

To get to the regional semifinals Wichita State clobbered Southern 95–70 in the first round, rallied to beat Iowa in the second 60–56, then just edged Kansas 66–65 in the regional semifinal on a 24-foot jumper by Mike Jones with five seconds left in the game. The Shockers, coached by Gene Smithson, had a pair of strong, high-scoring forwards in Antoine Carr and Cliff Levingston and a first-rate guard in Randy Smithson, who also happened to be the coach's son.

The Staters from Wichita, however, were no match for those from Baton Rouge. LSU got the lead early and powered to a 48–33 halftime lead. When they came back on the floor the Tigers continued to control the game, and the closest the Shockers came was the 11 points (96–85) that divided the two teams at the final buzzer. For LSU it was a balanced team effort.

LSU forward Leonard Mitchell was one of the Tigers' steadiest performers in the 1981 tourney. With a total of 70 points, an average of 14, he was the tournament's ninth-highest scorer.

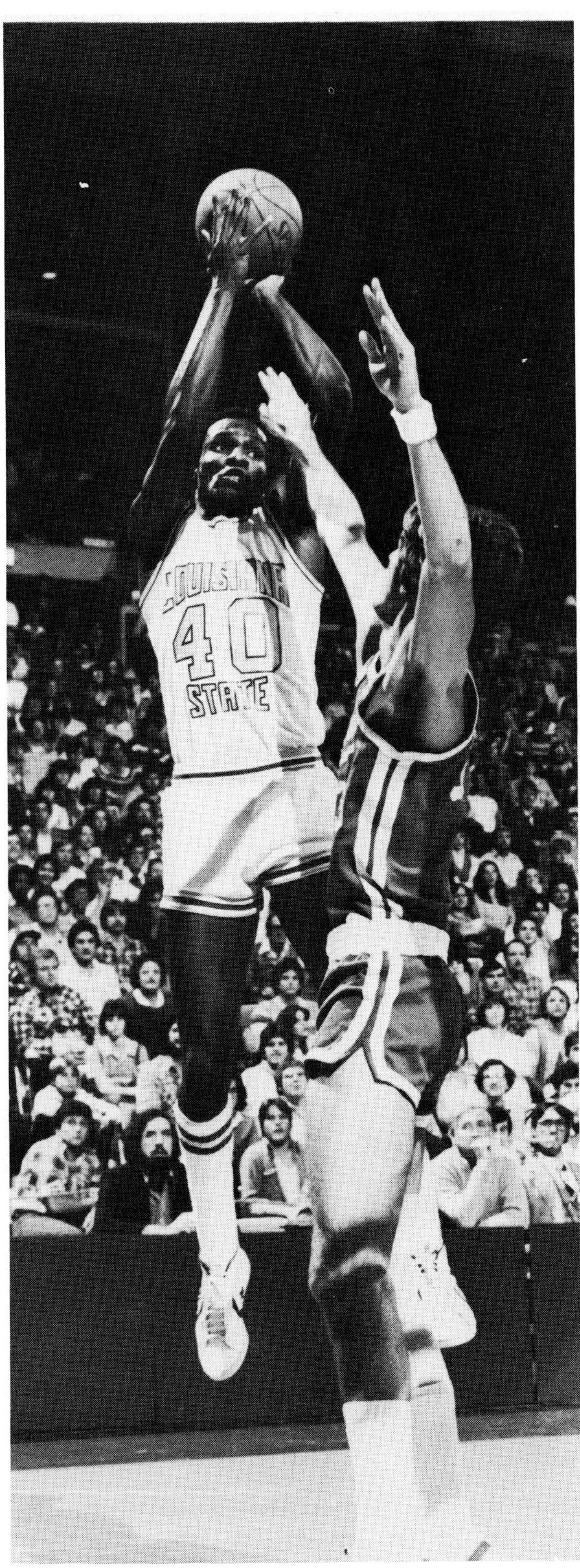

Durand Macklin (40), Louisiana State's contribution to the 1981 All-American squad, possessed a devastating jump shot. After scoring 31 points in LSU's second-round win over Lamar, however, Macklin was held to a paltry four points in the Tigers' semifinal loss to Indiana.

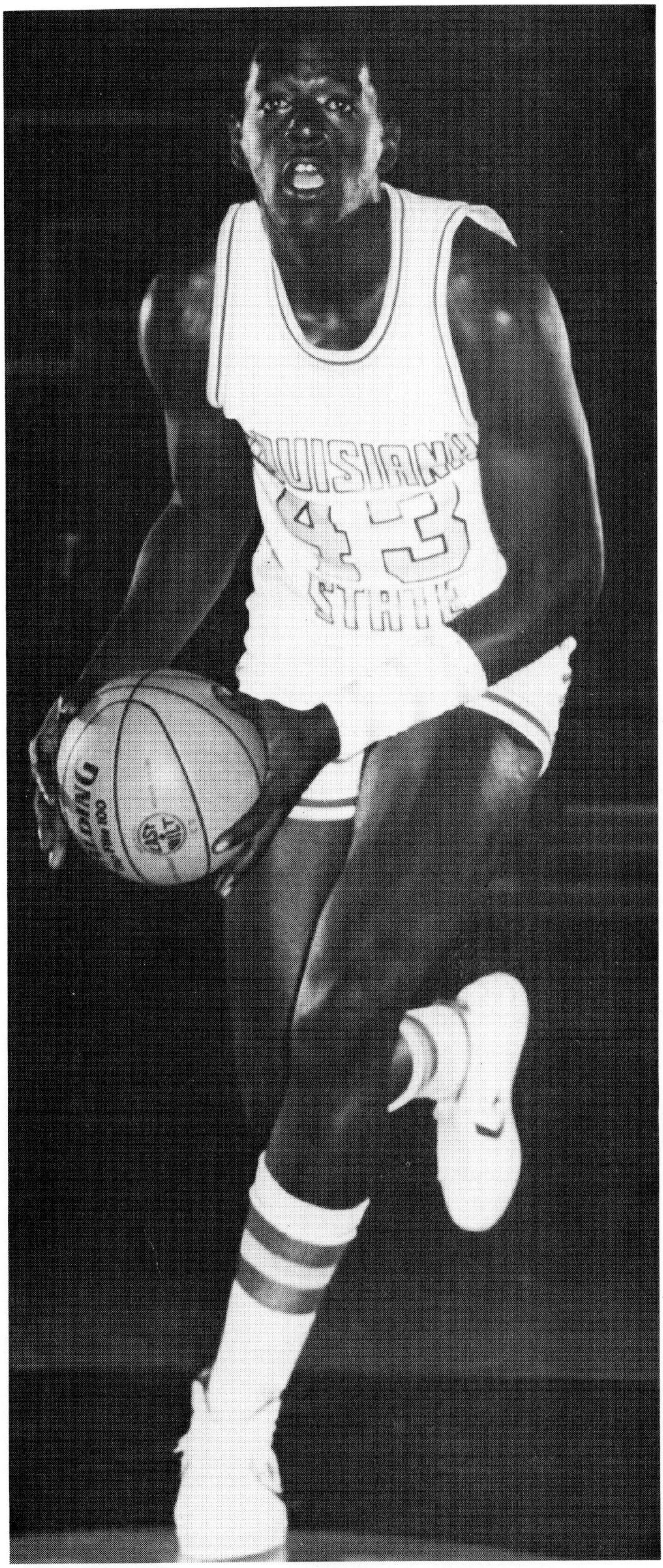

Greg "Cookieman" Cook, LSU's center in the 1981 tournament, grabbed 34 rebounds and averaged 13.4 points in the Tigers' five games.

Rudy Macklin was high with 21 points and 10 rebounds, but the other four starters were in double figures as well: Greg Cook, 19; Leonard Mitchell, 17; Ethan Martin, 13; and Howard Carter, 11. So Dale Brown and his Tigers had earned with relative ease a berth in the Final Four, the first time the school had done that since 1953.

In the Mideast, with the DePaul Blue Demons back in Chicago trying to figure out how they always seem to blow it in postseason play, the favorites appeared to be Bobby Knight's Indiana Hoosiers, that year's Big Ten champs. They were, in fact, the only seeded team to survive the Mideast's second round, but the Hoosiers had lost nine games during a very erratic regular season. Besides DePaul, other favored teams to fall were Wake Forest, upset by Boston College, and Kentucky, stunned by Alabama-Birmingham. Indiana, on the other hand, had humiliated Maryland 99-64 in its only tourney game before the regional semifinals. Consensus All-American Isiah Thomas, Indiana's 6′1″ guard and floor leader, scored 19 points himself against Maryland (nine of 11 field goals) and was credited with no fewer than 14 assists. Also contributing substantially to the massacre were Ray Tolbert, who tallied 26 points, and Landon Turner, with another 20.

Jim Thomas (20) came off the Indiana bench in the 1981 semifinal match-up with LSU to take over the ball-handling chores for his foul-plagued namesake, Isiah Thomas. The reserve guard not only led Indiana back from a three-point halftime deficit but also collected a Hoosier-high nine rebounds.

That win enabled Bobby Knight to take his team back to its home court in Bloomington, Indiana, for the regional semifinals—no small advantage. And there, amid the frenetic din made by Hoosier fans, the Indiana cagers glowed with a special incandescence and moved with ease into the Final Four. First they destroyed Alabama-Birmingham, turning a five-point halftime lead into an 87-72 victory. Again it was Isiah Thomas manipulating the game; this time he walked off with scoring honors, 27 points, while Randy Wittman added 20 and Ray Tolbert 17.

The only obstacle remaining was little St. Joseph's, now referred to as "giant-killer" after dispatching DePaul and then disposing of Boston College. But the festal ball ended for the Hawks in Bloomington, just as abruptly and definitively as Cinderella's had in fairyland. The Hawks could come up with only 16 points in the first half of the Mideast final while Indiana doubled that figure. It was more of the same in the last half, and when the final buzzer sounded Indiana was ahead 78-46. Now Knight and his Hoosiers would have to abandon their home-court advantage and do battle on the floorboards of the Spectrum in Philadelphia. But that arena held some choice memories for Hoosier fans because it was the site of Indiana's most recent moment of glory, where it had won its last NCAA crown just five years earlier.

Court wizard of the 1981 Boston College five was guard John Bagley (54), who averaged 21.7 points in the Eagles' three tourney games. In BC's upset win over Wake Forest Bagley hooped 35 points.

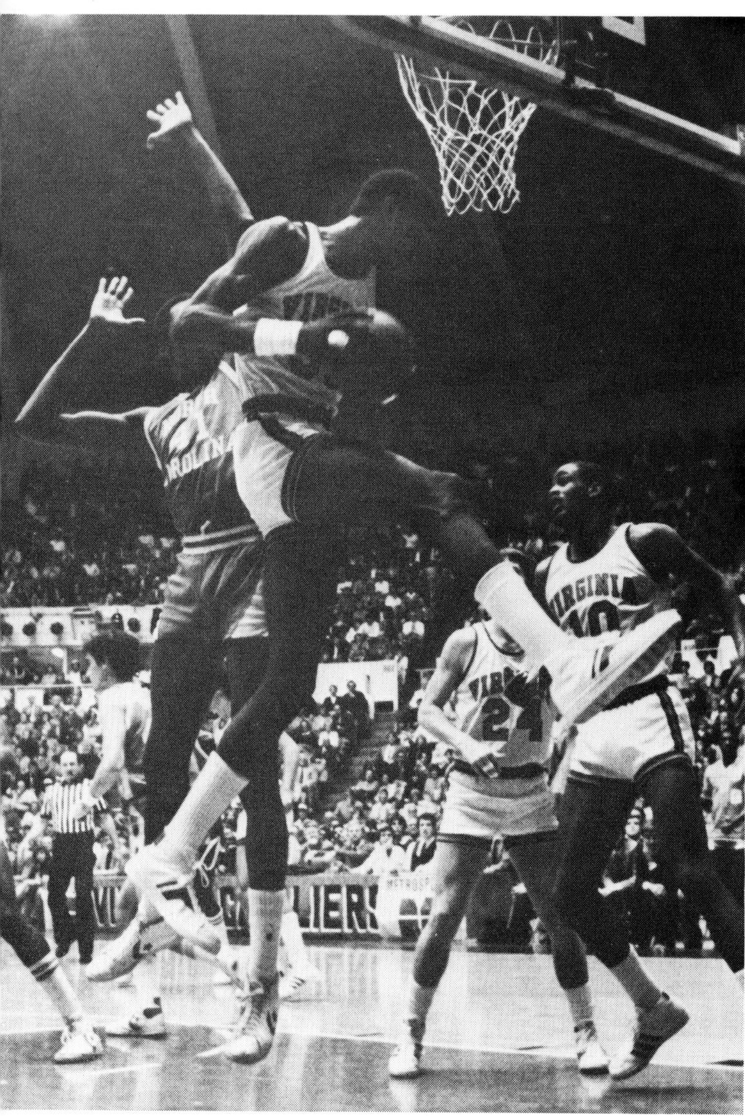

Virginia's skyscraper of a center, 7'4" Ralph Sampson, easily controls this rebound against ACC arch-rival North Carolina. A consensus All-American, Sampson averaged only 13.8 points in Virginia's five 1981 tournament games and was held to 11 in its semifinal loss to North Carolina.

In the East there was an imposing tower of a young man by the name of Ralph Sampson, and his 7′4″ All-American presence on the floor for Virginia was enough to make his team the favorite in that division. Sampson and the Virginia team were also enhanced by All-American guard Jeff Lamp. There were other fine teams in the East, all capable of taking the regional crown if they could avoid being too intimidated by the Sampson/Lamp duet, such seeds as Notre Dame and Tennessee and a streaking nonseed, Brigham Young, with All-American guard Danny Ainge leading that team.

None of those teams would, however, come close to beating Virginia, but unseeded Villanova would give the team a tough match. The Villanova team dogged Sampson throughout, holding him to a subpar 17 points and 12 rebounds. The upstarts from just outside Philadelphia had the Virginia Cavaliers by three points at the half, then stayed with them through most of the second period. The Cavaliers, however, pulled it out in the closing minutes, 54–50, and moved on to the regional semifinals in Atlanta.

Jeff Lamp, Virginia's floor leader, shown driving here, was the 1981 tournament's third-highest scorer, with 89 points and an average of 17.8. His 25 of 26 free throws was the tourney high.

Tennessee was also headed there after edging Virginia Commonwealth by a basket, 58–56. The Vols had a rugged center in Howard Wood and a dependable scorer in forward Dale Ellis (he posted 22 in their earlier tourney win). But they were simply no match for Virginia. In the middle Wood was nine inches shorter than Sampson, and the Vols had no one who could handle Jeff Lamp. Still, Tennessee gave the Virginians a fight well into the second half, even holding a five-point lead early in that period. But then the Cavaliers marched and left the Vols far behind. The final was 62–48, and the difference really was made by Jeff Lamp, who was the game's high scorer with 18. The Vols had stifled Sampson, who scored only nine points and grabbed but five rebounds, but that was little consolation.

Brigham Young made it to the semifinals in the East, principally on the gifted touch of Danny Ainge, who scored 21 points in the first-round win over Princeton and 37 in a second-round victory over UCLA. Brigham Young also got 19 and 17 points from Fred Roberts in those two games. The team faced its biggest challenge, however, in the semifinals with Notre Dame. The Fighting Irish, still under Digger Phelps and still claiming stars like Kelly Tripucka, Orlando Woolridge, and Tracy Jackson, had defeated James Madison in a low-scoring affair, 54–45, to gain admittance to the regional semifinals.

The Notre Dame game plan was to shut down Danny Ainge. And it worked—except for the last 10 seconds. The "wizard," as some scribes referred to Ainge, could manage only three baskets and four free throws in the first 39 minutes and 50 seconds of the game; the Notre Dame four-man zone, with the fifth player hounding Ainge at every step, worked well. At the same time Notre Dame was building a lead in the second period, one that reached 11 points before the Cougars started to squirm their way back into contention. Brigham Young not only got back into the game in the last eight minutes; it also stole the lead in the last minute, 49–48. But then Kelly Tripucka sank a long jumper with 10 seconds left and brought the entire stadium to their feet, most thinking they had just seen the game-winning bucket. Everybody sat back down when Utah took a time-out, but all were on their feet again to witness a most dazzling finale. Frank Deford described it in *Sports Illustrated:*

> Ainge did the most extraordinary thing. He took the inbounds pass, and guarded tight all the way, dashed up the right sideline and slashed through *three* men at midcourt, while dribbling behind his back. . . . Ainge then went left past the fourth of the Irish at the free throw line and slipped a shot over the fifth and final defender for a layup just before the buzzer, 51–50 BYU. It was the stuff of legends, and of winners. Long afterward, in the half-light of the darkened arena, Cougar coach Frank Arnold went up to Ainge's father and embraced him. "Don," he said, "I just want to thank you for giving us your boy."

So Brigham Young, far from its home in Provo, Utah, earned the right to challenge Virginia and Ralph Sampson in Atlanta. In the first half Jeff Lamp went head to head with Danny Ainge, and the Brigham Young star had a tough time of it. Still, the Cougars got ahead and went to the locker room with a 31–28 lead, the principal reason being that Brigham Young in turn had been able to stifle Ralph Sampson. But they could not keep it up, and Sampson became the game's force, leading the Cavaliers back to regain the lead midway through the second period. They never relinquished it after that, only built on it, and when the game ended the score was 74–60, Virginia's favor. Sampson ended up with 22 points and 12 rebounds, both game standards. Jeff Lamp had 18. For the Cougars, Danny Ainge was held to 13 points, their high. So Virginia advanced to the Final Four with more than a few people saying that the Cavaliers had to be *the* team to beat that year.

But another Atlantic Coast Conference team, which perhaps feared Virginia and Ralph Sampson but was not overawed, actually lusted for another chance at the Cavaliers. Dean Smith's North Carolina Tar Heels were moving impressively through the West, and one of their prime motivations was an overwhelming desire to get back at the Virginia Cavaliers, to whom they had twice blown

Highest scorer in the 1981 tourney was North Carolina's Al Wood with 109 points, an average of 21.8. Wood scored 39 in the Tar Heels' semifinal romp over Virginia.

double-digit leads during the regular season. Coach Smith had one of the most effective frontcourts in the game that year, with forwards James Worthy and Al Wood and center Sam Perkins. They had taken a variety of lumps during the season but always seemed to bounce back. They were seeded in the West and faced Pittsburgh in the second round, a laugher in which the Tar Heels cruised to a 14-point halftime lead, then turned it into a 74–57 rout. Worthy got 21 for North Carolina (eight of 10 from the floor), and Perkins picked up 19.

Step two would not be so easy. The West regionals were scheduled for Salt Lake City, and the displaced Tar Heels were slated to meet Utah on its home court there. The Utes were a highly regarded team, with big guns Danny Vraines and Tom Chambers and a fine point guard in Scott Martin. But the comforts of home were simply not enough when they took on the Tar Heels and their fine frontcourt. North Carolina played a precision game, scoring as needed and harassing the Utes on defense. Utah was also in the throes of experiencing its worst offensive game of the year, hitting on only 23 of 58 field goals (39.7 percent). The final score was 61–56, North Carolina on top. The Tar Heels got 15 points each from Worthy, Perkins, and Wood and another 12 from freshman guard Matt Doherty.

Meanwhile Kansas State, which had shocked both San Francisco and Oregon State in the first two rounds, confirmed its regional credentials by whipping Illinois in the West semifinal. Coached by Jack Hartman, the Wildcats from Manhattan, Kansas, were a forceful, almost brawling quintet on the floor, though they had an especially lithe forward-guard in Rolando Blackman. But as strong and relentless as they could be, the K-Staters also possessed a delicate touch when they needed it. And that's what they employed against the Illini. The game was won at the free-throw line. The often heavy-handed K-Staters in this game fouled Illinois only nine times, which resulted in two points for the Illini from the free-throw line. At the other end of the court Kansas State earned 17 points from its 25 free-throw attempts. It was enough to give the Wildcats a 57–52 victory.

Kansas State, surprisingly, was outmuscled in its next encounter with the frontcourt of North Carolina. The spread of Al Wood, Sam Perkins, and James Worthy was too much for K-State. The Tar Heels outrebounded the Wildcats 40–30, and they also outscored them 82–68, with North Carolina shooting 54 percent from the floor and Kansas State a disappointing 42 percent. Al Wood was the game's most noticeable presence, with game highs of 21 points and 17 rebounds. Sam Perkins and guard Matt Doherty contributed 16 points apiece, and James Worthy had 15. For the sixth time Dean Smith was taking a North Carolina team to the Final Four (it was the school's eighth visit, counting the two treks made by his predecessors). Twice Smith's team had been runners-up, losing out in the 1968 finals to John Wooden's UCLA and in 1977 to Al McGuire's Marquette. In the other appearances North Carolina had placed third once and fourth twice. The Tar Heels had not won the first-place trophy since Frank McGuire's North Carolina team earned it in a triple overtime win over Kansas back in 1957.

In the first semifinal game at the Spectrum in Philadelphia LSU coach Dale Brown knew what to expect from Indiana's marvelous floor leader, Isiah Thomas, and he geared his defense appropriately. What he did not expect was another sophomore Thomas, this one with the first name of Jim, to come off the bench and play with the same virtuosity as his namesake. In the first half the game was controlled by Louisiana State, which was three points ahead at the intermission. Because LSU players were continually swarming over him on defense and going at him on offense, Isiah Thomas collected three fouls in the first half and would spend the remainder of the game alternating between the bench and the floor, where he was forced to play with a limiting caution. But with Bobby Knight's less than gentle urgings and the playmaking slack picked up by Jim Thomas, the Hoosiers came raging back in the second period. They virtually tore the game away from LSU, dominating the boards, destroying the Tigers on defense, allowing them only a meager 19 points all period. The Hoosiers in turn put 40 points on the scoreboard. The final was a humiliating score of 67–49. Loser LSU did not have to look far for the key reason for its demise—the team had made only 19 of 59 field goals, an awful shooting percentage of 32.2. Only one Tiger scored in double figures, Howard Carter with 10. Landon Turner was Indiana's chief scorer with 20 points, while a foul-troubled Isiah Thomas was second with 14. The most rebounds (nine) for the Hoosiers were grabbed by reserve Jim Thomas.

It was all Atlantic Coast Conference in game two. Dean Smith had earned the opportunity to avenge the Tar Heels' humblings by Virginia earlier that year. And he got that satisfaction, which came as a manifest gift from his soaring forward Al Wood. The game was close through the first half, and Ralph Sampson was effectively bottled up by the Tar Heel defense. It was in the second half when Al Wood took over and Virginia crumbled under the onslaught. From a 37–37 tie in the second period, the Tar Heels, behind Wood,

Guard Howard Carter guided LSU's attack on the floor in the 1981 tourney. Besides being the key to getting the ball to Durand Macklin, Carter was also the tournament's tenth highest scorer with 69 points.

Randy Wittman (24) averaged 12.4 points a game to help Indiana gain the NCAA crown in 1981. His best efforts: 20 points against Alabama-Birmingham and 16 in the title game against North Carolina.

surged to a 74–58 lead (Wood contributed 22 points during a 10-minute run). When the game ended a few minutes later the Tar Heels had an impressive 78–65 triumph to make up for the discourtesies that Virginia had handed them in their two regular-season matches. And Al Wood had 39 points (14 of 19 from the floor, 11 of 13 from the line), the most points scored in any game that tourney and an all-time record high for a semifinal game. He also collected 10 rebounds, the most made by any player in the game. The vaunted Ralph Sampson had been held to 11 points (only three of 10 field goals) and nine rebounds.

So in 1981 it would be Bobby Knight in search of his second national championship and Dean Smith in pursuit of the first of his career.

During the regular season the two teams had met once, and North Carolina had triumphed 65–56. But that did not worry Bobby Knight. This team of his, he said, had not really gotten going until February; they were true late bloomers. At the same time, he must have been aware that no team that had lost as many as nine games in the regular season had ever won the national championship (Marquette, with seven losses in 1977, was the champ with the worst regular-season record up until that time). Knight, however, was counting on Isiah Thomas to alter that NCAA mark by leading his team over the Tar Heels despite their awesome front line.

During the first half it was North Carolina dominating early, then a resurgent Indiana taking over. At the intermission, with the Hoosiers up by a single point, it was still anybody's game. But once again Knight stirred his team in the locker room, and they rallied on the floor. Isiah Thomas came on like a whirlwind—he had had only one basket in the first half—and the Hoosier defense held the Tar Heels in tight check. Midway through the period Indiana moved to a comfortable 11-point lead, and from that point on the game was Indiana's. The Tar Heels never came closer than seven points. At the end 13 points divided the two teams and Indiana had its fourth NCAA national basketball championship. Only UCLA, with its 10 first-place trophies, and Kentucky, with five, have won it more often.

Isiah Thomas, who ended the evening with 23 points and had been the Hoosier's rallying force in the second half of the championship game as well as their guiding force in the earlier games, received the Outstanding Player award. For the Hoosiers that championship night at the Spectrum, Ray Tolbert got the most rebounds with 11, Randy Wittman con-

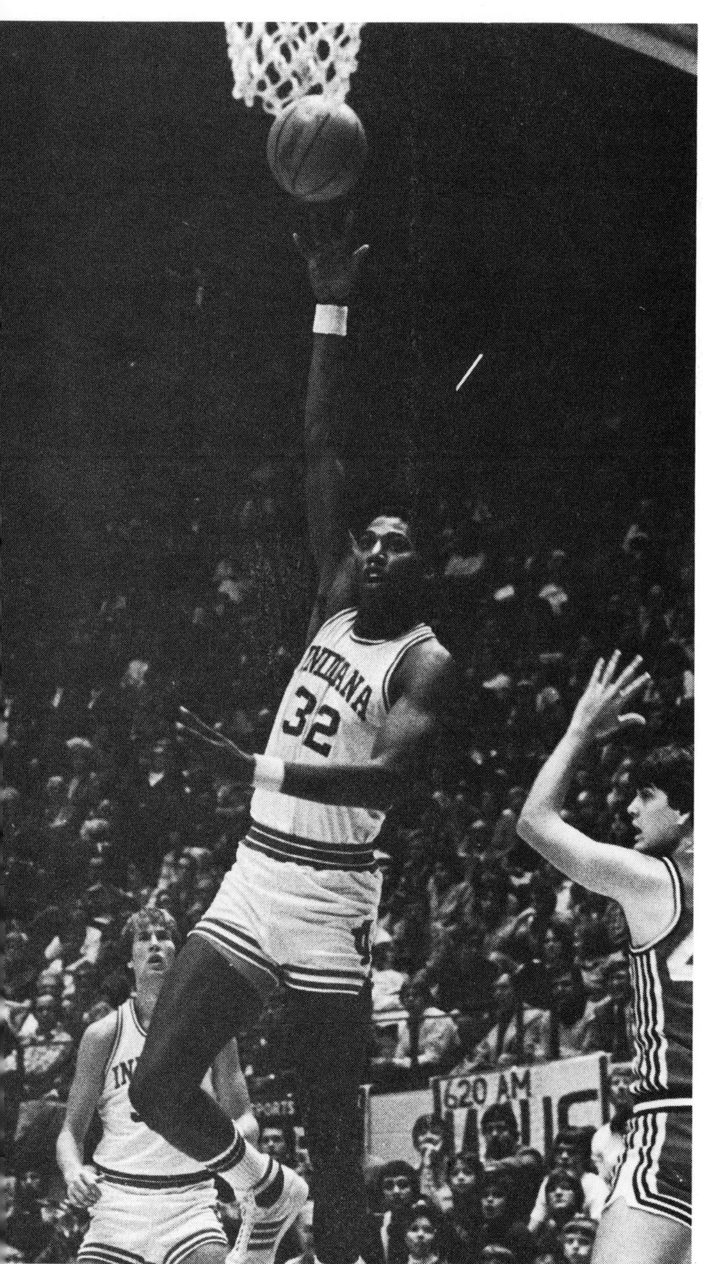

Forward Landon Turner (32) was a key figure in Indiana's luxury cruise to the 1981 national championship. The Hoosier forward averaged 13.2 points a game and snatched a total of 27 rebounds.

Bobby Knight won his second national championship in 1981 when his Hoosiers decisively defeated North Carolina 63–50.

Awards, 1981

Outstanding Player
Isiah Thomas (Indiana)

All-Tournament Team
Isiah Thomas (Indiana)
Jim Thomas (Indiana)
Landon Turner (Indiana)
Al Wood (North Carolina)
Jeff Lamp (Virginia)

tributed 16 points, and Landon Turner another 12. The Hoosier defense held Al Wood to 18 points and Sam Perkins to 11, the only Tar Heels to score in double figures.

Despite his limited performance in the championship game, North Carolina's Al Wood scored the most points in the 1981 NCAA tourney, 109. Hoosier Isiah Thomas was next with 91, and Jeff Lamp of Virginia had 89. Wood also posted the highest scoring average, 21.8 percent, only a fraction higher than the 21.7 percent recorded by John Bagley of Boston College and the 21.5 percent for Cliff Levingston of Wichita State. Levingston also collected the most rebounds that year, 53, while Virginia's Ralph Sampson grabbed 49, and Rudy Macklin of Louisiana State and Al Wood got 48 apiece. Isiah Thomas and Jeff Lamp scored the most free throws, 25, but Lamp had by far the best percentage, 96.2 (25 of 26).

Dean Smith, disappointed again, went back to Chapel Hill wondering if he was as jinxed in the Final Four as DePaul's Ray Meyer seemed to be in the early rounds of the NCAA tourney. Smith, however, would find a most satisfying answer to that question in 1982.

14
A Worthy North Carolina

When the 1981–82 regular season came to an end and the more fortunate teams were journeying to the various NCAA playoff sites, both AP and UPI agreed on the top team in the nation; in fact, they concurred on the first five. North Carolina headed the list, followed by DePaul, Virginia, Oregon State, and Missouri. And both wire services were in accordance on four of the five first-string All-Americans that year: center Ralph Sampson (Virginia); forward Terry Cummings (DePaul), and guards Eric "Sleepy" Floyd (Georgetown) and Quintin Dailey (San Francisco). AP favored Kevin Magee (University of California/Irvine) at the other forward position, while UPI gave its vote to James Worthy (North Carolina). But if the Associated Press had had the luxury of waiting until after the NCAA tournament, it would have been hard-pressed not to include Worthy on its list.

North Carolina's master strategist, Dean Smith, in his 21st year as head coach, was gunning for his seventh trek to the Final Four; six times before his Tar Heels had been there, each time emerging as an also-ran. This time they were the favorite. The phenomenal Al Wood was gone from the Carolina frontcourt, but James Worthy and Sam Perkins were still there. Matt Doherty had been moved to forward to replace Wood. Jimmy Black was back at one guard position, and Michael Jordan earned a starting berth at the other. The Tar Heels were able to run off an impressive 27 and two record during the regular season, despite an exceptionally arduous schedule,

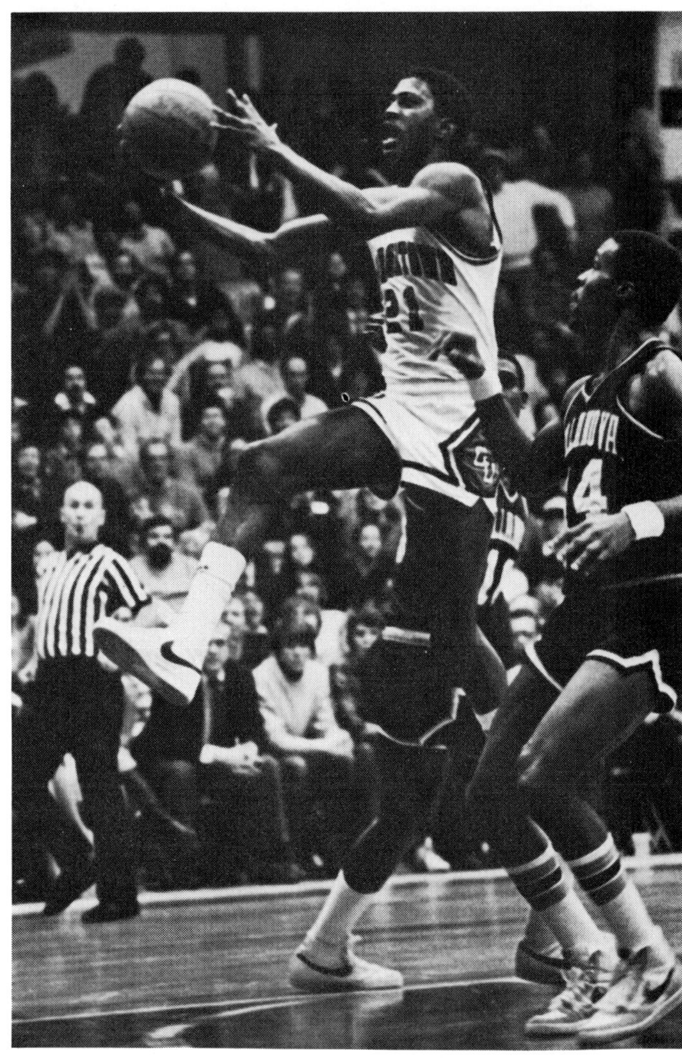

Eric "Sleepy" Floyd (21), going for a bucket against Villanova, sparkplugged Georgetown's offense in the 1981 and 1982 tourneys. In '82 he averaged 16 points in the Hoyas' five games and the year before scored a game-high 22 points in Georgetown's lone appearance against James Madison.

and also take the Atlantic Coast Conference crown.

In 1982, there were, however, some fine teams in the East regional that had every intention of depriving North Carolina of another trip to the Final Four. Among them were such nationally ranked teams as Memphis State (ninth in both), Alabama (12th in the AP and 13th in the UPI), and Wake Forest (18th in the AP and 19th in the UPI). Several unranked teams looked very tough, too, once the postseason activities got under way, especially Villanova and Northeastern.

There was also relatively unheralded James Madison, making only its second appearance ever in the tourney, which almost made the most sensational splash of that basketball year. The hoopsters from Harrisonburg, Virginia, upset Ohio State in the first round, overcoming a seven-point halftime deficit to turn in a seven-point win. Then it sent nightmarish chills through the bones of Dean Smith by almost doing the same thing to his top-seeded Tar Heels. North Carolina had to struggle just to get a 31–29 halftime lead, then battle desperately to ward off a determined James Madison in the second period. The Virginians came within a point with just more than a minute and a half left in the game, but Carolina was rescued by James Worthy, whose scoring and rebounding in the last minute of play brought the Tar Heels up and over, 52–50. It was, however, a game that, when it ended, elicited a collective sigh of relief from Dean Smith and his number-one-ranked cagers.

Another surprise in the East came from the Northeastern Huskies of Boston, who upset St. Joseph's of Philadelphia in the first round, then almost repeated the feat in the second. It took three overtimes for favored Villanova to scratch out a 76–72 win and overcome the 31-point performance by Northeastern guard Perry Moss.

Elsewhere in the East, Wake Forest, as expected, had no trouble with Old Dominion in the first round but did with Memphis State in the second. The Tigers from Tennessee proved to be too strong in the final minutes, though the game was a nerve racker all the way to the buzzer. Down four at the half, Memphis State regained the lead in the second period and then sneaked off with a 56–55 win, much the result of the 18 points and eight rebounds from the Tigers' freshman forward Keith Lee. Alabama, also a favorite in its encounter with St. John's, found the road no easier, that game going down to the wire as well. But in the end the Crimson Tide inched by St. John's 69–68. Just a basket or two difference in the four second-round games, and the East would have found James Madison, Northeastern, St. John's, and Wake Forest vying for the regional title instead of seeds North Carolina, Memphis State, Alabama, and Villanova.

In Raleigh, North Carolina, where the regional finals were held, North Carolina had its hands full with Alabama, and it took a superb performance from the free-throw line for the Tar Heels to emerge a winner, 74–69. Alabama was tagged with 27 fouls (13 more than North Carolina), and as a result the Tar Heels added 26 points from their 31 charity tosses. That was enough to override the 29 field goals Alabama sank to Carolina's 24. Again that night it was James Worthy who proved to be the controlling force, especially in the second half. The Tar Heels' forward ended the evening with 16 points, sharing scoring honors with Matt Doherty, and turned in a needed clutch performance from the free-throw line, eight for eight. He also collected eight rebounds for North Carolina, the most that game. Center Sam Perkins added 15 points and five rebounds for the Tar Heels.

Even closer was the semifinal match between Memphis State and Villanova. State was a slight favorite, but no one was underrating the Villanova Wildcats, who had come on strong at the end of the regular season and were champs of the Big East conference. The Wildcats were paced by a strong center, John Pinone, two fine forwards in Ed Pinckney and Aaron Howard, and an expert ball handler in point guard Stewart Granger. Memphis State's fortunes were woven around 6′10″ forward Keith Lee, but he was ably restrained during the first half as Villanova built a 35–31 lead. Frustrated by the preponderance of attention Villanova was paying him, Lee got himself into foul trouble in the first half and therefore had to tone down his otherwise aggressive play. Still, the game remained very close, but Villanova had a one-point advantage when Lee finally fouled out with just fewer than five minutes left in the game. But even with the loss of Lee, the Staters hung in and worked their way to a tie at the buzzer. They could not carry it further, however, and Villanova outlasted them in the overtime period, scoring eight points to their four to take a 70–66 victory. John Pinone was the Wildcat leader with 19 points and 12 rebounds, but Ed Pinckney was equally instrumental in the victory, scoring 16, grabbing 10 rebounds, and tormenting Keith Lee on defense. Aaron Howard had another 16 for Villanova. Memphis State's Lee had 14 points when he fouled out, which proved to be the most racked up by a Stater in that game.

Two nights later Villanova was back on the court against the North Carolina Tar Heels to determine who would represent the East in that year's semifinals. Going to the Final Four was old times to Dean Smith, but that certainly did not diminish his desire to make another appearance there. Villanova coach Rollie Massimino had never been there, and only one other Wildcat team had made it before: the 1971 squad coached by Jack Kraft and spearheaded by All-Americans Howard Porter and Hank Siemiontkowski. That team had come in second to UCLA but whose standing had later been erased by the NCAA as penalty for having allowed ineligible student athletes to play.

As primed as Villanova was, and as much as coach Massimino wanted to unseat the Tar Heels, his team was simply no match for Dean Smith's peaking North Carolinians. The Tar Heels controlled the game from start to finish; it was never a runaway, but Carolina always maintained a relatively comfortable margin. The Tar Heels led by six at the half and by 10 at the final buzzer. It was essentially a team effort, with five players for North Carolina in double figures: Mike Jordan, 15; James Worthy, 14; Matt Doherty and Sam Perkins, 13 apiece; and Jimmy Black, 11. Again the Tar Heels' superiority at the free-throw line played a vital role; they converted 20 of 24, while Villanova reaped only six points from its nine free throws. For Villanova Ed Pinckney scored 18 points and snatched 10 rebounds, and John Pinone bucketed another 14.

So it was that Dean Smith would go to test his Final Four jinx one more time and North Carolina would arrive in search of its second national championship, a spoil that had eluded the Tar Heels for the previous 25 years.

Number two DePaul did not fare as well as number one North Carolina. Ray Meyer, in his 40th year as head coach of the Chicago school, watched with mortification as his Blue Demons fell apart once again in the postseason tourney. Mark Aguirre had left after his junior year to join the pros, but forward Terry Cummings had picked up his All-American credentials. Skip Dillard still held court at guard, now accompanied by Kenny Patterson. Bernard Randolph had been impressive as Cummings' tandem forward; seven-foot Walter Downing held down the pivot spot.

DePaul was a heavy favorite to beat Boston College, the blue Demons' first encounter in the Midwest regional. The Blue Demons had won 26 of their 27 regular-season contests and claimed the number one ranking in the polls for much of that year. But second-seed DePaul, for the third straight year, was eliminated in its first game of the NCAA tournament. And no one could say it was undeserved. With 20 turnovers and an incredible 35 personal fouls (Dillard, Randolph, Patterson, and reserves Tyrone Corbin and Jerry McMillan all fouled out, and Cummings and Downing garnered four fouls each), the Blue Demons fell to Boston College 82–75. The Eagles did not take nearly as much advantage of DePaul's foul fever as they should have, making only 24 of 42 free throws, but it was enough. Another bleak Blue Demon statistic was that they shot only 44.4 percent from the floor (32 of 72 field goals). The only respectable performance by a Blue Demon was turned in by Terry Cummings, who was credited with a game-high 17 rebounds and 20 points. For Boston College guard John Bagley scored 26 points, and reserve Michael Adams came off the bench to add 21 (including nine of 11 free throws).

With DePaul out of it, a slight favorite in the Midwest was fifth-ranked Missouri, closely tailed by 10th-ranked Tulsa and 12th-ranked Arkansas. The Tigers of Missouri had lost

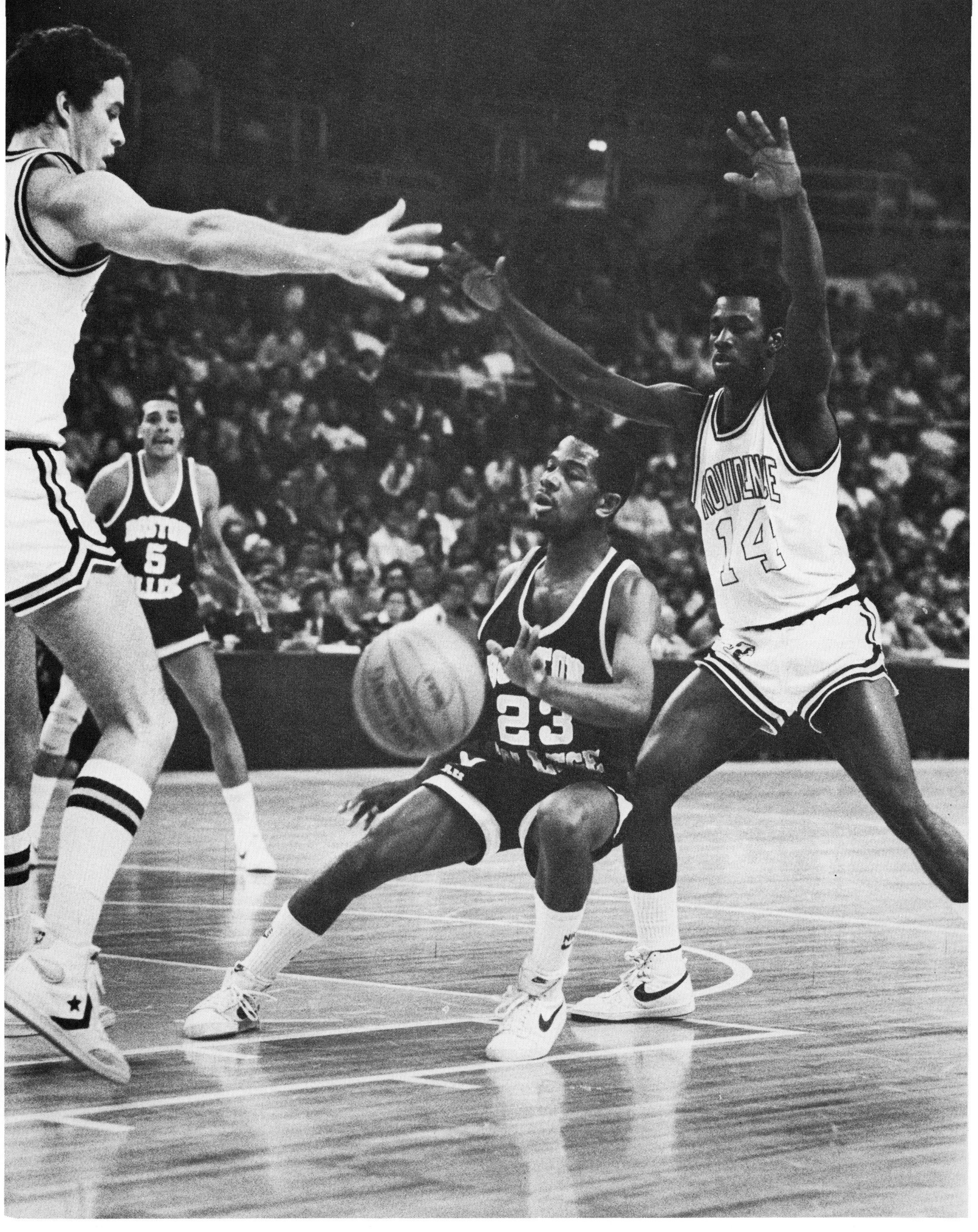

Michael Adams (23), maneuvering here against Providence, came off the bench to help lead Boston College to a startling upset of nationally ranked number two DePaul in the 1982 tourney. The reserve guard scored 21 points that game and 20 a few days later against Kansas State.

three games and won 26 during the regular season, had the deft services of All-American candidate Ricky Frazier at forward and an imposing center in Steve Stipanovich, and would be the only seeded team to survive the Midwest's second round. The Tigers did it with a clean win over Marquette, 73–69, a game in which Frazier posted 20 points and Stipanovich 19.

Sharing DePaul's sad fate were Tulsa, defeated by Houston, and Arkansas, victim of Kansas State. In the first of the two upsets Houston, which had knocked off Alcorn State in the first round behind guard Rob Williams' 25-point effort, dominated Tulsa throughout. The Cougars got another fine performance from Williams that night as he tallied 26 points (10 of 15 from the floor). The Houston defense also held Tulsa's All-American candidate Paul Pressey to 16 points, though he collected a game-high 12 rebounds. The final: Houston 78, Tulsa 74. In the other surprise, Kansas State got 21 points from guard Tyrone Adams and 13 from forward Ed Nealy, while as a team the Wildcats shot 60.4 percent from the floor. Arkansas, which had a one-point lead at the half, faltered, then fell 65–64 when it failed on a desperate jumper in the game's last few seconds.

In the first game of the Midwest regional semifinals at the Checkerdome in St. Louis, Kansas State took on Boston College, and most viewed it a toss-up. The Kansans forged to a five-point lead at the half and had effectively stopped BC's normally high-scoring guard John Bagley. The Wildcats continued to harass Bagley through the second period, but the Eagles' bench came to the rescue. Freshman guard Michael Adams and forward John Garris were brought in, and they more than picked up the slack; in fact, they could be credited with leading the Eagles to their 69–65 victory. Adams contributed 20 points (seven of eight from the floor) and Garris 18, while a frustrated Bagley made only four of 12 field goals as part of his total of 10 points.

Missouri was given the edge in the second Midwest semifinal. Houston had lost seven games before coming to the tournament that year and had come in second in the Southwest Conference, a record noticeably less lustrous than that of the Missourians. The Cougars, under Guy Lewis, in his 26th year as Houston head coach, were spearheaded on court by All-American candidate guard Rob Williams. But they would have to contend with Ricky Frazier, Missouri's potent scoring forward, and he was at his best that night, scoring a game-high 29 points. That performance was buttressed by Mizzou center Steve Stipanovich's 17 points and game-high 12 rebounds. But despite those two admirable performances, it was not enough to overcome Houston's beautifully balanced offensive attack. The Cougars drove to a six-point lead at the half, then fought off a second-period rally by Missouri to cop a 79–78 win and the right to meet Boston College for the Midwest title. Houston's Rob Williams had been held to 10 points (a lowly four of 15 field goals), but his fellow guard Lynden Rose scored 16, forwards Michael Young and Clyde Drexler added 15 and 14 respectively, center Larry Micheaux had 11, and seven-foot reserve center Akeem Olajuwon of Nigeria came off the bench to score 13 and take a team-high 11 rebounds.

Before the tourney began, the odds of a Houston–Boston College match-up for the Midwest title would have been astronomical. The two unseeded, unranked contenders had emerged from a division that claimed teams ranked number two, five, 10, 12, and 18 in the country. But they had prevailed and had insured that at least one unexpected team would join the 1982 Final Four. The game offered a fine match-up between top-notch guards John Bagley of Boston College and Rob Williams of Houston, and they were both at their best that night at the Checkerdome. With a multitude of fast breaks and some very hot-handed shooting, the game turned into one of the highest-scoring affairs in that year's tourney.

Houston led 46–43 at halftime in what had been a wide-open, frantic period, and the action was just as explosive in the second half. But Boston College was fouling, and the consequences of it were to be the deciding element in the outcome of the game. As the battle wore on, the Houston cagers took crucial advantage of their trips to the free-throw line. Boston College came as close as four points with about a minute and a half left, but then the

Houston guard Lynden Rose (00) goes up for an easy two against Missouri. Rose was the Cougars' high scorer, 20 points, in the 1982 semifinal game, but Houston fell to North Carolina that night 68–63. Number 23 on Houston is Clyde Drexler.

team had to foul intentionally to get the ball, and the Houston steady hands increased the lead to a game-winning 99–92. Four Eagles fouled out, and Boston College was assessed with 33 personal fouls. That resulted in 33 points from the free-throw line for Houston (BC got only 16 points on charity tosses), more than enough to offset the five-field-goal advantage Boston College had. Among the most clutch performances of the night was that of Houston's freshman guard Reid Gettys, who came off the bench midway through the second half and quickly became the object of Boston College fouls. With uncommon coolness for a fresh reserve, he sank 10 of 10, and that was one of the key deciders of the game. Rob Williams was the Cougar high scorer with 25 points, and center Larry Micheaux had 18, while Lyndon Rose and forward Clyde Drexler had 15 each. For Boston College John Bagley scored 26 points, center Jay Murphy added 23, and sub John Garris toted up another 19.

So Houston, for the first time since 1968, would go to the Final Four, where it would have the formidable job of taking on the nation's number-one-ranked team, North Carolina.

The Mideast was another division loaded with top-quality teams. Foremost was number-three-ranked Virginia, built around skyscraper Ralph Sampson. There were also two definite threats from the Blue Grass State, Kentucky and Louisville, both well-seasoned pros when it came to postseason play. Joe B. Hall's Kentucky Wildcats were ranked 14th in the nation by UPI and 15th by AP, though they had lost seven games that year. Denny Crum's Louisville Cardinals had lost nine games yet were ranked 20th in both wire service polls. There was also Big Ten champion Minnesota, ranked sixth by UPI and a slot lower in the AP poll. And last but certainly not least was Alabama–Birmingham, which had lost only five games and was ranked 17th in the AP poll.

The only early surprise of the regional was dealt to Kentucky. Against Middle Tennessee State, Joe Hall's Wildcats handled themselves respectably in the first half but had to settle for a 30–30 tie. After that it was sheer humiliation. The Kentucky cagers could find the basket on only the rarest of occasions, scoring a paltry 14 points that half and tumbling to defeat 50–44.

There were no major surprises in the second round, however. Louisville, with forward Derek Smith scoring 17 and guard Jerry Eaves

Lancaster Gordon (4), defending against Virginia, was one of Louisville's hottest hands in the 1982 tournament. His best effort was the game-high 23 points he scored when the Cardinals eliminated Minnesota in the Mideast regional. Number 22 on Louisville is forward Rodney McCray.

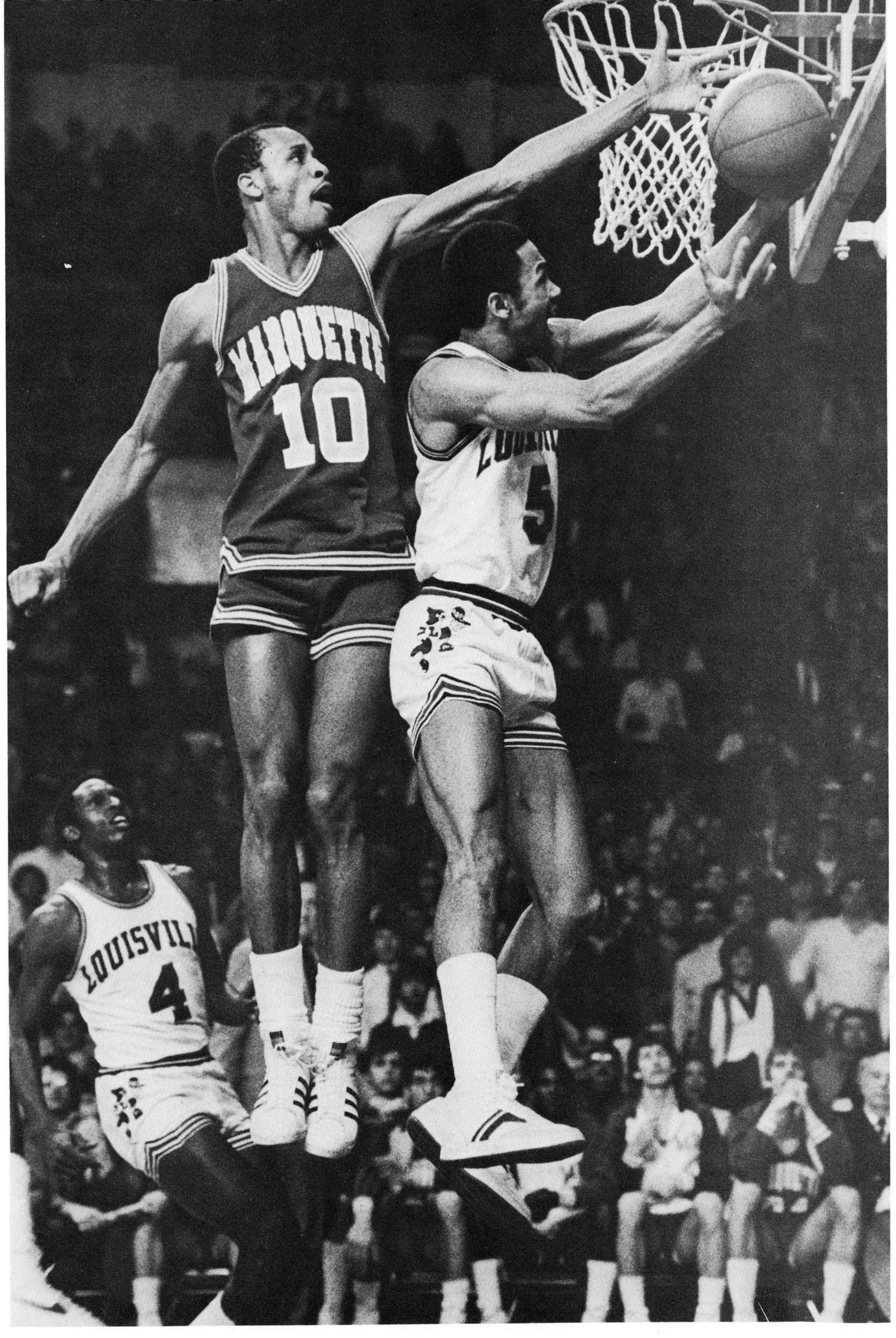

Jerry Eaves (5) of Louisville tries to sneak a lay-up under Marquette's Michael Wilson (10) in this 1982 game. Eaves had his best tourney game when he scored 13 points in the Cardinals' regional title win over Alabama-Birmingham. Number 4 is Lancaster Gordon.

13, decimated Middle Tennessee State 81–56. Alabama–Birmingham, coached by former UCLA headman Gene Bartow, had to face Big Ten also-ran Indiana, but it was a known fact that Bobby Knight's teams were always a threat in postseason play. The Blazers from Alabama, however, found this year to be an exception to that rule and handed the Hoosiers a resounding 80–70 defeat, despite a fine 24-point performance from Indiana forward Ted Kitchel. The Blazers' hotshot guard, Oliver Robinson, offset most of that with his 23 points, and forward Chris Giles added an important 17. The true margin of victory, however, was set at the free-throw line, where the Blazers converted 24 of 29 while Indiana harvested only six points from its 10 attempts. The Blazers also outshot the Hoosiers from the floor, 56 percent to 46.4 percent.

Regional favorite Virginia, down seven at the half, had to come from behind to slip barely by Tennessee 54–51. Ralph Sampson, with 19 points, and guard Jeff Jones, with 10, were the only Cavaliers in double figures. For Tennessee guard Michael Brooks had 24 and forward Dale Ellis 16. But Virginia did not look at all that impressive in its win over the Vols.

Minnesota had a lot more trouble with Tennessee–Chattanooga than anticipated. Losing by two at the half, the Gophers managed to escape with a razor-thin 62–61 win. The entire Minnesota frontcourt, including 7′3″ center Randy Breuer, had trouble with the Moccasins' two forwards, Willie White and Russ Schoene, who scored 22 and 20 points respectively. Schoene also took a game-high 12 rebounds. For the Gophers guard Trent Tucker was the biggest gun with 20 points, but Breuer added 17 and guard Darryl Mitchell had 16.

There were no surprises among the four teams that showed up in Birmingham for the regional semifinals, and no one was happier than the Blazers of Alabama–Birmingham and Gene Bartow because they would enjoy the advantage of playing on their own homecourt.

The Virginia Cavaliers would learn to their chagrin how potent that advantage was in their semifinal encounter with Bartow's Blazers. Despite 21 rebounds from Ralph Sampson and a 37–33 halftime lead, a favored Virginia would fade badly in the late going and fall to the Alabamans 68–66. And they did it to themselves with 18 turnovers to the Blazers' 11, six more fouls, and 10 fewer points from the free-throw line. Once again it was Oliver Robinson leading the Blazers, this time scoring a game-high 23 points. Sampson (only eight of 18 from the floor) and Jeff Jones had 19 and 18 points respectively for the Cavaliers.

Oliver Robinson, University of Alabama–Birmingham's star guard, averaged 22 points in UAB's three games in the 1982 tourney. He could not get his team past Louisville, however, in the Mideast regional final. Robinson averaged 17 points in UAB's three tourney games the year before.

Alabama–Birmingham would face Louisville in the regional final because Denny Crum's Cardinals had advanced by defeating Minnesota. The Gophers made a game of it in the first period, only a point down at the break, but Louisville pulled away in the second period: the final, 67–61. High scorer for the night was Louisville guard Lancaster Gordon with 23 points (10 of 14 field goals), followed by Gophers' Randy Breuer and Trent

One of the chief reasons for Georgetown's success in 1982 was awesome center Pat Ewing (33), rejecting a shot here. Ewing had 23 points and a game-high 11 rebounds in the Hoyas' championship loss to North Carolina. Other Hoyas are Fred Brown (20) and Anthony Jones (11).

Tucker, who posted 22 apiece. Cardinal Derek Smith also contributed 17 for Louisville.

Both Alabama–Birmingham and Louisville were teams that liked to run and gun, both liked to press on defense, and both played very physical basketball games underneath. Denny Crum had the advantage of experience in playoff competition; Gene Bartow had the benefit of playing before a very partisan hometown crowd. Louisville was the freshest at the beginning, getting off to an early lead and building it to a 40–32 halftime margin. Then it was the Blazers' turn. They powered back and finally snatched the lead away from the Cardinals. But they were unable to hold it in the game's last six minutes. Louisville regained it 56–54 and never gave it up again. The final was 75–68. The biggest hero for the Cardinals was reserve Charles Jones, who came off the bench to score 19 points, including nine free throws, all of which came in clutch situations. Derek Smith had another 14 for the Cardinals, Jerry Eaves 13, and Lancaster Gordon 11. For the disappointed Blazers, Oliver Robinson was high with 20. So Denny Crum and the Louisville Cardinals would get a shot at winning their second national championship in three years.

The power in the West, it was said in basketball circles, was a team from the East; or, as it was put in *Sports Illustrated,* "the beast of the East is the best of the West." The Georgetown Hoyas, under their always imposing coach John Thompson, was the team on

Georgetown coach John Thompson brought the Hoyas to the 1982 championship match, only to see them edged out by North Carolina 63–62 in a real heartbreaker.

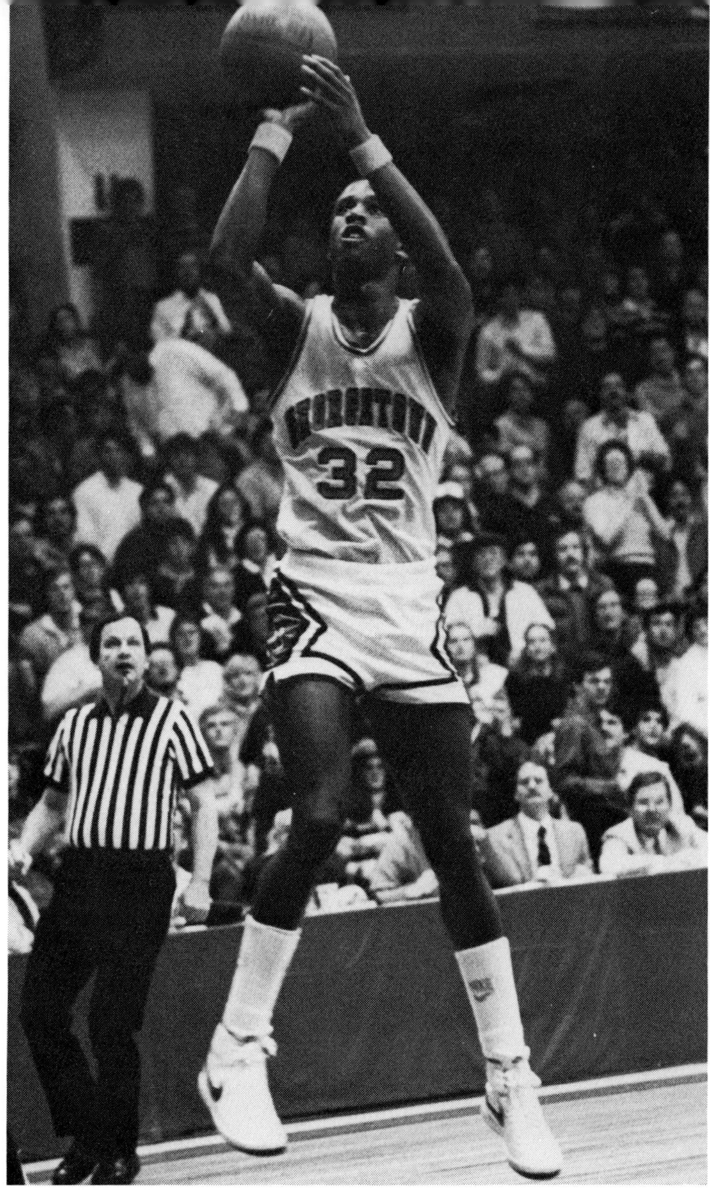

Eric Smith (32), about to hit an easy two here, scored 14 points for Georgetown in the 1982 semifinal and final games.

which the smart money was being laid. But there was also the Pac-10 champ, Oregon State, which had lost only four games that year, was ranked nationally number four, and was the West's top seed. Rumor had it, however, that the Beavers would not be able to contain the Hoyas' All-American guard Sleepy Floyd or their seven-foot freshman center Pat Ewing, nor would they be able to break Georgetown's reputedly inviolable defense.

Also from the West was Idaho, making its first tournament appearance ever but doing so as the nation's eighth-ranked team and one that had lost only two regular-season games. And the Fresno State Bulldogs, another newcomer, had a record identical to that of Idaho. The Bulldogs were ranked 10th by UPI and 11th by AP.

Everything went according to the odds makers' game plan out West. Georgetown, though playing sloppily and scoring far less than usual, outlasted Wyoming 51–43. No one had been very impressive on offense for the Hoyas. Sleepy Floyd, who spent many minutes on the bench as a result of committing four fouls, produced only 11 points, and big Pat Ewing got only seven, though his eight rebounds were the most in that game. But the Hoya's defense appeared to be everything it was cracked up to be.

Oregon State showed its offense as the Beavers demolished Pepperdine 70–51 in their second-round game. Forward Danny Evans banked 18 points for the Starters, guard Lester "Molester" Connor had 16, and center Charlie Sitton 14.

Idaho and Fresno State found their paths rutted and hazardous, but both managed to get by and advance to the regional semifinals in Provo, Utah. Fresno State, behind the 18-point performance of forward Rod Higgins, held off West Virginia 50–46, though it did not impress anyone with that win. And Idaho staved off a spirited finish by Iowa and sneaked away with a 69–67 overtime victory. For the Vandals, who tallied 29 of 35 field goals (to 11 of 19 for Iowa) and outscored the Hawkeyes 12–10 in the overtime period, it was a breathtaking victory. Forward Phil Lupson was high for Idaho with 21 points and nine rebounds, but center Kelvin Smith added 16 and guard Brian Kellerman another 14.

Against Fresno State, Georgetown's prized defense was stingier than ever, conceding only 20 points per half. While shutting down the Californians, the Hoyas also proved they had an offense, posting 58 points themselves on 21 of 33 field goals (63.6 percent) and failing on only two of 18 free-throw attempts. Sleepy Floyd had 16 points and Ewing 15 for the Hoyas in a game that was never in doubt.

Oregon State had just as easy a time with Idaho. Holding the normally volatile Vandals to 42 points, Oregon State cruised to an 18-point win behind Lester Conner's 24 points and 10 rebounds and Charlie Sitton's 16 points and seven rebounds.

To prove the pretourney prognosticators correct, Georgetown did almost nothing wrong when the team took the floor at Brigham Young University's arena against respected Oregon State in the West regional finals. At the half the Hoyas from Washington, DC, had compiled a 42–25 lead. Throughout, the Georgetown defense was as niggardly as ever, in the end allowing the Oregon State Beavers only 45 points, far below the 65 they had averaged in their two previous tournament games. The Hoyas, during the same 40 minutes of playing time, set an all-time NCAA record by shooting 74.4 percent from the floor (29 of 39 field goals). With Sleepy Floyd scoring 22 points and Pat Ewing 13, John Thompson's team impressed everyone who had witnessed the 24-point massacre in the West.

The Final Four for 1982 met at the Superdome in New Orleans, an arena that would enable the NCAA to attract the biggest crowd ever to a college basketball game.

North Carolina, most obvservers felt, had the easier task in the semifinals. Houston, after all, was the only unranked team in the Final Four and had been far from consistent during the year. But Dean Smith's Tar Heels had been less than consistent in their many appearances in Final Four competition. The chief threat that Houston had was Rob Williams, and Dean Smith set his Tar Heel defense to stop the high-scoring guard. It worked well. Everything worked well. Houston did not get onto the scoreboard until after the Tar Heels already had 14 points up there. But Houston did fight back and came within a basket by the half. North Carolina still dominated in the second half and never relinquished the lead. The final: North Carolina 68, Houston 63. When it was over, Houston's Rob Williams had only two points, the result of two free throws, and for the first time in his memory he had not scored a single field goal (zero for eight). The Tar Heel hero in that game was Sam Perkins, the veteran center racking up 25 points and 10 rebounds. Guard Michael Jordan had 18 points and James Worthy 14. For the Houston Cougars Lynden Rose scored 20, Larry Micheaux 18, and Clyde Drexler 17. But it had been North Carolina all the way, shooting a nifty 59.1 percent from the floor and 84.2 percent from the line, and living up to its number one billing. Now Dean Smith, for the second straight year and for the fourth time in his coaching career, was taking the Tar Heels to the NCAA championship game, hoping to banish forever their reputation for being unable to win the big one.

Georgetown was as ready as it would ever be, coach John Thompson said before its semifinal battle with Lousiville. No team had come anywhere close to beating Georgetown in its three preceding tournament games, and its vaunted defense had allowed an average of only 42.7 points a game. Denny Crum and his Cardinals were not intimidated by the Hoyas, however. After all, they still had four starters who had played on their 1979 national championship team. But they were far from complacent. "Put points on the board," Crum told

The tournament's Outstanding Player in 1982 was North Carolina's James Worthy. The All-American forward, masterful on defense as well as on offense, bucketed 28 points in the title game and averaged 17.4 over the Tar Heels' five games.

Center Sam Perkins was a viable force in North Carolina's tourney success in 1982. The strong center had game-high totals of 25 points and 10 rebounds in NC's semifinal victory over Houston.

North Carolina's coach, Dean Smith, finally won the national championship in 1982, his Tar Heels just edging Georgetown, 63–62.

Sophomore forward Matt Doherty averaged only 8.6 points for North Carolina in the 1982 tourney but was a hawk on defense.

Guard Michael Jordan contributed 16 points to North Carolina's championship win over Georgetown in 1982 and 18 points in the semifinal triumph over Houston. He averaged 13.2 points a game.

his team. "Break Georgetown's defensive stranglehold." At the same time Crum planned to give Georgetown a dose of its own strategy: full-court press and hound-dog defense from the very start.

As a result, it was a low-scoring game. The Hoyas led through almost all of the first half, allowing Louisville only 22 points during that period. But the Cardinals allowed the Hoyas only 24 during the same 20 minutes of playing time. The second half was also a period of defensive predomination, and again Georgetown came out two points ahead. The final was 50–46, and the Hoyas would make their first appearance in an NCAA championship game since 1943, when they lost to Wyoming. Forward Eric Smith was high for Georgetown with 14 points, and Sleepy Floyd had 13. Pat Ewing dominated the boards, grabbing a game-high 10 rebounds. For the Louisville Cardinals only Derek Smith scored in double figures, and just barely, with 10 points. As a team Louisville shot only 39.6 percent and were outrebounded 34–27.

The stage was set for a very exciting finale. It was a true pick-it game, and there were as many people who thought Georgetown would win as there were siding with North Carolina. At the opening tip-off the Superdome was filled with 61,612 spectators, the largest crowd ever to witness a college basketball game. And tens of millions more were watching it on television or listening to it on the radio. The NCAA college basketball championship was by 1982 as big a sports spectacular as the Super Bowl or the World Series. It had come a long way since that first battle for the college basketball crown back at a gymnasium on the Northwestern campus in 1939.

In 1982 the spectacle at the Superdome was surely worth it for all those who watched it, a thriller all the way to the final buzzer. But it was a strange game. Georgetown center Pat Ewing was apparently plagued with overwhelming anxiety at the outset; the first eight points scored by North Carolina were the result of four goaltending calls against him. Even so, the Hoyas maintained the lead until North Carolina tied it at 18. The Hoya defense, usually so effective, was having trouble containing Tar Heel superstar James Worthy. The big forward dropped nine field goals through the net during the first half. But still North Carolina trailed 32–31 at the end of the period.

The lead changed hands a number of times during the second period. With 6:04 left in the game, James Worthy dropped in two free throws to give the Tar Heels a 57–56 lead. They maintained that lead for the next 4½ minutes, but the game was far from over. With North Carolina ahead 61–58, Pat Ewing sank a 13-footer to bring the Hoyas within a point. Then he grabbed the rebound on a missed Tar Heel free throw; got the ball to Sleepy Floyd, who let fly a nine-foot jumper that threaded the net; and Georgetown had the lead with 57 seconds left. But then, 42 seconds later, Tar Heel freshman Michael Jordan went up with a 16-foot jumper to put North Carolina back on top 63–62, with only 15 seconds left on the clock.

Georgetown still had plenty of time to work for a last shot and wrench the game from the hands of the Tar Heels and the heart of Dean Smith. But then Hoya guard Fred Brown threw perhaps the most ill-starred pass in NCAA tourney history. Dribbling down the court, he suddenly wheeled and passed the ball to the side to a player he thought was Hoya forward Eric Smith. But the figure standing there was wearing a white uniform, none other than Tar Heel James Worthy. Flabbergasted, Worthy caught the ball, then began dribbling toward the other end of the court. In desperation, Smith fouled him intentionally, but only two seconds were left and it did not matter when Worthy missed both free throws. The score stood at 63–62 when the buzzer rang an end to the 1982 college basketball championship.

Dean Smith finally had a winner, and another NCAA trophy would go back to Chapel Hill. James Worthy had had his best game of the tourney that night, scoring 28 points (13 of 17 from the floor), and was a clear-cut choice for the Oustanding Player award. Guard Michael Jordan contributed 16 and Sam Perkins 10. For the Hoyas Pat Ewing had 23 points and a game-high 11 rebounds,

Awards, 1982

Outstanding Player
James Worthy (North Carolina)

All-Tournament Team
James Worthy (North Carolina)
Sam Perkins (North Carolina)
Michael Jordan (North Carolina)
Pat Ewing (Georgetown)
Eric Floyd (Georgetown)

while Sleepy Floyd dropped in 18 and Eric Smith 14.

It was a tournament blessed with a variety of excellent teams, fine individual performances, and numerous nail-biting games, but none was more breathtaking or more intricately played than the championship tilt between North Carolina and Georgetown. And Dean Smith had to have a good feeling. The jinx was finally broken.

15
Cinderella State

As the 1983 season came to a close, only two of the previous year's Final Four teams were ranked among the nation's top four teams and neither were from the final two. But runners-up Houston and Louisville were tabbed numbers one and two by both AP and UPI in 1983 and were considered in the dream class. Reigning champ North Carolina was rated no higher than eighth, and last year's second-place Georgetown barely made the national rankings at number 20.

Houston was almost a unanimous choice for the nation's top spot. The Cougars sported a record of 27–2, and were 16–0 in the Southwest Conference. Louisville was also dramatically impressive, 29–3 overall and 12–0 in the Metro Conference. But these two top-ranked teams could not meet in the NCAA championship game in 1983 because Houston was slated in the Midwest region and Louisville in the Mideast; the winners of those regions would face each other in the semifinals.

Houston, coached by Guy V. Lewis, was an awesome force, with the most intimidating frontcourt in the college game. At one forward was certified All-American Clyde Drexler, a 6′6″ leaper who could do things with his body that would astonish Rubber Man. At the other forward was 6′9″ Larry "Mr. Mean" Micheaux, and at center was 7′ Akeem Abdul Olajuwon from Nigeria. They called their act "Phi Slamma Jamma," a fraternity of slam-dunk artists. The Cougars also had Michael Young, a starter at forward the year before, in

Larry "Mr. Mean" Micheaux (40) and Clyde "the Glide" Drexler battle each other for a Houston rebound. Both charter members of "Phi Slamma Jamma," the two frontcourters were instrumental in bringing Houston to the Final Four in 1982 and 1983.

the backcourt, but he was as capable as anybody at stuffing the ball through the hoop. Houston also had the advantage of playing their first tournament game in their own hometown.

Their opponent was unranked Maryland who had won 19 of 29 regular season games and had ended up in a tie for third in the ever-rugged Atlantic Coast Conference (trailing Virginia and North Carolina and even-up with North Carolina State). Maryland had survived a 52–51 game against Tennessee-Chattanooga in the first round, but they proved to be no match for the classy Cougars.

The game was "boring," in the words of Houston coach Guy Lewis, as Maryland tried desperately to keep it at the slowest of paces. At first they succeeded, the score at half was only Houston 26, Maryland 24. But the strategy failed in the second period and Houston blew the game open, winning it 60–50.

Houston moved on to Kansas City for the regional playoffs where they would face Memphis State, who were 22–7 during the regular season and a team that had just done away with the Georgetown Hoyas and their towering center Pat Ewing. The five from Memphis had briefly been ranked number one early in the season, and they were getting great performances from 6′11″ sophomore forward Keith Lee (he had 28 points and 15 rebounds in State's win over Georgetown). Also slated to do battle with Houston's fabled frontcourt was State's 6′9″ center, Detrick Phillips.

It was a battle of the frontcourt, and Houston won it handily. The most devastating force was Akeem Abdul Olajuwon, who scored a game-high 21 points. He dominated the boards and intimidated Memphis on defense. Usually productive, Keith Lee was held to 13 points, a dismal 6 of 15 from the floor. The final score was 70–63. Everyone agreed, the Cougars were living up to the pre-tourney predictions that they would bring the 1983 trophy back to Texas.

Villanova was the Midwest's number three seed. They earned the right to try and derail the Houston express by virtue of surviving a 55–54 game with Iowa, a team that had stung second-seeded Missouri a week earlier. Villanova was paced by senior center John Pinone, who, at 6′8″, was considerably shorter than Houston's Olajuwon. Villanova also had a fine forward in 6′9″ Ed Pinckney and a deadly shooter in guard Stewart Granger.

Houston was a definite favorite in the regional final, and they showed why by decimating Villanova, 89–71, for their 25th consecutive victory. The overwhelming presence of Olajuwon and forward Larry Micheaux carried the game. Micheaux scored a career high 30 points and grabbed 12 rebounds; Olajuwon had 20 points, 13 rebounds, and rejected eight Villanova shots. Michael Young added another 20 points for the Cougars and Clyde Drexler slammed in 12. Villanova was never in the game. The Cougars, a surprise visitor to the previous year's Final Four, was no surprise at all in 1983. And there they would face Denny Crum's Louisville Cardinals.

Louisville did not have such a luxury cruise through their region as Houston did. Coach Crum, who guided the Cardinals to the national championship in 1980, had also brought them to the semifinals in 1982 only to lose a heartbreaker to Georgetown. Now, in 1983, his returning starters from that team included an All-American candidate, guard Lancaster Gordon, and forward Rodney McCray (who as a freshman started on the championship team of 1980). At the other forward was Rodney's brother, Scooter; at center 6′8″ Charles Jones; and at the other guard, Milt Wagner.

Louisville's first encounter was with Tennessee who had snuck by Marquette in the first round by a single point. The Vols, unranked and 19–11 during the regular season, were decided underdogs but they gave the Cardinals a run for their proverbial money through the first three quarters of the game. With 10 minutes remaining, only two points separated the two teams. But Louisville got its act together and pulled away to win 70–57. Lancaster Gordon and Charles Jones led the Cardinals with 18 points apiece.

The win qualified them to meet a very tough Arkansas team in the regionals at Knoxville. The Razorbacks were ranked ninth in the country, had lost only three of 28 regular season games, and had bombed a good Purdue team to get to the regionals. Arkansas had two

Rodney McCray (22) powers for two Louisville points in the Mideast regional title game against Kentucky. The Cardinals beat their intrastate rivals by 12 points, and McCray accounted for 15 Cardinal points and eight rebounds.

Louisville's Scooter McCray (21) battles for a rebound here in an early round game against Tennessee. The Scooter had 10 points that game.

dazzling guards in Darrell Walker and Alvin Robertson (they scored 49 points and accounted for 11 steals in the win over Purdue), and a fine center in Joe Kleine. They had it all together in the first half against Louisville, and when the buzzer sent the two teams to their respective locker rooms Arkansas was ahead, 37–27. Louisville, however, fought back and finally tied it at 61-all with less than two minutes left. Kleine dropped one in for the Razorbacks, but Lancaster Gordon tied it with a fade-away jumper with a little more than a minute left. Arkansas tried to hold the ball for the last shot but a traveling violation turned it over to Louisville. The Cardinals got the coveted last shot which bounced around on the rim until Scooter McCray managed to tip it in just as the buzzer ended the game. The final: Louisville 65, Arkansas 63.

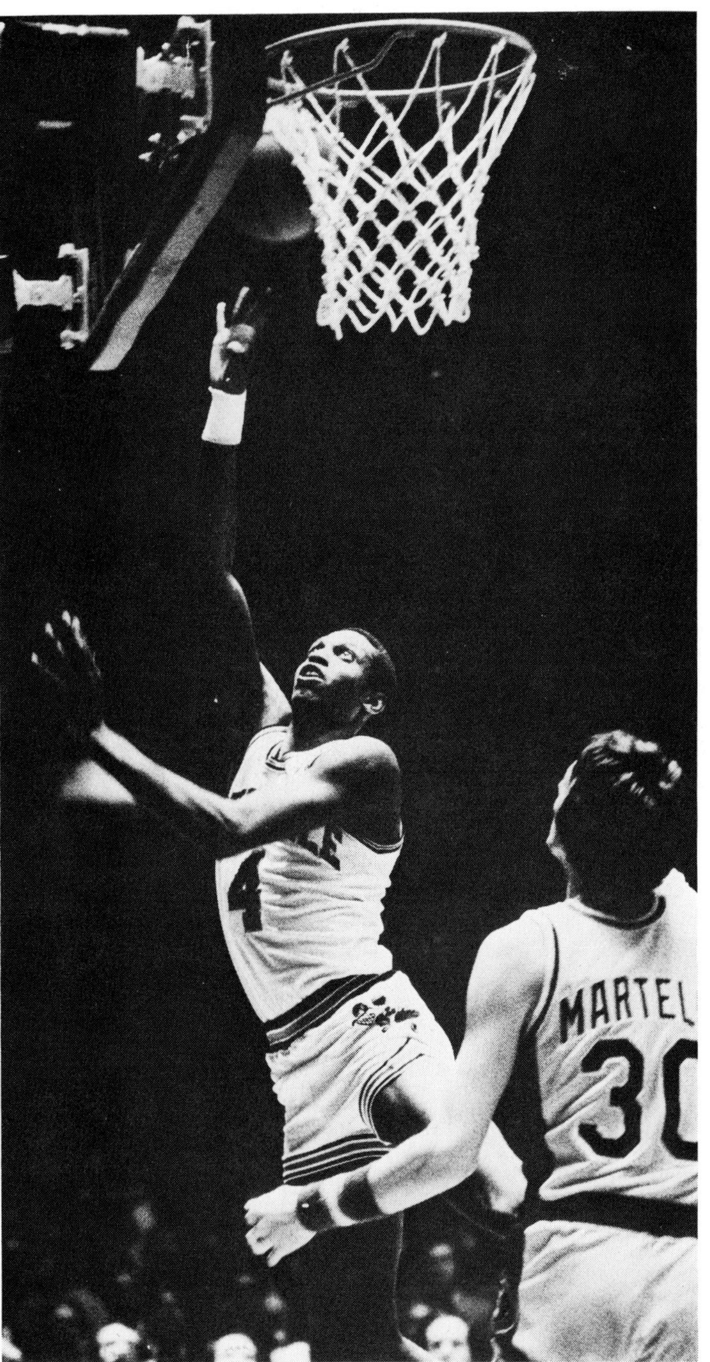

A gymnastic lay-up from the fingertips of Lancaster Gordon (4), Louisville's All-American guard. Gordon scored 24 points, the game-high in the Cardinal win over Kentucky, and 17 in their semifinal loss to Houston.

In the other Midwest regional, Kentucky surprised second-seed and nationally ranked number five Indiana, 64–59, setting up a confrontation between the two dogged arch-rivals of the Blue Grass State. Louisville and Kentucky had not faced each other in an NCAA basketball game since 1959, principally because Kentucky had consistently disdained to play the Cardinals in the regular season and a postseason encounter never materialized although both teams had made numerous trips to the NCAA tourney.

In 1983, Kentucky had won 21 of its 28 regular season games and was ranked tenth by UPI and twelfth by the AP. They were paced by guard Dirk Minniefield and 6′11″ center Melvin Turpin.

Kentucky governor John Y. Brown showed up at the game in Knoxville wearing a sportcoat one half of which was Louisville red and the other Kentucky blue. The entire state had taken sides, so had the Kentucky sportswriters. The game took on special meaning as it was hyped throughout the nation by the media. Louisville was a two-point favorite before the opening tip-off, but they certainly did not look like it during the first half. Kentucky outshot the Cardinals 62 percent to 40 percent and fashioned a 37–30 lead at the half.

But Louisville fought back in the second half, just as they had against Arkansas. As the game came down to the final buzzer, Louisville had rallied and taken a two-point lead, 62–60. But then Wildcat sharpshooter Jim Master let fly a long jumper from the corner that snapped the net and sent the game into overtime.

Louisville coach Denny Crum was worried and said so afterwards: "Usually when a team hits that kind of shot, that team goes on to win." But the momentum didn't shift to Kentucky, the adrenalin did not flow freely in the Wildcats' veins. Instead Louisville blew it apart in the overtime period and walked off with an 80–68 triumph. So, the "Comeback Kids," as some were calling them now, would return to the Final Four in '83 with the chance to take on the only team ranked above them in the national polls. It was already being touted, in effect, as the tourney's championship game.

Most felt the winner surely would have little trouble with the survivor of the other semifinal match.

The reason for such speculation was based on the fact that in the other two regionals, two very large surprises had emerged triumphant, Georgia in the East and North Carolina State in the West. Before the tourney, neither team had been given much of a chance at arriving in Alburquerque for the Final Four matchups. Georgia, although ranked 15th in the country by UPI and 18th by the AP, had an uninspiring record of 21–9 and had ended up in a four-way tie for fourth place in the Southeastern Conference. North Carolina State, 20–10, had rankings of 14 and 16 respectively in the UPI and AP polls, and they ended their season in a tie for third place in the Atlantic Coast Conference.

Georgia was, surprisingly, seeded fourth in the East where St. John's (nationally ranked number three) and reigning titleholder North Carolina were the strong favorites. The Bulldogs from Georgia, guided by coach Hugh Durham, were, in fact, making their very first appearance in the NCAA tourney. They had not won their conference basketball title since 1933. Georgia was led by forwards James Banks and Lamar Heard. Vern Fleming was considered to be the best guard in the Southeastern Conference. Although an eruptive scorer center Terry Fair was, however, only 6′7″ and the tallest of the starting five.

Unlikely Georgia came about as close to being eliminated in the first round as a team could. They had to come from behind to snatch the game from Virginia Commonwealth, a victory secured when James Banks sunk a 12-foot jump shot with three seconds left. The win was controversial as well because a lot of observers felt the ball had been touched by Banks' teammate Lamar Heard while it was on the rim and therefore should not have counted. Nevertheless, it did count and the Georgia Bulldogs survived to face the winner of the Rutgers–St. Johns confrontation.

St. Johns, dubbed the "Beast of the East," had won 27 games and lost only four during the regular season. Many NCAA watchers

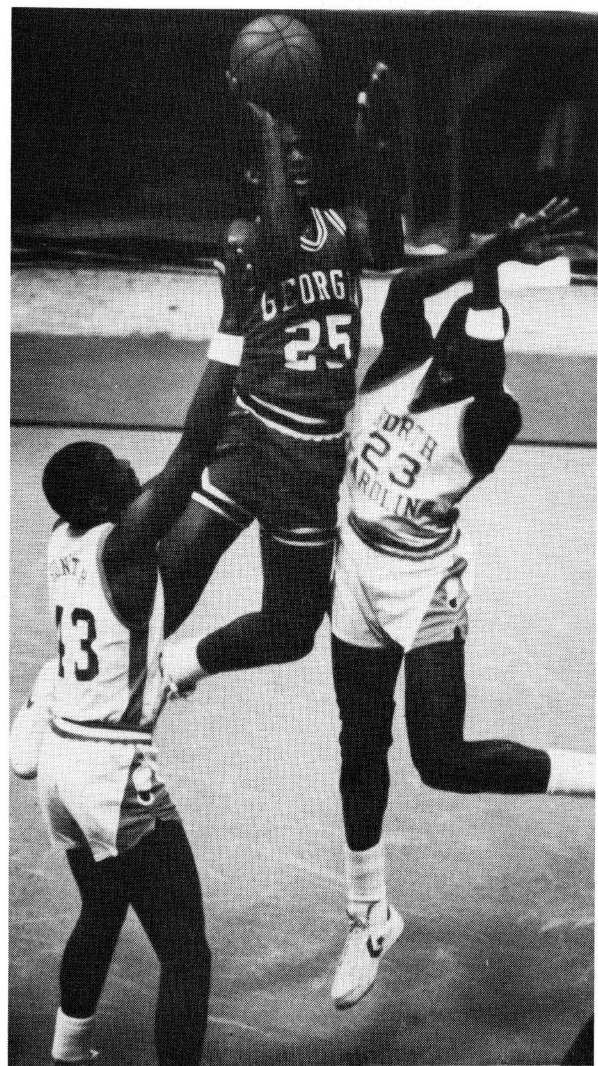

James Banks was Georgia's premier offensive threat in 1983, here going up for a soft jumper against North Carolina. Banks banked 20 points as the Bulldogs secured the title to the East regional. Tar Heel defenders are Curtis Hunter (43) and Michael Jordan (23).

thought they had just as good a shot at the tourney crown as Houston and Louisville. Chris Mullen was the Redmen's leader on the floor, and he was ably supported by David Russell, Kevin Williams, and Billy Goodwin. The 6′6″ Mullen scored 24 points as St. Johns sent Rutgers back to New Jersey.

He also scored 19 in the regional against Georgia, but notably favored St. Johns simply could not handle the Bulldogs, much to everyone's surprise. Most clearly they could not handle Bulldog center Terry Fair, who scored 27 points. Georgia dominated most of the second half, although the Redmen got within a point with five seconds left. But then Fair

Louisville's 6'8" center Charles Jones goes up for a slam-dunk here. He had 12 points, 11 rebounds, and his hands full with Akeem Abdul Olajuwon in the semifinal match-up with Houston.

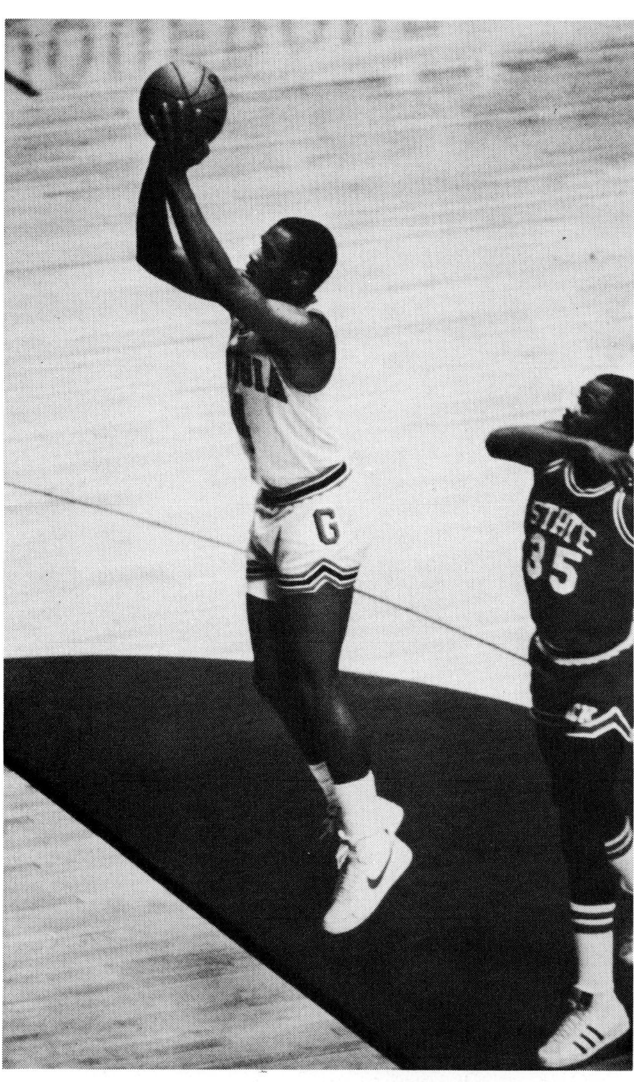

Georgia's Gerald Crosby goes up for a little jumper in the semifinal against NC State. Crosby had 12 points for the frustrated Bulldogs that game. Number 35 on NC State is guard Sidney Lowe.

Cozell McQueen (45), NC State center, hooks a short one here over Tar Heel star Sam Perkins (41). McQueen was an important factor in the Wolfpack's frontcourt throughout the 1983 tourney.

slam-dunked one to seal the Bulldogs victory, 70–67. Lamar Heard scored another 11 points for Georgia, and Vern Fleming and James Banks had 10 each.

The win gave Georgia the opportunity to face reigning champ North Carolina, who had demolished James Madison and Ohio State, in the East regionals. The Tar Heels had three starters back from the crown bearers of 1982: center Sam Perkins, guard Michael Jordan, and forward Matt Doherty. The Tar Heels were a heavy favorite, but they fell, and how the Bulldogs pulled off their second consecutive major upset had everyone scratching their heads. Georgia hung in there during the first half, trailing most of the time, but managing to end up on the better side of a 37–35 halftime score. Then, in the second half, their most fearsome scorer Terry Fair went to the bench with four fouls with the score Georgia 41, North Carolina 40. There was a long 18 minutes remaining in the game, and most thought the Tar Heels would now assert themselves and forge ahead to victory.

But Georgia was remarkable, and the Bulldogs steadily pulled ahead. With a minute and 20 seconds left, they had built an 80–65 lead. The final score was 82–77, but the Tar Heels had never really threatened. James Banks was the Bulldog high-point man with 20, while Vern Fleming and Gerald Crosby contributed 17 apiece. For the hapless Tar Heels, Michael Jordan scored 26. And so Georgia, in its first appearance in the tournament, would go on to Albuquerque to be part of the Final Four festivities.

There they would face the North Carolina State Wolfpack who also had overcome some rather enormous odds to reach the semifinals. Like Georgia, NC State had almost been eliminated in their first game, managing to pull off a 69–67 win in overtime against a feisty Pepperdine team. After that, it was one miracle after another. Under one of the game's most animated and entertaining coaches, Jim Valvano, the Wolfpack won 20 of 30 games that year. Their sparkplug was guard Dereck Whittenburg, but they counted on 6′11″ forward Thurl Bailey for much of their scoring. State also had a fine guard in Sidney Lowe and two strong frontcourt men in center Co-

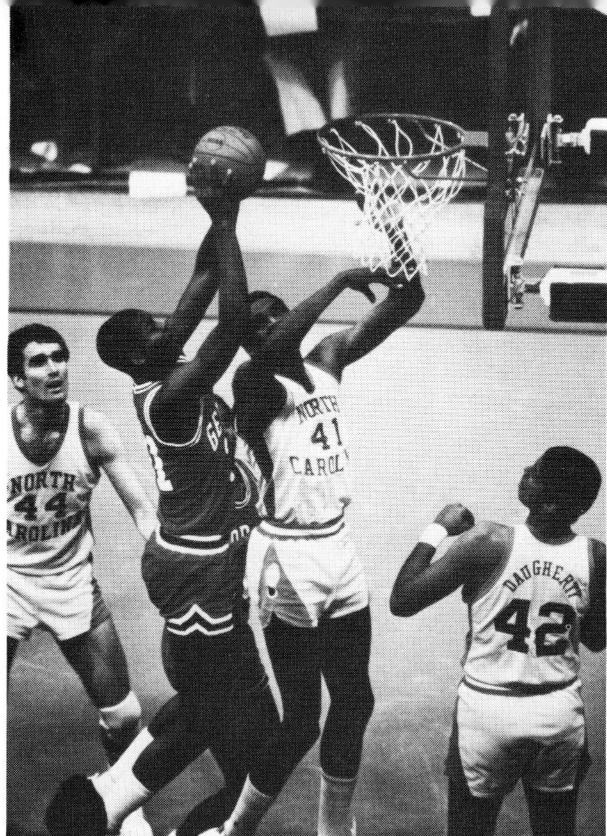

Richard Corhen is about to net two for the Georgia Bulldogs in their regional final win over North Carolina. Corhen came off the bench to contribute seven crucial points. Tar Heels in the picture are Matt Doherty (44), Sam Perkins (41), and Brad Daugherty (42).

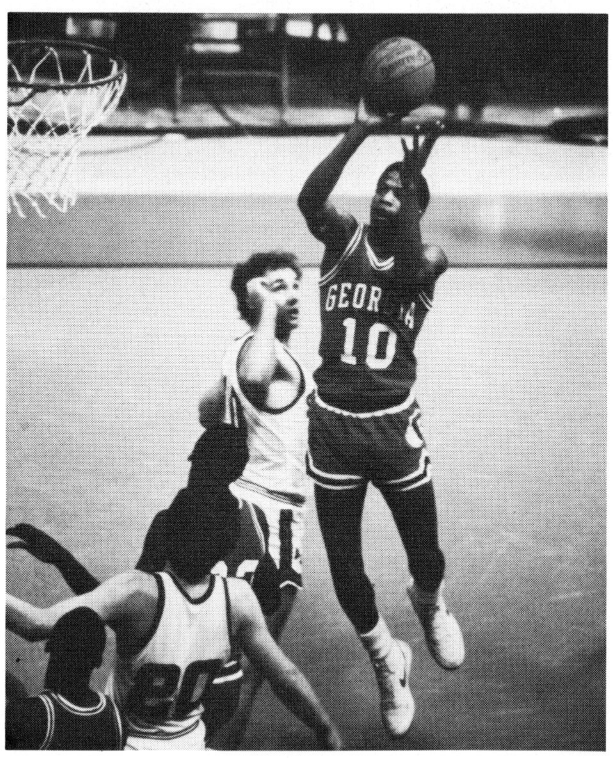

Vern Fleming, pegged as the SEC's best guard in 1983, goes up for two against St. Johns in the East regional. Fleming had 10 points, but would have his best game in the semifinal loss to NC State when he had team highs of 14 points and 11 rebounds.

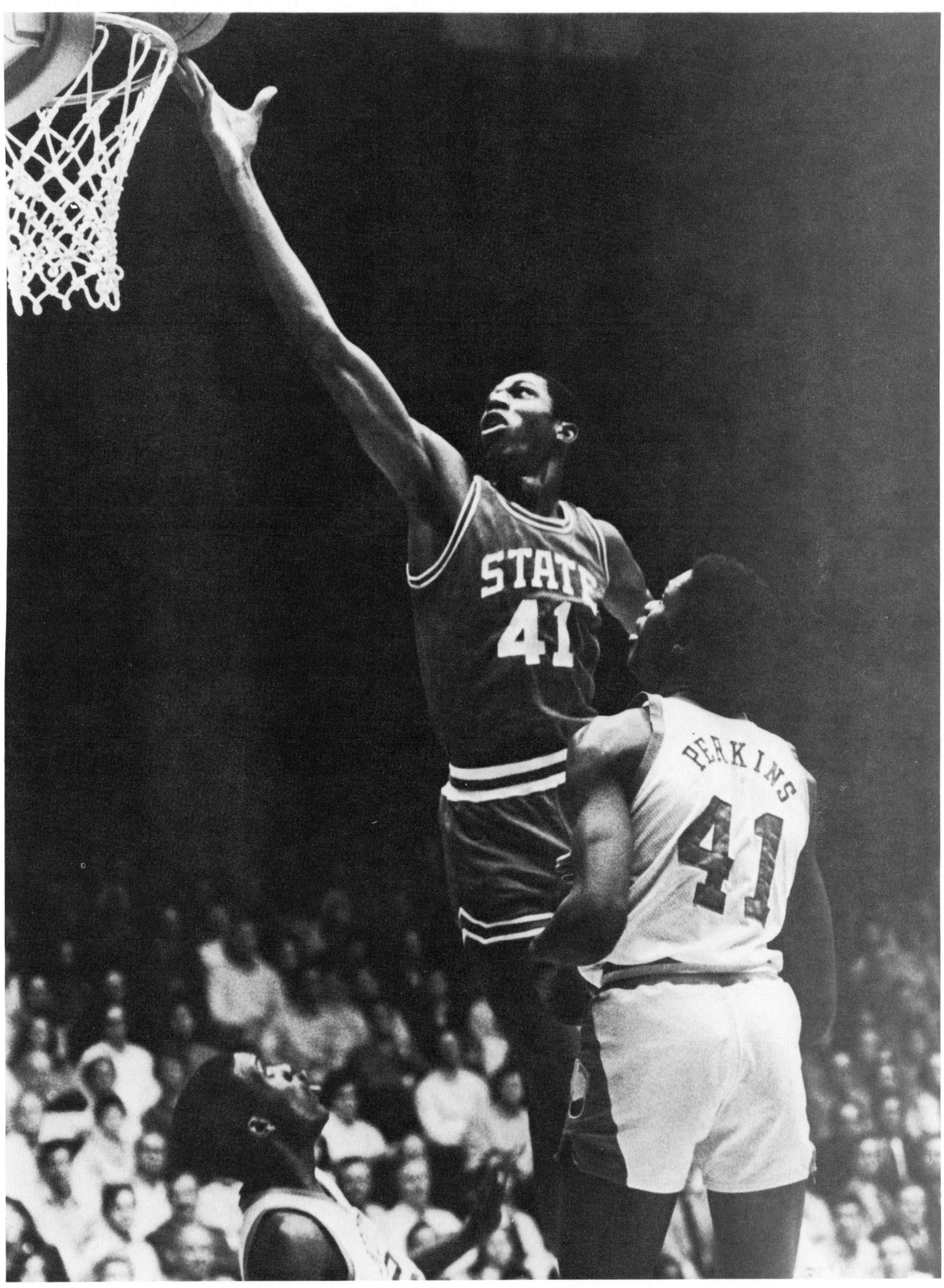

Thurl Bailey (41), with the touch of an angel, deposits two here for North Carolina State. Bailey was the tournament's second highest scorer with 101 points, an average of 16.8 per game. Looking on is North Carolina All-American Sam Perkins (41).

zell McQueen and forward Lorenzo Charles.

The road to the Final Four was beset with many obstacles for the Wolfpack. After the Pepperdine scare, sixth-ranked Nevada-Las Vegas lay in wait. Jerry Tarkanian's Rebel five was a decided favorite, and they led by as many as 12 points midway through the second half. But here came NC State again, whittling away at the UNLV lead.

Then, with the Rebels up by a point and only seconds remaining, hot-hand Dereck Whittenburg lofted a 20-footer for the desperate Wolfpack. But it didn't go in. It came off the rim and Thurl Bailey tipped it back. Again it bounded away. Bailey went back up, managed to grab the ball, then tossed up an off-balance jumper just before the buzzer rang. It looped over the rim and into the net to give the Wolfpack an upset victory, 71–70. Bailey had 25 points and Lorenzo Charles 17, while Whittenburg had been held to a disappointing 13.

The victory sent them to Ogden, Utah, for the regional playoffs where they had to face the Utah Utes, who had surprised seventh-ranked UCLA a week earlier. To most, it seemed a toss-up. NC State did come from a much tougher conference, yet on the other hand the Utes had knocked off second-seed UCLA and a good Illinois team.

The game was close, at least through the first half and the first two minutes of the second. At that point Utah led 32–30, but then the incredibly resilient Wolfpack exploded. They shot better than 68 percent, and outscored the Utes 45–24 in the remaining 18 minutes of the game. The final: NC State 75, Utah 56. The most productive member of the Wolfpack was Whittenburg, who tallied 27 points.

That victory left one more obstacle, and it was a considerable one. Fourth-ranked Virginia (27–4) the region's top seed, with everybody's All-American center, 7′4″ Ralph Sampson, had disposed of Washington State and Boston College to get to the West regional final. State had beaten the Virginia Cavaliers in the Atlantic Coast Conference playoffs, but the Virginians had defeated them twice during the season. And besides Sampson, Virginia had proven scorers in guards Othell Wilson and Rick Carlisle and forward Craig Robinson. The odds makers liked Virginia by five.

The odds makers were wrong, however. Ralph Sampson's college basketball career came to a premature end that night in Ogden, Utah. Virginia, who led through much of the first half and held a five-point lead at intermission, could not handle the "Come-From-Behind-Boys" from North Carolina and the exceptional play of Whittenburg and Thurl Bailey. Although State was down by as much as seven points in the second half, they kept pace with Sampson and Company and eventually the Wolfpack tied the game. But Virginia went ahead 63–62. State, however, had the ball, and Whittenburg was maneuvering for a last shot, one that would win the game with a true Frank Merriwell finish. He didn't get the shot because suddenly he spotted Lorenzo Charles under the basket and rifled the ball to him.

The Wolfpack forward went up for the lay-up but a desperate Ralph Sampson denied it by fouling him. After a seemingly endless time-out, Charles, a sophomore, went to the free throw line and methodically sunk both charity tosses. Still, seconds remained. The Wolfpack collapsed on Sampson and no one could get him the ball. So Tim Mullen tried to change the outcome with a long jumper, but he missed. Cavalier guard Othell Wilson got the rebound and another chance, but he too missed and the buzzer heralded another NC State upset. Whittenburg had 24 points for the night and Bailey 14. Lorenzo Charles added 11 points and a team-high 10 rebounds. Ralph Sampson in his swan song game scored 23 points and collected 11 rebounds.

The Final Four gathered in neutral Albuquerque, New Mexico, a city with a mile-high elevation, where, as the sportscasters kept telling everybody, the oxygen was thin and everybody was sure to get tired. The first game on the slate pitted the Georgia Bulldogs against the Wolfpack from North Carolina State.

Between the two, they had lost 19 regular season games. The semifinal match-up between such improbables caused some to call it

The 1983 champs, the Wolfpack from North Carolina State. **Top row** (left to right): Craig Sink (head trainer), Gary Bryant (manager), Ed McLean (assistant coach), Ray Martin (assistant coach), Jim Valvano (head coach), Tom Abatemarco (assistant coach), Max Perry (graduate assistant coach), Steve Whitt (manager), Jim Rehbok (assistant trainer). **Middle row** (left to right): George McClain, Walt Densmore, Dinky Proctor, Cozell McQueen, Lorenzo Charles, Mike Warren, Terry Gannon, Ernie Myers. **Bottom row** (left to right): Alvin Battle, Thurl Bailey, Sidney Lowe, Dereck Whittenburg, Quinton Leonard, Harold Thompson.

North Carolina State coach Jim Valvano, shouting words of encouragement, discontent, or derision here, brought the Wolfpack's Cinderella team to the 1983 NCAA national championship.

the "Cinderella Bowl," while others referred to it as "the Jayvee prelim before *the* varsity game." State's coach Jim Valvano conceded that the winner of it would certainly be the underdog in the championship game. But his ace guard Dereck Whittenburg added, with keen insight, "Cinderella means they don't expect you to be here. It doesn't mean you aren't good."

Jimmy the Greek gave Georgia a two-point edge in his odds assessment. Moments after the opening tip, however, the Bulldogs set out to prove him decisively wrong. Whether it was the altitude or the fact that it was the Georgians first trip to the classic—or perhaps just an outrageously bad night—Georgia floundered miserably through the first half. After 11 minutes they had made only four of 24 shots and trailed 19–10. At the intermission they trailed 33–22, having sunk only 10 of 36 shots, a 28 percent shooting average. The usually deft Georgia shooter James Banks was as cold as the tips of some of the neighboring mountaintops.

The Bulldogs did rally a bit in the second half and came as close as eight points, but it was not long before the Wolfpack ran it back up to an 18-point deficit. The final score, 67–60, was a misleadingly close set of figures because Georgia was never in the game. Whittenburg had hooped 20 points for the Staters and Thurl Bailey had slammed in another 20. Center Cozell McQueen collected a game-high 13 rebounds. For the battered Bulldogs, guard Vern Fleming was high with 14 points but he was only seven for 17 from the floor. Banks accounted for 13 points, sinking only five of 19 shots.

The "varsity game" which followed lived up to all expectations. The Phi Slamma Jamma dunking fraternity from Houston and the satin-smooth Louisville Cardinals played a precision-perfect first half, trading the lead time and time again (there were a total of 10 ties during that period). By the time the intermission came, Louisville had edged out to a 41–36 lead, principally the result of outrebounding the Cougars 26–15 and the deadliness of guard Milt Wagner, who dumped in 16 points.

The second half was another matter altogether, perhaps one of the most dazzling displays of power basketball ever put on in the NCAA tournament. Louisville built a lead of 57–49, but then Houston erupted with the ferocity of Mt. St. Helens and in just a little more than five minutes of play outscored Louisville 17–1, and commanded a 66–58 lead.

As Phil Hersh of the Chicago *Sun Times* described it:

> "In the telling stretch, which lasted 5:28, Michael Young flew out of the corner to dunk Clyde Drexler's lob, Drexler dunked a pass from Alvin Franklin, Benny Anders stole the ball and dunked over Charles Jones, and Drexler had a driving, dipsy-do, who coulda thunk he'd do it dunk."

Besides those events, there was the predominant force of Akeem Abdul Olajuwon, who,

Milt Wagner (20) displays pure perfection of style with this jumper. Wagner was the only All-Tournament selection from outside the final two in 1983. He had a game-high 24 points in Louisville's semifinal loss to Houston.

The NCAA's 1983 Outstanding Player, 7' Akeem Abdul Olajuwon slam-dunks one here. One of the chief brothers of "Phi Slamma Jamma," Olajuwon grabbed 22 rebounds and scored 21 points in Houston's semifinal win over Louisville. He had 20 points in the championship game but despite his brilliant performance the Cougars fell to North Carolina State..

when the final buzzer rang had registered a total of 22 rebounds, 21 points, eight blocks, and four dunks. Houston's amazing second half propelled them to a 94–81 victory, and left all eyewitnesses in imponderable awe at the magnitude of their basketball brilliance.

Besides Olajuwon's impressive stats, Drexler had 21 points, Young 16, and Franklin 13. Milt Wagner was high for the disappointed Wolfpack with 24.

To the championship, Houston brought a 26-game winning streak; North Carolina State, only the fact that if they won they would become the first team ever to have taken the NCAA crown after losing 10 regular season games. And after the display Houston put on in the semifinals, there was little reason to question why the Phi Slamma Jammers were favored by as much as eight points by some oddsmakers. The only voice of guarded dissent heard was that of former Marquette coach and current basketball broadcaster Al McGuire, who raised more than a few eyebrows when he said if the winning point total was only in the 50s the winning team would be North Carolina State.

The strategies were predictable. Guy Lewis wanted his Cougars to run, gun, and slam-dunk. NC State's Jim Valvano said before the game, "If we get the opening tip, we won't take a shot till Tuesday morning."

The Wolfpack did not wait until Tuesday morning, however, and began shooting early and effectively, in fact scored the games's first six points. The underdog suddenly became the top dog as the Staters smoothly controlled the first half of play, building a 33–25 lead. It was Thurl Bailey who dominated the inside, scor-

Sidney Lowe was good enough to make the 1983 All-Tournament team. A deadly outside shooter and deft ballhandler, Lowe scored 10 points and had a crucial 11 assists in the Wolfpack's semifinal game against Georgia.

The keynote of NC State's 1983 success story was provided by Dereck Whittenburg (4), laying up an uncontested two here against Duke. Whittenburg was the 1983 tourney's top scorer, 120 points, an average of 20 per game.

ing 15 points that half, and not the tourney's otherwise most imposing force, Akeem Abdul Olajuwon. And the most dazzling of the Phi Slamma Jammers, Clyde Drexler, had only one basket in those 20 minutes of play, and most disturbing, four fouls.

Still, no one could forget the remarkable turnaround Houston had staged against Louisville in that pyrotechnical second half of the semifinal game. And from the moment this second half began, it appeared that there was a repeat performance in the making. The Cougars, playing without Drexler, surged, and the Wolfpack stumbled. In the first 11 minutes of the half, Houston outscored State 15–2. With the score now 42–35 in their favor, Houston surprisingly chose to steal Jim Valvano's tactic and slow the game to a crawl; it was a method of play the Phi Slamma Jammers seldom even thought about and one they would live to rue. Although the Cougars could slam and stuff, they were not subtle ballhandlers and soon the turnovers enabled State to inch back into the game. With just under two minutes remaining, the Wolfpack tied the score at 52 apiece. Houston's lead had melted away under their own mistakes and the superb outside shooting of Dereck Whittenburg, Sidney Lowe, and reserve Terry Gannon.

Houston had the ball, and the strategy now selected by Guy Lewis was to hold it for the remaining minute and a half and take the last shot. Jim Valvano's counter-strategy, however, was not to let them do that. Aware the Cougars were less than invincible from the free-throw line, he told his team to foul. With just over a minute left, Whittenburg fouled guard Alvin Franklin. He missed the first of a one-and-one and Cozell McQueen swept in the rebound for the Wolfpack. There were 44 seconds to go when State took a time-out. Now, it was their turn to hold for the last shot.

The plan was for Whittenburg to loft one of his deadly jumpers just before the buzzer. He was hounded, however, and could not get in range for a decent shot, but finally managed to pump off a 35-footer. It didn't get to the rim, but it did get to the hands of a leaping Lorenzo Charles under the basket. He went right back up and slam-dunked it through. North Carolina State was a winner, 54–52, ironically climaxing it with the Phi Slamma Jamma's own patented weapon, the stuff.

Thurl Bailey was high for the Wolfpack with 15 points (all in the first half) and Dereck Whittenburg had 14. For Houston, Akeem Abdul Olajuwon had 20 points and was named the tourney's Outstanding Player.

When it was all over, there were two voices ringing loud with truth. The final score was in the 50s and, as Al McGuire had predicted, underdog North Carolina State was on the elevated end of it. And now, no one was apt to dispute Dereck Whittenburg's observation that being a Cinderella team "doesn't mean you aren't good."

Appendix

1939 Tournament Stats

Semifinals

Ohio State	fg	ft-fta	pf	tp
Hull	10	8- 8	1	28
Baker	2	0- 0	2	4
Schick	3	1- 1	3	7
Dawson	1	0- 2	1	2
Lynch	0	0- 1	3	0
Mickelson	1	0- 0	0	2
Stafford	1	0- 0	0	2
Sattler	3	2- 3	1	8
Maag	0	0- 0	0	0
Boughner	0	0- 0	0	0
Mees	0	0- 0	0	0
Scott	0	0- 0	0	0
Totals	21	11-15	11	53

Villanova	fg	ft-fta	pf	tp
Lazorchak	2	0- 0	1	4
Montgomery	1	1- 3	4	3
Dubino	1	0- 3	3	2
Krutulis	2	1- 1	2	5
Nugent	7	2- 3	2	16
Duzminski	2	2- 3	3	6
Sinnott	0	0- 0	0	0
Rice	0	0- 0	0	0
Robinson	0	0- 0	0	0
Yung	0	0- 0	0	0
Totals	15	6-13	15	36

Oregon	fg	ft-fta	pf	tp
Gale	3	5- 7	4	11
Hardy	0	3- 3	1	3
Sarpola	0	0- 0	0	0
Mullen	0	1- 2	0	1
Dick	6	2- 2	1	14
Wintermute	4	2- 2	1	10
Johansen	4	0- 1	3	8
Pavalunas	1	0- 0	1	2
Anet	1	4- 5	2	6
Totals	19	17-22	13	55

Oklahoma	fg	ft-fta	pf	tp
McNatt	5	2- 3	1	12
Roop	1	1- 2	2	3
Walker	1	0- 1	0	2
Corbin	1	0- 0	0	2
Scheffler	2	2- 2	4	6
Mullen	0	0- 0	1	0
Kerr	3	3- 3	0	9
Mesch	1	0- 1	4	2
Zoller	0	0- 0	2	0
Snodgrass	0	1- 1	1	1
Totals	14	9-13	15	37

Championship

Oregon	fg	ft-fta	pf	tp
Gale	2	4- 5	1	8
Dick	5	5- 5	3	15
Wintermute	2	0- 1	1	4
Anet	4	2- 3	3	10
Johansen	4	1- 2	1	9
Mullen	0	0- 0	0	0
Pavalunas	0	0- 0	0	0
Totals	17	12-16	9	46

Ohio State	fg	ft-fta	pf	tp
Hull	5	2- 2	2	12
Baker	0	0- 1	0	0
Schick	1	0- 0	1	2
Dawson	1	0- 0	4	2
Lynch	3	1- 3	3	7
Maag	0	0- 0	0	0
Scott	0	1- 1	1	1
Boughner	1	0- 0	0	2
Sattler	3	1- 2	0	7
Mickelson	0	0- 0	2	0
Stafford	0	0- 0	0	0
Totals	14	5- 9	13	33

1940 Tournament Stats

Semifinals

Indiana	fg	ft	pf	tp
McCreary	0	0	3	0
Schaefer	2	4	3	8
W. Menke	4	2	4	10
Dro	2	1	2	5
Huffman	2	2	3	6
Zimmer	1	1	0	3
Dorsey	0	0	0	0
Armstrong	2	3	0	7
Totals	13	13	15	39

Duquesne	fg	ft	pf	tp
Becker	2	2	4	6
Milkovich	4	2	4	10
Lacey	1	0	3	2
Debnar	0	2	2	2
Widowitz	3	1	3	7
Reiber	0	0	0	0
Kasperik	1	1	1	3
Totals	11	8	17	30

Kansas	fg	ft-fta	pf	tp
Ebling	2	4- 8	1	8
Engleman	3	0- 0	1	6
Allen	3	2- 2	2	8
Miller	2	2- 4	2	6
Harp	6	3- 4	3	15
Voran	0	0- 1	0	0
Kline	0	0- 0	0	0
Totals	16	11-19	9	43

Southern California	fg	ft-fta	pf	tp
Vaughn	2	2- 5	2	6
Morrison	0	0- 0	3	0
Sears	8	3- 4	2	19
McGavin	3	0- 0	4	6
Lippert	4	0- 1	3	8
Lambert	0	1- 2	2	1
Luber	1	0- 1	0	2
Totals	18	6-13	16	42

Championship

Indiana	fg	ft-fta	pf	tp
Schaefer	4	1- 1	1	9
McCreary	6	0- 0	2	12
W. Menke	2	1- 2	3	5
Huffman	5	2- 3	4	12
Dro	3	1- 1	4	7
Armstrong	4	2- 3	3	10
Gridley	0	0- 0	0	0
R. Menke	0	0- 0	0	0
Zimmer	2	1- 1	1	5
Dorsey	0	0- 0	0	0
Francis	0	0- 0	1	0
Totals	26	8-11	19	60

Kansas	fg	ft-fta	pf	tp
Ebling	1	2- 5	0	4
Engleman	5	2- 3	3	12
Allen	5	3- 4	3	13
Miller	0	2- 2	4	2
Harp	2	1- 3	1	5
Hunter	0	1- 1	0	1
Hogben	2	0- 0	0	4
Kline	0	0- 0	0	0
Voran	0	1- 2	0	1
Sands	0	0- 0	0	0
Johnson	0	0- 0	0	0
Totals	15	12-20	11	42

1941 Tournament Stats

Semifinals

Arkansas	fg	ft-fta	pf	tp
J. Adams	10	2- 5	1	22
Carpenter	2	1- 3	2	5
Freiberger	1	3- 5	3	5
Pitts	5	2- 4	2	12
Robbins	0	0- 1	3	0
Hickey	1	1- 2	2	3
Wynne	0	0- 1	2	0
O. Adams	2	2- 2	3	6
Totals	21	11-23	18	53

Washington State	fg	ft-fta	pf	tp
Gentry	4	1- 2	2	9
Butts	5	1- 1	1	11
Gilberg	3	0- 3	4	6
Zimmerman	0	0- 0	2	0
Lindeman	4	6- 9	2	14
Gebert	5	2- 2	1	12
Sundquist	2	2- 2	2	6
Hunt	1	0- 0	3	2
Akins	0	0- 0	0	0
Hooper	2	0- 0	4	4
Totals	26	12-19	21	64

Championship

Wisconsin	fg	ft-fta	pf	tp
Epperson	2	0- 0	3	4
Schrage	0	0- 0	1	0
Kotz	5	2- 3	2	12
Englund	5	3- 4	2	13
Timmerman	1	0- 0	1	2
Rehm	2	0- 1	2	4
Strain	0	2- 2	1	2
Alwin	1	0- 0	0	2
Totals	16	7-10	12	39

Wisconsin	fg	ft-fta	pf	tp
Kotz	3	4- 4	1	10
Scott	0	0- 0	0	0
Epperson	2	3- 4	0	7
Englund	2	7- 8	4	11
Schrage	0	0- 0	0	0
Timmerman	0	0- 1	0	0
Strain	2	0- 2	3	4
Alwin	0	0- 0	0	0
Rehm	1	2- 2	0	4
Schiewe	0	0- 0	0	0
Totals	10	16-21	8	36

Pittsburgh	fg	ft-fta	pf	tp
Straloski	6	0- 1	4	12
Swacus	0	0- 0	0	0
Egan	0	0- 0	0	0
Kocheran	1	2- 2	0	4
Port	1	2- 3	4	4
Paffrath	1	1- 1	1	3
Milanovich	2	0- 0	3	4
Ziolkowski	0	0- 0	2	0
Artman	0	0- 0	0	0
Klein	0	0- 0	1	0
Malarkey	1	1- 1	3	3
Totals	12	6- 8	18	30

Washington State	fg	ft-fta	pf	tp
Gentry	0	1- 2	1	1
Gilberg	1	0- 2	1	2
Butts	1	1- 1	1	3
Lindeman	0	3- 4	1	3
Zimmerman	0	0- 0	0	0
Gebert	10	1- 2	1	21
Hunt	0	0- 0	0	0
Sundquist	2	0- 1	3	4
Hooper	0	0- 0	0	0
Totals	14	6-12	8	34

1942 Tournament Stats

Semifinals

Stanford	fg	ft-fta	pf	tp
Dana	3	1- 2	1	7
Pollard	8	1- 1	2	17
Madden	0	0- 0	0	0
Voss	4	2- 5	3	10
Linari	0	0- 0	0	0
Eikelman	0	0- 0	1	0
Cowden	2	3- 5	2	7
McCaffrey	0	0- 0	0	0
Dallmar	2	1- 1	0	5
Oliver	0	0- 0	0	0
Totals	19	8-14	9	46

Dartmouth	fg	ft-fta	pf	tp
Myers	4	1- 2	2	9
Pogue	0	0- 0	0	0
Munroe	9	2- 4	2	20
Briggs	0	0- 0	0	0
Olsen	5	1- 3	2	11
Shaw	1	0- 0	0	2
Pearson	0	3- 3	1	3
Parmer	0	0- 1	2	0
Skaug	1	0- 1	4	2
McKernan	0	0- 0	0	0
Totals	20	7-14	13	47

Colorado	fg	ft-fta	pf	tp
McCloud	1	1- 2	2	3
Huggins	0	0- 0	0	0
Nuckolls	0	0- 1	3	0
Putman	3	0- 0	1	6
Doll	3	5- 5	3	11
Hamburg	3	2- 2	2	8
Kirchner	3	1- 1	0	7
Totals	13	9-11	11	35

Kentucky	fg	ft-fta	pf	tp
White	0	0- 0	2	0
Ramsey	0	0- 0	0	0
Allen	2	2- 4	2	6
Ticco	0	1- 1	1	1
Brewer	1	2- 4	1	4
King	1	2- 2	0	4
Staker	0	0- 0	4	0
England	1	0- 0	1	2
Akers	5	1- 2	3	11
Totals	10	8-13	14	28

Championship

Stanford	fg	ft-fta	pf	tp
Dana	7	0- 0	0	14
Eikelman	0	0- 0	0	0
Burness	0	0- 0	0	0
Linari	3	0- 0	0	6
Voss	6	1- 1	2	13
Madden	0	0- 0	0	0
Cowden	2	1- 2	3	5
McCaffrey	0	0- 0	0	0
Dallmar	6	3- 5	0	15
Oliver	0	0- 0	0	0
Totals	24	5- 8	5	53

Dartmouth	fg	ft-fta	pf	tp
Meyers	4	0- 1	1	8
Parmer	1	0- 0	0	2
Munroe	5	2- 2	1	12
Shaw	0	0- 0	0	0
Olsen	4	0- 0	0	8
Pogue	0	0- 0	0	0
Pearson	2	2- 2	3	6
McKernan	0	0- 0	0	0
Skaug	1	0- 0	2	2
Briggs	0	0- 0	0	0
Totals	17	4- 5	7	38

1943 Tournament Stats

Semifinals

Wyoming	fg	ft-fta	pf	tp
Sailors	4	4- 6	3	12
Weir	6	1- 1	3	13
Waite	0	0- 0	1	0
Komenich	8	1- 4	2	17
Volker	3	1- 3	4	7
Roney	1	2- 3	3	4
Collins	2	1- 2	2	5
Totals	24	10-19	18	58

Texas	fg	ft-fta	pf	tp
Overall	5	4- 7	3	14
Hargis	11	7-11	3	29
Langdon	1	2- 3	2	4
Brahaney	1	0- 0	3	2
Fitzgerald	1	0- 0	4	2
Wright	1	1- 1	2	3
Cox	0	0- 0	3	0
Totals	20	14-22	20	54

Georgetown	fg	ft-fta	pf	tp
Gabbianelli	3	0- 0	1	6
Fenney	0	0- 0	2	0
Duffey	0	0- 0	0	0
Potolicchio	5	1- 3	1	11
Reilly	0	0- 0	0	0
Mahnken	8	1- 2	4	17
Hyde	1	0- 0	2	2
Hassett	2	7- 7	0	11
Kraus	1	4- 6	3	6
Totals	20	13-18	13	53

DePaul	fg	ft-fta	pf	tp
Jorgenson	6	2- 3	2	14
Frailey	0	0- 0	0	0
Cominsky	5	1- 3	3	11
Mikan	3	5- 8	1	11
Starzyk	3	1- 1	2	7
Kelly	2	2- 2	4	6
Ryan	0	0- 0	3	0
Totals	19	11-17	15	49

Championship

Georgetown	fg	ft-fta	pf	tp
Reilly	1	0- 0	0	2
Potolicchio	1	2- 3	1	4
Gabbianelli	1	2- 3	3	4
Hyde	0	0- 0	0	0
Mahnken	2	2- 3	2	6
Hassett	3	0- 3	4	6
Finnerty	0	0- 0	0	0
Kraus	2	0- 1	3	4
Fenney	4	0- 0	1	8
Duffey	0	0- 0	0	0
Totals	14	6-13	14	34

Wyoming	fg	ft-fta	pf	tp
Sailors	6	4- 5	2	16
Collins	4	0- 0	1	8
Weir	2	1- 3	2	5
Waite	0	0- 0	0	0
Komenich	4	1- 4	2	9
Volker	2	1- 2	3	5
Roney	0	1- 2	1	1
Reese	1	0- 0	0	2
Totals	19	8-16	11	46

1944 Tournament Stats

Semifinals

Utah	fg	ft	tp
Ferrin	3	0	6
Smuin	2	1	5
Sheffield	4	1	9
Misaka	4	1	9
Wilkinson	1	2	4
B. Lewis	3	1	7
Totals	17	6	40

Iowa State	fg	ft	tp
Ray Wehde	2	1	5
Block	2	1	5
Roy Wehde	2	0	4
Brookfield	3	0	6
Ewoldt	0	0	0
Oulman	2	1	5
Sauer	0	2	2
Meyers	2	0	4
Totals	13	5	31

Championship

Utah	fg	ft-fta	pf	tp
Ferrin	8	6- 7	0	22
Smuin	0	0- 0	2	0
Sheffield	1	0- 0	1	2
Misaka	2	0- 0	1	4
Wilkinson	3	1- 4	0	7
Lewis	2	3- 3	2	7
Totals	16	10-14	6	42

Dartmouth	fg	ft-fta	pf	tp
Gale	3	1- 1	2	7
Leggat	5	2- 4	2	12
Brindley	13	2- 3	3	28
McGuire	4	1- 3	1	9
Vancisin	0	0- 0	2	0
Monahan	2	0- 0	1	4
Totals	27	6-11	11	60

Ohio State	fg	ft-fta	pf	tp
Grate	3	1- 2	2	7
Dugger	3	2- 6	4	8
Gunton	0	0- 0	0	0
Risen	8	5- 6	0	21
Caudill	0	0- 0	1	0
Bowen	3	0- 0	1	6
Fink	0	0- 0	0	0
Huston	5	1- 1	3	11
Totals	22	9-15	11	53

Dartmouth	fg	ft-fta	pf	tp
Gale	5	0- 2	1	10
Mercer	0	1- 1	3	1
Leggat	4	0- 0	1	8
Nordstrom	0	0- 0	0	0
Brindley	5	1- 1	3	11
McGuire	3	0- 1	3	6
Murphy	0	0- 0	0	0
Vancisin	2	0- 0	3	4
Goering	0	0- 0	0	0
Totals	19	2- 5	14	40

Half time: Dartmouth 18–17 Regulation Score: 36–36.

1945 Tournament Stats

Semifinals

New York Univ.	fg	ft-fta	pf	tp
Grenert	2	2- 5	3	6
Benanti	0	0- 0	1	0
Forman	4	2- 2	2	10
Schayes	5	4- 8	4	14
Walsh	2	2- 3	5	6
Most	1	0- 1	2	2
Tannenbaum	5	3- 3	2	13
Mangiapane	7	3- 5	4	17
Goldstein	1	0- 0	2	2
Totals	27	16-27	25	70

Ohio State	fg	ft-fta	pf	tp
Grate	2	2- 3	4	6
Sims	2	3- 4	3	7
Snyder	0	0- 0	0	0
Dugger	1	2- 5	5	4
Caudill	3	1- 1	3	7
Risen	8	10-13	5	26
Huston	2	1- 3	5	5
Amling	5	0- 2	1	10
Totals	23	19-31	26	65

Regulation score: 62-62.

Oklahoma A&M	fg	ft	pf	tp
Hankins	8	6	1	22
Kern	3	0	2	6
Kurland	6	3	3	15
Halbert	0	0	1	0
Williams	2	3	2	7
Parks	1	0	1	2
Parrack	7	2	1	16
Wylie	0	0	0	0
Totals	27	14	11	68

Arkansas	fg	ft	pf	tp
Richie	2	0	0	4
Byles	1	0	1	2
M. Schumchyk	1	2	·3	4
F. Schumchyk	0	0	1	0
Kearne	1	1	2	3
Kok	4	4	2	12
Joliff	0	0	3	0
Flynt	5	1	2	11
Copeland	0	1	0	1
Wheeler	2	0	3	4
Totals	16	9	17	41

Championship

Oklahoma A&M	fg	ft-fta	pf	tp
Hankins	6	3- 6	3	15
Parks	0	0- 0	3	0
Kern	3	0- 4	3	6
Wylie	0	0- 0	0	0
Kurland	10	2- 3	3	22
Parrack	2	0- 1	3	4
Williams	1	0- 1	1	2
Totals	22	5-15	16	49

New York Univ.	fg	ft-fta	pf	tp
Grenert	5	2- 3	3	12
Forman	5	1- 2	1	11
Goldstein	0	2- 2	2	2
Schayes	2	2- 6	2	6
Walsh	0	0- 0	2	0
Tannenbaum	2	0- 0	2	4
Mangiapane	2	2- 4	3	6
Most	1	2- 3	2	4
Totals	17	11-20	17	45

1946 Tournament Stats

Semifinals

North Carolina	fg	ft-fta	pf	tp
Dillon	5	6-13	4	16
Anderson	3	0- 1	2	6
Scholbe	0	0- 0	1	0
Paxton	4	0- 2	3	8
McKinney	4	1- 3	5	9
White	2	3- 4	4	7
Thorne	1	0- 0	1	2
Jordan	4	4- 5	3	12
Totals	23	14-28	23	60

Ohio State	fg	ft-fta	pf	tp
Bowen	3	6- 6	4	12
Snyder	4	3- 7	3	11
Wells	0	0- 0	4	0
Underman	8	7- 8	4	23
Huston	3	3- 6	5	9
Johnston	0	0- 0	0	0
Amling	1	0- 1	5	2
Totals	19	19-28	25	57

Regulation Score: 54-54.

Oklahoma A&M	fg	ft-fta	pf	tp
Aubrey	0	0- 0	0	0
Bennett	1	2- 2	1	4
Kern	2	0- 0	1	4
Geyman	0	0- 0	0	0
Kurland	12	5- 6	3	29
Steinmier	0	0- 0	0	0
Halbert	0	0- 0	0	0
Bell	1	2- 2	2	4
Bradley	1	1- 2	1	3
Williams	1	1- 1	0	3
Parks	2	1- 1	1	5
Totals	20	12-14	9	52

California	fg	ft-fta	pf	tp
LaFaille	4	2- 2	4	10
Wolfe	7	0- 1	2	14
Dean	0	0- 0	0	0
Smith	0	1- 3	3	1
Walker	2	2- 3	2	6
Wray	1	0- 0	2	2
Larner	0	0- 0	0	0
Hogeboom	0	2- 3	0	2
Totals	14	7-12	13	35

Championship

North Carolina	fg	ft-fta	pf	tp
Dillon	5	6- 6	5	16
Anderson	3	2- 3	3	8
Paxton	2	0- 0	4	4
McKinney	2	1- 3	5	5
White	0	1- 1	0	1
Thorne	1	0- 0	2	2
Jordan	0	4- 8	3	4
Totals	13	14-21	22	40

Oklahoma A&M	fg	ft-fta	pf	tp
Aubrey	0	1- 2	1	1
Bennett	3	0- 0	4	6
Kern	3	1- 3	2	7
Bradley	1	1- 2	1	3
Kurland	9	5- 9	5	23
Halbert	0	0- 0	0	0
Williams	0	2- 4	2	2
Bell	0	1- 1	1	1
Parks	0	0- 0	2	0
Totals	16	11-21	18	43

1947 Tournament Stats

Semifinals

Oklahoma	fg	ft	tp
Reich	4	3	11
Courty	3	2	8
Pryor	1	0	2
Tucker	6	3	15
Paine	4	0	8
Merchant	0	1	1
Landon	2	2	6
Waters	1	2	4
Totals	21	13	55

Texas	fg	ft	tp
Hargis	3	3	9
Hamilton	0	1	1
Martin	8	2	18
Langdon	3	1	7
Madsen	1	4	6
Cox	1	0	2
Wagner	5	1	11
Totals	21	12	54

Championship

Oklahoma	fg	ft-fta	pf	tp
Reich	3	2- 2	3	8
Courty	3	2- 3	4	8
Tucker	6	10-12	3	22
Paine	2	2- 2	0	6
Landgon	1	0- 1	4	2
Waters	0	0- 0	0	0
Day	0	0- 0	0	0
Pryor	0	1- 1	2	1
Merchant	0	0- 0	1	0
Totals	15	17-21	17	47

Holy Cross	fg	ft-fta	pf	tp
Kaftan	11	8–12	2	30
O'Connell	2	1– 2	1	5
Oftring	2	3– 3	3	7
Mullaney	0	3– 5	2	3
Haggerty	2	0– 0	3	4
Cousy	2	1– 2	3	5
McMullen	1	1– 3	2	3
Laska	1	0– 0	1	2
Curran	0	1– 2	2	1
Totals	21	18–29	19	60

CCNY	fg	ft-fta	pf	tp
Trubowitz	2	0– 1	1	4
Dambrot	5	4– 7	3	14
Galiber	1	3– 5	4	5
Shapiro	2	1– 1	3	5
Malamed	1	1– 1	2	3
Jameson	1	1– 1	5	3
Farbman	0	1– 1	1	1
Benson	0	0– 0	1	0
Finestone	4	1– 2	4	9
Schmones	0	1– 1	1	1
Totals	16	13–20	25	45

Holy Cross	fg	ft-fta	pf	tp
Kaftan	7	4– 9	4	18
O'Connell	7	2– 4	3	16
Oftring	6	2– 3	5	14
Mullaney	0	0– 0	2	0
Haggerty	0	0– 0	0	0
Laska	0	0– 0	0	0
Curran	0	0– 1	2	0
Reilly	0	0– 0	1	0
McMullin	2	4– 4	0	8
Cousy	0	2– 2	1	2
Bollinger	0	0– 0	0	0
Graver	0	0– 0	0	0
Totals	22	14–23	18	58

1948 Tournament Stats

Semifinals

Kansas State	fg	ft	pf	tp
Harman	3	6	4	12
Krone	0	2	0	2
Howey	3	3	5	9
Langton	1	1	3	3
Weatherby	0	0	2	0
Brannum	3	1	5	7
Clark	1	3	5	5
Dean	3	2	4	8
Shannon	1	4	1	6
Totals	15	22	29	52

Kentucky	fg	ft	tp
Jones	4	4	12
Barker	2	0	4
Line	0	0	0
Groza	10	3	23
Holland	0	0	0
Beard	6	1	13
Rollins	3	2	8
Barnstable	0	0	0
Totals	25	10	60

Baylor	fg	ft	pf	tp
Owens	3	2	5	8
Kichman	0	0	2	0
DeWitt	3	0	5	6
Preston	1	3	1	5
Pulley	1	0	0	2
Heathington	3	9	2	15
Johnson	4	5	3	13
Robinson	5	1	4	11
Totals	20	20	22	60

Holy Cross	fg	ft	tp
Oftring	4	4	12
McMullan	0	0	0
Cousy	1	3	5
O'Connell	3	3	9
Kaftan	6	3	15
Bollinger	1	0	2
Curran	3	1	7
Formon	0	0	0
Mullaney	0	0	0
Laska	1	0	2
Totals	19	14	52

Championship

Kentucky	fg	ft	tp
Jones	4	1	9
Barker	2	1	5
Groza	6	2	14
Beard	4	4	12
Rollins	3	3	9
Line	3	1	7
Holland	1	0	2
Barnstable	0	0	0
Totals	23	12	58

Baylor	fg	ft	tp
Owens	2	1	5
DeWitt	3	2	8
Heathington	3	2	8
Johnson	3	4	10
Robinson	3	2	8
Pulley	0	1	1
Hickman	1	0	2
Preston	0	0	0
Srack	0	0	0
Totals	15	12	42

1949 Tournament Stats

Semifinals

Kentucky	fg	ft	pf	tp
Jones	4	1	3	9
Line	6	3	0	15
Groza	10	7	4	27
Beard	4	1	2	9
Barker	3	2	3	8
Hirsch	3	0	1	6
Barnstable	1	0	1	2
Totals	31	14	14	76

Illinois	fg	ft	pf	tp
Eddleman	3	0	1	6
Kersulis	3	3	2	9
Green	3	1	2	7
Osterkorn	2	1	5	5
Erickson	2	1	2	5
Foley	1	1	1	3
Gatewood	3	0	0	6
Marks	1	0	2	2
Cottrell	0	0	1	0
Anderson	0	0	1	0
Beach	1	0	0	2
Sunderlage	0	2	2	2
Totals	19	9	19	47

Oklahoma A&M	fg	ft-fta	pf	tp
Shelton	3	7- 8	3	13
Hobbs	0	0- 0	0	0
Yates	0	0- 0	0	0
McArthur	0	0- 0	2	0
Pilgrim	0	0- 0	4	0
Harris	8	7- 7	1	23
Bradley	3	1- 1	1	7
Jaquet	0	0- 0	0	0
Allen	0	0- 0	1	0
Parks	2	4- 6	2	8
Smith	1	2- 2	1	4
Hayes	0	0- 0	1	0
Totals	17	21-24	16	55

Oregon State	fg	ft-fta	pf	tp
Petersen	2	0- 3	5	4
Catterall	0	1- 2	1	1
Sliper	0	0- 0	1	0
Fleming	1	0- 1	0	2
Snyder	1	0- 0	1	2
Watt	0	0- 0	1	0
Rinearson	0	0- 0	2	0
Crandall	4	3- 4	3	11
Harper	1	0- 1	1	2
Ballantyne	1	1- 1	2	3
Torrey	0	1- 1	0	1
Holman	1	2- 2	1	4
Totals	11	8-15	18	30

Championship

Kentucky	fg	ft	pf	tp
Jones	1	1	3	3
Line	2	1	3	5
Groza	9	7	5	25
Beard	1	1	4	3
Barker	1	3	4	5
Barnstable	1	1	1	3
Hirsch	1	0	1	2
Totals	16	14	21	46

Oklahoma A&M	fg	ft	pf	tp
Yates	1	0	1	2
Shelton	3	6	4	12
Harris	3	1	5	7
Bradley	0	3	3	3
Parks	2	3	5	7
Jaquet	0	1	0	1
McArthur	0	2	1	2
Pilgrim	0	2	1	2
Smith	0	0	1	0
Totals	9	18	21	36

1950 Tournament Stats

Semifinals

CCNY	fg-fga	ft-fta	pf	tp
Dambrot	5-14	3- 6	3	13
Warner	5-18	7-11	3	17
Roman	9-17	3- 4	5	21
Galiber	0- 0	0- 0	1	0
Nadell	2- 2	0- 1	2	4
Roth	2- 6	0- 0	5	4
Mager	4-11	1- 2	5	9
Layne	3-13	4- 5	2	10
Cohen	0- 0	0- 2	0	0
Totals	30-81	18-31	26	78

North Carolina State	fg-fga	ft-fta	pf	tp
Ranzino	9-30	6- 9	5	24
Stine	1- 2	0- 0	0	2
Dickey	7-19	2- 6	5	16
Horvath	4- 4	6- 8	4	14
Bubas	0- 2	2- 2	4	2
Harand	0- 0	2- 2	2	2
Cartier	4- 8	3- 4	5	11
Cook	1- 3	0- 0	0	2
Totals	26-68	21-31	25	73

Championship

CCNY	fg-fga	ft-fta	pf	tp
Dambrot	7-14	1- 2	0	15
Roman	6-17	0- 2	5	12
Warner	4- 9	6-14	2	14
Roth	2- 7	1- 5	2	5
Mager	4-10	6- 6	3	14
Galiber	0- 0	0- 0	1	0
Layne	3- 7	5- 6	3	11
Nadell	0- 0	0- 0	1	0
Totals	26-64	19-35	17	71

Bradley	fg-fga	ft-fta	pf	tp
Mann	4- 7	5- 8	4	13
Chianakas	1- 5	0- 0	0	2
Schlictman	0- 0	0- 0	0	0
Melchiorre	4-11	3- 3	4	11
Unruh	2-11	3- 4	2	7
Behnke	1- 7	0- 1	0	2
Preece	4- 6	4- 6	3	12
Kelly	3- 7	2- 2	2	8
Grover	6-14	1- 1	2	13
Totals	25-68	18-25	17	68

Baylor	fg-fga	ft-fta	pf	tp
Hickman	3- 7	0- 0	3	6
Cobb	3- 8	1- 2	3	7
Carrington	0- 0	0- 0	0	0
Heathington	10-20	6- 6	5	26
Fleetwood	0- 0	0- 0	0	0
Preston	4-11	6- 7	4	14
Hovde	0- 0	0- 0	0	0
DeWitt	1- 6	2- 3	5	4
Johnson	0- 2	0- 0	0	0
Srack	3- 7	3- 3	3	9
Totals	24-61	18-21	23	66

Bradley	fg-fga	ft-fta	pf	tp
Grover	0-10	2- 3	3	2
Schlictman	0- 3	0- 0	2	0
Unruh	4- 9	0- 0	5	8
Behnke	3-10	3- 3	4	9
Kelly	0- 1	0- 2	0	0
Mann	2- 7	5- 5	5	9
Preece	6-11	0- 0	5	12
D. Melchiorre	0- 0	0- 0	0	0
G. Melchiorre	7-16	2- 4	4	16
Chianakas	5- 7	1- 3	4	11
Stowell	0- 0	1- 1	0	1
Totals	27-74	14-21	32	68

1951 Tournament Stats

Semifinals

Kentucky	fg-fga	ft-fta	rb	pf	tp
Hagan	3- 9	2- 2	4	5	8
Linville	7-12	0- 0	4	4	14
Spivey	11-21	6-10	16	5	28
Watson	5-17	0- 0	8	4	10
Ramsey	2-19	1- 3	12	2	5
Tsioropoulos	0- 2	1- 2	1	1	1
Whitaker	4-11	2- 4	4	5	10
Newton	0- 0	0- 0	0	1	0
Totals	32-91	12-21	49	27	76

Kansas State	fg-fga	ft-fta	rb	pf	tp
Head	4- 9	1- 1	5	3	9
Gibson	0- 0	0- 2	3	0	0
Schuyler	2- 4	0- 1	0	1	4
Stone	5- 5	0- 0	1	2	10
Peck	0- 1	1- 1	1	2	1
Hitch	4-11	4- 6	8	2	12
Knostman	4- 8	3- 6	3	0	11
Iverson	3- 4	3- 3	2	0	9
Rousey	0- 1	1- 4	0	2	1
Barrett	1- 7	3- 3	4	4	5
Upson	3- 4	0- 0	1	2	6
Team			8		
Totals	26-54	16-27	36	18	68

Illinois	fg-fga	ft-fta	rb	pf	tp
Follmer	2- 3	2- 3	5	2	6
Bemoras	5- 8	2- 3	7	2	12
Peterson	3-11	2- 3	5	5	8
Fletcher	8-19	5-11	10	0	21
Sunderlage	6-15	8-11	3	2	20
Beach	2-12	3- 3	6	1	7
Baumgardner	0- 2	0- 1	1	4	0
Totals	26-70	22-35	37	16	74

Oklahoma A&M	fg-fga	ft-fta	rb	pf	tp
Johnson	2-10	3- 3	5	4	7
McAfee	0- 1	0- 0	0	3	0
Miller	0- 2	0- 0	2	3	0
Stockton	0- 0	1- 1	1	0	1
Ward	1- 2	0- 0	0	1	2
Darcey	2- 5	0- 1	1	4	4
Pager	5-10	1- 2	2	3	11
Smith	0- 0	1- 1	1	2	1
Amaya	1- 2	0- 0	1	0	2
Rogers	2- 5	0- 0	0	2	4
McArthur	1-11	5- 5	2	2	7
Sheets	2- 4	1- 1	0	1	5
Team			10		
Totals	16-52	12-14	25	25	44

Championship

Kentucky	fg-fga	ft-fta	rb	pf	tp
Whitaker	4- 5	1- 1	2	2	9
Linville	2- 7	4- 8	8	5	8
Spivey	9-29	4- 6	21	2	22
Ramsey	4-10	1- 3	4	5	9
Watson	3- 8	2- 4	3	3	8
Hagan	5- 6	0- 2	4	5	10
Tsioropoulos	1- 4	0- 0	3	1	2
Newton	0- 0	0- 0	0	0	0
Totals	28-69	12-24	45	23	68

Kansas State	fg-fga	ft-fta	rb	pf	tp
Head	3-11	2- 2	3	2	8
Stone	3- 8	6- 8	6	2	12
Hitch	6-15	1- 1	9	3	13
Barrett	2-12	0- 2	3	1	4
Iverson	3-12	1- 2	0	3	7
Rousey	2-10	0- 0	2	3	4
Gibson	0- 2	1- 1	1	5	1
Upson	0- 1	0- 0	2	1	0
Knostman	1- 4	1- 2	3	1	3
Peck	2- 3	0- 1	0	0	4
Schuyler	1- 2	0- 1	1	2	2
Totals	23-80	12-20	30	23	58

1952 Tournament Stats

Semifinals

St. John's	fg	ft	tp
McMahon	3	3	9
Davis	1	0	2
Walsh	2	0	4
Zawoluk	9	6	24
MacGilvray	2	2	6
Duckett	4	3	11
Walker	2	1	5
Totals	23	15	61

Illinois	fg	ft	tp
C. Follmer	4	2	10
Bemoras	1	1	3
Peterson	2	0	4
Kerr	3	2	8
Bredar	7	0	14
Fletcher	5	4	14
Gerecke	3	0	6
Totals	25	9	59

Kansas	fg	ft	tp
Kenney	3	1	7
Liennard	0	0	0
Hoag	4	2	10
Keller	1	2	4
Lovellette	12	9	33
Born	1	2	4
D. Kelley	4	2	10
Heitholt	2	0	4
Davenport	0	2	2
Totals	27	20	74

Santa Clara	fg	ft	tp
Sears	0	1	1
Young	3	2	8
Garibaldi	1	0	2
Gatzert	1	1	3
Schoenstein	6	1	13
Peters	1	1	3
Brock	3	1	7
Benedetti	1	0	2
Soares	7	2	16
Totals	23	9	55

Championship

Kansas	fg-fga	ft-fta	rb	pf	tp
Kenney	4-11	4- 6	4	2	12
Keller	1- 1	0- 0	4	2	2
Lovellette	12-25	9-11	17	4	33
Lienhard	5- 8	2- 2	4	4	12
D. Kelley	2- 5	3- 6	3	5	7
Hoag	2- 6	5- 7	4	5	9
Houghland	2- 5	1- 3	6	2	5
Davenport	0- 0	0- 0	0	1	0
Heitholt	0- 0	0- 0	0	0	0
Born	0- 0	0- 0	0	0	0
A. Kelley	0- 0	0- 0	1	0	0
Totals	28-63	24-35	42	25	80

St. John's	fg-fga	ft-fta	rb	pf	tp
McMahon	6-12	1- 4	2	4	13
Davis	1- 4	2- 3	2	4	4
Zawoluk	7-12	6-11	9	5	20
Duckett	2- 5	2- 2	2	4	6
MacGilvray	3- 8	2- 5	10	3	8
Walsh	3- 6	0- 0	4	3	6
Walker	0- 2	0- 0	2	4	0
McMorrow	1- 3	0- 0	0	3	2
Sagona	2- 2	0- 0	0	5	4
Giancontieri	0- 0	0- 2	1	0	0
Peterson	0- 1	0- 0	0	0	0
Totals	25-55	13-27	32	35	63

1953 Tournament Stats

Semifinals

Indiana	fg	ft	tp
Kraak	2	5	9
Farley	4	2	10
DeaKyne	0	0	0
Schlundt	8	13	29
White	0	3	3
Leonard	9	4	22
Byers	0	0	0
Poff	0	0	0
Scott	2	3	7
Totals	25	30	80

Louisiana State	fg	ft	tp
Belcher	4	2	10
Clark	0	2	2
Freshley	0	1	1
Loughmiller	0	0	0
Pettit	10	9	29
Magee	6	5	17
McArdie	1	1	3
Bridges	1	3	5
Totals	22	23	67

Championship

Kansas	fg	ft-fta	pf	tp
Patterson	1	7- 8	3	9
A. Kelley	7	6- 8	3	20
Davenport	0	0- 0	0	0
Born	8	10-12	5	26
Smith	0	1- 1	1	1
Alberts	0	0- 0	1	0
D. Kelley	3	2- 4	2	8
Reich	2	0- 0	2	4
Totals	21	26-33	17	68

Kansas	fg	ft	tp
Patterson	6	5	17
Smith	0	0	0
Alberts	0	0	0
A. Kelley	3	1	7
Davenport	0	2	2
Born	9	7	25
D. Kelley	8	2	18
Heitholt	1	0	2
Reich	3	2	8
Totals	30	19	79

Washington	fg	ft	tp
McCutchen	0	3	3
Halle	0	1	1
McClary	2	2	6
Parsons	0	1	1
Houbregs	8	2	18
Elliott	1	1	3
Cipriano	4	3	11
Apeland•	1	0	2
Koon	3	2	8
Totals	19	15	53

Indiana	fg	ft-fta	pf	tp
Kraak	5	7-10	5	17
DeaKyne	0	0- 0	1	0
Farley	1	0- 0	5	2
Schlundt	11	8-11	3	30
White	1	0- 0	2	2
Leonard	5	2- 4	2	12
Poff	0	0- 0	0	0
Scott	2	2- 3	3	6
Byers	0	0- 0	1	0
Totals	25	19-28	22	69

1954 Tournament Stats

Semifinals

La Salle	fg	ft	tp
Singley	4	2	10
Maples	3	1	7
Blatcher	7	5	19
Gola	5	9	19
O'Malley	3	3	9
O'Hara	2	1	5
Totals	24	21	69

Penn State	fg	ft	tp
Weidenhammer	1	1	3
Haag	2	0	4
Fields	2	1	5
Brewer	3	0	6
Arnelle	5	8	18
Rohland	2	0	4
Blocker	2	0	4
Sherry	1	4	6
Edwards	2	0	4
Totals	20	14	54

Bradley	fg	ft	tp
Petersen	1	3	5
Gower	1	0	2
King	6	5	17
Kilcullen	0	0	0
Estergard	7	7	21
Utt	0	0	0
Carney	6	8	20
O'Connell	0	0	0
Kent	3	1	7
Babetch	1	0	2
Totals	25	24	74

Southern Cal.	fg	ft	tp
Pausig	5	2	12
Carr	1	1	3
Psaltis	2	0	4
Dunne	1	0	2
Irvin	9	5	23
Ludecke	1	0	2
Hammer	2	3	7
Welsh	6	7	19
Totals	27	18	72

Championship

La Salle	fg	ft-fta	pf	tp
Singley	8	7-10	4	23
Greenberg	2	1- 2	1	5
Maples	2	0- 0	4	4
Blatcher	11	1- 2	4	23
Gola	7	5- 5	5	19
O'Malley	5	1- 1	4	11
Yodsnukis	0	0- 0	5	0
O'Hara	2	3- 4	1	7
Totals	37	18-24	28	92

Bradley	fg	ft-fta	pf	tp
Petersen	4	2- 2	2	10
Babetch	0	0- 0	0	0
King	3	6- 7	4	12
Gower	0	1- 2	1	1
Estergard	3	11-12	1	17
Carney	3	11-17	4	17
Utt	0	0- 0	1	0
Kent	8	0- 2	2	16
Riley	1	1- 2	1	3
Totals	22	32-44	16	76

1955 Tournament Stats

Semifinals

La Salle	fg	ft	tp
O'Malley	1	4	6
Maples	1	2	4
Singley	5	6	16
Blatcher	2	1	5
Gola	8	7	23
Lewis	5	4	14
Greenberg	4	0	8
Totals	26	24	76

Iowa	fg	ft	tp
Davis	1	0	2
School	3	0	6
Cain	8	1	17
Logan	7	6	20
Seaberg	5	5	15
Scheuerman	1	11	13
Totals	25	23	73

San Francisco	fg	ft	tp
Wiebusch	1	0	2
King	1	2	4
Buchanan	0	6	6
Russell	10	4	24
Jones	3	2	8
Baxter	2	3	7
Bush	0	1	1
Perry	5	0	10
Zannini	0	0	0
Kirby	0	0	0
Totals	22	18	62

Colorado	fg	ft	tp
Jeangerard	1	2	4
Coffman	1	2	4
Ranglos	1	2	4
Yardley	1	2	4
Halderson	3	3	9
Hannah	2	5	9
Mock	2	0	4
Mansfield	0	4	4
Grant	1	0	2
Peterson	2	2	6
Totals	14	22	50

Championship

San Francisco	fg	ft-fta	pf	tp
Mullen	4	2- 5	5	10
Buchanan	3	2- 2	1	8
Russell	9	5- 7	1	23
Jones	10	4- 4	2	24
Perry	1	2- 2	4	4
Wiebusch	2	0- 0	0	4
Zannini	1	0- 0	0	2
Lawless	1	0- 0	0	2
Kirby	0	0- 0	1	0
Totals	31	15-20	14	77

La Salle	fg	ft-fta	pf	tp
O'Malley	4	2- 3	1	10
Singley	8	4- 4	1	20
Gola	6	4- 5	4	16
Lewis	1	4- 9	1	6
Greenberg	1	1- 2	4	3
Blatcher	4	0- 0	1	8
Maples	0	0- 0	0	0
Fredericks	0	0- 0	0	0
Totals	24	15-23	12	63

1956 Tournament Stats

Semifinals

Iowa	fg	ft	tp
Cain	8	4	20
Schoof	5	8	18
Logan	13	10	36
Seaberg	1	0	2
Scheuerman	1	2	4
Martel	1	1	3
Totals	29	25	83

Temple	fg	ft	tp
Reinfeld	1	0	2
Norman	1	0	2
Fleming	2	0	4
Cohen	3	0	6
Van Patton	1	0	2
Rodgers	12	4	28
Lear	15	2	32
Totals	35	6	76

Championship

San Francisco	fg	ft-fta	pf	tp
Boldt	7	2- 2	4	16
Farmer	0	0- 0	2	0
Preaseau	3	1- 2	3	7
Russell	11	4- 5	2	26
Nelson	0	0- 0	0	0
Perry	6	2- 2	2	14
Brown	6	4- 4	0	16
Baxter	2	0- 0	0	4
Totals	35	13-15	13	83

San Francisco	fg	ft	tp
Boldt	3	1	7
Farmer	11	4	26
Preaseau	1	0	2
King	0	0	0
Russell	8	1	17
Perry	6	2	14
Brown	5	2	12
Baxter	4	0	8
Totals	38	10	86

Southern Methodist	fg	ft	tp
Showalter	4	0	8
Krog	3	0	6
McGregor	1	1	3
Krebs	10	4	24
Miller	1	0	2
Mills	1	9	11
Morris	4	2	10
Herrscher	1	2	4
Totals	25	18	68

Iowa	fg	ft-fta	pf	tp
Cain	7	3- 4	1	17
Schoof	5	4- 4	3	14
Logan	5	2- 2	3	12
George	0	0- 0	0	0
Scheuerman	4	3- 4	2	11
Seaberg	5	7-10	1	17
Martel	0	0- 0	0	0
McConnell	0	0- 0	0	0
Totals	26	19-24	10	71

1957 Tournament Stats

Semifinals

Kansas	fg-fga	ft-fta	rb	pf	tp
M. King	6- 8	1- 1	4	1	13
Elston	8-12	0- 0	6	3	16
Chamberlain	12-22	8-11	11	0	32
Parker	1- 1	0- 0	3	0	2
Loneski	2- 6	3- 4	7	3	7
L. Johnson	1- 3	0- 0	8	0	2
Billings	0- 1	0- 0	0	0	0
Hollinger	1- 1	0- 1	0	0	2
Dater	1- 1	0- 0	0	2	2
Green	1- 1	0- 0	2	1	2
Kindred	0- 0	0- 2	2	0	0
M. Johnson	1- 1	0- 0	0	0	2
Team			1		
Totals	34-57	12-19	44	10	80

Michigan State	fg-fga	ft-fta	rb	pf	tp
Quiggle	6-21	8-10	10	1	20
Green	4-12	3- 6	19	2	11
Ferguson	4- 8	2- 3	1	5	10
Hedden	4-20	6- 7	15	5	14
Wilson	0- 3	2- 2	5	1	2
Anderegg	2- 7	3- 6	3	2	7
Bencie	1- 6	0- 0	2	1	2
Scott	2- 3	0- 2	3	1	4
Team			7		
Totals	23-80	24-36	65	18	70

Half time: 29-29. Regulation Score: 58-58. First Overtime: 64-64. Second Overtime: 66-66.

North Carolina	fg-fga	ft-fta	rb	pf	tp
Rosenbluth	11-42	7- 9	3	1	29
Cunningham	9-18	3- 5	12	5	21
Brennan	6-16	2- 4	17	5	14
Kearns	1- 8	4- 5	6	4	6
Quigg	0- 1	2- 3	4	5	2
Lotz	0- 1	0- 0	4	1	0
Young	1- 3	0- 1	2	1	2
Searcy	0- 0	0- 0	1	0	0
Team			5		
Totals	28-89	18-27	54	22	74

San Francisco	fg-fga	ft-fta	rb	pf	tp
Day	3-14	3- 8	7	2	9
Dunbar	2- 8	0- 0	4	1	4
Brown	5-14	0- 0	2	2	10
Farmer	6-15	2- 2	4	2	14
Preaseau	5- 8	2- 2	2	2	12
Mallen	0- 2	0- 0	1	1	0
Lillevand	1- 3	0- 0	0	1	2
Koljian	0- 1	3- 4	0	0	3
J. King	0- 3	0- 0	0	1	0
Russell	0- 0	0- 0	1	0	0
Radanovich	0- 1	0- 0	0	0	0
Mancasola	1- 2	0- 0	0	1	2
Team			4		
Totals	23-71	10-16	25	10	56

Championship

North Carolina	fg-fga	ft-fta	rb	pf	tp
Rosenbluth	8-15	4- 4	5	5	20
Cunningham	0- 3	0- 1	5	4	0
Brennan	4- 8	3- 7	11	3	11
Kearns	4- 8	3- 7	1	4	11
Quigg	4-10	2- 3	9	4	10
Lotz	0- 0	0- 0	2	0	0
Young	1- 1	0- 0	3	1	2
Team			6		
Totals	21-45	12-22	42	21	54

Kansas	fg-fga	ft-fta	rb	pf	tp
Chamberlain	6-13	11-16	14	3	23
King	3-12	5- 6	4	4	11
Elston	4-12	3- 6	4	2	11
Parker	2- 4	0- 0	0	0	4
Loneski	0- 5	2- 3	3	2	2
L. Johnson	0- 1	2- 2	0	1	2
Billings	0- 0	0- 0	0	2	0
Team			3		
Totals	15-47	23-33	28	14	53

Half time: North Carolina 29-22. Regulation Score: 46-46. First Overtime: 48-48. Second Overtime: 48-48.

1958 Tournament Stats

Semifinals

Kentucky	fg-fga	ft-fta	rb	pf	tp
Crigler	3-11	0- 2	9	4	6
Cox	6-17	10-11	13	4	22
Collinsworth	0- 0	0- 0	0	1	0
Beck	3- 9	2- 2	15	2	8
Hatton	5-16	3- 4	2	3	13
Smith	2-10	8- 9	5	3	12
Team			5		
Totals	19-63	23-28	49	17	61

Temple	fg-fga	ft-fta	rb	pf	tp
Norman	7-17	2- 3	6	3	16
Brodsky	2- 5	0- 2	14	2	4
Van Patton	1- 1	1- 2	3	4	3
Fleming	3- 7	3- 6	5	1	9
Rodgers	9-24	4- 6	5	4	22
Kennedy	3- 7	0- 1	3	4	6
Team			5		
Totals	25-61	10-20	41	18	60

Seattle	fg-fga	ft-fta	rb	pf	tp
Ogorek	3- 9	1- 2	4	4	7
Frizzell	2- 4	6- 7	2	2	10
Petrie	0- 0	0- 0	0	0	0
Baylor	9-21	5- 7	22	3	23
Humphries	0- 0	0- 0	0	0	0
Harney	0- 4	0- 0	2	1	0
Brown	5- 6	4- 5	13	2	14
Saunders	5-11	2- 3	8	1	12
Piasecki	1- 1	3- 4	0	1	5
Kootnekoff	1- 1	0- 0	0	0	2
Team			5		
Totals	26-57	21-28	56	14	73

Kansas State	fg-fga	ft-fta	rb	pf	tp
Boozer	6-15	3- 5	4	4	15
Frank	6-12	3- 4	7	4	15
Abbott	0- 4	0- 0	2	1	0
Long	2- 6	0- 1	4	2	4
Fischer	0- 1	0- 0	0	1	0
Parr	2-11	0- 1	8	1	4
Matuszak	3- 8	1- 3	7	1	7
DeWitz	2- 7	2- 3	0	2	6
Holwerda	0- 2	0- 0	1	2	0
Team			1		
Totals	21-66	9-17	33	18	51

Championship

Kentucky	fg-fga	ft-fta	rb	pf	tp
Cox	10-23	4- 4	16	3	24
Crigler	5-12	4- 7	14	4	14
Beck	0- 1	0- 1	3	4	0
Mills	4- 9	1- 4	5	3	9
Hatton	9-20	12-15	3	3	30
Smith	2- 8	3- 5	6	4	7
Team			8		
Totals	30-73	24-36	55	21	84

Seattle	fg-fga	ft-fta	rb	pf	tp
Frizzell	4- 6	8-11	5	3	16
Ogorek	4- 7	2- 2	11	5	10
Baylor	9-32	7- 9	19	4	25
Harney	2- 5	0- 1	1	1	4
Brown	6-17	5- 7	5	5	17
Saunders	0- 2	0- 0	2	3	0
Piasecki	0- 0	0- 0	0	0	0
Team			3		
Totals	25-69	22-30	46	21	72

1959 Tournament Stats

Semifinals

California	fg-fga	ft-fta	rb	pf	tp
McClintock	2-11	2- 4	11	1	6
Dalton	2- 4	3- 4	7	5	7
Imhoff	10-25	2- 5	16	4	22
Fitzpatrick	2- 9	0- 0	3	4	4
Buch	7-15	4- 6	6	2	18
Grout	2- 7	1- 2	2	1	5
Simpson	1- 2	0- 0	3	0	2
Team			8		
Totals	26-73	12-21	56	17	64

Cincinnati	fg-fga	ft-fta	rb	pf	tp
Robertson	5-16	9-11	19	4	19
Wiesenhahn	5-11	0- 0	3	1	10
Tenwick	2- 6	1- 1	4	1	5
Davis	6-15	1- 2	2	2	13
Whitaker	4- 7	0- 2	3	3	8
Landfried	0- 1	3- 5	4	3	3
Bouldin	0- 0	0- 1	0	1	0
Team			7		
Totals	22-56	14-22	42	15	58

Championship

West Virginia	fg-fga	ft-fta	rb	pf	tp
West	10-21	8-12	11	4	28
Akers	5- 8	0- 1	6	0	10
Clousson	4- 7	2- 3	4	4	10
Smith	2- 5	1- 1	2	3	5
Bolyard	1- 4	4- 4	3	4	6
Retton	0- 0	2- 2	0	0	2
Ritchie	1- 4	2- 2	4	0	4
Patrone	2- 6	1- 2	4	1	5
Team			7		
Totals	25-55	20-27	41	16	70

West Virginia	fg-fga	ft-fta	rb	pf	tp
West	12-21	14-20	15	3	38
Akers	2- 5	1- 2	8	5	5
Clousson	5- 5	2- 2	4	4	12
Smith	5- 9	2- 4	5	0	12
Bolyard	4-10	5- 7	3	1	13
Ritchie	2- 6	0- 2	5	1	4
Patrone	1- 4	0- 0	1	0	2
Retton	3- 4	0- 0	0	1	6
Schertzinger	0- 0	0- 0	0	0	0
Posch	1- 2	0- 0	0	0	2
Goode	0- 0	0- 0	0	0	0
Visnic	0- 0	0- 0	0	0	0
Team			8		
Totals	35-66	24-37	49	15	94

Louisville	fg-fga	ft-fta	rb	pf	tp
Goldstein	6-10	9- 9	9	4	21
Turner	8-16	2- 5	7	4	18
Sawyer	2- 6	3- 4	2	5	7
Tieman	1- 7	1- 1	0	0	3
Andrews	9-15	1- 1	2	3	19
Kitchen	3- 7	0- 0	5	4	6
Leathers	2- 8	1- 1	3	3	5
Geiling	0- 0	0- 0	0	1	0
Stacey	0- 0	0- 0	2	1	0
Team			7		
Totals	31-69	17-21	37	25	79

California	fg-fga	ft-fta	rb	pf	tp
McClintock	4-13	0- 1	10	1	8
Dalton	6-11	3- 4	2	4	15
Imhoff	4-13	2- 2	9	3	10
Buch	0- 4	2- 2	2	3	2
Fitzpatrick	8-13	4- 7	2	1	20
Simpson	0- 1	0- 0	2	2	0
Grout	4- 5	2- 2	3	1	10
Doughty	3- 6	0- 0	1	3	6
Team			7		
Totals	29-66	13-18	38	18	71

1960 Tournament Stats

Semifinals

California	fg-fga	ft-fta	rb	pf	tp
McClintock	5-12	8-10	10	3	18
Gillis	5-10	3- 3	4	4	13
Imhoff	10-21	5- 5	11	4	25
Shultz	4- 7	3- 5	3	1	11
Wendell	0- 4	4- 7	3	2	4
Stafford	1- 4	2- 2	0	2	4
Doughty	1- 3	0- 0	2	1	2
Team			10		
Totals	26-61	25-32	43	17	77

Cincinnati	fg-fga	ft-fta	rb	pf	tp
Robertson	4-16	10-12	10	4	18
Willey	4- 9	1- 2	4	4	9
Hogue	5- 9	4- 6	11	5	14
Davis	4- 8	2- 2	2	1	10
Bouldin	4- 7	0- 0	0	4	8
Sizer	0- 0	0- 1	1	0	0
Wiesenhahn	5- 8	0- 0	9	3	10
Bryant	0- 1	0- 0	1	3	0
Pomerantz	0- 0	0- 0	0	0	0
Team			2		
Totals	26-58	17-23	40	24	69

Ohio State	fg-fga	ft-fta	rb	pf	tp
Nowell	3- 8	0- 0	0	4	6
Gearhart	1- 3	1- 1	1	3	3
Havlicek	2- 8	2- 2	10	0	6
Cedargren	1- 1	0- 0	1	0	2
Lucas	9-15	1- 1	13	2	19
Furry	4- 7	2- 3	7	2	10
Hoyt	0- 0	2- 2	0	0	2
Roberts	3- 6	1- 2	7	0	7
Barker	1- 1	0- 0	0	0	2
Siegfried	7-11	5- 5	3	3	19
Knight	0- 0	0- 0	1	0	0
Nourse	0- 0	0- 0	0	0	0
Team			5		
Totals	31-60	14-16	48	14	76

New York Univ.	fg-fga	ft-fta	rb	pf	tp
DiNapoli	0- 0	0- 0	1	0	0
Paprocky	4-17	1- 2	0	3	9
Cunningham	4-14	6- 8	3	2	14
Loche	0- 3	1- 1	0	0	1
Murphy	1- 1	0- 1	0	0	2
Barden	2-11	4- 4	8	2	8
Sanders	4-13	0- 3	22	2	8
Reiss	0- 0	0- 0	1	1	0
Keith	0- 1	0- 0	0	0	0
Filardi	6-12	0- 1	6	3	12
Regan	0- 1	0- 0	0	1	0
Midoinoff	0- 1	0- 0	0	0	0
Team			3		
Totals	21-74	12-20	44	14	54

Championship

Ohio State	fg-fga	ft-fta	rb	pf	tp
Havlicek	4- 8	4- 5	6	2	12
Roberts	5- 6	0- 1	5	1	10
Lucas	7- 9	2- 2	10	2	16
Nowell	6- 7	3- 3	4	2	15
Siegfried	5- 6	3- 6	1	2	13
Gearhart	0- 1	0- 0	1	0	0
Cedargren	0- 0	1- 2	1	1	1
Furry	2- 4	0- 0	3	1	4
Hoyt	0- 1	0- 0	0	0	0
Barker	0- 0	0- 0	0	0	0
Knight	0- 1	0- 0	0	1	0
Nourse	2- 3	0- 0	3	1	4
Team			1		
Totals	31-46	13-19	35	13	75

California	fg-fga	ft-fta	rb	pf	tp
McClintock	4-15	2- 3	3	3	10
Gillis	4- 9	0- 0	1	1	8
Imhoff	3- 9	2- 2	5	2	8
Wendell	0- 6	4- 4	0	2	4
Shultz	2- 8	2- 2	4	4	6
Mann	3- 5	1- 1	0	0	7
Doughty	4- 5	3- 3	6	1	11
Stafford	0- 1	1- 2	0	1	1
Morrison	0- 0	0- 0	1	1	0
Averbuck	0- 0	0- 1	1	0	0
Pearson	0- 1	0- 0	0	0	0
Alexander	0- 0	0- 0	0	0	0
Team			7		
Totals	20-59	15-18	28	15	55

1961 Tournament Stats

Semifinals

Cincinnati	fg-fga	ft-fta	rb	pf	tp
Wiesenhahn	5- 7	4- 6	5	4	14
Thacker	1- 7	5- 6	6	3	7
Hogue	9-16	0- 4	14	4	18
Bouldin	7-14	7- 8	3	0	21
Yates	4- 6	5- 7	5	2	13
Heidotting	3- 8	1- 1	6	1	7
Sizer	1- 1	0- 0	0	0	2
Dierking	0- 0	0- 0	1	1	0
Altenau	0- 0	0- 0	0	0	0
Shingleton	0- 0	0- 0	0	0	0
Calhoun	0- 0	0- 0	0	0	0
Team			5		
Totals	30-59	22-32	45	15	82

Utah	fg-fga	ft-fta	rb	pf	tp
Ruffell	6-11	2- 2	5	4	14
Rhead	2- 5	4- 6	10	4	8
McGill	11-31	3- 4	8	4	25
Morton	3- 9	1- 1	1	4	7
Rowe	1- 3	0- 0	1	2	2
Crain	2- 5	0- 1	5	4	4
Aufderheide	2- 3	2- 2	3	1	6
Cozby	0- 0	0- 0	0	0	0
Thomas	0- 0	1- 2	0	0	1
Jenson	0- 0	0- 0	0	0	0
Team			6		
Totals	27-67	13-18	39	23	67

Ohio State	fg-fga	ft-fta	rb	pf	tp
Nowell	7-11	1- 1	0	2	15
Havlicek	5- 6	1- 2	9	2	11
Lucas	10-11	9-10	13	2	29
Hoyt	2- 6	0- 0	1	3	4
Siegfried	8-11	5- 7	9	4	21
Knight	2- 5	1- 2	3	2	5
McDonald	1- 4	0- 0	2	1	2
Gearhart	0- 2	2- 2	1	2	2
Reasbeck	0- 1	0- 1	1	1	0
Lee	1- 1	0- 0	2	0	2
Miller	0- 0	0- 0	0	0	0
Landes	2- 2	0- 0	0	1	4
Team			9		
Totals	38-60	19-25	50	20	95

St. Joseph's	fg-fga	ft-fta	rb	pf	tp
Lynam	2- 5	3- 4	0	0	7
Hoy	6-17	1- 1	2	2	13
Majewski	4-12	5- 7	4	1	13
Egan	3-15	2- 3	5	2	8
Kempton	5- 9	8- 8	8	3	18
Wynne	1- 9	2- 2	2	4	4
Booth	0- 3	2- 2	2	3	2
Gormley	1- 5	2- 2	1	3	4
Westhead	0- 1	0- 1	2	0	0
Bugey	0- 0	0- 0	0	0	0
Dickey	0- 0	0- 0	0	0	0
Team			9		
Totals	22-76	25-30	35	18	69

Championship

Cincinnati	fg-fga	ft-fta	rb	pf	tp
Wiesenhahn	8-15	1- 1	9	3	17
Thacker	7-21	1- 4	7	0	15
Hogue	3- 8	3- 6	7	3	9
Yates	4- 8	5- 5	2	3	13
Bouldin	7-12	2- 3	4	4	16
Sizer	0- 0	0- 0	1	0	0
Heidotting	0- 0	0- 0	0	0	0
Team			6		
Totals	29-64	12-19	36	13	70

Ohio State	fg-fga	ft-fta	rb	pf	tp
Havlicek	1- 5	2- 2	4	2	4
Hoyt	3- 5	1- 1	1	3	7
Lucas	10-17	7- 7	12	4	27
Nowell	3- 9	3- 3	3	1	9
Siegfried	6-10	2- 3	3	2	14
Knight	1- 3	0- 0	1	1	2
Gearhart	1- 1	0- 0	0	1	2
Team			8		
Totals	25-50	15-16	32	14	65

Half time: Ohio State 39-38. Regulation Score: 61-61.

1962 Tournament Stats

Semifinals

UCLA	fg-fga	ft-fta	rb	pf	tp
Blackman	2- 3	0- 0	2	5	4
Cunningham	8-14	3- 3	9	2	19
Slaughter	1- 4	0- 0	7	5	2
Green	9-16	9-11	7	1	27
Hazzard	5-10	2- 3	6	2	12
Waxman	2- 3	2- 3	3	1	6
Stewart	0- 0	0- 0	1	2	0
Totals	27-50	16-20	35	18	70

Cincinnati	fg-fga	ft-fta	rb	pf	tp
Bonham	8-14	3- 6	2	4	19
Wilson	1- 6	1- 2	4	1	3
Hogue	12-18	12-17	19	3	36
Thacker	1- 7	0- 0	4	3	2
Yates	4-10	2- 3	3	3	10
Sizer	1- 3	0- 0	1	3	2
Totals	27-58	18-28	33	17	72

Championship

Cincinnati	fg-fga	ft-fta	rb	pf	tp
Bonham	3-12	4- 4	6	3	10
Wilson	1- 6	4- 4	11	2	6
Hogue	11-18	0- 2	19	2	22
Thacker	6-14	9-11	6	2	21
Yates	4- 8	4- 7	1	1	12
Sizer	0- 0	0- 0	0	0	0
Totals	25-58	21-28	43	10	71

Wake Forest	fg-fga	ft-fta	rb	pf	tp
Chappell	10-24	7-11	18	5	27
Christie	0- 2	1- 1	4	2	1
Wollard	1- 3	1- 2	3	2	3
Wiedeman	5-16	3- 6	8	0	13
Packer	8-14	1- 2	5	3	17
Hull	0- 2	0- 0	2	2	0
McCoy	0- 1	2- 2	1	1	2
Carmichael	0- 0	0- 0	1	1	0
Hassell	1- 2	0- 0	0	0	2
Zawacki	0- 0	1- 3	0	0	1
Koehler	0- 1	0- 0	0	0	0
Brooks	0- 1	2- 2	1	1	2
Totals	25-66	18-29	43	17	68

Ohio State	fg-fga	ft-fta	rb	pf	tp
Havlicek	9-19	7- 9	16	3	25
McDonald	5-10	1- 2	5	3	11
Lucas	8-16	3- 4	16	1	19
Nowell	2-11	0- 0	2	2	4
Reasbeck	5- 7	0- 0	3	4	10
Gearhart	2- 5	0- 0	0	4	4
Doughty	2- 4	4- 4	5	1	8
Bradds	0- 0	0- 1	4	3	0
Knight	0- 2	0- 0	2	2	0
Flatt	0- 0	1- 2	0	0	1
Taylor	0- 0	0- 0	0	1	0
Frazier	1- 1	0- 0	0	0	2
Totals	34-75	16-22	53	24	84

Ohio State	fg-fga	ft-fta	rb	pf	tp
Havlicek	5-14	1- 2	9	1	11
McDonald	0- 1	3- 3	1	2	3
Lucas	5-17	1- 2	16	3	11
Reasbeck	4- 6	0- 0	0	4	8
Nowell	4-16	1- 1	6	2	9
Doughty	0- 1	0- 0	2	2	0
Gearhart	1- 4	0- 0	4	3	2
Bradds	5- 7	5- 6	4	2	15
Totals	24-66	11-14	42	19	59

1963 Tournament Stats

Semifinals

Cincinnati	fg-fga	ft-fta	rb	pf	tp
Bonham	3-12	8- 9	5	3	14
Thacker	5- 8	4- 8	11	3	14
Wilson	8- 9	8-12	13	2	24
Yates	5- 9	2- 3	5	1	12
Shingleton	1- 2	0- 0	2	1	2
Heidotting	0- 0	1- 2	2	1	1
Cunningham	2- 3	0- 0	0	1	4
Meyer	1- 1	1- 2	1	1	3
Smith	1- 3	0- 2	1	1	2
Elsasser	1- 2	0- 1	1	0	2
Abernethy	1- 2	0- 0	3	0	2
Totals	28-51	24-39	44	14	80

Oregon State	fg-fga	ft-fta	rb	pf	tp
Pauly	2- 8	0- 1	3	5	4
Kraus	1- 6	1- 1	3	3	3
Counts	8-14	4- 4	9	5	20
Peters	1- 5	2- 2	4	4	4
Baker	0- 9	0- 1	2	0	0
Jarvis	1- 6	3- 4	0	3	5
Rossi	1- 3	0- 0	0	1	2
Campbell	0- 2	1- 1	2	2	1
Torgerson	1- 2	0- 0	0	0	2
Hayward	0- 2	1- 1	2	3	1
Benner	2- 2	0- 0	1	0	4
Totals	17-59	12-15	26	26	46

Loyola	fg-fga	ft-fta	rb	pf	tp
Harkness	7-18	6- 9	11	3	20
Rouse	6-12	1- 2	6	4	13
Hunter	11-20	7- 9	18	3	29
Egan	4- 9	6- 7	3	2	14
Miller	8-11	2- 2	5	4	18
Wood	0- 1	0- 0	3	0	0
Rochelle	0- 0	0- 0	0	0	0
Reardon	0- 0	0- 0	0	0	0
Connaughton	0- 0	0- 0	0	0	0
Team			5		
Totals	36-71	22-29	51	16	94

Duke	fg-fga	ft-fta	rb	pf	tp
Heyman	11-30	7- 9	12	5	29
Mullins	10-20	1- 3	9	4	21
Buckley	4-10	2- 4	13	3	10
Schmidt	0- 2	0- 0	2	3	0
Harrison	0- 3	2- 3	3	0	2
Herbster	0- 2	0- 0	0	1	0
Ferguson	1- 2	0- 0	0	1	2
Jamison	0- 0	0- 0	0	1	0
Cox	0- 0	0- 0	0	0	0
Mann	0- 1	0- 0	0	0	0
Tison	5-12	1- 3	8	3	11
Team			5		
Totals	31-82	13-22	52	21	75

Championship

Loyola	fg-fga	ft-fta	rb	pf	tp
Harkness	5-18	4- 8	6	4	14
Rouse	6-22	3- 4	12	4	15
Hunter	6-22	4- 4	11	3	16
Egan	3- 8	3- 5	3	3	9
Miller	3-14	0- 0	2	3	6
Team			11		
Totals	23-84	14-21	45	17	60

Cincinnati	fg-fga	ft-fta	rb	pf	tp
Bonham	8-16	6- 6	4	3	22
Thacker	5-12	3- 4	15	4	13
Wilson	4- 8	2- 3	13	4	10
Yates	4- 6	1- 4	8	4	9
Shingleton	1- 3	2- 3	4	0	4
Heidotting	0- 0	0- 0	1	2	0
Team			7		
Totals	22-45	14-20	52	17	58

Half time: Cincinnati 29-21. Regulation Score: 54-54.

1964 Tournament Stats

Semifinals

Duke	fg-fga	ft-fta	rb	pf	tp
Ferguson	6-11	0- 1	0	0	12
Buckley	11-16	3- 5	14	4	25
Tison	3-10	6-10	13	4	12
Harrison	6-15	2- 3	2	2	14
Mullins	8-19	5- 6	8	1	21
Marin	1- 2	0- 0	2	1	2
Vacendak	2- 5	1- 2	2	1	5
Herbster	0- 0	0- 0	0	0	0
Totals	37-78	17-27	41	13	91

Michigan	fg-fga	ft-fta	rb	pf	tp
Buntin	8-18	3- 3	9	5	19
Cantrell	6-10	0- 0	4	2	12
Russell	13-19	5- 6	8	5	31
Tregoning	3-11	2- 2	6	4	8
Darden	2- 6	1- 1	9	5	5
Myers	2- 5	0- 0	5	2	4
Pomey	0- 1	1- 2	0	0	1
Herner	0- 1	0- 0	0	0	0
Totals	34-71	12-14	41	23	80

UCLA	fg-fga	ft-fta	rb	pf	tp
Goodrich	7-18	0- 0	6	3	14
Slaughter	2- 6	0- 0	5	4	4
Hazzard	7-10	5- 7	7	2	19
Hirsch	2-11	0- 0	1	4	4
Erickson	10-21	8- 9	10	2	28
McIntosh	3- 5	2- 3	10	3	8
Washington	5-11	3- 4	6	1	13
Totals	36-82	18-23	45	19	90

Kansas State	fg-fga	ft-fta	rb	pf	tp
Moss	3- 9	1- 1	5	3	7
Robinson	2- 7	0- 1	5	4	4
Simons	10-17	4- 6	7	3	24
Suttner	3- 9	0- 5	10	2	6
Murrell	13-22	3- 5	13	3	29
Paradis	5- 9	0- 0	1	0	10
Williams	1- 1	2- 3	1	2	4
Nelson	0- 1	0- 0	0	1	0
Gottfrid	0- 0	0- 0	0	1	0
Barnard	0- 1	0- 0	0	0	0
Totals	37-76	10-21	42	19	84

Championship

UCLA	fg-fga	ft-fta	rb	pf	tp
Goodrich	9-18	9- 9	3	1	27
Slaughter	0- 1	0- 0	1	0	0
Hazzard	4-10	3- 5	3	5	11
Hirsch	5- 9	3- 5	6	3	13
Erickson	2- 7	4- 4	5	5	8
McIntosh	4- 9	0- 0	11	2	8
Washington	11-16	4- 4	12	4	26
Darrow	0- 1	3- 4	1	2	3
Stewart	0- 1	0- 0	0	1	0
Huggins	0- 1	0- 1	1	2	0
Hoffman	1- 2	0- 0	0	0	2
Levin	0- 1	0- 0	0	0	0
Totals	36-76	26-32	43	25	98

Duke	fg-fga	ft-fta	rb	pf	tp
Ferguson	2- 6	0- 1	1	3	4
Buckley	5- 8	8-12	9	4	18
Tison	3- 8	1- 1	1	2	7
Harrison	1- 1	0- 0	1	2	2
Mullins	9-21	4- 4	4	5	22
Marin	8-16	0- 1	10	3	16
Vacendak	2- 7	3- 3	6	4	7
Herbster	1- 4	0- 2	0	0	2
Kitching	1- 1	0- 0	1	0	2
Mann	0- 0	3- 4	2	1	3
Harscher	0- 0	0- 0	0	0	0
Cox	0- 0	0- 0	0	0	0
Totals	32-72	19-28	35	24	83

1965 Tournament Stats

Semifinals

Princeton	fg-fga	ft-fta	rb	pf	tp
Bradley	12-25	5- 5	5	7	29
Haarlow	4-10	1- 4	1	3	9
Brown	2- 6	0- 0	5	3	4
Walters	5-10	1- 2	1	3	11
Rodenbach	2- 5	2- 2	3	1	6
Hummer	4-10	4- 5	4	9	12
Koch	1- 4	1- 2	1	4	3
Kingston	0- 1	2- 2	1	2	2
Totals	30-71	16-22	21	32	76

Michigan	fg-fga	ft-fta	rb	pf	tp
Tregoning	6- 9	1- 1	2	10	13
Darden	6-13	1- 3	3	9	13
Buntin	7-13	8-10	4	14	22
Russell	10-21	8- 9	0	10	28
Pomey	2- 8	2- 2	4	3	6
Myers	1- 4	0- 0	1	4	2
Thompson	0- 1	2- 2	0	0	2
Dill	0- 0	3- 4	2	1	3
Ludwig	0- 0	0- 0	1	0	0
Clawson	2- 2	0- 1	0	1	4
Totals	34-71	25-32	17	52	93

Championship

UCLA	fg-fga	ft-fta	rb	pf	tp
Erickson	1- 1	1- 2	1	1	3
Lacey	5- 7	1- 2	7	3	11
McIntosh	1- 2	1- 2	0	2	3
Goodrich	12-22	18-20	4	4	42
Goss	4-12	0- 0	3	1	8
Washington	7- 9	3- 4	5	2	17
Lynn	2- 3	1- 2	6	1	5
Lyons	0- 0	0- 0	0	1	0
Galbraith	0- 0	0- 0	0	0	0
Hoffman	1- 1	0- 0	1	0	2
Levin	0- 1	0- 0	1	0	0
Chambers	0- 0	0- 1	0	0	0
Team			6		
Totals	33-58	25-33	34	15	91

Wichita	fg-fga	ft-fta	rb	pf	tp
Smith	4-11	0- 1	2	3	8
Thompson	13-19	10-11	6	2	36
Leach	6-14	0- 1	10	3	12
Pete	6-11	5- 5	6	5	17
Criss	4-13	0- 0	4	4	8
Reed	2- 3	1- 1	4	4	5
Davis	1- 2	0- 0	1	0	2
Trope	0- 1	0- 0	0	0	0
Nosich	0- 0	1- 3	0	0	1
Reimond	0- 1	0- 0	1	0	0
Team			4		
Totals	36-75	17-22	38	21	89

UCLA	fg-fga	ft-fta	rb	pf	tp
Lacey	9-13	6-10	2	13	24
Erickson	1- 6	0- 0	2	5	2
McIntosh	4- 5	3- 4	2	4	11
Goodrich	11-21	6- 8	2	5	28
Goss	8-13	3- 3	2	9	19
Washington	4-13	2- 4	1	7	10
Lynn	5- 9	0- 0	1	8	10
Chambers	0- 5	0- 0	1	2	0
Lyons	2- 3	0- 0	2	1	4
Levin	0- 1	0- 0	1	1	0
Galbraith	0- 0	0- 0	1	0	0
Hoffman	0- 0	0- 0	0	0	0
Totals	44-89	20-29	17	55	108

Michigan	fg-fga	ft-fta	rb	pf	tp
Darden	8-10	1- 1	4	5	17
Pomey	2- 5	0- 0	2	2	4
Buntin	6-14	2- 4	6	5	14
Russell	10-16	8-10	5	2	28
Tregoning	2- 7	1- 1	5	5	5
Myers	0- 4	0- 0	3	2	0
Brown	0- 0	0- 0	0	0	0
Ludwig	1- 2	0- 0	0	0	2
Thompson	0- 0	0- 0	0	0	0
Bankey	0- 0	0- 0	0	0	0
Clawson	3- 4	0- 0	0	2	6
Dill	1- 2	2- 2	1	1	4
Team			7		
Totals	33-64	14-18	33	24	80

1966 Tournament Stats

Semifinals

Utah	fg-fga	ft-fta	rb	pf	tp
Tate	0- 4	1- 3	2	5	1
Jackson	3- 9	2- 2	2	1	8
Mackay	4-10	6- 9	7	2	14
Ockel	1- 1	3- 3	9	3	5
Chambers	14-31	10-12	17	3	38
Black	3- 8	2- 4	2	3	8
Lake	1- 1	0- 0	0	3	2
Day	1-2	0-0	0	0	2
Totals	27-66	24-33	39	20	78

Texas Western	fg-fga	ft-fta	rb	pf	tp
Hill	5-20	8-10	11	4	18
Artis	10-20	2- 3	5	2	22
Shed	2- 3	5- 6	3	3	9
Lattin	5- 7	1- 1	4	5	11
Flournoy	3- 6	2- 2	9	5	8
Cager	2- 5	1- 1	0	3	5
Worsley	5- 8	2- 3	5	3	12
Armstrong	0- 2	0- 1	3	2	0
Totals	32-71	21-27	40	27	85

Duke	fg-fga	ft-fta	rb	pf	tp
Marin	11-18	7-10	7	2	29
Riedy	2- 7	2- 2	8	3	6
Lewis	9-13	3- 3	6	3	21
Verga	2- 7	0- 0	3	1	4
Vacendak	7-16	3- 3	3	5	17
Wendelin	1- 4	0- 1	2	4	2
Liccardo	0- 1	0- 0	0	0	0
Barone	0- 0	0- 0	0	1	0
Team			7		
Totals	32-66	15-19	36	19	79

Kentucky	fg-fga	ft-fta	rb	pf	tp
Conley	3- 5	4- 4	1	0	10
Riley	8-17	3- 4	8	5	19
Jaracz	3- 5	2- 3	4	5	8
Dampier	11-20	1- 2	4	3	23
Kron	5-13	2- 2	10	1	12
Tallent	1- 2	2- 2	1	0	4
Berger	1- 4	5- 6	5	1	7
Gamble	0- 0	0- 1	0	1	0
Team			8		
Totals	32-66	19-24	41	16	83

Championship

Kentucky	fg-fga	ft-fta	rb	pf	tp
Dampier	7-18	5- 5	9	4	19
Kron	3- 6	0- 0	7	2	6
Conley	4- 9	2- 2	8	5	10
Riley	8-22	3- 4	4	4	19
Jaracz	3- 8	1- 2	5	5	7
Berger	2- 3	0- 0	0	0	4
Gamble	0- 0	0- 0	0	1	0
LeMaster	0- 1	0- 0	0	1	0
Tallent	0- 3	0- 0	0	1	0
Totals	27-70	11-13	33	23	65

Texas Western	fg-fga	ft-fta	rb	pf	tp
Hill	7-17	6- 9	3	3	20
Artis	5-13	5- 5	8	1	15
Shed	1- 1	1- 1	3	1	3
Lattin	5-10	6- 6	9	4	16
Cager	1- 3	6- 7	6	3	8
Flournoy	1- 1	0- 0	0	0	2
Worsley	2- 4	4- 6	4	0	8
Totals	22-49	28-34	35	12	72

1967 Tournament Stats

Semifinals

Dayton	fg-fga	ft-fta	rb	pf	tp
May	16-22	2- 6	15	2	34
Sadlier	4- 7	0- 1	0	0	8
Obrovac	0- 0	0- 0	1	1	0
Klaus	3- 6	9-10	8	4	15
Hooper	1- 7	3- 4	4	1	5
Torain	4-14	6- 8	11	5	14
Wannemacher	0- 0	0- 2	0	0	0
Waterman	0- 0	0- 0	0	0	0
Team			5		
Totals	28-56	20-31	44	13	76

UCLA	fg-fga	ft-fta	rb	pf	tp
Heitz	0- 0	1- 1	0	1	1
Shackelford	11-19	0- 1	8	1	22
Alcindor	6-11	7-13	20	1	19
Allen	6-15	5- 5	9	2	17
Warren	4-10	6- 7	9	0	14
Nielsen	0- 3	0- 0	3	5	0
Sweek	0- 4	0- 0	1	2	0
Saffer	0- 0	0- 0	0	0	0
Team			1		
Totals	27-62	19-27	51	12	73

North Carolina	fg-fga	ft-fta	rb	pf	tp
Miller	6-18	1- 1	13	4	13
Bunting	1- 3	1- 1	5	4	3
Clark	8-14	3- 5	11	4	19
Lewis	5-18	1- 1	3	3	11
Grubar	2- 7	3- 3	2	4	7
Gauntlett	1- 4	0- 0	3	0	2
Brown	0- 3	0- 0	0	0	0
Tuttle	3- 5	1- 1	1	3	7
Team			5		
Totals	26-72	10-12	43	22	62

Houston	fg-fga	ft-fta	rb	pf	tp
Hayes	12-31	1- 2	24	4	25
Bell	3-11	4- 7	11	4	10
Kruse	2- 5	1- 1	0	2	5
Grider	2- 7	0- 0	2	2	4
Chaney	3-11	0- 2	4	4	6
Lentz	1- 2	0- 3	4	1	2
Spain	1- 5	0- 0	4	2	2
Lewis	0- 0	0- 1	0	1	0
Lee	2- 3	0- 0	1	0	4
Team			1		
Totals	26-75	6-16	51	20	58

Championship

UCLA	fg-fga	ft-fta	rb	pf	tp
Heitz	2- 7	0- 0	6	2	4
Shackelford	5-10	0- 2	3	1	10
Alcindor	8-12	4-11	18	0	20
Allen	7-15	5- 8	9	2	19
Warren	8-16	1- 1	7	1	17
Nielsen	0- 1	0- 1	1	3	0
Sweek	1- 1	0- 0	0	1	2
Saffer	2- 5	0- 0	0	1	4
Saner	1- 1	0- 0	2	2	2
Chrisman	0- 0	1- 2	1	2	1
Sutherland	0- 0	0- 0	0	0	0
Lynn	0- 1	0- 0	0	0	0
Team			7		
Totals	34-69	11-25	54	15	79

Dayton	fg-fga	ft-fta	rb	pf	tp
May	9-23	3- 4	17	4	21
Sadlier	2- 5	1- 2	7	5	5
Obrovac	0- 2	0- 0	2	1	0
Klaus	4- 7	0- 0	0	1	8
Hooper	2- 7	2- 4	5	2	6
Torain	3-14	0- 0	4	3	6
Waterman	4-11	2- 3	1	3	10
Sharpenter	2- 5	4- 5	5	1	8
Samanich	0- 2	0- 0	2	0	0
Beckman	0- 0	0- 0	0	0	0
Inderrieden	0- 0	0- 0	0	0	0
Wannemacher	0- 0	0- 0	0	0	0
Team			8		
Totals	26-76	12-18	51	20	64

1968 Tournament Stats

Semifinals

Ohio State	fg-fga	ft-fta	rb	pf	tp
Howell	6-17	1- 2	3	2	13
Hosket	4-11	6- 9	9	5	14
Sorenson	5-17	1- 3	11	3	11
Schnabel	0- 1	0- 0	2	1	0
Meadors	3-13	2- 2	3	3	8
Finney	8-13	0- 2	4	2	16
Smith	2- 6	0- 0	5	1	4
Andreas	0- 0	0- 0	0	0	0
Barclay	0- 1	0- 0	0	0	0
Geddes	0- 0	0- 0	1	1	0
Team			11		
Totals	28-79	10-18	49	18	66

North Carolina	fg-fga	ft-fta	rb	pf	tp
Miller	10-23	0- 1	6	2	20
Bunting	4- 7	9-10	12	2	17
Clark	7- 9	1- 1	11	4	15
Scott	6-16	1- 4	5	3	13
Grubar	4- 9	3- 3	6	0	11
Fogler	1- 2	0- 0	0	1	2
Brown	0- 4	0- 0	4	2	0
Tuttle	1- 1	0- 1	0	0	2
Team			10		
Totals	33-71	14-20	54	14	80

Championship

UCLA	fg-fga	ft-fta	rb	pf	tp
Shackelford	3- 5	0- 1	2	0	6
Lynn	1- 7	5- 7	6	3	7
Alcindor	15-21	4- 4	16	3	34
Warren	3- 7	1- 1	3	2	7
Allen	3- 7	5- 7	5	0	11
Nielsen	1- 1	0- 0	1	1	2
Heitz	3- 6	1- 1	2	3	7
Sutherland	1- 2	0- 0	2	1	2
Sweek	0- 1	0- 0	0	1	0
Saner	1- 3	0- 0	2	2	2
Team			9		
Totals	31-60	16-21	48	16	78

Houston	fg-fga	ft-fta	rb	pf	tp
Lee	2-15	0- 0	4	4	4
Hayes	3-10	4- 7	5	4	10
Spain	4-12	7-10	13	1	15
Chaney	5-13	5- 7	7	2	15
Lewis	2- 8	2- 2	5	0	6
Hamood	3- 5	4- 6	0	2	10
Gribben	0- 5	0- 1	5	1	0
Bell	3- 8	3- 4	5	0	9
Taylor	0- 0	0- 0	0	0	0
Cooper	0- 2	0- 0	1	0	0
Team			9		
Totals	22-78	25-37	54	14	69

UCLA	fg-fga	ft-fta	rb	pf	tp
Shackelford	6-10	5- 5	3	4	17
Lynn	8-10	3- 3	8	4	19
Alcindor	7-14	5- 6	18	3	19
Warren	7-18	0- 0	5	3	14
Allen	9-18	1- 2	9	1	19
Nielsen	2- 3	0- 0	1	4	4
Heitz	3- 6	1- 1	1	1	7
Sweek	1- 1	0- 1	0	0	2
Sutherland	0- 1	0- 0	0	1	0
Saner	0- 2	0- 0	1	2	0
Team			11		
Totals	43-83	15-18	57	23	101

North Carolina	fg-fga	ft-fta	rb	pf	tp
Miller	5-13	4- 6	6	3	14
Bunting	1- 3	1- 2	2	5	3
Clark	4-12	1- 3	8	3	9
Scott	6-17	0- 1	3	3	12
Grubar	2- 5	1- 2	0	2	5
Fogler	1- 4	2- 2	0	0	4
Brown	2- 5	2- 2	5	1	6
Tuttle	0- 0	0- 0	0	0	0
Frye	1- 2	0- 1	1	0	2
Whitehead	0- 0	0- 0	0	0	0
Delany	0- 1	0- 0	0	0	0
Fletcher	0- 1	0- 0	0	0	0
Team			10		
Totals	22-63	11-19	35	17	55

1969 Tournament Stats

Semifinals

Drake	fg-fga	ft-fta	rb	pf	tp
Pulliam	4-14	4- 5	5	4	12
Williams	0- 1	0- 0	1	4	0
Wise	5- 7	3- 4	16	3	13
McCarter	10-27	4- 4	1	3	24
Draper	5-13	2- 2	1	2	12
Odom	0- 2	0- 1	2	4	0
Wanamaker	4- 7	1- 1	7	4	9
Zeller	4-12	4- 6	3	3	12
Gwin	0- 0	0- 1	1	3	0
Team			4		
Totals	32-83	18-24	41	30	82

UCLA	fg-fga	ft-fta	rb	pf	tp
Shackelford	2- 5	2- 3	2	4	6
Rowe	6- 9	2- 2	13	2	14
Alcindor	8-14	9-16	21	3	25
Heitz	3- 6	1- 3	1	5	7
Vallely	9-11	11-14	6	5	29
Wicks	0- 2	0- 0	1	1	0
Sweek	0- 0	0- 0	0	1	0
Patterson	0- 0	2- 2	0	0	2
Schofield	0- 3	2- 4	0	0	2
Team			4		
Totals	28-50	29-44	48	21	85

North Carolina	fg-fga	ft-fta	rb	pf	tp
Bunting	7-13	5- 7	7	2	19
Scott	6-19	4- 6	6	3	16
Clark	7- 9	6-10	9	2	20
Fogler	1- 4	0- 0	2	2	2
G. Tuttle	2- 4	0- 1	3	3	4
Delany	0- 2	0- 0	1	4	0
Dedmon	0- 1	0- 1	4	2	0
Brown	1- 4	0- 0	1	0	2
Gipple	0- 3	0- 0	1	0	0
Chadwick	1- 2	0- 0	2	0	2
R. Tuttle	0- 1	0- 0	0	0	0
Eggleston	0- 0	0- 0	0	0	0
Team			1		
Totals	25-62	15-25	37	18	65

Purdue	fg-fga	ft-fta	rb	pf	tp
Gilliam	3-11	0- 0	8	0	6
Faerber	3- 3	2- 2	9	3	8
Johnson	2- 5	1- 3	5	4	5
Mount	14-28	8- 9	4	0	36
Keller	9-19	2- 3	5	3	20
Kaufman	0- 1	2- 3	6	4	2
Weatherford	3- 6	1- 1	2	1	7
Bedford	3- 3	0- 0	5	4	6
Taylor	1- 1	0- 1	3	0	2
Longfellow	0- 1	0- 0	2	0	0
Reasoner	0- 0	0- 0	0	1	0
Young	0- 0	0- 0	0	0	0
Team			2		
Totals	38-78	16-22	51	20	92

Championship

UCLA	fg-fga	ft-fta	rb	pf	tp
Shackelford	3- 8	5- 8	9	3	11
Rowe	4-10	4- 4	12	2	12
Alcindor	15-20	7- 9	20	2	37
Heitz	0- 3	0- 1	3	4	0
Vallely	4- 9	7-10	4	3	15
Sweek	3- 3	0- 1	1	3	6
Wicks	0- 1	3- 6	4	1	3
Schofield	1- 2	0- 0	0	0	2
Patterson	1- 1	2- 2	2	0	4
Seibert	0- 0	0- 0	1	0	0
Farmer	0- 0	0- 0	0	1	0
Ecker	1- 1	0- 0	0	0	2
Team			5		
Totals	32-58	28-41	61	19	92

Purdue	fg-fga	ft-fta	rb	pf	tp
Gilliam	2-14	3- 3	11	2	7
Faerber	1- 2	0- 0	3	5	2
Johnson	4- 9	3- 4	9	2	11
Mount	12-36	4- 5	1	3	28
Keller	4-17	3- 4	4	5	11
Kaufman	0- 0	2- 2	5	5	2
Bedford	3- 8	1- 3	8	3	7
Weatherford	1- 5	2- 2	1	3	4
Reasoner	0- 1	0- 1	1	2	0
Taylor	0- 0	0- 0	0	0	0
Team			5		
Totals	27-92	18-24	48	30	72

1970 Tournament Stats

Semifinals

Jacksonville	fg-fga	ft-fta	rb	pf	tp
Wedeking	7-15	1- 1	6	4	15
Morgan	6-15	5- 6	5	3	17
Burrows	2- 4	1- 1	4	4	5
McIntyre	0- 3	0- 0	3	1	0
Gilmore	9-14	11-15	21	2	29
Dublin	1- 3	9- 9	2	2	11
Nelson	1- 7	10-12	7	3	12
Blevins	1- 1	0- 0	0	1	2
Baldwin	0- 1	0- 1	0	1	0
Team			4		
Totals	27-63	37-45	52	21	91

St. Bonaventure	fg-fga	ft-fta	rb	pf	tp
Kalbaugh	5- 8	2- 2	4	3	12
Hoffman	4-14	2- 4	6	3	10
Gary	2- 7	5- 8	13	5	9
Baldwin	2-10	1- 2	4	5	5
Gantt	8-17	0- 0	8	5	16
Kull	4- 7	0- 0	0	5	8
Thomas	7-17	1- 2	4	3	15
Grys	1- 5	2- 2	1	2	4
Tepas	0- 0	2- 2	1	0	2
Fahey	1- 1	0- 0	0	1	2
Team			6		
Totals	34-86	15-22	47	32	83

UCLA	fg-fga	ft-fta	rb	pf	tp
Rowe	4- 7	7-11	15	0	15
Patterson	5- 9	2- 2	6	3	12
Wicks	10-12	2- 5	16	3	22
Vallely	7-19	9-10	4	3	23
Bibby	8-13	3- 3	2	5	19
Booker	0- 1	0- 0	0	2	0
Betchley	0- 0	0- 0	0	0	0
Schofield	0- 0	0- 0	0	1	0
Ecker	0- 0	0- 0	0	0	0
Seibert	0- 1	0- 0	1	0	0
Hill	0- 0	0- 1	0	1	0
Chapman	1- 1	0- 0	1	0	2
Team			0		
Totals	35-63	23-32	45	18	93

New Mexico State	fg-fga	ft-fta	rb	pf	tp
Criss	6-16	7- 9	2	5	19
Collins	13-23	2- 3	0	3	28
Burgess	1- 6	0- 0	2	2	2
Smith	4-11	2- 3	7	5	10
Lacey	3- 9	2- 3	16	3	8
Reyes	1- 6	0- 0	4	2	2
Neal	2- 4	0- 0	6	2	4
Horne	0- 4	2- 2	1	2	2
Moore	1- 1	0- 0	1	0	2
Lefevre	0- 0	0- 0	1	0	0
Franco	0- 0	0- 0	0	0	0
McCarthy	0- 0	0- 0	0	0	0
Team			5		
Totals	31-80	15-20	45	24	77

Championship

Jacksonville	fg-fga	ft-fta	rb	pf	tp
Wedeking	6-11	0- 0	2	2	12
Blevins	1- 2	1- 2	0	1	3
Morgan	5-11	0- 0	4	5	10
Burrows	6- 9	0- 0	6	1	12
Gilmore	9-29	1- 1	16	5	19
Nelson	3- 9	2- 2	5	1	8
Dublin	0- 5	2- 2	1	4	2
Baldwin	0- 0	0- 0	0	0	0
McIntyre	1- 3	0- 0	3	4	2
Hawkins	0- 1	1- 1	1	1	1
Selke	0- 0	0- 0	0	0	0
Team			2		
Totals	31-80	7- 8	40	24	69

UCLA	fg-fga	ft-fta	rb	pf	tp
Rowe	7-15	5- 5	8	4	19
Patterson	8-15	1- 4	11	1	17
Wicks	5- 9	7-10	18	3	17
Vallely	5-10	5- 7	7	2	15
Bibby	2-11	4- 4	4	1	8
Booker	0- 0	2- 3	0	0	2
Seibert	0- 1	0- 0	1	1	0
Ecker	1- 1	0- 0	0	0	2
Betchley	0- 0	0- 1	0	0	0
Chapman	0- 1	0- 0	1	0	0
Hill	0- 0	0- 1	0	0	0
Schofield	0- 0	0- 0	0	0	0
Team			3		
Totals	28-63	24-35	53	12	80

1971 Tournament Stats

Semifinals

Villanova	fg-fga	ft-fta	rb	pf	tp
Smith	5-14	3- 6	11	1	13
Porter	10-20	2- 3	16	4	22
Siemiontkowski	11-20	9-10	15	5	31
Ingelsby	5-10	4- 7	4	1	14
Ford	3- 6	2- 2	1	4	8
McDowell	2- 3	0- 3	3	1	4
Team			4		
Totals	36-73	20-31	54	16	92

Half time: Western Kentucky 38-35. Regulation Score: 74-74. First Overtime: 85-85.

Western Kentucky	fg-fga	ft-fta	rb	pf	tp
Glover	5- 15	2- 4	20	4	12
Dunn	11- 33	3- 6	8	5	25
McDaniels	10- 24	2- 4	17	5	22
Rose	8- 21	2- 3	8	2	18
Bailey	5- 11	2- 3	8	1	12
Witt	0- 1	0- 0	0	3	0
Sundmacker	0- 0	0- 0	0	1	0
Team			8		
Totals	39-105	11-20	69	21	89

Championship

Villanova	fg-fga	ft-fta	rb	pf	tp
Smith	4-11	1- 1	2	4	9
Porter	10-21	5- 6	8	1	25
Siemiontkowski	9-16	1- 2	6	3	19
Ingelsby	3- 9	1- 1	4	2	7
Ford	0- 4	2- 3	5	4	2
McDowell	0- 1	0- 0	2	0	0
Fox	0- 0	0- 0	0	0	0
Team			4		
Totals	26-62	10-13	31	14	62

Kansas	fg-fga	ft-fta	rb	pf	tp
Robisch	7–19	3– 6	6	3	17
Russell	5–12	2– 2	4	4	12
Brown	3– 8	1– 3	9	4	7
Stallworth	5–10	2– 4	5	5	12
Nash	3– 9	1– 2	3	1	7
Kivisto	1– 1	1– 4	1	2	3
Canfield	0– 0	0– 0	0	1	0
Williams	0– 1	2– 2	0	2	2
Mathews	0– 0	0– 0	0	0	0
Douglas	0– 0	0– 0	1	0	0
Team			3		
Totals	24–60	12–23	32	22	60

UCLA	fg-fga	ft-fta	rb	pf	tp
Rowe	7–10	2– 4	15	2	16
Wicks	5– 9	11–13	8	2	21
Patterson	3–11	0– 0	6	2	6
Bibby	6– 9	6– 6	4	3	18
Booker	1– 2	1– 2	5	3	3
Schofield	1– 3	0– 1	0	3	2
Farmer	0– 2	0– 1	2	1	0
Betchley	0– 0	0– 1	0	0	0
Ecker	0– 1	2– 2	1	0	2
Hill	0– 0	0– 0	0	0	0
Chapman	0– 0	0– 0	1	2	0
Team			5		
Totals	23–47	22–30	47	18	68

UCLA	fg-fga	ft-fta	rb	pf	tp
Rowe	2– 3	4– 5	8	0	8
Wicks	3– 7	1– 1	9	2	7
Patterson	13–18	3– 5	8	1	29
Bibby	6–12	5– 5	2	1	17
Booker	0– 0	0– 0	0	0	0
Schofield	3– 9	0– 0	1	4	6
Betchley	0– 0	1– 2	1	1	1
Team			5		
Totals	27–49	14–18	34	9	68

1972 Tournament Stats

Semifinals

Florida State	fg-fga	ft-fta	rb	pf	tp
Garrett	4– 8	3– 7	5	4	11
King	6–17	10–10	5	1	22
Royals	6– 8	6– 7	10	5	18
McCray	3– 6	3– 6	9	3	9
Samuel	2– 4	1– 4	1	0	5
Harris	1– 6	2– 2	4	2	4
Petty	3– 5	4– 7	1	5	10
Gay	0– 1	0– 0	0	0	0
Team			6		
Totals	25–55	29–43	41	20	79

North Carolina	fg-fga	ft-fta	rb	pf	tp
Jones	4– 8	1– 1	9	3	9
Wuycik	7–16	6– 6	6	4	20
McAdoo	10–19	4– 5	15	5	24
Previs	1– 5	3– 6	3	4	5
Karl	5–14	1– 3	6	3	11
Huband	0– 1	0– 0	2	2	0
Chamberlain	2– 5	2– 3	10	4	6
Johnston	0– 1	0– 0	0	1	0
Chambers	0– 1	0– 1	0	1	0
Team			1		
Totals	29–70	17–25	52	27	75

Louisville	fg-fga	ft-fta	rb	pf	tp
Lawhon	0– 7	1– 2	3	3	1
Thomas	2– 4	0– 0	3	5	4
Vilcheck	3– 6	0– 0	1	5	6
Price	11–23	8– 9	5	3	30
Bacon	5–11	5– 7	4	0	15
Carter	4– 8	0– 0	2	0	8
Bunton	1– 5	1– 1	4	1	3
Bradley	1– 3	0– 0	2	1	2
Stallings	1– 2	0– 1	1	2	2
Cooper	0– 1	2– 2	1	1	2
Pry	2– 3	0– 0	1	1	4
Meiman	0– 1	0– 0	1	0	0
Team			4		
Totals	30–74	17–22	32	22	77

UCLA	fg-fga	ft-fta	rb	pf	tp
Wilkes	5–11	2– 2	6	0	12
Farmer	6–12	3– 5	4	2	15
Walton	11–13	11–12	21	2	33
Lee	3– 6	4– 6	4	1	10
Bibby	1– 5	0– 0	3	5	2
Curtis	4– 5	0– 0	2	2	8
Hollyfield	3– 6	0– 0	4	1	6
Carson	1– 1	0– 0	0	1	2
Nater	0– 0	2– 4	1	1	2
Hill	1– 1	4– 4	0	1	6
Chapman	0– 0	0– 1	1	0	0
Franklin	0– 1	0– 0	2	0	0
Team			3		
Totals	35–61	26–34	51	16	96

Championship

Florida State	fg-fga	ft-fta	rb	pf	tp
Garrett	1– 9	1– 1	5	1	3
King	12–20	3– 3	6	1	27
Royals	5– 7	5– 6	10	5	15
McCray	3– 6	2– 5	6	4	8
Samuel	3–10	0– 0	1	1	6
Harris	7–13	2– 3	6	1	16
Petty	0– 0	1– 1	0	1	1
Cole	0– 2	0– 0	2	1	0
Team			6		
Totals	31–67	14–19	42	15	76

UCLA	fg-fga	ft-fta	rb	pf	tp
Wilkes	11–16	1– 2	10	4	23
Farmer	2– 6	0– 0	6	2	4
Walton	9–17	6–11	20	4	24
Lee	0– 0	0– 0	2	0	0
Bibby	8–17	2– 3	3	2	18
Curtis	4–14	0– 1	4	1	8
Hollyfield	1– 6	0– 0	2	2	2
Nater	1– 2	0– 1	1	0	2
Team			2		
Totals	36–78	9–18	50	15	81

1973 Tournament Stats

Semifinals

Providence	fg-fga	ft-fta	rb	pf	tp
Crawford	5-12	0- 0	15	3	10
Costello	5- 5	1- 1	8	5	11
Barnes	5- 7	2- 3	3	4	12
DiGregorio	15-36	2- 2	2	4	32
Stacom	6-15	3- 3	5	5	15
King	2- 6	0- 0	1	1	4
Baker	0- 0	0- 0	1	0	0
Dunphy	0- 1	1- 2	1	0	1
Bello	0- 0	0- 0	0	0	0
Team			3		
Totals	38-82	9-11	39	22	85

Memphis State	fg-fga	ft-fta	rb	pf	tp
Buford	3- 7	0- 0	3	2	6
Kenon	14-27	0- 4	22	1	28
Robinson	11-17	2- 3	16	2	24
Laurie	1- 3	2- 3	1	4	4
Finch	7-16	7- 9	6	4	21
Cook	3- 6	2- 3	1	2	8
Westfall	2- 3	3- 4	2	0	7
Jones	0- 1	0- 0	0	0	0
Team			3		
Totals	41-80	16-26	54	15	98

UCLA	fg-fga	ft-fta	rb	pf	tp
Wilkes	5-10	3- 4	6	3	13
Farmer	3- 6	1- 2	3	4	7
Walton	7-12	0- 0	17	4	14
Lee	0- 1	0- 0	0	0	0
Hollyfield	5- 6	0- 0	2	1	10
Curtis	9-15	4- 7	2	2	22
Meyers	2- 3	0- 0	5	1	4
Nater	0- 0	0- 0	0	1	0
Team			3		
Totals	31-53	8-13	38	16	70

Indiana	fg-fga	ft-fta	rb	pf	tp
Buckner	3-10	0- 1	5	2	6
Crews	4-10	0- 0	2	3	8
Downing	12-20	2- 4	5	5	26
Green	1- 7	0- 0	5	2	2
Ritter	6-10	1- 1	2	3	13
Laskowski	1- 8	0- 0	4	0	2
Abernethy	0- 1	0- 0	1	1	0
Smock	0- 0	0- 0	0	0	0
Noort	0- 0	0- 0	1	0	0
Wilson	0- 0	0- 0	0	0	0
Morris	0- 0	0- 0	0	0	0
Ahlfield	0- 0	0- 0	0	0	0
Allen	1- 1	0- 0	0	0	2
Memering	0- 0	0- 0	0	0	0
Team			4		
Totals	28-67	3- 6	29	16	59

Championship

UCLA	fg-fga	ft-fta	rb	pf	tp
Wilkes	8-14	0- 0	7	2	16
Farmer	1- 4	0- 0	2	2	2
Walton	21-22	2- 5	13	4	44
Lee	1- 1	3- 3	3	2	5
Hollyfield	4- 7	0- 0	3	4	8
Curtis	1- 4	2- 2	3	1	4
Meyers	2- 7	0- 0	3	1	4
Nater	1- 1	0- 0	3	2	2
Franklin	1- 2	0- 1	1	0	2
Carson	0- 0	0- 0	0	0	0
Webb	0- 0	0- 0	0	0	0
Team			2		
Totals	40-62	7-11	40	18	87

Memphis State	fg-fga	ft-fta	rb	pf	tp
Buford	3- 7	1- 2	3	1	7
Kenon	8-16	4- 4	8	3	20
Robinson	3- 6	0- 1	7	4	6
Laurie	0- 1	0- 0	0	0	0
Finch	9-21	11-13	1	2	29
Westfall	0- 1	0- 0	0	5	0
Cook	1- 4	2- 2	0	1	4
McKinney	0- 0	0- 0	0	0	0
Jones	0- 0	0- 0	0	0	0
Tetzlaff	0- 0	0- 2	0	1	0
Liss	0- 1	0- 0	0	0	0
Andrews	0- 0	0- 0	0	0	0
Team			2		
Totals	24-57	18-24	21	17	66

1974 Tournament Stats

Semifinals

UCLA	fg-fga	ft-fta	rb	pf	tp
Meyers	6- 9	0- 1	8	4	12
Wilkes	5-17	5- 5	7	5	15
Walton	13-21	3- 3	18	2	29
Curtis	4- 8	3- 4	5	4	11
Lee	4-11	0- 0	4	2	8
Johnson	0- 3	0- 0	0	0	0
McCarter	1- 2	0- 0	0	0	2
Team			2		
Totals	33-71	11-13	44	18	77

North Carolina State	fg-fga	ft-fta	rb	pf	tp
Stoddard	4-11	1- 2	9	5	9
Thompson	12-25	4- 6	10	3	28
Burleson	9-20	2- 6	14	4	20
Rivers	3- 8	1- 2	2	3	7
Towe	4-10	4- 4	2	4	12
Spence	2- 3	0- 0	5	0	4
Hawkins	0- 0	0- 0	0	0	0
Team			2		
Totals	34-77	12-20	44	19	80

Half time: 35-35. Regulation Score: 65-65. First Overtime: 77-77.

Championship

Marquette	fg-fga	ft-fta	rb	pf	tp
Ellis	6-16	0- 0	11	5	12
Tatum	2- 7	0- 0	3	4	4
Lucas	7-13	7- 9	13	4	21
Walton	4-10	0- 0	2	2	8
Washington	3-13	5- 8	4	3	11
Delsman	0- 0	0- 0	0	2	0
Daniels	1- 3	1- 2	0	3	3
Campbell	2- 3	0- 0	1	3	4
Homan	0- 4	1- 2	6	2	1
Brennan	0- 0	0- 0	0	1	0
Team			3		
Totals	25-69	14-21	43	29	64

Kansas	fg-fga	ft-fta	rb	pf	tp
Cook	1- 3	2- 4	5	5	4
Morningstar	5-13	0- 0	5	4	10
Knight	0- 5	0- 0	5	3	0
Greenlee	3- 7	0- 0	3	4	6
Kivisto	2- 7	2- 5	2	4	6
Suttle	8-13	3- 4	9	2	19
Smith	3- 4	0- 0	4	3	6
Team			4		
Totals	22-52	7-13	37	25	51

Marquette	fg-fga	ft-fta	rb	pf	tp
Ellis	2- 9	1- 2	10	3	5
Tatum	5-11	4- 6	3	3	14
Lucas	7-11	4- 4	14	2	18
Walton	2- 7	3- 4	1	4	7
Washington	5-12	6-11	3	4	16
Daniels	0- 2	0- 0	0	1	0
Campbell	0- 1	0- 0	1	0	0
Homan	1- 2	0- 0	0	2	2
Delsman	0- 1	2- 2	0	1	2
Brennan	0- 0	0- 0	0	0	0
Bryant	0- 0	0- 0	0	0	0
Vollmer	0- 0	0- 0	0	0	0
Johnson	0- 0	0- 0	0	0	0
Team			6		
Totals	22-56	20-29	38	20	64

North Carolina State	fg-fga	ft-fta	rb	pf	tp
Stoddard	3- 4	2- 2	7	5	8
Thompson	7-12	7- 8	7	3	21
Burleson	6- 9	2- 6	11	4	14
Rivers	4- 9	6- 9	2	2	14
Towe	5-10	6- 7	3	1	16
Spence	1- 2	1- 2	3	2	3
Moeller	0- 0	0- 0	0	0	0
Team			1		
Totals	26-46	24-34	34	17	76

1975 Tournament Stats

Semifinals

Louisville	fg-fga	ft-fta	rb	pf	tp
Murphy	14-28	5- 7	2	2	33
Cox	5- 8	4-11	16	2	14
Bunton	3- 4	1- 2	7	2	7
Bridgeman	4-15	4- 4	15	4	12
Bond	2- 6	2- 2	3	1	6
Whitfield	0- 0	0- 0	1	1	0
Gallon	0- 3	0- 0	2	2	0
Brown	1- 1	0- 0	1	0	2
Wilson	0- 0	0- 0	0	0	0
Howard	0- 0	0- 1	0	0	0
Team			2		
Totals	29-65	16-27	49	14	74

UCLA	fg-fga	ft-fta	rb	pf	tp
Meyers	6-16	4- 6	7	3	16
Johnson	5-10	0- 0	11	2	10
Washington	11-19	4- 6	8	4	26
Trgovich	6-12	0- 0	2	5	12
McCarter	3-12	0- 0	2	2	6
Drollinger	1- 2	1- 2	4	5	3
Olinde	0- 0	0- 0	0	0	0
Spillane	1- 2	0- 0	1	1	2
Team			1		
Totals	33-73	9-14	36	22	75

Half time: Louisville 37-33. Regulation Score: 65-65.

Syracuse	fg-fga	ft-fta	rb	pf	tp
Hackett	4- 6	6- 9	5	5	14
Sease	7-11	4- 4	10	4	18
Seibert	2- 3	0- 2	6	5	4
Lee	10-17	3- 3	3	4	23
Williams	2- 9	0- 1	2	5	4
King	2- 8	1- 3	5	1	5
Kindel	1- 3	1- 2	1	1	3
Shaw	0- 0	0- 0	2	2	0
Parker	2- 3	4- 7	2	3	8
Byrnes	0- 0	0- 1	1	0	0
Kelley	0- 1	0- 0	0	0	0
Meadors	0- 0	0- 0	1	0	0
Team			2		
Totals	30-61	19-32	40	30	79

Kentucky	fg-fga	ft-fta	rb	pf	tp
Grevey	5-13	4- 5	3	5	14
Guyette	2- 3	3- 4	6	3	7
Robey	3- 8	3- 7	11	4	9
Conner	5- 9	2- 4	5	4	12
Flynn	4- 9	3- 5	3	4	11
Givens	10-20	4- 8	11	2	24
Johnson	2- 4	0- 0	1	3	4
Phillips	5- 6	0- 2	4	4	10
Lee	1- 4	0- 1	2	1	2
Haskins	0- 0	2- 2	1	0	2
Hale	0- 1	0- 0	3	0	0
Hall	0- 0	0- 0	1	1	0
Warford	0- 0	0- 0	0	0	0
Smith	0- 1	0- 0	0	0	0
Team			6		
Totals	37-78	21-38	57	31	95

Championship

UCLA	fg-fga	ft-fta	rb	pf	tp
Meyers	9-18	6- 7	11	4	24
Johnson	3- 9	0- 1	7	2	6
Washington	12-23	4- 5	12	4	28
Trgovich	7-16	2- 4	5	4	16
McCarter	3- 6	2- 3	2	1	8
Drollinger	4- 6	2- 5	13	4	10
Team			5		
Totals	38-78	16-25	55	19	92

Kentucky	fg-fga	ft-fta	rb	pf	tp
Grevey	13-30	8-10	5	4	34
Guyette	7-11	2- 2	7	3	16
Robey	1- 3	0- 0	9	5	2
Conner	4-12	1- 2	5	1	9
Flynn	3- 9	4- 5	3	4	10
Givens	3-10	2- 3	6	3	8
Johnson	0- 3	0- 0	3	3	0
Phillips	1- 7	2- 3	6	4	4
Hall	1- 1	0- 0	1	0	2
Lee	0- 0	0- 0	0	1	0
Team			4		
Totals	33-86	19-25	49	28	85

1976 Tournament Stats

Semifinals

UCLA	fg-fga	ft-fta	rb	pf	tp
Washington	6-15	3- 4	8	3	15
Johnson	6-10	0- 1	6	2	12
Greenwood	2- 5	1- 2	10	2	5
Townsend	2-10	0- 0	3	1	4
McCarter	2- 9	0- 0	4	5	4
Drollinger	0- 3	2- 2	1	3	2
Holland	0- 2	0- 0	0	0	0
Spillane	0- 2	0- 0	1	0	0
Smith	3- 4	0- 0	0	3	6
Hamilton	0- 1	1- 2	0	0	1
Vroman	0- 0	0- 0	1	2	0
Lippert	0- 0	2- 2	0	0	2
Olinde	0- 0	0- 0	0	0	0
Team			3		
Totals	21-61	9-13	37	21	51

Michigan	fg-fga	ft-fta	rb	pf	tp
Britt	5- 9	1- 1	5	4	11
Robinson	8-13	4- 5	16	2	20
Hubbard	8-13	0- 3	13	4	16
Green	7-16	2- 2	6	4	16
Grote	4-13	6- 6	4	4	14
Baxter	2- 5	1- 2	3	0	5
Staton	1- 1	2- 2	0	1	4
Bergen	0- 0	0- 0	0	0	0
Thompson	0- 0	0- 0	0	0	0
Schinnerer	0- 0	0- 0	0	1	0
Hardy	0- 0	0- 0	0	0	0
Jones	0- 0	0- 0	0	0	0
Lillard	0- 0	0- 0	0	0	0
Team			3		
Totals	35-70	16-21	50	20	86

Indiana	fg-fga	ft-fta	rb	pf	tp
Abernethy	7- 8	0- 1	6	3	14
May	5-16	4- 6	4	2	14
Benson	6-15	4- 6	9	4	16
Wilkerson	1- 5	3- 4	19	3	5
Buckner	6-14	0- 1	3	3	12
Crews	1- 1	2- 3	3	0	4
Team			1		
Totals	26-59	13-21	45	15	65

Rutgers	fg-fga	ft-fta	rb	pf	tp
Sellers	5-13	1- 3	8	4	11
Copeland	7-12	1- 1	5	3	15
Bailey	1- 3	4- 6	6	0	6
Jordan	6-20	4- 4	4	4	16
Dabney	5-17	0- 1	5	4	10
Anderson	3- 8	0- 1	6	3	6
Conlin	2- 2	0- 0	1	2	4
Hefele	1- 1	0- 0	1	2	2
Team			2		
Totals	30-76	10-16	38	22	70

Championship

Michigan	fg-fga	ft-fta	rb	pf	tp
Britt	5- 6	1- 1	3	5	11
Robinson	4- 8	0- 1	6	2	8
Hubbard	4- 8	2- 2	11	5	10
Green	7-16	4- 5	6	3	18
Grote	4- 9	4- 6	1	4	12
Bergen	0- 1	0- 0	0	1	0
Staton	2- 5	3- 4	2	3	7
Baxter	0- 2	0- 0	0	2	0
Thompson	0- 0	0- 0	0	0	0
Hardy	1- 2	0- 0	2	0	2
Team			1		
Totals	27-57	14-19	32	25	68

Indiana	fg-fga	ft-fta	rb	pf	tp
Abernethy	4- 8	3- 3	4	2	11
May	10-17	6- 6	8	4	26
Benson	11-20	3- 5	9	3	25
Wilkerson	0- 1	0- 0	0	1	0
Buckner	5-10	6- 9	8	4	16
Radford	0- 1	0- 0	1	0	0
Crews	0- 1	2- 2	1	1	2
Wisman	0- 1	2- 3	1	4	2
Valavicius	1- 1	0- 0	0	0	2
Haymore	1- 1	0- 0	1	0	2
Bender	0- 0	0- 0	0	0	0
Team			3		
Totals	32-61	22-28	36	19	86

1977 Tournament Stats

Semifinals

North Carolina	fg-fga	ft-fta	rb	pf	tp
Davis	7- 7	5- 6	5	3	19
O'Koren	14-19	3- 5	8	1	31
Yonakor	5- 7	1- 4	9	0	11
Ford	4-10	4- 5	6	2	12
Kuester	2- 5	5- 7	6	0	9
Zaliagiris	0- 1	0- 0	0	0	0
Krafcisin	0- 0	0- 1	2	1	0
Buckley	1- 5	0- 0	2	3	2
Bradley	0- 1	0- 0	1	0	0
Wolf	0- 1	0- 0	1	0	0
Colescott	0- 0	0- 0	0	1	0
Team			1		
Totals	33-56	18-28	41	11	84

Nevada-Las Vegas	fg-fga	ft-fta	rb	pf	tp
Owens	7-15	0- 0	2	4	14
Gondrezick	4- 8	0- 0	5	4	8
Moffett	6- 9	1- 2	9	5	13
R. Smith	4-11	0- 1	1	1	8
S. Smith	10-18	0- 0	2	1	20
T. Smith	6- 8	0- 2	1	3	12
Theus	4-11	0- 0	5	4	8
Brown	0- 0	0- 0	1	0	0
Team			3		
Totals	41-80	1- 5	29	22	83

Championship

North Carolina	fg-fga	ft-fta	rb	pf	tp
Davis	6-13	8-10	8	4	20
O'Koren	6-10	2- 4	11	5	14
Yonakor	3- 5	0- 0	4	0	6
Ford	3-10	0- 0	2	3	6
Kuester	2- 6	1- 2	0	5	5
Krafcisin	1- 1	0- 0	0	0	2
Zaliagiris	2- 3	0- 0	0	3	4
Bradley	1- 1	0- 0	0	2	2
Buckley	0- 1	0- 0	0	1	0
Wolf	0- 1	0- 0	1	0	0
Colescott	0- 0	0- 0	0	0	0
Coley	0- 0	0- 0	0	0	0
Doughton	0- 0	0- 0	0	0	0
Virgil	0- 0	0- 0	0	1	0
Team			2		
Totals	24-51	11-16	28	24	59

Marquette	fg-fga	ft-fta	rb	pf	tp
Ellis	2- 8	0- 0	5	4	4
Neary	0- 1	0- 0	2	3	0
Whitehead	10-16	1- 2	16	1	21
Lee	5-18	1- 1	3	3	11
Boylan	4- 9	0- 0	3	2	8
Toone	2- 6	2- 2	1	3	6
Rosenberger	0- 0	1- 2	1	0	1
Team			2		
Totals	23-58	5- 7	33	16	51

N.C.-Charlotte	fg-fga	ft-fta	rb	pf	tp
Massey	7-13	0- 0	8	1	14
King	2- 7	0- 0	5	2	4
Maxwell	5- 6	7- 9	12	2	17
Kinch	1- 7	2- 2	4	2	4
Watkins	2- 4	2- 3	0	5	6
Gruber	2- 6	0- 0	0	0	4
Scott	0- 0	0- 0	0	0	0
Team			1		
Totals	19-43	11-14	30	12	49

Marquette	fg-fga	ft-fta	rb	pf	tp
Ellis	5- 9	4- 5	9	4	14
Neary	0- 2	0- 0	0	1	0
Whitehead	2- 8	4- 4	11	2	8
Lee	6-14	7- 7	3	1	19
Boylan	5- 7	4- 4	4	3	14
Rosenberger	1- 1	4- 4	1	1	6
Toone	3- 6	0- 1	0	1	6
Team			1		
Totals	22-47	23-25	29	13	67

1978 Tournament Stats

Semifinals

Arkansas	fg-fga	ft-fta	rb	pf	tp
Counce	2- 2	2- 3	2	4	6
Delph	5-13	5- 6	8	3	15
Schall	3- 5	0- 0	3	5	6
Brewer	5-12	6- 8	5	2	16
Moncrief	5-11	3- 7	5	3	13
Zahn	1- 1	1- 2	2	3	3
Reed	0- 0	0- 0	0	2	0
Team			1		
Totals	21-44	17-26	26	22	59

Kentucky	fg-fga	ft-fta	rb	pf	tp
Givens	10-16	3- 4	9	2	23
Robey	3- 6	2- 2	8	2	8
Phillips	1- 6	3- 4	2	4	5
Macy	2- 8	3- 4	3	4	7
Claytor	1- 2	0- 1	0	4	2
Shidley	3- 5	0- 0	2	4	6
Lee	4- 8	5- 5	8	4	13
Casey	0- 0	0- 0	0	0	0
Stephens	0- 0	0- 0	0	0	0
Cowan	0- 0	0- 0	0	1	0
Williams	0- 0	0- 0	0	1	0
Team			0		
Totals	24-51	16-20	32	26	64

Duke	fg-fga	ft-fta	rb	pf	tp
Banks	8-15	6- 7	12	1	22
Dennard	2- 3	3- 5	7	5	7
Gminski	13-17	3- 4	5	2	29
Harrell	0- 2	6- 6	2	2	6
Spanarkel	4-11	12-12	4	1	20
Bender	0- 1	2- 3	2	2	2
Goetsch	1- 1	0- 0	0	0	2
Suddath	1- 3	0- 0	0	2	2
Team			2		
Totals	29-53	32-37	34	15	90

Notre Dame	fg-fga	ft-fta	rb	pf	tp
Tripucka	5-17	2- 2	9	3	12
Batton	3- 6	4- 4	2	1	10
Flowers	5- 8	0- 0	6	3	10
Branning	4-10	0- 0	1	3	8
Williams	8-15	0- 1	2	2	16
Laimbeer	1- 5	5- 6	10	5	7
Hanzlik	3- 8	2- 2	6	5	8
Jackson	5- 6	1- 2	0	4	11
Wilcox	2- 2	0- 0	0	0	4
Team			1		
Totals	36-77	14-17	37	26	86

Championship

Duke	fg-fga	ft-fta	rb	pf	tp
Banks	6-12	10-12	8	2	22
Dennard	5- 7	0- 0	8	5	10
Gminski	6-16	8- 8	12	3	20
Harrell	2- 2	0- 0	0	3	4
Spanarkel	8-16	5- 6	2	4	21
Suddath	1- 3	2- 3	2	1	4
Bender	1- 2	5- 5	1	3	7
Goetsch	0- 1	0- 0	1	1	0
Team			1		
Totals	29-59	30-34	35	22	88

Kentucky	fg-fga	ft-fta	rb	pf	tp
Givens	18-27	5- 8	8	4	41
Robey	8-11	4- 6	11	2	20
Phillips	1- 4	2- 2	2	5	4
Macy	3- 3	3- 4	0	1	9
Claytor	3- 5	2- 4	0	2	8
Lee	4- 8	0- 0	4	4	8
Shidler	1- 5	0- 1	1	3	2
Aleksinas	0- 0	0- 0	0	1	0
Williams	1- 3	0- 0	4	2	2
Cowan	0- 2	0- 0	2	1	0
Stephens	0- 0	0- 0	0	0	0
Courts	0- 0	0- 0	0	0	0
Gettelfinger	0- 0	0- 0	0	0	0
Casey	0- 0	0- 0	0	1	0
Team			0		
Totals	39-68	16-25	32	26	94

1979 Tournament Stats

Semifinals

DePaul	fg-fga	ft-fta	rb	pf	tp
Watkins	8-11	0- 0	2	4	16
Aguirre	9-18	1- 2	5	3	19
Mitchem	6-11	0- 0	5	4	12
Bradshaw	4- 8	0- 0	3	1	8
Garland	9-18	1- 3	4	2	19
Team			2		
Totals	36-66	2- 5	21	14	74

Indiana State	fg-fga	ft-fta	rb	pf	tp
Miley	2- 2	0- 0	3	1	4
Gilbert	6- 7	0- 1	5	2	12
Bird	16-19	3- 4	16	3	35
Nicks	4-13	2- 2	1	3	10
Reed	3- 5	0- 0	2	0	6
Heaton	3- 6	0- 0	3	2	6
Staley	1- 4	1- 2	2	3	3
Team			2		
Totals	35-56	6- 9	34	14	76

Pennsylvania	fg-fga	ft-fta	rb	pf	tp
Price	7-18	4- 4	7	5	18
Smith	0- 6	0- 0	0	5	0
White	5-12	3- 4	11	4	13
Salters	1- 5	0- 0	1	2	2
Willis	4-13	1- 3	6	2	9
Ross	2- 6	0- 0	6	3	4
Hall	3- 8	0- 1	2	1	6
Reynolds	1- 3	0- 0	0	3	2
Leifsen	0- 1	1- 2	4	1	1
Flick	0- 6	6- 6	2	3	6
Jackson	1- 2	4- 4	1	0	6
Kuhl	0- 2	0- 0	0	0	0
Condon	0- 0	0- 0	2	2	0
Team			2		
Totals	24-82	19-24	44	31	67

Michigan State	fg-fga	ft-fta	rb	pf	tp
Brkovich	6-10	0- 0	1	4	12
Kelser	12-19	4- 6	9	2	28
Charles	2- 2	0- 0	6	4	4
Donnelly	3- 5	0- 0	3	0	6
Johnson	9-10	11-12	10	2	29
Vincent	0- 1	3- 4	1	2	3
Gonzalez	1- 5	0- 0	3	2	2
Longaker	2- 2	0- 0	2	0	4
Lloyd	0- 2	6- 7	0	1	6
Kaye	2- 2	1- 3	2	1	5
Huffman	0- 0	0- 1	2	2	0
Gilkie	0- 1	0- 0	1	1	0
Brkovich	1- 1	0- 1	1	1	2
Team			3		
Totals	38-60	25-34	44	22	101

Championship

Indiana State	fg-fga	ft-fta	rb	pf	tp
Miley	0- 0	0- 1	3	1	0
Gilbert	2- 3	0- 4	4	4	4
Bird	7-21	5- 8	13	3	19
Nicks	7-14	3- 6	2	5	17
Reed	4- 9	0- 0	0	4	8
Heaton	4-14	2- 2	6	2	10
Staley	2- 2	0- 1	3	2	4
Nemcek	1- 1	0- 0	0	3	2
Team			3		
Totals	27-64	10-22	34	24	64

Michigan State	fg-fga	ft-fta	rb	pf	tp
Brkovich	1- 2	3- 7	4	1	5
Kelser	7-13	5- 6	8	4	19
Charles	3- 3	1- 2	7	5	7
Donnelly	5- 5	5- 6	4	2	15
Johnson	8-15	8-10	7	3	24
Vincent	2- 5	1- 2	2	4	5
Gonzalez	0- 0	0- 0	0	0	0
Longaker	0- 0	0- 0	0	0	0
Team			2		
Totals	26-43	23-33	34	19	75

1980 Tournament Stats

Semifinals

Purdue	fg-fga	ft-fta	rb	pf	tp
Morris	5-14	2- 2	6	2	12
Hallman	1- 7	0- 0	7	4	2
Carroll	8-14	1- 4	8	3	17
Edmonson	9-16	5- 6	3	3	23
Walker	1- 3	4- 5	1	4	6
Stallings	0- 0	0- 0	0	0	0
Scearce	0- 2	0- 0	3	0	0
Barnes	1- 1	0- 0	0	1	2
Walker	0- 1	0- 0	1	4	0
Team			3		
Totals	25-58	12-17	32	21	62

UCLA	fg-fga	ft-fta	rb	pf	tp
Wilkes	2- 2	0- 0	1	5	4
Vandeweghe	9-12	6- 6	5	1	24
Sanders	3- 7	6- 6	6	2	12
Foster	4- 7	1- 2	3	5	9
Holton	1- 3	2- 2	1	1	4
Allums	0- 0	0- 2	4	3	0
Daye	1- 5	4- 5	3	2	6
Sims	0- 3	0- 0	3	1	0
Pruitt	3- 7	2- 2	1	1	8
Team			3		
Totals	23-46	21-25	30	21	67

Championship

Louisville	fg-fga	ft-fta	rb	pf	tp
Brown	4-12	0- 2	7	3	8
Smith	3- 9	3- 4	5	2	9
McCray	2- 4	3- 4	11	4	7
Eaves	4- 7	0- 2	3	3	8
Griffith	9-16	5- 8	2	3	23
Burkman	0- 1	0- 0	1	4	0
Wright	2- 4	0- 0	4	1	4
Branch	0- 0	0- 0	0	0	0
Team			3		
Totals	24-53	11-20	36	20	59

1981 Tournament Stats

Semifinals

Iowa	fg-fga	ft-fta	rb	pf	tp
Brookins	6-18	2- 2	6	5	14
Boyle	0- 8	0- 0	7	2	0
Krafcisin	4- 5	4- 4	3	5	12
Lester	4- 4	2- 2	1	2	10
Arnold	9-17	2- 2	3	1	20
Waite	4- 6	1- 1	2	5	9
Hansen	2- 8	3- 4	4	2	7
Gannon	0- 0	0- 0	0	0	0
Henry	0- 0	0- 0	0	1	0
Team			0		
Totals	29-66	14-15	26	23	72

Louisville	fg-fga	ft-fta	rb	pf	tp
Brown	1- 3	0- 2	5	4	2
Smith	3- 7	7- 8	8	2	13
McCray	5- 7	4- 4	9	2	14
Eaves	2- 4	4- 5	4	1	8
Griffith	14-21	6- 8	5	1	34
Wright	1- 2	0- 0	3	1	2
Burkman	2- 3	3- 4	2	3	7
Branch	0- 0	0- 0	0	0	0
Deuser	0- 0	0- 0	0	0	0
Cleveland	0- 0	0- 0	0	0	0
Pulliam	0- 0	0- 0	0	0	0
Team			0		
Totals	28-47	24-31	36	14	80

UCLA	fg-fga	ft-fta	rb	pf	tp
Wilkes	1- 4	0- 0	6	3	2
Vandeweghe	4- 9	6- 6	7	3	14
Sanders	4-10	2- 4	6	4	10
Foster	6-15	4- 4	1	3	16
Holton	1- 3	2- 2	2	2	4
Pruitt	2- 8	2- 2	6	2	6
Daye	1- 3	0- 0	1	1	2
Allums	0- 0	0- 0	2	0	0
Anderson	0- 0	0- 0	0	0	0
Team			3		
Totals	19-52	16-18	34	18	54

Virginia	fg-fga	ft-fta	rb	pf	tp
Lamp	7-18	4- 4	7	5	18
Gates	1- 1	0- 0	4	4	2
Sampson	3-10	5- 7	9	3	11
Wilson	4- 7	0- 0	2	4	8
Jones	5-13	1- 1	3	3	11
Stokes	0- 2	0- 0	1	3	0
Raker	5- 9	3- 3	5	5	13
Lattimore	1- 1	0- 0	1	0	2
Team			2		
Totals	26-61	13-15	34	27	65

North Carolina	fg-fga	ft-fta	rb	pf	tp
Wood	14-19	11-13	10	3	39
Worthy	2- 8	4- 7	3	2	8
Perkins	4- 7	3- 5	9	4	11
Pepper	0- 4	0- 0	1	2	0
Black	4- 6	2- 3	1	4	10
Doherty	0- 1	8- 9	4	1	8
Braddock	0- 1	0- 0	0	0	0
Kenny	1- 1	0- 0	1	0	2
Team			2		
Totals	25-47	28-37	31	16	78

Indiana	fg-fga	ft-fta	rb	pf	tp
Kitchel	3- 8	4- 4	6	3	10
Turner	7-19	6- 7	8	1	20
Tolbert	3- 7	1- 2	6	3	7
I. Thomas	6- 8	2- 3	2	4	14
Wittman	3-10	2- 2	2	0	8
Risley	0- 2	1- 2	2	0	1
J. Thomas	0- 4	2- 2	9	1	2
Bouchie	0- 1	0- 0	2	0	0
Grunwald	1- 2	1- 2	2	1	3
Brown	0- 1	0- 1	0	0	0
Isenbarger	0- 1	0- 0	0	0	0
Franz	0- 0	2- 2	0	1	2
LaFave	0- 0	0- 0	2	1	0
Team			3		
Totals	23-63	21-27	44	15	67

Louisiana State	fg-fga	ft-fta	rb	pf	tp
Mitchell	3-10	3- 4	10	3	9
Macklin	2-12	0- 0	8	1	4
Cook	3- 5	0- 0	5	5	6
Martin	2- 8	3- 3	3	4	7
Carter	5-10	0- 0	6	3	10
Sims	2- 8	1- 2	1	0	5
Jones	0- 2	0- 1	2	3	0
Tudor	1- 3	4- 4	2	3	6
Bergeron	0- 0	0- 0	0	0	0
Costello	0- 0	0- 0	0	0	0
Black	1- 1	0- 0	1	0	2
Team			4		
Totals	19-59	11-14	42	22	49

Championship

Indiana	fg-fga	ft-fta	rb	pf	tp
Kitchel	0- 1	0- 0	0	3	0
Turner	5- 8	2- 2	6	5	12
Tolbert	1- 4	3- 6	11	0	5
I. Thomas	8-17	7- 8	2	4	23
Wittman	7-13	2- 2	4	2	16
Risley	1- 1	3- 4	4	1	5
J. Thomas	1- 4	0- 0	4	2	2
Team			2		
Totals	23-48	17-22	33	17	63

North Carolina	fg-fga	ft-fta	rb	pf	tp
Wood	6-13	6- 9	6	4	18
Worthy	3-11	1- 2	6	5	7
Perkins	5- 8	1- 2	8	3	11
Pepper	2- 5	2- 2	1	1	6
Black	3- 4	0- 0	2	5	6
Budko	0- 1	0- 0	1	0	0
Doherty	1- 2	0- 1	4	4	2
Braddock	0- 2	0- 0	0	1	0
Brust	0- 0	0- 0	0	0	0
Kenny	0- 1	0- 0	1	0	0
Team			0		
Totals	20-47	10-16	29	23	50

1982 Tournament Stats

Semifinals

Houston	fg-fga	ft-fta	rb	pf	tp
Drexler	6-12	5- 6	9	3	17
Young	1- 7	0- 1	3	0	2
Micheaux	8-14	2- 3	6	2	18
Rose	10-15	0- 2	2	2	20
R. Williams	0- 8	2- 2	1	1	2
B. Williams	0- 1	0- 0	1	2	0
Olajuwon	1- 3	0- 0	6	4	2
Davis	1- 2	0- 0	0	3	2
Anders	0- 2	0- 0	0	2	0
Totals	27-64	9-14	33	19	63

Louisville	fg-fga	ft-fta	rb	pf	tp
Brown	2- 5	0- 0	1	1	4
Smith	4- 8	2- 4	6	4	10
McCray	2- 5	4- 4	5	5	8
Lancaster	1- 6	0- 0	1	2	2
Eaves	4- 9	0- 0	4	1	8
Wagner	1- 4	0- 0	2	3	2
Jones	4- 7	0- 2	6	0	8
McCray	0- 1	0- 0	0	1	0
Wright	1- 3	2- 2	0	1	4
Totals	19-48	8-12	27	18	46

North Carolina	fg-fga	ft-fta	rb	pf	tp
Doherty	2- 7	1- 2	1	1	5
Worthy	7-10	0- 0	4	3	14
Perkins	9-11	7- 7	10	1	25
Black	1- 2	4- 6	3	4	6
Jordan	7-14	4- 4	5	4	18
Peterson	0- 0	0- 0	1	0	0
Brust	0- 0	0- 0	0	1	0
Martin	0- 0	0- 0	0	0	0
Braddock	0- 0	0- 0	0	0	0
Totals	26-44	16-19	26	14	68

Georgetown	fg-fga	ft-fta	rb	pf	tp
E. Smith	6-10	2- 4	2	2	14
Hancock	1- 3	0- 0	2	0	2
Ewing	3- 8	2- 2	10	2	8
Brown	1- 3	2- 3	3	4	4
Floyd	3-11	7- 8	5	4	13
Spriggs	2- 2	1- 3	7	2	5
G. Smith	0- 0	0- 0	0	1	0
Jones	2- 4	0- 0	3	1	4
Martin	0- 0	0- 0	1	0	0
Totals	18-41	14-20	34	16	50

Championship

Georgetown	fg-fga	ft-fta	rb	pf	tp
E. Smith	6- 8	2- 2	3	5	14
Hancock	0- 2	0- 0	0	1	0
Ewing	10-15	3- 3	11	4	23
Brown	1- 2	2- 2	2	4	4
Floyd	9-17	0- 0	3	2	18
Spriggs	0- 2	1- 2	1	2	1
Jones	1- 3	0- 0	0	0	2
Martin	0- 2	0- 0	0	1	0
G. Smith	0- 0	0- 0	0	1	0
Totals	27-51	8- 9	22	20	62

North Carolina	fg-fga	ft-fta	rb	pf	tp
Doherty	1- 3	2- 3	3	0	4
Worthy	13-17	2- 7	4	3	28
Perkins	3- 7	4- 6	7	2	10
Black	1- 4	2- 2	3	2	4
Jordan	7-13	2- 2	9	2	16
Peterson	0- 3	0- 0	1	0	0
Braddock	0- 0	0- 0	0	1	0
Brust	0- 0	1- 2	1	1	1
Totals	25-47	13-22	30	11	63

1983 Tournament Stats

Semifinals

Georgia	fg-fga	ft-fta	rb	pf	tp
Banks	5-19	3- 5	2	3	13
Heard	3- 5	2- 3	10	2	8
Fair	2- 9	1- 2	6	3	5
Crosby	5-15	2- 2	1	3	12
Fleming	7-17	0- 0	11	4	14
Cohren	3- 6	0- 1	7	2	6
Hartry	1- 3	0- 0	0	3	2
Floyd	0- 0	0- 0	0	0	0
Total					60

North Carolina State	fg-fga	ft-fta	rb	pf	tp
Bailey	9-17	2- 5	10	3	20
Charles	2- 2	1- 2	6	1	5
McQueen	4- 5	0- 0	13	5	8
Whittenburg	8-18	4- 4	0	1	20
Lowe	4- 6	2- 2	5	3	10
Battle	0- 0	0- 0	2	0	0
Gannon	1- 4	2- 2	1	0	4
Total					67

Houston	fg-fga	ft-fta	rb	pf	tp
Drexler	10-15	1- 2	7	2	21
Micheaux	4- 7	0- 1	3	5	8
Olajuwon	9-14	3- 7	22	4	21
Franklin	5- 8	3- 4	1	0	13
Young	7-18	2- 3	4	2	16
Gettys	0- 0	0- 0	1	2	0
Anders	5- 9	3- 5	6	4	13
Rose	0- 2	0- 0	0	3	0
Williams	1- 1	0- 0	0	0	2
Giles	0- 0	0- 1	0	0	0
Total					94

Louisville	fg-fga	ft-fta	rb	pf	tp
S. McCray	5- 8	0- 0	6	4	10
R. McCray	3- 6	2- 8	5	4	8
Jones	3-10	6- 8	11	3	12
Gordon	6-15	5- 6	6	3	17
Wagner	12-23	0- 0	2	4	24
Thompson	1- 4	4- 5	5	4	6
Hall	2- 4	0- 0	1	0	4
West	0- 0	0- 0	0	1	0
Valentine	0- 0	0- 0	0	0	0
Total					81

Championship

Houston	fg-fga	ft-fta	rb	pf	tp
Drexler	1- 5	2- 2	2	4	4
Micheaux	2- 6	0- 0	6	1	4
Olajuwon	7-15	6- 7	18	1	20
Franklin	2- 6	0- 1	0	0	4
Young	3-10	0- 4	8	0	6
Anders	4- 9	2- 5	2	2	10
Gettys	2- 2	0- 0	2	3	4
Rose	0- 1	0- 0	1	2	0
Williams	0- 1	0- 0	4	3	0
Total					52

North Carolina State	fg-fga	ft-fta	rb	pf	tp
Bailey	7-16	1- 2	5	1	15
Charles	2- 7	0- 0	7	2	4
McQueen	1- 5	2- 2	12	4	4
Whittenburg	6-17	2- 2	5	3	14
Lowe	4- 9	0- 1	0	2	8
Battle	0- 1	2- 2	1	1	2
Gannon	3- 4	1- 2	1	3	7
Myers	0- 0	0- 0	1	0	0
Total					54

TOURNAMENT RECORDS

Individual

Most Points, One Game
61, Austin Carr, Notre Dame (112) vs. Ohio (82), first round, 3/7/70

Most Points, Three-Game Series
158, Austin Carr, Notre Dame, 1970 (61 vs. Ohio, 52 vs. Kentucky, 45 vs. Iowa)

Most Points, Four-Game Series
143, Jerry Chambers, Utah, 1966 (40 vs. Pacific, 33 vs. Oregon, 38 vs. Texas-El Paso, 32 vs. Duke)

Most Points, Five-Game Series
177, Bill Bradley, Princeton, 1965 (22 vs. Penn State, 27 vs. North Carolina State, 41 vs. Providence, 29 vs. Michigan, 58 vs. Wichita State)

Most Points, Six-Game Series
158, Joe Barry Carroll, Purdue, 1980 (33 vs. La Salle, 36 vs. St. John's, 11 vs. Indiana, 26 vs. Duke, 17 vs. UCLA, 35 vs. Iowa)

Most Points, Career
358, Elvin Hayes, Houston, 1966-67-68

Most Field Goals, One Game
25, Austin Carr, Notre Dame (112) vs. Ohio (82), 44 attempts, first round, 3/7/70

Most Field Goals, Three-Game Series
68, Austin Carr, Notre Dame, 1970 (25 vs. Ohio, 22 vs. Kentucky, 21 vs. Iowa)

Most Field Goals, Four-Game Series
57, Bob Houbregs, Washington, 1953 (20 vs. Seattle, 12 vs. Santa Clara, 8 vs. Kansas, 17 vs. Louisiana State)

Most Field Goals, Five-Game Series
70, Elvin Hayes, Houston, 1968 (20 vs. Loyola, Ill., 16 vs. Louisville, 17 vs. Texas Christian, 3 vs. UCLA, 14 vs. Ohio State)

Most Field Goals, Six-Game Series
63, Joe Barry Carroll, Purdue, 1980 (12 vs. La Salle, 14 vs. St. John's, 5 vs. Indiana, 10 vs. Duke, 8 vs. UCLA, 14 vs. Iowa)

Most Field Goals, Career
152, Elvin Hayes, Houston, 1966-67-68

Highest Field Goal Percentage in One Year (min. 25 made)
76.5% (26-34), Alex Gilbert, Indiana State, 1979

Highest Field Goal Percentage in One Year (min. 40 made)
76.3% (45-59), Bill Walton, UCLA, 1973

Highest Field Goal Percentage, Career (min. 60 made)
68.6% (109-159), Bill Walton, UCLA, 1972-74

Most Free Throws, One Game
23, Bob Carney, Bradley (76) vs. Colorado (64), 26 attempts, second round, 3/12/54

Most Free Throws, Three-Game Series
38, Johnny O'Brien, Seattle, 1953 (8 vs. Idaho State, 12 vs. Washington, 18 vs. Wyoming)

Most Free Throws, Four-Game Series
49, Don Schlundt, Indiana, 1953 (13 vs. DePaul, 15 vs. Notre Dame, 13 vs. LSU, 8 vs. Kansas)

Most Free Throws, Five-Game Series
55, Bob Carney, Bradley, 1954 (9 vs. Oklahoma City, 23 vs. Colorado, 4 vs. Oklahoma State, 8 vs. Southern California, 11 vs. LaSalle)

Most Free Throws, Six-Game Series
39, Kiki Vandeweghe, UCLA, 1980 (12 vs. Old Dominion, 1 vs. DePaul, 6 vs. Ohio State, 8 vs. Clemson, 6 vs. Purdue, 6 vs. Louisville)

Most Free Throws, Career
90, Oscar Robertson, Cincinnati, 1958-59-60

Highest Free Throw Percentage in One Year (min. 20 made)
96.2% (25-26), Jeff Lamp, Virginia, 1981

Highest Free Throw Percentage in One Year (min. 35 made)
94.1% (48-51), Bill Bradley, Princeton, 1965

Highest Free Throw Percentage, Career (min. 50 made)
91.7% (88-96), Bill Bradley, Princeton, 1963-65

Most Rebounds, One Game
31, Nate Thurmond, Bowling Green (60) vs. Mississippi State (65), regional third-place, 1963

Most Rebounds, Three-Game Series
70, Nate Thurmond, Bowling Green, 1963 (20 vs. Notre Dame, 19 vs. Illinois, 31 vs. Mississippi State)

Most Rebounds, Four-Game Series
77, John Green, Michigan State, 1957 (27 vs. Notre Dame, 18 vs. Kentucky, 19 vs. North Carolina, 13 vs. San Francisco)

Most Rebounds, Five-Game Series
105, Elvin Hayes, Houston, 1968 (27 vs. Loyola, Ill., 24 vs. Louisville, 25 vs. Texas Christian, 13 vs. UCLA, 16 vs. Ohio State)

Most Rebounds, Six-Game Series
60, Mike Sanders, UCLA, 1980 (10 vs. Old Dominion, 12 vs. DePaul, 8 vs. Ohio State, 10 vs. Clemson, 6 vs. Purdue, 6 vs. Louisville)

Most Rebounds, Career
222, Elvin Hayes, Houston, 1966-67-68

Team

Most Points, One Game
121, Iowa vs. Notre Dame (106), regional third place, 3/14/70
121, Nevada-Las Vegas vs. San Francisco (95), first round, 3/12/77

Most Points, Both Teams, One Game
227, Iowa (121) vs. Notre Dame (106), regional third place, 3/14/70

Most Points, Three-Game Series
317, Notre Dame, 1970, 105.7 per game (112–82 vs. Ohio, 99–109 vs. Kentucky, 106–121 vs. Iowa)

Most Points, Four-Game Series
400, UCLA, 1965, 100.0 per game (100–76 vs. Brigham Young, 101–93 vs. San Francisco, 108–89 vs. Wichita State, 91–80 vs. Michigan)

Most Points, Five-Game Series
505, Nevada–Las Vegas 1977, 101.0 per game (121–95 vs. San Francisco, 88–83 vs. Utah, 107–90 vs. Idaho State, 83–84 vs. North Carolina, 106–94 vs. UNC–Charlotte)

Most Points, Six-Game Series
462, Iowa, 1980 (86 vs. Virginia Commonwealth, 77 vs. North Carolina State, 88 vs. Syracuse, 81 vs. Georgetown, 72 vs. Louisville, 58 vs. Purdue)

Most Field Goals, One Game
52, Iowa (121) vs. Notre Dame (106), regional third place, 3/14/70

Most Field Goals, Four-Game Series
162, UCLA, 1965 (44 vs. Brigham Young, 41 vs. San Francisco, 44 vs. Wichita State, 33 vs. Michigan)

Most Field Goals, Five-Game Series
218, Nevada–Las Vegas, 1977 (49 vs. San Francisco, 37 vs. Utah, 44 vs. Idaho State, 41 vs. North Carolina, 47 vs. North Carolina–Charlotte)

Most Field Goals, Six-Game Series
173, Pennsylvania, 1979 (26 vs. Iona, 29 vs. North Carolina, 31 vs. Syracuse, 22 vs. St. John's, 24 vs. Michigan State, 41 vs. DePaul)

Most Free Throws, One Game
41, Utah (89) vs. Santa Clara (81), regional third place, 3/12/60

Most Free Throws, Four-Game Series
108, Indiana, 1953 (29 vs. Notre Dame, 30 vs. DePaul, 30 vs. LSU, 19 vs. Kansas)

Most Free Throws, Five-Game Series
146, Bradley, 1954 (23 vs. Oklahoma City, 38 vs. Colorado, 29 vs. Oklahoma State, 24 vs. Southern California, 32 vs. La Salle)

Most Free Throws, Six-Game Series
136, UCLA, 1980 (29 vs. Old Dominion, 17 vs. DePaul, 28 vs. Ohio State, 25 vs. Clemson, 21 vs. Purdue, 16 vs. Louisville)

Most Personal Fouls, One Game
39, Kansas (71) vs. Notre Dame (77), 3/15/75

Rebounds

One Game
76, Houston vs. Texas Christian, regional championship, 1968.

Three-Game Series
169, Notre Dame (66 vs. Houston, 60 vs. Drake, 43 vs. TCU), 1971.

Four-Game Series
236, Michigan State (60 vs. San Francisco, 65 vs. North Carolina, 51 vs. Kentucky, 66 vs. Notre Dame), 1957.

Five-Game Series
306, Houston (54 vs. Ohio State, 54 vs. UCLA, 76 vs. TCU, 59 vs. Louisville, 63 vs. Loyola, Ill.), 1968.

Six-Game Series
218, Pennsylvania (33 vs. Iona, 28 vs. North Carolina, 35 vs. Syracuse, 28 vs. St. John's, 44 vs. Michigan State, 50 vs. DePaul), 1979.

CHAMPIONSHIP GAME RECORDS

Individual

Field Goals Made—21 (22), Bill Walton, UCLA vs. Memphis State, St. Louis, 1973.

Field Goals Attempted—36 (12), Rick Mount, Purdue vs. UCLA, Louisville, 1969.

Field Goal Percentage—95.5* (21 of 22), Bill Walton, UCLA vs. Memphis State, St. Louis, 1973.

Free Throws Made—18 (20), Gail Goodrich, UCLA vs. Michigan, Portland, 1965.

Free Throws Attempted—20 (18), Gail Goodrich, UCLA vs. Michigan, Portland, 1965.

Free Throw Percentage—91.7* (11 of 12), Dick Estergard, Bradley vs. La Salle, Kansas City, 1954.

Most Rebounds—21, Bill Spivey, Kentucky vs. Kansas State, Minneapolis, 1951.

Most Points—44, Bill Walton, UCLA vs. Memphis State, St. Louis, 1973.

* Minimum 10 made.

Team

Field Goals Made—40 (62), UCLA vs. Memphis State, St. Louis, 1973.

Field Goals Attempted—92 (27), Purdue vs. UCLA, Louisville, 1969.

Field Goal Percentage—67.4* (31 of 46), Ohio State vs. California, San Francisco, 1960.

Free Throws Made—32 (44), Bradley vs. La Salle, Kansas City, 1954.

Free Throws Attempted—44 (32), Bradley vs. La Salle, Kansas City, 1954.

Free Throw Percentage—93.8* (15 of 16), Ohio State vs. Cincinnati, Kansas City, 1961.

Most Rebounds—61, UCLA vs. Purdue, Louisville, 1969.

Most Personal Fouls—36, Oklahoma State vs. Kentucky, Washington, 1949.

Most Points—98, UCLA vs. Duke, Kansas City, 1964.

* Minimum 15 made

Two-Team

Field Goals Made—71, UCLA (38) vs. Kentucky (33), San Diego, 1975.

Field Goals Attempted—164, UCLA (78) vs. Kentucky (86), San Diego, 1975.

Free Throws Made—50, Bradley (32) vs. La Salle (18), Kansas City, 1954.

Free Throws Attempted—68, Bradley (44), vs. La Salle (24), Kansas City, 1954.

Most Rebounds—109, UCLA (61) vs. Purdue (48), Louisville, 1969.

Most Personal Fouls—57, Oklahoma State (36) vs. Kentucky (21), Washington, 1949.

Most Points—181, UCLA (98), vs. Duke (83), Kansas City, 1964.

NATIONAL SEMIFINAL GAME RECORDS

Individual

Field Goals Made—16 (19), Larry Bird, Indiana State vs. DePaul, Salt Lake City, 1979.

Field Goals Attempted—36 (15), Ernie DiGregorio, Providence vs. Memphis State, St. Louis, 1973.

Field Goal Percentage—90.9* (10 of 11), Jerry Lucas, Ohio State vs. St. Joseph's, Kansas City, 1961.

Free Throws Made—14 (20), Jerry West, West Virginia vs. Louisville, Louisville, 1959.

Free Throws Attempted—20 (14), Jerry West, West Virginia vs. Louisville, Louisville, 1959.

Free Throw Percentage—100.0* (12 of 12), Jim Spanarkel, Duke vs. Notre Dame, St. Louis, 1978.

Most Rebounds—24, Elvin Hayes, Houston vs. UCLA, Louisville, 1967.

Most Points—39, Al Wood, North Carolina vs. Virginia, Philadelphia, 1981.

* Minimum 10 made.

Team

Field Goals Made—44 (89), UCLA vs. Wichita State, Portland, 1965.

Field Goals Attempted—91 (32), Kentucky vs. Illinois, Minneapolis, 1951.

Field Goal Percentage—63.3* (38 of 60), Ohio State vs. St. Joseph's, Kansas City, 1961.

Free Throws Made—37 (45), Jacksonville vs. St. Bonaventure, College Park, 1970.

Free Throws Attempted—45 (37), Jacksonville vs. St. Bonaventure, College Park, 1970.

Free Throw Percentage—87.5* (21 of 24), Oklahoma State vs. Oregon State, Seattle, 1949.

Most Rebounds—65, Michigan State vs. North Carolina, Kansas City, 1957.

Most Personal Fouls—32, St. Bonaventure vs. Jacksonville, College Park, 1970.

Most Points—108, UCLA vs. Wichita State, Portland, 1965.

* Minimum 15 made.

Two-Team

Field Goals Made—80, UCLA (44) vs. Wichita State (36), Portland, 1965.

Field Goals Attempted—169, North Carolina (89) vs. Michigan State (80), Kansas City, 1957.

Free Throws Made—52, Jacksonville (37) vs. St. Bonaventure (15), College Park, 1970.

Free Throws Attempted—70, Kentucky (38) vs. Syracuse (32), San Diego, 1975.

Most Rebounds—119, Michigan State (65) vs. North Carolina (54), Kansas City, 1957.

Most Personal Fouls—61, Kentucky (31) vs. Syracuse (30), San Diego, 1975.

Most Points—197, UCLA (108) vs. Wichita State (89), Portland, 1965.

CHAMPIONSHIP RESULTS

Year	Champion	Score	Runner-Up	Third Place	Fourth Place
1939	Oregon	46–33	Ohio State	*Oklahoma	*Villanova
1940	Indiana	60–42	Kansas	*Duquesne	*USC
1941	Wisconsin	39–34	Washington State	*Pittsburgh	*Arkansas
1942	Stanford	53–38	Dartmouth	*Colorado	*Kentucky
1943	Wyoming	46–34	Georgetown	*Texas	*DePaul
1944	Utah	42–40†	Dartmouth	*Iowa State	*Ohio State
1945	Oklahoma A&M	49–45	New York U.	*Arkansas	*Ohio State
1946	Oklahoma A&M	43–40	North Carolina	Ohio State	California
1947	Holy Cross	58–47	Oklahoma	Texas	CCNY
1948	Kentucky	58–42	Baylor	Holy Cross	Kansas State
1949	Kentucky	46–36	Oklahoma A&M	Illinois	Oregon State
1950	CCNY	71–68	Bradley	N.C. State	Baylor
1951	Kentucky	68–58	Kansas State	Illinois	Oklahoma A&M
1952	Kansas	80–63	St. John's	Illinois	Santa Clara
1953	Indiana	69–68	Kansas	Washington	Louisiana State
1954	La Salle	92–76	Bradley	Penn State	USC
1955	San Francisco	77–63	La Salle	Colorado	Iowa
1956	San Francisco	83–71	Iowa	Temple	SMU
1957	North Carolina	54–53‡	Kansas	San Francisco	Michigan State
1958	Kentucky	84–72	Seattle	Temple	Kansas State
1959	California	71–70	West Virginia	Cincinnati	Louisville
1960	Ohio State	75–55	California	Cincinnati	New York U.
1961	Cincinnati	70–65†	Ohio State	Vacated	Utah
1962	Cincinnati	71–59	Ohio State	Wake Forest	UCLA
1963	Loyola (Ill.)	60–58†	Cincinnati	Duke	Oregon State
1964	UCLA	98–83	Duke	Michigan	Kansas State
1965	UCLA	91–80	Michigan	Princeton	Wichita State
1966	Texas-Western	72–65	Kentucky	Duke	Utah
1967	UCLA	79–64	Dayton	Houston	North Carolina
1968	UCLA	78–55	North Carolina	Ohio State	Houston
1969	UCLA	92–72	Purdue	Drake	North Carolina
1970	UCLA	80–69	Jacksonville	New Mexico St.	St. Bonaventure
1971	UCLA	68–62	Vacated**	Vacated**	Kansas
1972	UCLA	81–76	Florida State	North Carolina	Louisville
1973	UCLA	87–66	Memphis State	Indiana	Providence
1974	N.C. State	76–64	Marquette	UCLA	Kansas
1975	UCLA	92–85	Kentucky	Louisville	Syracuse
1976	Indiana	86–68	Michigan	UCLA	Rutgers
1977	Marquette	67–59	North Carolina	Nev.-Las Vegas	N.C.-Charlotte
1978	Kentucky	94–88	Duke	Arkansas	Notre Dame
1979	Michigan State	75-64	Indiana State	DePaul	Penn
1980	Louisville	59–54	Vacated**	Purdue	Iowa
1981	Indiana	63–50	North Carolina	Virginia	LSU
1982	North Carolina	63–62	Georgetown	Louisville	Houston
1983	N.C. State	54–52	Houston	Louisville	Georgia

*Tied for third place

**Student athletes representing Villanova (1971), Western Kentucky (1971), and UCLA (1980) were declared ineligible subsequent to the tournament. Under NCAA rules, the teams' and ineligible student-athletes' records were deleted; and the teams' places in the standings were vacated. In the one case of an outstanding player, Howard Porter (Villanova) was vacated.

†Overtime.

‡Three overtimes.

Site of Finals	Coaches of Team Champions	Outstanding Player Award
Evanston, Ill.	Howard Hobson, Oregon	None Selected
Kansas City, Mo.	Branch McCracken, Indiana	Marvin Huffman, Indiana
Kansas City, Mo.	Harold Foster, Wisconsin	John Kotz, Wisconsin
Kansas City, Mo.	Everett Dean, Stanford	Howard Dallmar, Stanford
New York City	Everett Shelton, Wyoming	Ken Sailors, Wyoming
New York City	Vadal Peterson, Utah	Arnie Ferrin, Utah
New York City	Henry Iba, Oklahoma A&M	Bob Kurland, Okla. A&M
New York City	Henry Iba, Oklahoma A&M	Bob Kurland, Okla. A&M
New York City	Alvin Julian, Holy Cross	George Kaftan, Holy Cross
New York City	Adolph Rupp, Kentucky	Alex Groza, Kentucky
Seattle, Wash.	Adolph Rupp, Kentucky	Alex Groza, Kentucky
New York City	Nat Holman, CCNY	Irwin Dambrot, CCNY
Minneapolis, Minn.	Adolph Rupp, Kentucky	None Selected
Seattle, Wash.	Forrest Allen, Kansas	Clyde Lovellette, Kansas
Kansas City, Mo.	Branch McCracken, Indiana	B. H. Born, Kansas
Kansas City, Mo.	Kenneth Loeffler, La Salle	Tom Gola, La Salle
Kansas City, Mo.	Phil Woolpert, San Francisco	Bill Russell, San Francisco
Evanston, Ill.	Phil Woolpert, San Francisco	Hal Lear, Temple
Kansas City, Mo.	Frank McGuire, N. Carolina	Wilt Chamberlain, Kansas
Louisville, Ky.	Adolph Rupp, Kentucky	Elgin Baylor, Seattle
Louisville, Ky.	Pete Newell, California	Jerry West, West Virginia
San Francisco, Cal.	Fred Taylor, Ohio State	Jerry Lucas, Ohio State
Kansas City, Mo.	Edwin Jucker, Cincinnati	Jerry Lucas, Ohio State
Louisville, Ky.	Edwin Jucker, Cincinnati	Paul Hogue, Cincinnati
Louisville, Ky.	George Ireland, Loyola (Ill.)	Art Heyman, Duke
Kansas City, Mo.	John Wooden, UCLA	Walt Hazzard, UCLA
Portland, Oregon	John Wooden, UCLA	Bill Bradley, Princeton
College Park, Md.	Don Haskins, Texas-Western	Jerry Chambers, Utah
Louisville, Ky.	John Wooden, UCLA	Lew Alcindor, UCLA
Los Angeles, Cal.	John Wooden, UCLA	Lew Alcindor, UCLA
Louisville, Ky.	John Wooden, UCLA	Lew Alcindor, UCLA
College Park, Md.	John Wooden, UCLA	Sidney Wicks, UCLA
Houston, Texas	John Wooden, UCLA	Vacated**
Los Angeles, Cal.	John Wooden, UCLA	Bill Walton, UCLA
St. Louis, Mo.	John Wooden, UCLA	Bill Walton, UCLA
Greensboro, N.C.	Norman Sloan, N.C. State	David Thompson, N.C. State
San Diego, Calif.	John Wooden, UCLA	Richard Washington, UCLA
Philadelphia, Pa.	Bobby Knight, Indiana	Kent Benson, Indiana.
Atlanta, Georgia	Al McGuire, Marquette	Butch Lee, Marquette
St. Louis, Mo.	Joe Hall, Kentucky	Jack Givens, Kentucky
Salt Lake City, Utah	Jud Heathcote, Michigan St.	Earvin Johnson, Mich. St.
Indianapolis, Ind.	Denny Crum, Louisville	Darrell Griffith, Louisville
Philadelphia, Pa.	Bobby Knight, Indiana	Isiah Thomas, Indiana
New Orleans, La.	Dean Smith, North Carolina	James Worthy, North Carolina
Albuquerque, N.M.	Jim Valvano, N.C. State	Akeem Abdul Olajuwan, Houston

BEST SINGLE-GAME SCORING PERFORMANCES

Player, Institution vs. Opponent, Year	FG	FT	TP
Austin Carr, Notre Dame vs. Ohio, 1970	25	11	61
Bill Bradley, Princeton vs. Wichita State, 1965	22	14	58
Oscar Robertson, Cincinnati vs. Arkansas, 1958	21	14	56
Austin Carr, Notre Dame vs. Kentucky, 1970	22	8	52
Austin Carr, Notre Dame vs. Texas Christian, 1971	20	12	52
Elvin Hayes, Houston vs. Loyola (Ill.), 1968	20	9	49
Hal Lear, Temple vs. Southern Methodist, 1956	17	14	48
Austin Carr, Notre Dame vs. Houston, 1971	17	13	47
Dave Corzine, DePaul vs. Louisville, 1978	18	10	46
Bob Houbregs, Washington vs. Seattle, 1953	20	5	45
Austin Carr, Notre Dame vs. Iowa, 1970	21	3	45
Clyde Lovellette, Kansas vs. St. Louis, 1952	16	12	44
Bill Walton, UCLA vs. Memphis State, 1973	21	2	44
Rod Thorn, West Virginia vs. St. Joseph's (Pa.), 1963	16	12	44
Dan Issel, Kentucky vs. Notre Dame, 1970	17	10	44
Oscar Robertson, Cincinnati vs. Kansas, 1960	19	5	43
Jeff Mullins, Duke vs. Villanova, 1964	19	5	43
Willie Smith, Missouri vs. Michigan, 1976	18	7	43
Johnny O'Brien, Seattle vs. Idaho State, 1953	17	8	42
Bob Houbregs, Washington vs. Louisiana State, 1953	17	8	42
John Clune, Navy vs. Connecticut, 1954	16	10	42
Jim Barnes, Texas-El Paso vs. Texas A&M, 1964	16	10	42
Gail Goodrich, UCLA vs. Michigan, 1965	12	18	42
Don Schlundt, Indiana vs. Notre Dame, 1953	13	15	41
Jack Givens, Kentucky vs. Duke, 1978	18	5	41
David Thompson, N.C. State vs. Providence, 1974	16	8	40

HIGHEST SCORING AVERAGE

(Minimum: 50% of maximum tournament games)

Year	Player	School	G	FG	FT	Pts	Avg
1939	Jim Hull	Ohio State	3	22	14	58	19.0
1940	Howard Engleman	Kansas	3	18	3	39	13.0
	Bob Kinney	Rice	2	12	2	26	13.0
1941	John Adams	Arkansas	2	21	6	48	24.0
1942	Chet Palmer	Rice	2	19	5	43	21.5
	Jim Pollard	Stanford	2	20	3	43	21.5
1943	John Hargis	Texas	2	21	17	59	29.5
1944	Nick Bozolich	Pepperdine	2	17	11	45	22.5
1945	Dick Wilkins	Oregon	2	19	6	44	22.0
1946	Bob Kurland	Oklahoma State	3	28	16	72	24.0
1947	George Kaftan	Holy Cross	3	25	13	63	21.0
1948	Jack Nichols	Washington	2	13	13	39	19.5

Year	Player	School	G	FG	FT	Pts	Avg
1949	Alex Groza	Kentucky	3	31	20	82	27.3
1950	Sam Ranzino	North Carolina St.	3	25	25	75	25.0
1951	William Kukoy	North Carolina St.	3	25	19	69	23.0
1952	Clyde Lovellette	Kansas	4	53	35	141	35.3
1953	Bob Houbregs	Washington	4	57	25	139	34.8
1954	John Clune	Navy	3	30	19	79	26.3
1955	Terry Rand	Marquette	3	31	11	73	24.3
1956	Hal Lear	Temple	5	63	34	160	32.0
1957	Wilt Chamberlain	Kansas	4	40	41	121	30.3
1958	Wayne Embry	Miami (Ohio)	3	32	19	83	27.7
1959	Jerry West	West Virginia	5	57	46	160	32.0
1960	Jerry West	West Virginia	3	35	35	105	35.0
1961	Bill McGill	Utah	4	49	21	119	29.8
1962	Len Chappell	Wake Forest	5	45	44	134	26.8
1963	Barry Kramer	NYU	3	31	28	100	33.3
1964	Jeff Mullins	Duke	4	50	16	116	29.0
1965	Bill Bradley	Princeton	5	65	47	147	35.4
1966	Jerry Chambers	Utah	4	55	33	143	35.8
1967	Lew Alcindor	UCLA	4	39	28	106	26.5
1968	Elvin Hayes	Houston	5	70	27	167	33.4
1969	Rick Mount	Purdue	4	49	24	122	30.5
1970	Austin Carr	Notre Dame	3	68	22	158	52.7
1971	Austin Carr	Notre Dame	3	48	29	125	41.7
1972	Dwight Lamar	SW Louisiana	4	41	18	100	33.3
1973	Larry Finch	Memphis State	4	34	39	107	26.8
1974	John Shumate	Notre Dame	3	35	16	86	28.7
1975	Adrian Dantley	Notre Dame	3	29	34	92	30.7
1976	Willie Smith	Missouri	3	38	18	94	31.3
1977	Cedric Maxwell	N.C.-Charlotte	5	39	45	123	24.6
1978	Dave Corzine	DePaul	3	33	16	82	27.3
1979	Larry Bird	Indiana State	5	52	32	136	27.2
1980	Joe Barry Carroll	Purdue	6	63	32	158	26.3
1981	Al Wood	North Carolina	5	44	21	109	21.8
1982	Oliver Robinson	UAB	3	27	12	66	22.0
1983	D. Whittenburg	North Carolina St.	6	47	26	120	20.0

* The tournament's leading scorer was Jim McDaniels of Western Kentucky (147 points). However, student athletes representing that institution were declared ineligible subsequent to the tournament; under NCAA rules the team's and ineligible student athletes' records were deleted, and the team's place in the final standings was vacated.

MOST POINTS

Year	Player	School	G	FG	FT	Pts	Avg
1939	Jim Hull	Ohio State	3	22	14	58	19.3
1940	Howard Engleman	Kansas	3	18	3	39	13.0
1941	John Adams	Arkansas	2	21	6	48	24.0
1942	Chet Palmer	Rice	2	19	5	43	21.5
	Jim Pollard	Stanford	2	20	3	43	21.5
1943	John Hargis	Texas	2	21	17	59	29.5
1944	Aud Brindley	Dartmouth	3	24	4	52	17.3
1945	Bob Kurland	Oklahoma A&M	3	30	5	65	21.7
1946	Bob Kurland	Oklahoma A&M	3	28	16	72	24.0
1947	George Kaftan	Holy Cross	3	25	13	63	21.0
1948	Alex Groza	Kentucky	3	23	8	54	18.0
1949	Alex Groza	Kentucky	3	31	20	82	27.3
1950	Sam Ranzino	North Carolina St.	3	25	25	75	25.0
1951	Don Sunderlage	Illinois	4	28	27	83	20.8
1952	Clyde Lovellette	Kansas	4	53	35	141	35.3
1953	Bob Houbregs	Washington	4	57	25	139	34.8
1954	Tom Gola	La Salle	5	38	38	114	22.8
1955	Bill Russell	San Francisco	5	49	20	118	23.6
1956	Hal Lear	Temple	5	63	34	160	32.0
1957	Len Rosenbluth	North Carolina	5	53	34	140	28.0
1958	Elgin Baylor	Seattle	5	48	39	135	27.0
1959	Jerry West	West Virginia	5	57	46	160	32.0
1960	Oscar Robertson	Cincinnati	4	47	28	122	30.5
1961	Bill McGill	Utah	4	49	21	119	29.8
1962	Len Chappell	Wake Forest	5	45	44	134	26.8
1963	Jerry Harkness	Loyola (Ill.)	5	41	24	106	21.2
1964	Jeff Mullins	Duke	4	50	16	116	29.0
1965	Bill Bradley	Princeton	5	65	47	147	35.4
1966	Jerry Chambers	Utah	4	55	33	143	35.8
1967	Elvin Hayes	Houston	5	57	14	128	25.6
1968	Elvin Hayes	Houston	5	70	27	167	33.4
1969	Rick Mount	Purdue	4	49	24	122	30.5
1970	Austin Carr	Notre Dame	3	68	22	158	52.7
1971	Vacated*						
1972	Jim Price	Louisville	4	41	21	103	25.7
1973	Ernie DiGregorio	Providence	5	59	10	128	25.6
1974	David Thompson	North Carolina St.	4	38	21	97	24.3
1975	Jim Lee	Syracuse	5	51	17	119	23.8
1976	Scott May	Indiana	5	45	23	113	22.6
1977	Cedric Maxwell	N.C.-Charlotte	5	39	45	123	24.6
1978	Mike Gminski	Duke	5	45	19	109	21.8
1979	Tony Price	Pennsylvania	6	58	26	142	23.7
1980	Joe Barry Carroll	Purdue	6	63	32	158	26.3
1981	Al Wood	North Carolina	5	44	21	109	21.8
1982	Rob Williams	Houston	5	30	28	88	17.6
1983	D. Whittenburg	North Carolina St.	6	47	26	120	20.0

* Howard Porter, Villanova. Student athletes representing Villanova were declared ineligible subsequent to the tournament. Under NCAA rules, Villanova's and ineligible student athletes' records were deleted; and Villanova's place in the final standings was vacated.

LEADING REBOUNDER

Year	Player, Institution	g	rb	avg.
1951	Bill Spivey, Kentucky	4	65	16.3
1957	John Green, Michigan State	4	77	19.3
1958	Elgin Baylor, Seattle	5	91	18.2
1959	Don Kojis, Marquette	3	56	18.7
1960	Howard Jolliff, Ohio	3	64	21.3
1961	Jerry Lucas, Ohio State	4	73	18.3
1962	Len Chappell, Wake Forest	5	86	17.2
1963	Nate Thurmond, Bowling Green	3	70	23.3
1964	Paul Silas, Creighton	3	57	19.0
1965	Bill Bradley, Princeton	5	57	11.4
1966	Elvin Hayes, Houston	3	50	16.7
1967	Elvin Hayes, Houston	5	75	15.0
1968	Elvin Hayes, Houston	5	97	19.4
1969	Lew Alcindor, UCLA	4	64	16.0
1970	Sam Lacey, New Mexico State	5	90	18.0
1971	Sidney Wicks, UCLA	4	52	13.0
1972	Bill Walton, UCLA	4	64	16.0
1973	Bill Walton, UCLA	4	58	14.5
1974	Tom Burleson, North Carolina State	4	61	15.3
1975	Richard Washington, UCLA	5	60	12.0
1976	Phil Hubbard, Michigan	5	51	10.2
1977	Cedric Maxwell, North Carolina-Charlotte	5	64	12.8
1978	Eugene Banks, Duke	5	50	10.0
1979	Larry Bird, Indiana State	5	67	13.4
1980	Mike Sanders, UCLA	6	60	10.0
1981	Cliff Levingston, Wichita State	4	53	13.3
1982	Clyde Drexler, Houston	5	42	8.4
1983	Akeem Abdul Olajuwon, Houston	6	65	13.0

CAREER SCORING

Player, Institution (Years Competed)	Games	FG	FT	Points	Avg.
Elvin Hayes, Houston (1966-67-68)	13	152	54	358	27.5
Oscar Robertson, Cincinnati (1958-59-60)	10	117	90	324	32.4
Lew Alcindor, UCLA (1967-68-69)	12	115	74	304	25.3
Bill Bradley, Princeton (1963-64-65)	9	108	87	303	33.7
Austin Carr, Notre Dame (1969-70-71)	7	117	55	289	41.3
Jerry West, West Virginia (1958-59-60)	9	97	81	275	30.6
Jerry Lucas, Ohio State (1960-61-62)	12	104	58	266	22.2
Bill Walton, UCLA (1972-73-74)	12	109	36	254	21.2
Gail Goodrich, UCLA (1963-64-65)	10	84	67	235	23.5
Marques Johnson, UCLA (1974-75-76-77)	16	96	42	234	14.6
Tom Gola, La Salle (1954-55)	10	77	75	229	22.9
Cazzie Russell, Michigan (1964-65-66)	9	81	64	226	25.1
Len Chappell, Wake Forest (1961-62)	8	72	77	221	27.6
Paul Hogue, Cincinnati (1960-61-62)	12	93	35	221	18.4
Jimmy Collins, New Mexico St. (1968-69-70)	11	91	37	219	19.9
Jack Givens, Kentucky (1975-77-78)	13	89	34	212	16.3
Bill Russell, San Francisco (1955-56)	9	89	31	209	23.2
Richard Washington, UCLA (1974-75-76)	13	94	21	209	16.1
Adrian Dantley, Notre Dame (1974-75-76)	8	73	57	203	25.4
Eddie Owens, Nev.-Las Vegas (1975-76-77)	10	88	26	202	20.2
Jeff Mullins, Duke (1963-64)	8	84	32	200	25.0

CAREER REBOUNDING

Player, Institution (Years Competed)	g	rb	avg.
Elvin Hayes, Houston (1966-67-68)	13	222	17.1
Lew Alcindor, UCLA (1967-68-69)	12	201	16.8
Jerry Lucas, Ohio State (1960-61)	12	197	16.4
Bill Walton, UCLA (1972-73-74)	12	159	13.3
Sam Lacey, New Mexico State (1968-69-70)	11	157	14.3
Marques Johnson, UCLA (1974-75-76-77)	16	138	8.6
Curtis Rowe, UCLA (1969-70-71)	12	131	10.9
Mel Counts, Oregon State (1962-63-64)	9	127	14.1
John Green, Michigan State (1957, 1959)	6	118	19.7
Artis Gilmore, Jacksonville (1970-71)	6	115	19.2
Sidney Wicks, UCLA (1969-70-71)	12	112	9.3
Paul Silas, Creighton (1962, 1964)	6	111	18.5
Bill Bradley, Princeton (1963-64-65)	9	108	12.0
Phil Hubbard, Michigan (1976-77)	8	96	12.0

BEST SINGLE-GAME REBOUNDING PERFORMANCE

Player, Institution vs. Opponent, Year	Rebounds
Nate Thurmond, Bowling Green vs. Mississippi State, 1963	31
Jerry Lucas, Ohio State vs. Kentucky, 1961	30
Toby Kimball, Connecticut vs. St. Joseph's (Pa.), 1965	29
Elvin Hayes, Houston vs. Pacific, 1966	28
John Green, Michigan State vs. Notre Dame, 1957	27
Paul Silas, Creighton vs. Oklahoma City, 1964	27
Elvin Hayes, Houston vs. Loyola (Ill.), 1968	27
Howard Joliff, Ohio vs. Georgia Tech, 1960	26
Phil Hubbard, Michigan vs. Detroit, 1977	26
Jerry Lucas, Ohio State vs. Western Kentucky, 1960	25
Elvin Hayes, Houston vs. Texas Christian, 1968	25

Index

A

Abernathy, Tom, 114, 116, 117
Adams, Johnny, 8
Adams, Michael, 172, 173, 174
Adams, Tyrone, 174
Adler, Frank, 84
Aguirre, Mark, 136, 137, 140, 142, 145, 150, 151, 158, 172
Ainge, Danny, 164, 165
Akers, Willie, 55
Alabama, 115, 171
Alabama-Birmingham Blazers, 162, 168, 176, 177, 178, 179
Albers, Jerry, 41
Alcindor, Lew, 21, 77, 79, 80, 81, 82, 83, 84, 85, 86, 87, 98, 90, 92, 94
Alcorn State, 174
Allen, Bob, 7
Allen, Forrest C. "Phog", 5, 7, 34, 36, 38, 41, 45, 48, 80, 81, 82, 83, 84
Allen, Lucius, 80, 81, 82, 83, 84
All-Tournament Team Awards, in 1940, 6; in 1952, 38; in 1953, 42; in 1954, 44; in 1955, 46; in 1956, 48; in 1957, 51; in 1958, 53; in 1959, 56; in 1960, 60; in 1961, 62; in 1962, 64; in 1963, 66; in 1964, 72; in 1965, 74; in 1966, 76; in 1967, 81; in 1968, 84; in 1969, 87; in 1970, 89; in 1971, 95; in 1972, 99; in 1973, 102; in 1974, 107; in 1975, 113; in 1976, 117; in 1977, 126; in 1978, 133; in 1979, 144; in 1980, 156; in 1981, 169; in 1982, 184
Anders, Benny, 196
Anderson, Forddy, 30, 44
Anderson, Keith, 130
Anderson, Kim, 115
Andrews, Jim, 99
Anet, Bobby, 3, 4
Arcaro, Eddie, 8
Arizin, Paul, 21, 26
Arizona State, 65, 100, 151
Arizona Wildcats, 115, 116
Arkansas Razorbacks, 8, 9, 15, 53, 119, 129-30, 132, 136, 137, 140, 142, 144, 157, 160, 172, 174, 186-87, 188
Armstrong, Curley, 6
Arnelle, Jesse, 44
Arnold, Frank, 165
Arnold, Ken, 146, 154, 156
Artis, Orsten, 76
Aubrey, Sam, 20
Avers, Randy, 128
Awtrey, Dennis, 85

B

Baer, Buddy, 7
Bagley, John, 163, 169, 172, 174, 176
Bailey, Thurl, 192, 193, 194, 196, 197, 199
Baker, Dick, 3, 4
Baker, Terry, 65
Ball, Odell, 136
Banks, Gene, 130, 131, 133, 134, 136, 152
Banks, James, 189, 192, 196
Barker, Cliff, 24, 26, 27, 28
Barnes, Marvin, 99, 100
Barnstable, Dale, 25, 26
Bartow, Gene, 100, 102, 115, 178, 179
Batleff, Ed, 99
Batton, Dave, 131
Baylor Bears, 20, 25, 30
Baylor, Elgin, 52, 53
Beard, Butch, 83
Beard, Ralph, 21, 24, 25, 26, 27, 28
Benson, Kent, 114, 115, 116, 117
Bertrand, Joe, 38
Betchley, Rich, 95
Bibby, Henry, 88, 92, 93, 94, 95, 96, 97, 98, 99
Bird, Larry, 135, 136, 137, 139-40, 141, 142, 143, 144
Black, Jimmy, 170, 172
Blackman, Rolando, 158, 166
Blatcher, Frank, 44
Boldt, Carl, 48
Bond, Phil, 109
Bonham, Ron, 62, 63, 64, 65, 67, 68
Booker, Kenny, 92, 95
Boozer, Bob, 52, 54, 55
Born, B. H., 40, 41, 42
Boston College Eagles, 81, 162, 163, 169, 172, 173, 174, 176, 194
Boudreau, Lou, 2
Bouldin, Carl, 62, 63
Bouldin, Paul, 61
Boylan, Jim, 118, 119, 123, 125, 126, 127
Boyle, Kevin, 146, 147, 148, 153-54
Bradds, Gary, 64
Bradley Braves, 28, 30, 43, 44, 45, 141, 145, 150
Bradley, Bill, 72, 73, 74
Bradshaw, Clyde, 136, 142, 150, 151
Branch, Tony, 148
Branning, Rich, 120, 131, [32], 36
Bredar, Jim, 36
Bremoras, Irv, 36
Brennan, Pete, 49, 51
Breuer, Randy, 178
Brewer, Ron, 129, 130, 132, 133
Bridgeman, Junior, 109, 112
Brigham Young, 32, 33, 73, 94, 137, 164, 165, 181
Brindley, Audley, 15, 16
Brookins, Vince, 146, 148, 151
Brooks, Michael, 178
Brown, Charley, 53
Brown, Dale, 158, 160, 162, 167
Brown, Fred, 179, 183
Brown, Gene, 47, 48, 51
Brown, John Y., 188
Brown, Larry, 151, 154, 156
Brown, Lewis, 121
Brown, Skip, 118, 119
Brown University, 2

Brown, Wiley, 148, 150, 155
Brucker, Steve, 72
Bubas, Vic, 71, 76
Buch, Al, 54, 55
Buckley, Jay, 71, 72
Buckner, Quinn, 99, 101, 114, 115, 116, 117
Bunch, Greg, 130
Buntin, Bill, 71, 72, 73, 74
Burkman, Roger, 148, 153, 155
Burleson, Tom, 105, 106, 108
Burness, Don, 10, 11
Butrym, Craig, 125
Bynum, Will, 115
Byrd, Robert, 125

C

Cain, Carl "Sugar," 46, 47, 48
California Golden Bears, 20, 54, 55, 57, 58, 60
Canisius College, 46, 49
Cann, Howard, 17
Carlisle, Rick, 194
Carnavale, Ben, 23
Carney, Bob, 44
Carr, Antoine, 159, 160
Carr, Austin, 85, 87, 88, 89, 92
Carroll, Joe Barry, 152, 153, 154, 156, 158
Carter, Butch, 153
Carter, Howard, 160, 162, 167
Carter, Reggie, 137, 138, 139
Carter, Ron, 115
Cartwright, Bill, 136, 137, 141, 144
Casey, Mike, 82
Catholic University of Washington, 15
Central Michigan, 118
Chamberlain, Wilt "the Stilt," 34, 48, 50, 77
Chambers, Jerry, 75, 76
Chambers, Tom, 166
Chaney, Don, 78, 82, 83
Chapman, Bob, 128
Chapman, John, 95
Chappell, Len, 63, 64
Charles, Lorenzo, 194, 199
Chenetz, Ed, 30
Chones, Jim, 92, 93
Cincinnati Bearcats, 52, 54, 55, 60, 61, 62, 64-65, 66, 76, 109, 120
City College of New York (CUNY) Beavers, 23, 28, 29, 32
Clark, Rusty, 82, 85
Claytor, Truman, 128, 128
Clemson Tigers, 151
Cohen, Herb, 30
Collins, Jimmy, 14, 85, 88, 89, 92
Colorado Buffalos, 5, 10, 20, 44, 46, 63, 65, 85
Colorado State, 85
Columbia, 31
Combes, Harry, 31, 35
Connaughton, Dan, 68
Conn, Billy, 7
Connecticut, 42, 71, 116
Connor, Lester "Molester," 180, 181
Cook, Greg "Cookieman," 158, 160, 161, 162
Corbin, Tyrone, 172
Corhen, Richard, 192
Corzine, Dave, 115, 131, 132
Counts, Mel, 65
Cousy, Bob, 21, 22, 23, 24, 25, 29
Cowan, Fred, 152
Cowden, Bill, 10, 11
Cox, John, 53
Cox, Wesley, 112
Creighton, 8, 70, 105, 131-32, 158
Crigler, John, 53
Crimson Tide, 171
Crosby, Gerald, 191, 192
Crum, Denny, 95, 97, 109, 148, 154-55, 155, 156, 157, 176, 178, 179, 181, 183, 186, 188
Cummings, Terry, 145, 150, 151, 170, 172
Cunningham, Bob, 49
Cunningham, Gary, 63, 64, 95, 136
Curtis, Tommy, 96, 100, 101, 106

D

Dabney, Mike, 115
Dailey, Quintin, 170
Dallmar, Howie, 11
Dalton, Bob, 57
Dambrot, Irwin, 28, 29, 30
Dampier, Louie, 75-76, 76
Dana, Jack, 10
Dantley, Adrian, 115, 120
Darden, Oliver, 73, 74
Darrow, Chuck, 72
Dartmouth College, 10, 15-17, 52, 54, 73
Dassie, Larry, 118
Daughterty, Brad, 192
Davidson College, 82, 85, 89
Davis, Bob, 97
Davis, Dwight, 92
Davis, Jim, 37
Davis, Walter, 120, 122, 126
Dayton Flyers, 73, 81, 103, 105
Dean, Everett, 9, 10, 11
Debusschere, Dave, 63
Dee, Johnny, 92
Deford, Frank, 165
Delph, Marvin, 129, 130, 132
Dennard, Kenny, 131, 152
DePaul Blue Demons, 12, 14, 20, 38, 40, 55, 60, 112, 115, 116, 131, 132, 136, 137, 138, 140, 141, 142, 144, 145, 150, 158, 162, 169, 170, 172, 173, 174
Detroit, 63
Dickey, Dick, 29
Dick, John, 4
DiGregorio, Ernie, 99, 100, 102
Dillard, Mickey, 128
Dillard, Skip, 150, 158, 172
Dillon, John, 20
DiMaggio, Joe, 7-8
Doctor of Dunk. *See* Griffith, Darrell
Doherty, Matt, 166, 170, 171, 172, 182, 192
Donnelly, Terry, 144
Donoher, Don, 82
Donoher, Mickey, 81
Dorsey, Ralph, 6
Downing, Steve, 99, 101, 102
Downing, Walter, 172
Drake Bulldogs, 85, 86, 88, 94
Drake, Ducky, 72, 84, 95
Drexler, Clyde, 174, 175, 176, 181, 185, 186, 196, 197, 199
Dro, Bob, 6
Drollings, Ralph, 113
DuChateau, David, 125
Dudley, Jim, 125
Duke Blue Devils, 60, 66, 68, 71-72, 75-76, 85, 104, 130-34, 136, 137, 151, 152, 153, 198
Dunn, Jerry, 94
Duquesne, 5, 36, 85
Durham, Hugh, 97, 189
Durham, Jarrett, 85
DuVal, Dennis, 99
Dye, Tippy, 40

E

Eaves, Jerry, 148, 155, 177, 179
Ecker, John, 90, 95
Eddleman, Dike, 26
Edmonson, Keith, 152, 153, 156
Egan, John, 62, 66, 68
Ellis, Bo, 105, 115, 118, 120, 125, 126
Ellis, Dale, 178
Elstun, Gene, 51
Engleman, Howard, 5, 7
Englund, Gene, 8
Erickson, Keith, 70, 71, 72, 73
Evans, Danny, 180
Evans, Mike, 118
Ewing, Pat, 179, 180, 181, 183, 184, 186

F

Fair, Terry, 189, 192
Farmer, Larry, 95, 98, 101, 102
Farmer, Mike, 47, 96, 97, 105
Feiereisel, Ron, 38, 40
Ferrin, Arnie, 15, 16, 17, 21, 61-62
Finch, Larry, 99, 100, 101, 102
Fitzpatrick, Denny, 56, 57
Fleming, Vern, 189, 192, 196
Florida State Seminoles, 97-98, 99, 128
Flowers, Bruce, 115, 120, 132, 136
Floyd, Eric "Sleepy," 146, 147-48, 157-58, 170, 180, 181, 183, 184
Flynn, Mike, 109
Fordham, 42, 92, 93
Ford, Phil, 120, 122, 126, 127
Foster, Bill, 130, 133
Foster, Bud, 8
Foster, Rod, 150, 151, 156
Francis, Chet, 6
Franklin, Alvin, 196, 197, 199
Frazier, Ricky, 174
Fresno State Bulldogs, 180, 181
Friel, Jack, 8
Fullerton State, 129, 130

G

Gabcik, John, 68
Gale, Bob, 16
Gale, Laddie, 3, 4
Galiber, Joe, 30
Gannon, Terry, 199
Garland, Gary, 132, 136, 140, 142
Garris, John, 174, 176
Georgetown Hoyas, 14, 146-48, 157-58, 179, 180, 181, 183, 185, 186
Georgia Bulldogs, 189, 191, 192, 194, 195-96
Georgia Tech, 60
Gettys, Reid, 176
Giles, Chris, 178
Gilmore, Artis, 87, 89, 92
Givens, Jack, 111, 120, 127, 128, 129, 132, 133, 134
Glass, Arthur, 30
Glenn, Mike, 119
Gminski, Mike, 130, 131, 133, 134, 136, 152, 153
Goins, Rick, 128
Gola, Tom, 34, 38, 42, 43, 44, 46
Goldstein, Don, 56
Gondrezick, Glen, 121
Goodrich, Gail, 69, 70, 71, 72, 73, 74
Goodwin, Billy, 189
Gordon, Lancaster, 176, 177, 178, 179, 186, 187, 188
Gosnell, Al, 52
Goss, Fred, 73
Gowdy, Curt, 2
Graham, Kent, 72
Graham, Otto, 2
Graham, Ralph, 6
Graney, Mike, 52
Granger, Stewart, 171, 186
Green, John, 51, 63, 64
Green, Rickey, 115, 116, 117, 118
Greenwood, David, 115, 116, 120, 128, 129, 136, 137, 141, 142, 144
Grevey, Kevin, 99, 109, 113
Gridley, Jim, 6
Griffin, Rod, 118, 119
Griffith, Darrell, 131, 148, 150, 153, 154, 155, 156, 157
Grote, Steve, 117
Grout, Jack, 57
Groza, Alex, 21, 22, 24, 25, 26, 27, 28, 62, 84
Guyette, Bob, 109

H

Hackett, Rudy, 111
Hagan, Cliff, 31, 32, 33, 35, 36, 42
Halbrook, Swede, 46
Hall, Joe B., 97, 109, 127, 128, 134, 152, 176
Hamilton, Roy, 136, 139, 141
Hamline College, 2
Hankins, Cecil, 17
Hanzlik, Bill, 136
Hargis, John, 12, 13, 14, 23
Harkness, Jerry, 66, 67, 68, 70
Harlem Globetrotters, 52
Harp, Dick, 48
Harris, Bob, 27
Harris, Herman, 115
Hartman, Jack, 158, 166
Haskins, Don, 74, 76
Hatton, Vern, 50, 52, 53
Havlicek, John, 59, 60, 61, 63, 64, 82
Hawaii, 97
Hawkins, Tom, 49, 52
Hayden, Tom, 125
Hayes, Elvin, 77, 81, 82, 83, 84
Hays, Eric, 109
Hays, Steve, 120
Hazzard, Walt, 63, 64, 70, 71, 72, 73
Head, Ed, 32, 33
Heard, Lamar, 189, 192
Heathcote, Jud, 128, 129, 137, 142, 144
Heaton, Bob, 140, 142
Heenan, Kevin, 130
Heisman Trophy, 65
Heitz, Kenny, 81, 82, 84
Henderson, Bill, 25
Herron, Keith, 131
Hersh, Phil, 196
Heyman, Art, 66, 68, 71
Higgins, Mike, 72
Higgins, Rod, 181
Hill, Andy, 95, 96, 97
Hill, Bobby Joe, 75, 76
Hirsch, Jack, 70, 71, 72
Hitch, Lew, 33
Hobson, Howard "Hobby," 2
Hodges, Bill, 139, 144
Hoffman, Vaughn, 72
Hogue, Paul, 57, 61, 62, 63, 64
Holland, Brad, 136, 141
Hollyfield, Larry, 95, 96, 100, 102
Holman, Nat, 28, 29, 30
Holton, Michael, 150
Holy Cross Crusaders, 22-23, 24, 29, 117-18
Hosket, Bill, 82
Houbregs, Bob, 26, 38, 40, 41, 42
Houston Cougars, 77, 78, 81, 82, 84, 92, 93, 94, 132, 174, 176, 181, 185, 186, 188, 196, 197, 199
Howard, Aaron, 171, 172
Howard, Terry, 112
Howell, Steve, 82
Hoyt, Rickie, 61, 62
Hubbard, Phil, 115, 116, 117, 118
Huffman, Marv, 5, 6
Hull, Jimmy, 3, 4, 13
Hultberg, Jordy, 139, 150
Hunter, Les, 66, 67, 68

I

Iba, Hank, 17, 20, 27, 32, 40, 42
Idaho State Bengals, 40, 60, 120, 121
Idaho Vandals, 180, 181
Illinois Illini, 12, 26, 31, 32, 36, 66, 166
Imhoff, Darall, 54, 55, 56, 57, 58, 60
Indiana Hoosiers, 5-7, 8, 33, 38, 40, 41, 42, 96, 99, 100, 101, 109, 114, 115-17, 131, 151, 152, 162, 167, 168, 178, 188
Indiana State Sycamores, 135, 136, 137, 139-40, 141, 142, 143, 144
Iowa Hawkeyes, 45, 46, 47, 48, 82, 89, 136, 145, 146-48, 160, 181
Iowa State University, 15
Ireland, George, 65, 68, 70
Irvin, Roy, 44
Issel, Dan, 82, 85
Iverson, Jim, 33

J

Jabbar, Karem Abdul. *See* Alcindor, Lew

Jackson, Tracy, 136, 165
Jacksonville Dolphins, 87, 88, 89, 92, 93
James Madison Hoopsters, 157, 165, 170, 171, 192
John, Maurice, 85, 86
Johnson, Earvin "Magic," 128, 129, 135, 136-37, 139-40, 142, 143, 144
Johnson, Marques, 108, 112, 115, 116, 117, 120
Johnson, Steve, 158
Jones, Anthony, 179
Jones, Charles, 179, 186, 190, 196
Jones, Jeff, 178
Jones, K. C., 45, 46, 47, 49, 99
Jones, Mike, 160
Jones, Wallace "Wah Wah," 24, 25, 27, 28
Jordan, Ed, 115
Jordan, Michael, 170, 172, 181, 182, 183, 184, 189, 192
Jucker, Ed, 61, 62, 64, 65, 66
Julian, Alvin "Doggie," 23, 25

K

Kaftan, George, 23, 24, 25
Kansas Jayhawks, 5-7, 8, 10, 36, 38, 40, 41, 42, 48, 49, 50, 52, 60, 75, 76, 78, 92, 93, 94, 104, 105, 106, 160
Kansas State Wildcats, 22, 32, 33, 52, 53, 54, 55, 61, 71, 88, 97, 101, 111, 117, 118, 120, 148, 150, 158, 166-67, 173, 174
Karl, George, 97
Kearns, Tommy, 49, 50, 51
Keith, Larry, 142
Keller, Bill, 86
Kellerman, Brian, 181
Kelley, Al, 42
Kelley, Dean, 38, 40, 41
Kellogg, Clark, 151
Kelser, Greg "Special K," 128, 129, 135, 136, 139, 142, 144
Kennedy, Jim, 115
Kenney, Bob, 37
Kenon, Larry, 99, 100, 101, 102
Kentucky Wildcats, 10, 15, 22-34, 35, 39, 42, 45, 47, 48, 50, 52, 53, 63, 64, 70, 75, 76, 82, 85, 87, 89, 92, 93, 97, 99, 101, 109, 111, 112-13, 117, 120-26, 127-34, 151, 152, 162, 176, 188
Kerris, Jack, 25, 26
Kerr, Johnny "Red," 35, 36, 38
Kinch, Chad, 118
King, Nehru, 100
King, Ron, 97, 98, 99
Kirkpatrick, Curry, 155
Kitchel, Ted, 178
Klaerich, Ralph, 25, 26
Kleine, Joe, 187
Knight, Bobby, 60, 100, 101, 109, 114, 116, 117, 152, 153, 162, 167, 168, 169, 178
Knight, Toby, 120
Knostmar, Dick, 33
Komenich, Milo, 12, 13, 14
Kotz, Johnny, 8
Kraak, Charley, 42
Krafcisin, Steve, 146
Kraft, Jack, 172
Kuehl, Fred, 68
Kuester, John, 120
Kurland, Bob, 17, 20, 21, 27, 36, 62, 77, 81

L

Lacey, Edgar, 73, 74
Lacey, Sam, 85, 88
Laimbeer, Bill, 131, 132, 136
Lamar, Dwight, 99, 136, 160
Lamkin, Jim, 38, 40
Lamp, Jeff, 164, 169
Lane, Floyd, 29
Lanier, Bob, 82, 83, 89, 92
LaSalle Explorers, 38, 42, 43, 44, 45, 46-47, 11, 131, 145, 152
Lattin, Dave, 75
Lavelli, Tony, 26
Layne, Floyd, 30
Lear, Hal, 47, 48, 57, 71
Lee, Butch, 115, 118, 120, 124, 125, 126, 127
Lee, Greg, 96, 98, 102
Lee, Jim, 111, 113
Lee, Keith, 171, 186
Lee, Oliver, 136
Lee, Theodis, 82, 83
Leonard, Bob, 40, 41, 42, 101
Lester, Ronnie, 145-46, 153, 154
Levey, Seymour, 30
Levingston, Cliff, 159, 160, 169
Levin, Rich, 72
Lewis, Bob, 15
Lewis, Guy, 82, 174, 185, 186, 197, 199
Lienhard, Bill, 37
Lindemann, Paul, 8
Line, Jimmy, 25, 26, 27, 28
Linville, Shelby, 31, 32, 33
Loeffler, Ken, 42, 44
Logan, Bill, 46, 47, 48
Long Beach State, 88, 94, 97, 99, 100, 120
Louisiana State Tigers, 38, 39, 40-41, 44, 139, 150, 158, 159, 160, 167, 169
Louis, Joe, 7
Louisville Cardinals, 31, 77, 83, 97, 98, 109, 111, 112, 120, 131, 132, 140, 148-56, 157, 176, 177, 178, 181, 183, 185, 186, 187, 188, 190, 197, 199
Lovellette, Clyde, 12, 34, 36-37, 38, 40, 74, 77
Lowe, Sidney, 191, 194, 198, 199
Loyola Ramblers, 25, 26, 65-68, 69, 70, 77, 83, 99, 114
Lucas, Jerry, 21, 58, 59, 60, 61, 62, 63, 64, 82, 84
Lucas, Maurice, 99, 104, 105, 106
Luisetti, Hank, 2, 69
Lupson, Phil, 181
Lynam, Jimmy, 158
Lyne, Jerry, 68
Lynn, Mike, 82, 83, 84

M

MacCauley, "Easy" Ed, 21
MacGilvay, Ron, 38
Macklin, Durand, 160, 161, 167
Macklin, Rudy, 150, 158, 162, 169
Macy, Kyle, 127, 129, 152
Magee, Kevin, 170
Mager, Norm, 29, 30
Mahneken, John, 141
Majerus, Rick, 125
Maloy, Mike, 85
Mann, Bill, 28, 29
Marin, Jack, 75-76, 76
Marquette Warriors, 46, 85, 86, 92, 99, 100, 101, 104, 105, 106, 114-15, 116, 118, 119, 121-26, 127, 128, 136, 137, 140, 166, 168, 174, 186
Marshall, 55
Martin, Ethan, 160, 162
Martin, Scott, 166
Martin, Slater, 23, 24
Maryland, 100, 109, 146, 162, 186
Massey, Lew, 118, 122
Massimino, Rollie, 172
Master, Jim, 188
Mathisen, Art, 12
Maxwell, Cedric "Cornbread," 118, 126
May, Don, 80, 81, 82
May, Scott, 114, 115, 116, 117
McAdoo, Bob, 97, 99
McCarter, Andre, 108, 111, 115
McCarter, John, 87
McCarter, Willie, 85, 86

McCarthy, John, 52
McClary, Doug, 40
McClintock, Bill, 56, 57, 59, 60
McCoy, Tommy, 63
McCracken, Branch, 5, 6, 34, 42
McCray, Rodney, 148, 154, 155, 156, 176, 186, 187
McCray, Scooter, 186, 187, 188
McCreary, Jay, 6
McDaniels, Jim, 93, 94, 95
McDonald, Keven, 130
McFarlan, Lonnie, 158
McGilray, Ron, 37
McGuire, Al, 31, 85, 92, 93, 100, 106, 114, 119, 120, 122, 125, 126, 136, 166-67, 197, 199
McGuire, Dick, 15, 16, 37
McGuire, Frank, 34, 35, 48, 50, 92
McIntosh, Doug, 72
McKenna, Dennis, 68
McKinney, Horace "Boness," 20, 63
McKoy, Wayne, 137
McMahon, Jack, 36, 37
McMillan, Jerry, 172
McMullan, Bob, 23
McQueen, Cozell, 191, 194, 196, 199
Meely, Cliff, 85
Melchiorre, Gene, 28, 29, 30
Meminger, Dean, 85, 86, 92
Memphis State Tigers, 99, 100, 101, 102, 115, 171, 172, 186
Menke, Bill, 5, 6
Menke, Bob, 6
Menke, Ken, 12
Mercer University, 157
Merriwell, Frank, 5
Meyer, Larry, 30
Meyer, Ray, 14, 40, 115, 131, 136, 140, 141, 142, 150, 151, 158, 169, 172
Meyers, Dave, 105, 107, 108, 112, 113, 115
Miami (Ohio) University, 86, 127, 128
Micheaux, Larry, 174, 176, 181, 185, 186
Michigan State Spartans, 50, 55, 128-29, 135-44
Michigan Wolverines, 22, 70, 71, 73, 75, 105, 108, 115
Middle Tennessee State, 176, 178
Mikan, George, 9, 14, 17, 18, 20, 36, 69, 77
Miller, Eldon, 151
Miller, Larry, 82, 84
Miller, Ralph, 158
Miller, Ron, 63, 66, 68
Minishian, Dennis, 72
Minnesota Gophers, 97, 176, 178
Minnesota State School of Agriculture, 2
Minniefield, Dirk, 188
Misaka, Wat, 15
Mississippi State, 66
Missouri Tigers, 115, 170, 172, 174, 175
Mitchell, Darryl, 178
Mitchell, Leonard, 160, 162
Mitchem, James, 142, 150
Moncrief, Sidney, 129, 130, 132, 136, 137, 140, 144
Montana Grizzlies, 109
Montana State, 32
Moore, Jack, 38
Morehead State, 55
Morgan, George, 95
Morgan, Rex, 89, 92
Morningstar, Roger, 105
Morris, Drake, 152, 153
Morrison, Jack, 5
Moss, Perry, 171
Mount, Rick, 85, 87
Mullaney, Jim, 23, 24
Mullen, Chris, 189
Mullen, Jerry, 46
Mullen, Tim, 194
Mullins, Jeff, 66, 71, 72
Munroe, George, 10
Murphy, Allen, 109, 112, 113
Murphy, Jay, 176
Murray State, 70
Myers, Bob, 16

N

Nadell, Ronald, 30
Nagle, Gerry, 25
Naismith, James, 1, 2
Nash, Cotton, 63
Nater, Sven, 96, 97, 102
National Association of Basketball Coaches, 36
Navy, 23, 42
NCAA
laying of ground rules by, 2
original eight districts, 2
NCAA national championship finals; in 1939, 1, 2-4; in 1940, 4-7; in 1941, 8; in 1942, 9-11; in 1943, 12-15; in 1944, 15-17; in 1945, 17-20; in 1946, 20-21; in 1947, 22-24; in 1948, 24-25; in 1949, 25-27; in 1950, 28-31; in 1951, 31-34; in 1952, 35-38; in 1953, 38-42; in 1954, 42-44; in 1955, 44-46; in 1956, 47-48; in 1957, 48-52; in 1958, 52-53; in 1959, 54-57; in 1960, 57-61; in 1961, 61-62; in 1962, 62-64; in 1963, 64-68; in 1964, 69-72; in 1965, 72-74; in 1966, 75-76; in 1967, 77-82; in 1968, 82-84; in 1969, 85-87; in 1970, 87-92; in 1971, 92-95; in 1972, 96-99; in 1973, 99-102; in 1974, 102-8; in 1975, 108-13; in 1976, 114-17; in 1977, 117-26; in 1978, 127-34; in 1979, 135-44; in 1980, 145-56; in 1981, 159-69; in 1982, 170-81; in 1983, 185-99
Nealy, Ed, 174
Neary, Bill, 125
Nevada-Las Vegas, 115, 117, 121, 122, 127, 194
Newell, Pete, 54, 55
New Mexico, 130
New Mexico State Aggies, 81, 83-84, 85, 88, 92
New York University, 17, 20, 60
Nicks, Carl, 137, 140, 143
Nielsen, Jim, 84
Norman, Jerry, 72, 84
North Carolina 49ers, 118, 120, 121-26, 127, 152
North Carolina State Wolfpack, 28, 29, 31, 42, 73, 89, 103, 104, 105-8, 108, 116, 146, 186, 189, 191, 192, 193, 194, 195, 197, 198, 199
North Carolina Tar Heels, 20, 48-52, 63, 77, 81, 82, 84, 85, 86, 97, 108, 111, 117, 120, 121, 122, 129, 136, 137, 138, 150, 165-66, 167-69, 270-72, 175-76, 181-84, 186, 192
Northeastern Huskies, 171
Norwood, Ron, 115
Notre Dame Fighting Irish, 38, 40, 42, 50, 52, 85, 87, 89, 92, 102, 105, 115, 116, 117, 120, 121, 131, 132, 136, 137, 139, 164, 165
Nowell, Mel, 59, 60, 61

O

O'Brien, Johnny, 38, 40, 42
O'Connell, Dermie, 23, 24
Oftring, Frank, 24, 25
Ohio State Buckeyes, 1-4, 13, 15, 17, 20, 28, 58, 59, 60-61, 62, 63, 64, 66, 82, 84, 92, 93, 151, 171, 192
Ohio University, 70, 71, 87, 105
Oklahoma, 2, 4, 23, 136
Oklahoma A & M, 17, 20, 27, 32, 33, 40, 42, 44, 48, 64
Oklahoma City, 44
Oklahoma Sooners, 139-40

Oklahoma State, 52
O'Koren, Mike, 120, 122, 126, 127, 136
Olajuwaon, Akeem Abdul, 174, 185, 186, 190, 196, 197, 199
Old Dominion, 150, 171
Olsen, Harold, 3, 4
Olsen, Jim, 10, 11
Olsen, Lute, 146, 147, 153
Oral Roberts, 105
Oregon, 1-4, 9, 60
Oregon State Beavers, 23, 46, 63, 65, 70, 75, 109, 158, 170, 180, 181
Orr, Johnny, 116
Orr, Louis, 146
Ostrkorn, Wally, 26
Outstanding player awards, in 1940, 6; in 1941, 8; in 1942, 10, 11; in 1944, 16, 17; in 1948, 26; in 1949, 26; in 1952, 38; in 1953, 42; in 1954, 44; in 1955, 46; in 1956, 48; in 1957, 51; in 1958, 53; in 1959, 56; in 1960, 60; in 1961, 62; in 1962, 64; in 1963, 66; in 1964, 72; in 1965, 74; in 1966, 76; in 1967, 81; in 1968, 84; in 1969, 87; in 1970, 89; in 1971, 95; in 1972, 99; in 1973, 102; in 1974, 107; in 1975, 113; in 1976, 117; in 1977, 126; in 1978, 133; in 1979, 144; in 1980, 156; in 1982, 184; in 1983, 199
Owen, Mickey, 8
Owens, Eddie, 115, 121

P

Pacific, 137
Packer, Billy, 63
Parrack, Doyle, 17
Paterno, Bill, 115, 120
Patterson, Kenny, 172
Patterson, Steve, 88, 90, 92, 94, 95, 96
Payne, Ulice, 125
Pennsylvania Quakers, 92, 93, 94, 97, 100, 130-31, 136, 137, 138, 139, 142, 144, 151
Pennsylvania State, 10, 35, 44, 45, 46, 145
Pepperdine College, 15, 116, 137, 180, 192, 194
Perkins, Sam, 166, 169, 170, 171, 172, 181, 183, 184, 189, 191, 192, 193
Perry, Hal, 47, 48
Pete, Kelly, 73, 74
Peterson, Vadal, 15
Pettit, Bob, 26, 38, 39, 40, 41, 44
Phelps, Digger, 115, 120, 132, 133, 136, 165
Phillip, Andy, 12
Phillips, Detrick, 186
Phillips, Mike, 127, 128, 129
Pinckney, Ed, 171, 172, 186
Pinone, John, 171, 172, 186
Pittsburgh, 8, 20, 105, 166
Plair, Ron, 139
Pollard, Jim, 9, 21
Ponsetto, Joe, 115, 131
Porter, Howard, 93, 94, 95, 172
Pressey, Paul, 174
Price, Jim, 97, 98, 99
Price, Tony, 130, 138, 139, 142, 144
Princeton Tigers, 46, 72, 73, 81, 116, 165
Providence Friars, 73, 99, 100, 101, 102, 103, 105, 120, 173
Pruitt, Cliff, 151
Pryor, Ken, 23
Purdue Boilermakers, 85, 86, 120, 145, 151-52, 153, 187

Q-R

Quick, Mike, 99
Quigg, Joe, 51
Ragusa, Al, 30
Ramsey, Frank, 31, 34, 42
Ramsey, Randy, 115, 131
Randolph, Bernard, 172
Ranglos, Jim, 46
Ransey, Kelvin, 151, 156
Ranzino, Sam, 29
Rappis, Jim, 115
Ratleff, Ed, 97, 99
Ratterman, George, 2
Raymonds, Hank, 125, 136
Reading, Curtis, 118, 120
Reardon, Jim, 68
Red Cross Classic, 15, 17
Reed, U. S., 157
Rhode Island, University of, 22, 130
Rice, Greg, 8
Rice University, 10, 88
Riley, Pat, 76
Risen, Arnie, 15, 16, 19, 20
Rivers, Moe, 106
Roberts, Fred, 165
Roberts, Joe, 58, 59, 60, 61
Robertson, Alvin, 187
Robertson, Oscar, 52, 53, 54, 55, 56, 57, 60, 61
Robey, Rick, 108, 109, 120, 127, 128, 133, 134
Robinson, Craig, 194
Robinson, Jackie, 2
Robinson, John, 115, 116, 117, 118
Robinson, Oliver, 178, 179
Robinson, Reggie, 131
Robinson, Ronnie, 101, 102
Robisch, Dave, 94
Rochelle, Rich, 68
Rodgers, Guy, 52, 53
Rollins, Ken, 24, 25, 26
Roman, Ed, 28, 30
Rose, Jim, 93, 94
Rose, Lee, 118, 122, 152, 153, 154
Rose, Lynden, 174, 175, 176, 181
Rosenberger, Gary, 125
Rosenbluth, Lennie, 49, 50, 51
Ross, Vincent, 142
Roth, Al, 30
Rouse, Vic, 66, 67, 68
Rousey, Bob, 33
Rowe, Curtis, 85, 87, 88, 89, 91, 92, 94, 95, 96
Royals, Reggie, 97, 98
Rupp, Adolph, 22, 24, 25, 26, 28, 31, 33, 35, 39, 42, 53, 61, 63, 76, 82, 97, 127, 134
Russell, Bill, 34, 45, 46, 47, 48, 49, 77, 99
Russell, Cazzie, 70, 71, 72, 73, 74, 75
Russell, David, 189
Rutgers Scarlet Knights, 115, 116, 137, 189

S

Sailors, Kenny, 8, 12, 13, 14, 21
St. Bonaventure, 82, 83, 88, 89, 92, 130
St. John's Redmen, 15, 31, 35, 36, 37, 115, 136, 137, 138, 139, 152, 171, 189, 192
St. Joseph's Hawks, 55, 61, 62, 93, 100, 159, 162, 171
St. Louis, 31, 36
St. Mary's of California, 55
Salters, James, 138, 139, 142
Sampson, Ralph, 164, 167, 168, 169, 170, 176, 178, 194
Sand, Bobby, 30
Sanders, Frank, 99
Sanders, Mike "Slew," 150, 151, 154, 156
Sanders, Tom, 60
San Diego State, 116
Saner, Neville, 84
San Francisco Dons, 45, 46, 48, 49, 64, 65, 70-71, 73, 99, 100, 105, 121, 127, 129, 130, 136, 137, 139, 140, 141, 166
San Jose State, 111
Santa Clara, 36, 60, 83-84, 85
Scals, DeWayne "Astronaut," 150

Scearce, Mike, 153
Schaefer, Herm, 5, 6
Schall, Steve, 137
Schayes, Dolph, 17, 20
Schellenberg, Jerry, 118, 119
Schlundt, Don, 34, 38, 40, 41, 42, 101
Schnittker, Dick, 28
Schoene, Russ, 178
Schofield, Terry, 95
Scott, Charlie, 85, 87
Seattle, 38, 52, 53, 55, 65, 70
Sellers, Phil, 115
Shackelford, Lynn, 81, 83-84, 87
Sheffield, Fred, 15
Shelton, Ev, 12, 13
Shelton, Jack, 27
Shidler, Jay, 127, 152
Shingleton, Larry, 64, 67
Shoemaker, John, 128
Shyman, Bill, 40
Siegfried, Larry, 59, 60, 61, 62
Siemiontkowski, Hank, 93, 94, 95, 172
Sims, Willie, 150
Singley, Charlie, 42, 43, 44, 46
Sitton, Charlie, 180, 181
Slaughter, Fred, 70, 72
Sloan, Norm, 105, 106
Smiley, Jack, 12
Smith, Arnold, 30
Smith, Dean, 82, 84, 97, 120, 121-26, 136, 165, 167, 168, 169, 170, 171, 172, 181, 183, 184
Smith, Derek, 148, 149, 154, 179, 183
Smith, Eric, 180, 183
Smith, John, 158
Smith Kelvin, 181
Smith, Phil, 99
Smith, Robert, 121
Smith, Sam, 115, 121, 122
Smithson, Gene, 160
Smithson, Randy, 160
Smith, Timn, 138
Smith, Tony, 121
Smith, Willie, 115, 116
Smuin, Dick, 15
Sorenson, Dave, 82
South Carolina, 92, 97, 100, 101, 103
Southern, 160
Southern California, 5, 9, 44, 137, 145
Southern Illinois-Carbondale, 119
Southern Methodist, 47, 49, 77
Southwestern Louisiana, 97, 99
Spain, Ken, 82
Spanarkel, Jim, 130, 131, 133, 134, 136
Spivey, Bill, 28, 31, 32, 33, 35
Springfield College, 5
Stack, Greg, 125
Stacom, Kevin, 100
Stagg, Amos Alonzo, 2
Stallworth, Bud, 94
Stanford Indians, 9-11
Stewart, Kim, 72
Stipanovich, Steve, 174
Stone, Jack, 32, 33
Strack, Dave, 73
Sunderlage, Don, 31, 32
Sutherland, Gene, 84
Suttle, Rick, 105
Sutton, Eddie, 129, 136, 140, 160
Swaney, Jim, 139
Sweek, Bill, 84
Sylvester, Mike, 103, 105
Syracuse Orangemen, 50, 100, 109, 111, 137-38, 146

T

Tannenbaum, Sid, 17, 20
Tarkanian, Jerry, 97, 121, 194
Tatum, Earl, 106, 115
Taylor, Fred, 60, 61, 63
Taylor, Phil, 115
Taylor, Vince, 152
Temple, 47, 48, 52, 53
Tennessee-Chattanooga Moccasins, 178, 186
Tennessee Tech, 66
Tennessee Volunteers, 81, 116, 137, 164, 165, 178, 186
Texas, 2, 4, 13, 14, 23, 24, 65, 136
Texas A & M Aggies, 85, 148, 150
Texas Christian, 36, 55, 83, 89
Texas Tech, 61
Texas Western (Texas-El Paso) Miners, 70, 74, 75, 76, 77, 109
Thacker, Tom, 61, 63, 64, 65, 66
Theus, Reggie, 121
Thomas, Isiah, 162, 167, 168, 169
Thomas, Jim, 162, 167, 169
Thomas, Ron, 97
Thompson, David, 103, 105, 106, 107, 108
Thompson, George, 85
Thompson, John, 146, 179, 180, 181
Tolbert, Ray, 153, 162, 168
Toledo, 136, 139
Toone, Bernard, 118, 125, 127, 136, 137, 140
Towe, Monte, 104, 105, 106, 108
Townsend, Ray, 115, 116, 129
Trgovich, Pete, 108, 110, 113, 115
Tripucka, Kelly, 131, 132, 133, 136, 139, 165
Tucker, Gerry, 23
Tucker, Trent, 178
Tulsa, 172, 174
Turner, Bobby, 131
Turner, Landon, 162, 167, 169
Turpin, Melvin, 188

U

UCLA Bruins, 33, 47, 63, 64, 65, 69-74, 77, 79, 80, 81, 82, 83, 84, 85, 86, 87, 88, 90, 91, 92, 93, 94, 95, 96-116, 117, 120, 127, 129, 136, 137, 139, 140, 141, 142, 145, 148, 150-51, 154-55, 165, 172, 178, 194
Unruh, Paul, 28, 29
Unseld, Wes, 83
Utah State, 2, 63, 88
Utah Utes, 15-17, 46, 47, 54, 55, 61-62, 75, 76, 165, 166, 194

V

Vallely, John, 85, 86, 87, 88, 89, 92
Valvano, Jim, 192, 194, 197, 199
Vance, Gene, 12
Vanderbilt, 31, 73, 105
Vandeweghe, Kiki, 136, 141, 145, 150, 151, 154, 156
Vilcheck, Al, 98
Villanova Wildcats, 2, 4, 26, 70, 71, 89, 92, 93, 94, 95, 131, 164, 171, 172, 186
Vincent, Jay, 128
Virginia Cavaliers, 63, 164, 165, 167, 169, 170, 176, 178, 186, 194
Virginia Commonwealth, 146, 189
Virginia Military Institute, 115, 116
Virginia Tech, 81, 137
Voss, Ed, 10, 11
Vraines, Danny, 166

W

Wagner, Milt, 186, 196, 197
Waite, Steve, 146, 147, 148
Wake Forest Demon Deacons, 2, 4, 63, 117, 118, 119-20, 162, 163, 171
Walker, Darrell, 187
Walton, Bill, 21, 90, 96, 97, 98, 99, 100, 101, 102, 105, 106
Walton, John, 108
Warner, Ed, 29, 30
Warren, Mike, 80, 81, 82, 84
Washington, Kenny, 72, 74
Washington, Marcus, 99, 105, 106
Washington, Richard, 108, 112, 113, 115, 116

Washington State, 8, 9
Washington, University of, 13, 27, 31, 32, 38, 40, 41, 42
Watkins, Curtis, 131, 136, 137, 138, 140, 142
Watkins, Leroy, 30
Watson, Bobby, 28, 31, 33, 34
Watson, Lloyd, 115
Weber State, 97, 129, 137
Wehrle, Mark, 90
Weingart, Bob, 125
Weir, Jimmy, 13, 14
Western Kentucky Hilltoppers, 60, 63, 81, 89, 92, 93, 94, 128-29
West, Jerry, 52, 54, 55, 56, 57
West Virginia, 46, 52, 54, 55, 57, 60, 132
Whitaker, Skip, 31, 32, 33
Whitehead, Jerome, 115, 118, 120, 122, 123, 125, 126, 127
White, Willie, 178
Whitman, Randy, 168
Whittenburg, Dereck, 194, 195, 198, 199
Wichita State Shockers, 71, 72, 73, 116, 159, 160, 169
Wicks, Sidney, 85, 88, 89, 92, 94, 95, 96
Wiesenhahn, Bob, 61, 62
Wilkerson, Bob, 114, 116, 117
Wilkes, James, 150, 151, 154
Wilkes, Keith (Jamaal), 96, 97, 98, 99, 101, 102, 103, 105, 106, 107
Wilkinson, Bill, 16, 17
Wilkinson, Herb, 15
Williams, Don "Duck," 115, 120, 131, 132
Williams, Herb, 151
Williams, Kevin, 189
Williams, Larry, 131
Williams, LaVon, 152
Williams, Rob, 174, 176, 181
Wilson, George, 62, 63, 64, 65, 66
Wilson, Othell, 194
Wilson, Rick, 131
Wintermute, Slim, 4
Wisconsin Badgers, 8, 23
Wittlin, Mike, 30
Wittman, Randy, 162, 168
Wood, Al, 166, 168, 169, 170
Wood, Chuck, 68
Wood, Dale, 164
Wooden, John, 47, 63, 69, 70, 72, 73, 77, 81, 83, 84, 85, 86, 87, 88, 92, 94, 95, 96, 97, 98, 102, 108, 111, 112, 113, 115, 126, 141, 148, 150, 155, 166
Wood, Howard, 165
Woolpert, Phil, 45, 46, 47, 48, 49
Woolridge, Orlando, 136, 165
Worthen, Sam, 136, 137
Worthy, James, 166, 170, 171, 172, 181, 182, 183, 184
Wuycik, Dennis, 97
Wyoming Cowboys, 12-14, 15, 23, 27, 36, 81, 180

Y-Z

Yale, 49
Yates, Tony, 61, 62, 65, 66
Yelverton, Chuck, 92
Yonakor, Rich, 122
Young, Michael, 174, 185, 186, 196, 197
Zawoluk, Bob, 31, 35, 36, 37, 38
Zimmer, Andy, 6